The Steen Family In Europe And America

THE STEEN FAMILY

IN EUROPE AND AMERICA.

A GENEALOGICAL, HISTORICAL AND BIO-
GRAPHICAL RECORD OF NEARLY
THREE HUNDRED YEARS,

EXTENDING FROM

THE SEVENTEENTH TO THE TWENTIETH CENTURY.

BY THE

REV MOSES D A STEEN, DD

Pastor of the Presbyterian Church,
Woodbridge, Cal

Cincinnati, O
MONFORT & COMPANY,
1900

To
the memory of my revered father,

AARON FARIS STEEN,

whose counsel led to its production, this work
is affectionately inscribed by

THE AUTHOR

ANCIENT STEEN FAMILY CREST,

or coat-of-arms, which was in
use before A. D. 1650.

PREFACE.

This book, begun many years ago, has been of gradual growth. It was the writer's first intention to prepare only a genealogical record of his father's immediate family; afterwards he undertook to enlarge its scope so as to include the descendants of his grandfather, and then again at his father's request he began to trace backward the line of ancestry as far as possible, in order to connect the European with the American family.

In 1877 we visited Ireland, Scotland, England, Holland, etc., and while there obtained what information we could relative to the work, and began arranging the materials.

The preparation of this book has been a work of great difficulty which those only can appreciate who have themselves attempted to perform a similar task. Our early American ancestors, while engaged in subduing the forests and undergoing the hardships and dangers of frontier life, paid little attention to the recording of their family history, at least, but little has been preserved to posterity, or is now accessible. A great difficulty has also arisen in collecting information from the very many distant and scattered families in all parts of the land, by means of correspondence. While hundreds of letters of inquiry have been sent out, many remained unanswered, a large number of those received were very meager, and some of them almost illegible.

In the search for information concerning our own branch of the family we came into possession of much of the genealogy of other branches, which we thought ought to be preserved, and this has led still further to the enlargement of the work.

For the seeming partiality in the treating of some families and persons much more fully than others of equal, or more worthy

(7)

of like attention we offer this apology   Our own personal knowledge, or the information furnished by others, has enabled us to
enlarge in some cases, and the lack of these has compelled us
to be too brief in others   An earnest effort has been made to
secure accuracy and to render the work as complete as possible,
but owing to the deficiency of historical data, the *desired ideal
completeness* was not attainable by such time and attention as we
could give

   To make the work more easy for reference, it is divided
into books and chapters, each book presenting the descendants
of a large branch of the family, with a chapter devoted to each of
the children of that particular family   Thus BOOK ONE shows
the descendants of ROBERT STEEN, who was born in Ireland
about 1730, and Chapter V gives the particular descendants of
his fifth child, ALEXANDER STEEN, who was born in Lancaster
Co, Pa, Feb 14, 1773   The succeeding generations are shown
by Roman and Arabic numerals, which indicate the precise relationship of each individual to the person whose name appears at
the head of the chapter, thus V 3 1 1 6 shows that *Marme
Dewey Bogart*, who was born Jan 30, 1898, was the sixth child of
the first child of the first child of the third child of ALEXANDER
STEEN, and hence his great-great-grandson

   When a name is first recorded it is written *in full*, if the full
name is known to the writer, and whenever a contracted form
afterwards appears it indicates the name by which the individual
is known among his most intimate friends   Thus Robert Wilson
Steen when written R Wilson Steen indicates that he was fami-
larly called *Wilson* Steen, and John Work Steen, afterwards
written John W. Steen, intimates that among his friends he was
called *John* Steen

   This book is *not intended for general circulation*, but only for
those of our own name and relationship   These will find in it a
genealogical record of the past, and one that can at any time
be easily extended so as to include future generations   It is
hoped this record will prove both interesting and profitable to

the families and individuals chiefly concerned; for none of us
should willingly remain ignorant of our forefathers and kindred,
whose lives and character affect us more than those of any other
people.

The writer wishes to express his gratitude *to all* who have
rendered him assistance to any degree, by furnishing desired
information.   But thanks are *especially* due to the late Rev.
George Steen, of Limavady, Ireland; Mrs. Annie C. Steen, of
Belfast, Ireland; Mrs. Sarah Steen Irwin, of Toronto, Canada;
Mr. Nathaniel Steen, of Streetsboro, Ontario; the late Carroll J.
Steen, Esq., of Cato, Miss.; Mr. James P. Gossett, of Williams-
ton, S. C.; the Rev. John F. Steen, of New York, N. Y.; Mr.
James Steen Martin, of Philadelphia, Pa.; Miss Anna C. Steen, of
NewCastle, Pa.; Mrs. Eliza Steen Beveridge, of Buck Run, O.;
Mr. Benjamin W. Steen, of Glen Dale, Ind.; Miss Anna J. Steen,
of Martinstown, Mo., and others.

In our extensive correspondence we received very many
requests for personal photographs, which we were unable to
supply; and in order to gratify this expressed wish we have
taken the liberty to insert among the illustrations in the book
portraits of our own family.

It has been truly said that no one can climb very high on any
genealogical tree without finding some dead branches, yet the
writer feels a just pride in the good and honorable character of
the family as a whole — a fact which should stimulate us and
our posterity to act worthy of such parentage and relationship.

The book is now sent forth with the prayer that those who
read these pages may belong to the *Family of God*, and have their
names and *record* in the "LAMB'S BOOK OF LIFE."

Moses D. A. Steen,

THE MANSE, WOODBRIDGE, CAL., Oct. 1, 1900.

PORTRAITS.

CONTENTS.

BOOK FOUR.

BOOK FIVE

BOOK SIX

BOOK SEVEN

BOOK EIGHT

BOOK NINE

BOOK TEN

BOOK ELEVEN

BOOK TWELVE

BOOK THIRTEEN

BOOK FOURTEEN

BOOK EIGHTEEN

Miscellaneous Steen Families of Scotch-Irish Descent

BOOK NINETEEN

Miscellaneous Scandinavian Families.

BOOK TWENTY

INTRODUCTION.

The name STEEN seems to be of Scandinavian origin, and indicative of solidity, strength, or force of character. It is closely allied to such names as CEPHAS in the Aramaic language, *Peter* in the Greek, *Stein* in the German, and *Stone* in the English—all of which signify the same thing, a rock, or stone, which implies firmness.

The early possessors of the name seem also to have maintained something of the character indicated thereby. *Gustavus Adolphus*, King of Sweden, who came to the throne in 1611, as a Christian hero and patriot fought for liberty of conscience, and led an army of sixty thousand men into Germany for the noble purpose of rescuing Protestants from the tyranny of the house of Austria, had an *officer* under his command whose name was STEEN.

In Norway and Denmark the name is still not uncommon, and near the close of the nineteenth century a number of families from these countries have emigrated to America and settled in the Northwestern and Pacific Coast States, with some of whom the writer has had correspondence or personal intercourse.

In 1891 Oscar II., King of Norway and Sweden, appointed a *Mr Steen* to the position of Premier. The following is copied from a New York daily paper of May 25, 1891.

'The Conservative ministry has been overthrown because the Berner resolution was passed against its wishes by a vote of 59 to 55, and when the King requested the Radical Berner to form a new Cabinet he declined, and referred the King to his bitterest enemy, *Mr Steen*, who is undoubtedly, after Sverdrup the most eminent man in the party. King Oscar has, in acting on this advice, given a guarantee that he is a Constitutional King, who has accepted parliamentarism in good faith. *Mr Steen* who is the head master or principal of the public gymnasium in Stavenger, and has for many years been a leader of the more radical wing of the Liberal party in the Storthing, is personally obnoxious to the King, and the general impression in Norway has been that Oscar II would under no circumstances consent

(2)

to any public recognition of him   Mr Steen, as will be remembered, played a conspicuous part in the impeachment of the conservative ministry Selmer, and the contention of the Right has been that he prevaricated, and in other respects was unscrupulous in the selection of his means for ousting his enemies   He has, however, among the public-at-large the reputation of being an able and upright man, fearless and determined, and of great executive force   His radicalism is not at all alarming, referring chiefly to the extension of the suffrage, which ought long ago to have been granted, and the absolute equality of the two kingdoms   The only possible danger which the country may incur from his leadership is the further straining of the relations with Sweden, for the new Premier is not of a conciliatory temperament, and is imbued with a sense of 'Noise-Noise' independence to the very finger tips   It would be a great misfortune if the question of diplomatic representation were to be pressed to the point of arousing further hostility in Sweden, and thereby weakening the union

In Holland or The Netherlands the name has attracted greater attention from the fact that one of the most celebrated Dutch painters bore the name of Steen — the renowned Jan Steen — whose history is well known   The following item is copied from the Library of Universal Knowledge"

"Steen, Jan —A celebrated Dutch painter born in 1626, or according to others, in 1636 at Leyden, where his father was a brewer   He showed a predilection for art, which led to his being apprenticed to a German painter, Nicholas Knuepfer, of Utrecht. Subsequently he became a pupil of Van Goyen, whose daughter Margaret he married   Very soon his repute became established As he worked in a slow and elaborate manner, his gains were insufficient, and he started a brewery at Delft   Steen died in 1679 or 1689, leaving his family in very destitute case

"As an artist of the Dutch school he ranks high, and his works are now much valued   In humor and spirit they are scarcely surpassed, and their coloring is clear, fresh and delicate At times he attempted historical subjects, but his success in these was not great   It was in the homely and domestic scenes that his genius exhibited itself, and in this field he has scarcely since been equaled "

He was a relative of Rembrandt, and painted in all about three hundred pictures, among which is a fine portrait of himself

in the Ryks Museum at Amsterdam "The Feast of St
Nicholas" is one of his best and happiest productions and represents his own family His father and mother are in the back-
ground his wife, in the foreground, extends her arms to a happy
little girl, while six other children are included in the group At
the Louvre in Paris is one of his latest works dated 1674—'A
Feast at an Inn'— painted after he had opened his tavern, and
representing the actual interior of the place, and valued at thirty
thousand francs See *Century Magazine, Dec, 1893 pp 175-8
See also I Steen, Etude sur L'art en Hollande, by Van Westrheenen
(The Hague, 1856)*

   In visiting The Netherlands many years ago the writer found
in The Hague fifteen families who bore the name of Steen, and
in Amsterdam, Rotterdam and other cities a lesser number In
entering the Royal Museum and Picture Gallery at The Hague
we presented a card to the conductor who glanced at it a
moment, then clasped our hand in both of his, exclaiming with
animated countenance 'Steen' STEEN'" and then hurriedly led
us to several famous pictures, and pointing to them with enthusiasm and apparent joy cried out "*Jan Steen'* JAN STEEN! JAN
STEEN'" Thus, although we were far away from home a
stranger in a foreign land, the interest and pleasure of our sojourn
there was greatly increased by the simple fact that we belong to
The Steen Family

   In the sixteenth century the Roman Catholic persecution of
Protestants was most appalling The Duke of Alva, it is said,
even surpassed the persecuting heathen emperors of Rome in
his extreme cruelty while attempting to crush out the rising spirit
of religious and political liberty, and according to Grotius
destroyed the lives of one hundred thousand Protestants during
the six years of his regency (1567-1573) And in consequence of
these troubles many of the most upright citizens fled into other
countries for safety, among them a family of the name of Steen
crossed over the sea and located in Ayrshire, Scotland, where
the descendants remained for many generations They were a
noble stock of Protestant Christians of an unyielding type, who
had determined to maintain liberty of conscience and freedom
in the worship of God at every hazard The spirit of persecution which had prevailed so extensively in The Netherlands afterwards again arose in Scotland, and they were called to endure
hardness as good soldiers of Jesus Christ and suffer imprisonment for loyalty to God and the Gospel as they understood it

Our Scottish ancestral head, a devout and earnest Christian, was caused to languish for a considerable time at the 'Bass Rock" of historical fame as the prison house of the Covenanters, and was married to an estimable Christian woman on the very day of his release, probably at declaration of indulgence in 1672 This island rock is situated near the mouth of the frith of Forth, three miles northeast of North Berwick, in the North Sea It is nearly round, about one mile in circumference, four hundred feet high, traversed by a vast cavern, and inaccessible on all sides except at the southwest, where it is impossible to land in stormy weather After the Restoration, King Charles II purchased this island rock and fortress for £4 000, or about $20,000, as a prison for Covenanters It was a stronghold very difficult to capture, so much so that a mere handful of the partisans of James II held the place from June, 1691, to April, 1694, against all the forces sent against it by King William III, who afterwards had the fortifications demolished in 1701 It is now a private possession, let out to a keeper, who receives fees from visitors

As early as the reign of James I a family by the name of Steen crossed the Channel from Scotland into the North of Ireland, and located upon the banks of the Foyle, in the Province of Ulster, and County of Londonderry This was probably about 1620, or perhaps a few years later Here they continued to reside, notwithstanding the troublous times, and some at least escaped the terrible massacre of Protestants in Ireland in 1641 during the reign of Charles I Other families remained in Scotland until a much later period One family came over into Ireland during the protectorate of Oliver Cromwell, and settled first at Killinsky, in County Down, and afterwards located in Antrim, probably about 1653 or 1655 Still another family remained in Scotland until near the close of the reign of Charles II, under whom they had endured many privations, as well as imprisonment, for conscience sake These came into Ireland about 1684 or 1685, and located in County Antrim near a place called "The Vow,' on the banks of the River Bann, not many miles from Coleraine In the course of time there were families by the name of Steen living at Culmore, overlooking Loch Foyle in the vicinity of Londonderry Antrim, Coleraine, Balleney, Ballyghan, The Vow, etc These no doubt were all from the same original stock, and possessed the characteristics of their forefathers— firmness in Christian faith and fidelity to their principles in the midst of persecution and severe trials Some of these kindred

according to the flesh suffered in the terrible "siege of Derry,"
in 1688, when King James II endeavored to destroy by starva-
tion this stronghold of Protestantism The siege had been kept
up for one hundred and five days, when, under the command of
William the Prince of Orange, a man-of-war and two ships
loaded with provisions arrived It was with great difficulty that
they could gain even an approach to the city, for the army of
King James determined to prevent it if possible A great chain
had been stretched across the river to hinder the passage of any
vessel, but the warship of the Prince of Orange came against it
with such force as to break the chain yet the rebound was so
great as to throw the vessel near the shore, where it stuck in the
mud The enemy raised a shout of triumph and rushed forward
to board the ships and capture all the soldiers, crew, vessels and
provisions, but a broadside, simultaneously shot from all the can-
nons on board, not only arrested the attack, but the concussion
also drove the vessel from the mud-bank and caused it to float
out into deep water, to the great joy and relief of those on board
the ship They succeeded in running past all the batteries and
obstructions in the river, and in relieving the starving inhabitants
of the city of Londonderry The greatest cruelty had been practiced by the besiegers, and the utmost suffering endured by the
besieged, who had eaten all their horses and dogs, and were said
to be on their last ration of tallow and salted hide when the relief
came The garrison of SEVEN THOUSAND MEN had dwindled
down to THREE THOUSAND, many of them having died of starva-
tion while resenting the offer of a bribe of £2,000 or about $10,000
to any one who would open the gates to the enemy They sent
back their answer in the heroic message, "NO SURRENDER" and
remained steadfast to the last

In 1877 and again in 1896, the writer visited a number of
families by the name of Steen living in the northern counties of
Ireland, and in every instance found them to be earnest orthodox
Presbyterian Christian people several of whom were Presbyterian
clergymen in charge of congregations, while others were ruling
elders in the church During the latter visit he was driven to
the delightful home of John Steen, J P , near Castlerock, in
County Londonderry It was a fine old Episcopal residence,
which he had purchased at the time of the disestablishment A
flag was floating gracefully over it which he thought was some
British or Irish ensign, but it proved to be the *Scotch-Irish Steen
family Crest,* or ancient coat-of-arms, which had been in use for

more than two hundred and fifty years On a scroll beneath the figure was the motto, "Ad Diem Tendo" Its rightful color is Presbyterian true blue, which symbolizes fidelity The following is a small cut of the same, which he found in use among other Steen families, as in Belfast as their coat-of-arms, used on writing paper and visiting cards

It represents the fabled Phoenix bird rising from its own ashes, with extended wings, ready to fly away—an emblem of faith in God and hope of immortality, which even the dark days of fiery persecution could not destroy This steadfast faith and heroic endurance was characteristic of the Steen family in the sixteenth and seventeenth centuries The writer has also found Steen families in Scotland, England, Canada, and the United States possessing in general the same characteristics

Early in the eighteenth century several families of Steens removed from the North of Ireland to the British Colonies in America, settled in different localities, and have left a numerous posterity Other families came at different times later on, and located in various portions of the country They came with the great flow of population into the new country, which was mainly from the North of Ireland, and *almost entirely Presbyterians,* for the great Catholic-Irish immigration did not fairly commence until a much later period "These people spread themselves rapidly, from 1725 to 1765, through a large portion of Eastern and Western Pennsylvania and into North and South Carolina, becoming the basis of the Presbyterian Church in America", and 'constituting an element of the body politic second in value to no other, either in peace or war"

The writer remembers that when a mere child he heard his father speak of *his* Great-grandfather Steen and his large family His name, we believe, was *Richard Steen,* but of this we can not be certain Perhaps he came to the American Colonies with his children, but of this we have no record and do not know Of one thing, however, we may be sure, and that is, that he has left a very numerous posterity in this country We think there can be no reasonable doubt but that *Robert* and *Matthew Steen,* who resided in Pennsylvania, and *James* and *William Steen,* who

removed to South Carolina and were soldiers in the Revolutionary War, were all the sons of this man, and full brothers to each
other. We were told in childhood that our great-grandfather,
Robert Steen, had brothers who removed to South Carolina and
were soldiers in the Revolutionary Army

In the following pages we shall first of all give the record, so
far as known, of our great-grandfather ROBERT STEEN, and *his
descendants*, then present *separate* accounts of the various larger
branches of the related Steen families, devoting a "book," or a
section of the work, to each. An interrogation point (?) after a
name or date indicates doubt

REV. MOSES D. A. STEEN, D.D.

BOOK ONE.

DESCENDANTS OF ROBERT STEEN

Robert Steen was born near Coleraine, Ireland not far from a place called 'The Vow,' about 1730, removed to the British Colonies in America about 1755, was married to Elizabeth Boyd about 1757 or 1758, and brought up a family of five children in comfortable circumstances near Chestnut Level, in what is now Lancaster County, Pennsylvania

Robert Steen was one of the early immigrants who came over into the British Colonies in America from the North of Ireland, near the middle of the eighteenth century He was probably one of the elder sons of Richard Steen (?), who was born about A D 1700 and perhaps came to America with his large family, together with other relatives and friends, to make their future home in this new country, and whose ancestors came from Scotland into Ireland, where they had lived for several generations They belonged to a race of men of strong convictions, resolute purposes, and had already endured hardships for the sake of their religious principles They determined to brave the dangers of the ocean, the trials of frontier life, the deprivations incident to a new country, the struggles and difficulties necessary to fell the forest, and to build homes for themselves and families in the new world They landed in New York but soon afterwards made their way to Pennsylvania where free from the

(27)

depredations of the Indians, they would have a better opportunity to secure their own lands, and provide the necessaries of
life, with less of danger and more of comfort to themselves.   In
the large family of Richard Steen (?) there were several sons
among whom were Robert and Matthew, who settled in Pennsylvania, and James and William, who removed to the South and
located permanently in Union District, South Carolina, and each
became the paternal ancestor of a large branch of the Steen family residing in the Southern States.

Robert Steen was born not far from Coleraine, Ireland,
probably about 1730 (?), and most likely on the old "Green Hill"
farm, near a place called "The Vow," where there is a cemetery,
an old mill site, and a school, which the writer visited in 1896.
It is situated on the bank of the River Bann, about eight Irish
miles from Coleraine, in County Antrim, and Province of Ulster,
Ireland (?).   When about twenty-five years of age he removed to
the British Colonies with a large number of immigrants, relatives
and friends, about the year 1755 (?).   He was married to Miss
Elizabeth Boyd, probably about 1757 or 1758 (?), acquired a
farm, and established his home near Chestnut Level, in Lancaster
County, Pennsylvania, not far from the Susquehanna River, where
he brought up a family of three sons and two daughters in comfortable circumstances.   He was a man of influence, a devout
Presbyterian, a successful farmer, a patriotic citizen, opposed to
the Tories, and strongly favoring American independence, having
two brothers in the Revolutionary Army.   He was a fine singer,
especially fond of music and good society.   He lived to a ripe old
age, but the date of his death is not known to us.   The following are the names of his children.   Samuel, Robert, Mary, Elizabeth, and Alexander.

CHAPTER I

Samuel Steen, the eldest son of Robert and Elizabeth
Boyd Steen, was born near Chestnut Level, in Lancaster
County, Pennsylvania, about 1760 (?), and was brought up on
his father's farm.   He was an intelligent, industrious, and successful farmer.   He removed to Berkeley County, Virginia,

where he was married to Miss Mary Mayers, probably about
1790 (?), and brought up a large family of eleven children   He
was a man of influence and usefulness in society   a strict Presbyterian, who faithfully read the Bible, kept the Sabbath, observed
family worship, and was habitual and regular in his attendances
upon the ordinances and services of public worship in the sanc-
tuary   Late in life he removed with his wife and family to
Belmont County, Ohio, and located upon a farm near St Clairsville, where they spent the remainder of their lives   highly
respected by all

About 1850 all, or nearly all, of their children together with
their families, were living in that region, but now the children of
Samuel and Mary Mayers Steen are all dead, and their families
are very widely scattered

I —Alexander Steen, son of Samuel and Mary Mayers Steen
was born in Berkeley County, Virginia, in January 1800 and
removed with his parents to the farm near St Clairsville, Belmont Co , O   He afterwards lived in Franklin County, Pennsylvania, and in 1856 removed to Washington County, Illinois,
where he located upon a farm, and where he died Sept 25,
1869, in the 70th year of his age   Like his parents and all his
brothers and sisters, he was a Presbyterian in faith and practice
He was married in Franklin County, Pennsylvania   the exact
date being unknown   but probably about 1826 or 1827, to Miss
Rosanna Hunter, who died in Belmont County Ohio, March 6,
1848   To Alexander and Rosanna Hunter Steen were born
the following children:

1 Sarah Steen was born in Franklin County, Pennsylvania
    about 1828, and died in infancy

2 Mary Jane Steen was born in Franklin County Pennsyl-
    vania, in 1830   She was married to Samuel McElhenny,
    March 1, 1857 and died in Henderson County, Illinois, Dec
    26, 1864 in the 35th year of her age

    1 —James Lincoln Steen McElhenny, son of Samuel and
       Mary Jane Steen McElhenny was born about 1858 and
       died near Powersville, Putnam Co , Mo , in the spring of
       1892

3 Frances Ann Steen daughter of Alexander and Rosanna
    Hunter Steen, was born in Franklin County, Pennsylvania
    in 1832, and died in Topeka, Kan   in 1893

4 Samuel Giffen Steen, a farmer, a son of Alexander and
Rosanna Hunter Steen was born in Franklin County, Pennsylvania, in 1836 He was married in Belmont County,
Ohio, March 3 1859, to Miss Sarah E Bell, she having born
in Belmont County Ohio Aug 24, 1840 They removed
to Henderson County, Illinois, where all their children were
born They reside at present at Hawthorn, Montgomery
Co Ia The following are their children

I—Rosanna Steen, daughter of Samuel G and Sarah E
Steen was born in Henderson County, Illinois Jan 8
1860, and died in the same place April 3. 1860

II—William Taggart Steen—a farmer—a son of Samuel G
and Sarah E Steen, was born March 20 1861, and died
near Hawthorn, Montgomery Co Ia , May 28 1893, in
the 33d year of his age He was married to Miss Sarah
Smith, Feb 25. 1885. to whom the following three children were born, near Hawthorn, Ia

1 Edna May Steen was born Jan 17, 1887

2 Leroy Giffen Steen was born July 20, 1888

3 Mabel Fern Steen was born Aug. 29, 1891.

III—Hunter Adoniram Steen—a farmer—a son of Samuel
G and Sarah E Steen, was born in Henderson County,
Illinois, July 18, 1863 He was married Feb 22, 1888, to
Miss Clara Dixon, to whom were born four children, as
follows—residence, Hawthorn, Ia

1 De Ette E Steen, daughter of Hunter A and Clara
Steen, was born near Hawthorn, Ia , Jan 2, 1889

2 Vier Samuel Steen, son of Hunter A and Clara Steen
was born near Hawthorn, Ia , Sept 19 1890, and died
Oct 20, 1894

3 Ruby Irene Steen daughter of Hunter A and Clara
Steen, was born near Hawthorn Ia , Jan 2, 1893

4 William Henry Steen son of Hunter A and Clara
Steen was born near Hawthorn Montgomery Co , Ia
Nov 2 1895

5 James Alexander Steen son of Alexander and Rosanna
Steen was born near St Clairsville Belmont Co , O , Sept. 8.
1842 He was brought to the West with his father's family
in 1856 grew up to manhood upon his father's farm in
Washington County, Illinois, resided there till 1870, and

MR. AND MRS. SAMUEL G. STEEN.

then located near Hawthorn, Ia, where he continued until 1887, then removed to a farm near Powersville, Putnam Co, Mo, where he still lives—a practical farmer He was married in Springfield, Ill, March 28, 1867, to Miss Martha Jane Bloomfield, she having been born in Jessamine County, Kentucky, June 7, 1842, and died in Seymour, Wayne Co, Ia, July 18, 1881 He was married a second time Oct 17, 1882, to Miss Sarah Jane Lepper He was married a third time April 3, 1893, she having been born in Mercer County, Mo in 1851

I—Leona Steen, daughter of James A Steen and his first wife, was born in Henderson County, Illinois, Sept 1, 1868 and died in infancy

II—George Masters Steen, son of James A Steen and his second wife, was born near Hawthorn, Ia, July 22, 1883

III—Samuel Arnold Steen, son of James Alexander Steen and his third wife, was born near Powersville, Putnam Co, Mo, April 1, 1895

II—Elizabeth Steen a daughter of Samuel and Mary Mavers Steen, was born in Berkeley County, Virginia, in 1801 removed with her parents to Belmont County, Ohio, and lived with them upon her father's farm, near St Clairsville, until after his death She was an amiable and useful Christian woman, was never married, and died at the residence of her sister, Mrs Ann Steen Leech, in Winterset, Ia, in August, 1879, aged 78 years

III.—Jane Steen, a daughter of Samuel and Mary Mavers Steen, was born in Berkeley County, Virginia, Sept 6, 1804, and removed with her parents to their home, near St Clairsville, Belmont Co, O, where she lived until after her marriage She afterwards resided in the same neighborhood until her death, March 6, 1835, at the age of 30 years, 6 months, and 6 days. She was married near St Clairsville, O, in 1825 to Abner Stilwell, he having been born near Hancock, Ind, Nov 2, 1802, and died at the family residence, near St Clairsville, O, in March, 1889, in the 87th year of his age To Abner and Jane Steen Stilwell were born the following four children

1 John Crew Stilwell, the eldest son of Abner and Jane Steen Stilwell, was born near St Clairsville, Belmont Co, O,

(3)

March 22, 1827, and died in Richland Co , O , Aug 24, 1868, in the 42d year of his age   He was a farmer by occupation John C Stilwell was married, Feb 1, 1849, to Nancy Jane Collins, she having been born March 16 1832 and died in Richland County, Ohio, Dec 1, 1861, in the 30th year of her age   To them were born the following five children

I—Sarah Agnes Adams Stilwell, eldest child of John C. and Nancy J Stilwell, was born in Belmont County, Ohio, Feb 24, 1850, and was married in Knox County, Ohio, Aug 10, 1871. to LaFayette Zalmon, a farmer, who still resides near Greersville, Knox Co , O   To them were born the following

    1 William Lewis Zalmon was born April 22 1872, and died July 25, 1873

    2 John Edwin Zalmon was born Sept 24, 1873, and died March 7, 1875

II—William Collins Stilwell, the second child and eldest son of John C and Nancy J Stilwell, was born in Belmont County Ohio, June 21 1852, and is a carpenter by occupation   He was married at Fredericktown Knox Co , O , July 1, 1875, to Miss Elvina Mock, she having been born in Sauk County, Wisconsin, June 7, 1855, and died in Eaton County, Mich , Feb 23, 1884, in the 29th year of her age   William C Stilwell was married a second time in Charlotte, Eaton Co , Mich , to his cousin Miss Annie Belle Miller   Both are earnest and devout Presbyterian Christian people   Residence, Charlotte, Eaton Co , Mich   To William C and Elvina Mock Stilwell were born the following children

    1 Sheridan Mock Stilwell was born in Knox County, Ohio, Sept 27, 1877.

    2 Henry Harrison Stilwell was born in Eaton County, Michigan, Sept 10, 1880

III—Lucretia Jane Stilwell the third child and second daughter of John C and Nancy J Stilwell was born in Richland County Ohio, Nov 15, 1854, and was married in Knox County, Ohio March 6, 1880, to William McDonold, a farmer , residence near Belleville, Richland Co , O   To them was born one child

    1 —A daughter

IV—Iona Adella Stilwell (Collins) was born in Richland County, Ohio, June 29 1857, and was brought up by her grandparents, and took their name — the name of Collins — by which name she was known before her marriage She was married in Zanesville Logan County, Ohio. March 30 1895, to Noel Bradford Montgomery—a farmer — he having been born near Rich Hill Knox County, Ohio, March 31, 1873   Residence Raymonds, Union County Ohio

V—James Abel Stilwell, the fifth child and second son of John C and Nancy J Stilwell was born in Richland County, Ohio, April 25, 1861

2 James Alexander Stilwell the second son, and the second child of Abner and Jane Steen Stilwell, was born near St Clairsville Belmont County, Ohio September 25 1828 He has been a prosperous farmer, and now resides in Osceola, Polk County, Nebraska, his farm being about one-fourth mile from Shelby Nebraska   James A Stilwell was married, May 10, 1859, to Louisa Howard Shue she having been born December 27, 1840   To them were born the following children

I—Elizabeth Jane Stilwell was born near St Clairsville, Ohio, March 15 1861 and was married near Princeton, Illinois, March 3, 1884 to Peter Christian Sommerstedt — a farmer — he having been born in Denmark, February 24, 1856   To them have been born the following children Residence Osceola Polk County Nebraska

　　1 Myrtle Louetta Sommerstedt was born near Shelby, Nebraska, November 10, 1884

　　2 Ralph Howard Sommerstedt was born near Shelby, Nebraska January 1 1890

　　3 Grace Ruth Sommerstedt was born in Osceola Nebraska, February 10, 1898

II—George Crey Stilwell was born near St Clairsville, Ohio, May 30, 1863 and died May 20, 1884, in the 21st year of his age

III—Charles F Stilwell the third child and second son of James A and Louisa H Stilwell was born near St Clairsville Ohio, April 16, 1866, was a student at Wesley an University, at Lincoln Nebraska

IV —William Mitchell Stilwell was born near St Clairsville, Ohio, March 7, 1875, and died May 20, 1877, aged 2 years, 2 months, and 13 days

V —Grace Darling Stilwell, the fifth child and second daughter of James A and Louisa H Stilwell, was born near St Clairsville, Belmont County, Ohio, February 21, 1877, graduated from the Shelby High School in 1894, and from the Normal Department of Wesleyan University, at Lincoln, Neb , in 1895   Residence, Osceola, Nebraska

VI —Nola Leota Stilwell, the sixth child and third daughter of James A and Louisa H Stilwell, was born at Limerick, Bureau County, Illinois, January 6, 1880, a student of Wesleyan University, at Lincoln, Nebraska

VII —Viretta Luella Stilwell, the seventh child and fourth daughter of James A and Louisa H Stilwell, was born at Limerick, Illinois, May 9, 1881.   Residence. Osceola, Nebraska

VIII —Frank Enoch Stilwell, the fourth son, the eighth and youngest child of James and Louisa H Stilwell, was born at Shelby, Polk County, Illinois, October 17, 1887   Residence, Osceola, Nebraska

3   Mary Jane Stilwell, the third child and only daughter of Abner and Jane Steen Stilwell, was born near St Clairsville, Belmont County, Ohio, June 3, 1833, and was married to Joseph Miller September 8, 1849, he having been born August 27, 1823, and died December 28, 1866, in the 44th year of his age   Family residence, St Clairsville, Ohio   To Joseph and Mary Jane Miller were born, in St Clairsville, Ohio, the following children

I —Sarah Louisa Miller was born January 9, 1852, and was married by Rev George N Johnston, in Steubenville, Ohio, April 2, 1879, to Joseph Wood Bentley — a farmer Residence, St Clairsville, Ohio   To Joseph W and Sarah L Bentley were born the following children

   1. Cora Wood Bentley, born in 1880

   2 Harry Elwood Bentley born in 1889

II —Mary Agnes Miller was born March 2, 1854, and was married September 10, 1887, to George Armstrong Brokaw

III—Laura Jane Miller was born August 27, 1856, and was married by Rev Robert Alexander, December 28, 1883, to Walter John Cowans — a liveryman. Residence, Wellsburgh, West Virginia

IV—Annie Belle Miller was born August 24, 1858, and was married in Charlotte, Michigan, to William C. Stilwell. To them were born the following children. Residence, Charlotte. Michigan

   1 Ethel Anilla Stilwell, born in 1889

   2 Olive Jane Stilwell, born in 1891.

   3 William Joseph Stilwell, born in 1894

V.—Cornelia Adaline Miller was born January 9, 1860, and was married in St Clairsville, Ohio, by the Rev Mr Hingley, June 28, 1892, to Joseph Harper — a carpenter by occupation To them was born:

   1 Joseph Albert Harper, born in 1894

VI—Elizabeth Ross Miller was born April 2, 1862, and was married by Rev William Miller, March 7, 1883, to George Washington Brokaw — a farmer Residence, Flushing, Belmont County Ohio To them were born the following children

   1 Clarence Miller Brokaw, born in 1884

   2 Joseph Hacket Brokaw, born in 1888

   3. Wilella Jane Brokaw born in 1891

   4. Louisa S Brokaw, born in 1894

VII—William Newton Miller was born February 2, 1864; a stonemason by trade Residence, St Clairsville, Ohio

VIII—Alverda C Miller was born July 27, 1866 Residence, St Clairsville, Belmont County, Ohio

4 Samuel Steen Stilwell, the fourth child and youngest son of Abner and Jane Steen Stilwell, was born near St Clairsville, Belmont County, Ohio, May 15, 1834, and died at Bridgeport, Ohio, January 2 1889, in the 55th year of his age leaving a wife and nine children. He was married in St Clairsville, Ohio, August 7, 1856, to Anna Maria Geller she having been born in Bedford County, Pennsylvania, February 22, 1838 Family residence, No 3739 Harrison Street, Bellaire, Ohio To Samuel S and Anna M Stilwell were born the following children:

I—Abner Stilwell was born May 25, 1857, and died near
Steubenville, Ohio, May 5, 1888, killed by a railroad acci-
dent caused by obstructions on the Cleveland & Pittsburgh
Railroad, of which he was an engineer   He was married
in Wellsville, Ohio, August 5, 1883, to Annette King, she
having been born in Wellsville, Ohio, in August, 1862, and
now resides in Cleveland, Ohio   To Abner and Annette
King Stilwell were born the following

  1 Leona Stilwell was born June 5 1884, and died in
     August, 1885

  2 Ralph Stilwell was born in Bellaie, Ohio, December
     27, 1886

II—John W Stilwell, the second son of Samuel S and
Anna M Stilwell was born December 11, 1858 — by occupation a miller   He was married in West Alexandria,
Pennsylvania, March 22, 1884, to Mollie Oir, she having
been born in Bridgeport, Ohio, November 22, 1869   Residence, Martin's Ferry, Ohio   To them were born the
following

  1. Clyde Scott Stilwell was born in Bridgeport, Ohio,
     April 11, 1886

  2 Abner Jones Stilwell was born in Bellaie, Ohio, May
     15, 1888

  3 Lillian Stilwell was born in Martin's Ferry Ohio, Sep-
     tember 4 1891

  4 Louis Stilwell was born in Martin's Ferry, Ohio,
     December 19, 1894

III—Sophia Adaline Stilwell, the third child and eldest
daughter of Samuel S and Anna M Stilwell, was born
April 11, 1861   She was married at Bridgeport, Ohio,
February 19, 1886, to Albert Rogers — a farmer — he
having been born at Potomac, Ohio, July 5, 1852   Residence, Bellaire, Ohio   To them were born the following

  1 Grace Rogers was born in Bellaire, Ohio, June 14, 1890

  2 May Margaret Rogers was born in Bellaie, Ohio, May
     6, 1894

IV—George B McClellan Stilwell, the fourth child and third
son of Samuel S and Anna M Stilwell, was born April 11,

1863, and was married in St Clairsville, O , November 18, 1889, to Annie Elim she having been born at Brookside, Ohio, in January, 1865 Residence, Bridgeport, Ohio To them were born the following

1 Charles Louis Stilwell was born in Bellaire, Ohio, December 19 1890

2 Hilda Stilwell was born in Bellaire, Ohio, April 15, 1891.

3 Estella Stilwell was born in Bellaire Ohio, August 23, 1892

4 Hazel Stilwell was born in Bridgeport, Ohio, September 13, 1895

V —Craig Stilwell, the fifth child, and fourth son of Samuel S and Anna M Stilwell, was born April 18, 1865, and was married at Bridgeport, Ohio, in April, 1892, to Bertha Tarbott, she having been born at Kirkwood, Ohio, December 15, 1875 Residence, Bridgeport, Ohio To them the following child was born

1 Elizabeth Maria Stilwell was born in Bridgeport, Ohio, January 4, 1894

VI —Oscar D Stilwell, the sixth child, and fifth son of Samuel S and Anna M. Stilwell, was born September 23, 1867, and died April 9, 1868, aged 6 months and 26 days

VII —Lorena Stilwell, the seventh child and second daughter of Samuel S and Anna M Stilwell, was born November 22, 1869, and was married in Bellaire, Ohio, June 24, 1890, to Frank Hicks — a miller — he having been born in Uniontown, Ohio, February 14, 1864 Residence, Bellaire, Ohio To them were born the following

1 Helen Geneva Hicks was born in Bellaire, Ohio, May 8, 1891

2 Vera Hicks was born in Bellaire, Ohio, April 1, 1894, and died January 26, 1897.

VIII —Jennie Verlinda Stilwell, the eighth child and third daughter of Samuel S and Anna M Stilwell, was born December 23, 1871, and was married in Bellaire Ohio, January 19, 1891, to James G Crawford — a painter Residence, Bellaire, Ohio To them were born the following

1 Ralph Eugene Crawford was born in Bellaire, Ohio, July 1, 1892

2 Leo Crawford was born in Bellaire, Ohio, December 23, 1894

IX —Henry Ross Stilwell the ninth child and sixth son of Samuel S and Anna M Stilwell, was born December 20, 1873 Residence, Bellaire, Ohio

X —Margaret Myrtle Stilwell, the tenth child and fourth daughter of Samuel S. and Anna M Stilwell, was born March 25, 1876 She now resides with her mother in Bellaire, Ohio

XI —Samuel Joseph Stilwell, the eleventh child and seventh son of Samuel S and Anna M Stilwell, was born August 16, 1879 — a painter by occupation He resides with his mother at the family residence, No 3739 Harrison Street Bellaire Belmont County, Ohio

IV —James Steen, a son of Samuel and Mary Mayers Steen, was born in Berkeley County, Virginia He removed with his parents to the farm near St Clairsville, Ohio He is reported to have been married, but of this we have no record The later portion of his life was spent in Virginia, where he died

V —Anne Steen, a daughter of Samuel and Mary Mayers Steen, was born in Berkeley County, Virginia, in 1809 She removed with her parents to their farm, near St Clairsville, Belmont County, Ohio, where she resided until after marriage, her father having died before her marriage She, as well as her parents and all the family, was a strict Presbyterian, and until after 1850 all her father's children and their families were still living in that vicinity All the children of Samuel and Mary Mayers Steen are now dead, and their descendants are very widely scattered, some of whom are living in Ohio, Illinois, Iowa, Missouri, Virginia, etc

Anne Steen was married at St Clairsville, O , Aug 30, 1830. to Josiah Laughlin Leech, he having been born in Harrison County, Ohio, July 25, 1812, and died in Winterset, Madison County, Iowa, August 28, 1897 in the 86th year of his age Mrs Anne Steen Leech died in 1880 at Winterset, Iowa, aged 71 years The following are their children

1 Letitia Leech was born in Belmont County Ohio, May 25, 1831 She was married near Fairview, Guernsey County, Ohio, December 31, 1851, to John Boden — a farmer — he having been born near Morristown, Belmont County, Ohio, October 5, 1829 Residence, Hendrysburgh Ohio The following are their children

  I —M. A Boden was born near Hendrysburgh, Belmont County, Ohio, December 13, 1852 She was married to a Mr Boyd

  II —Mary Belle Boden was born near Cambridge, Guernsey County, Ohio, June 4, 1854 She was married to a Mr. Mead

  III —Wilbur L. Boden was born near Fairview, Guernsey County, Ohio, May 25, 1857.

  IV —Samuel E Boden was born near Morristown, Belmont County, Ohio, June 28, 1861

  V —Luella J. Boden was born near Fairview, Guernsey County, Ohio, February 13, 1868 She was married to a Mr Shepherd

2. Mary Jane Leech, the second daughter of Josiah L. and Anne Steen Leech, was born in Belmont County, Ohio, in 1833, and died when about two years old.

3 Sarah Elizabeth Leech, the third daughter of Josiah L and Anne Steen Leech, was born in Guernsey County, Ohio, March 30, 1835 She was married at Washington, Guernsey County, Ohio, May 23, 1865, to William Cunningham Henery, he having been born in Guernsey County, Ohio, February 23, 1833 Soon after marriage they located in Winterset, Madison County, Iowa, where they still reside Mr Henery is engaged in the insurance business The following are the children of William C and Sarah E Henery

  I —Josiah Wilbur Henery was born August 26, 1869

  II —Cora Mabel Henery was born January 13 1874

  III —John Alva Henery was born March 20, 1876

4 Nancy Eleanor Leech, the fourth daughter of Josiah L and Anne Steen Leech, was born in Belmont County, Ohio, February 12, 1837 She was married in Winterset, Iowa, November 17, 1870 to John McMillan Stewart, he having been born in Columbiana County, Ohio, October 4 1837 — a

farmer by occupation Residence, near Winterset, Madison
County, Iowa The following are their children

I —Frank Samuel Stewart was born August 2, 1871

II —Clyde Everett Stewart was born May 2, 1873

III —Nellie Leanne Stewart was born September 5, 1875

5 Robert Laughlin Leech, the fifth child and eldest son of
Josiah I and Anne Steen Leech, was born in Belmont
County, Ohio, June 15, 1839 — a State traveling salesman
He was married at Moorefield, Harrison County, Ohio,
August 30, 1864, to Miss Addie E Williams, she having been
born at Moorefield, Ohio January 6, 1847 Residence,
Winterset, Madison County, Iowa The following are their
children

I —Laura A Leech was born November 16 1865 — a
teacher

II —Benoni H Leech was born May 19, 1870

III —Jessie A Leech was born April 11, 1873

IV —Charles S Leech was born February 13, 1876

V —Flora Leech was born January 18, 1879

VI —John A Leech was born February 8, 1882

VII —Chester R Leech was born May 26, 1885

VIII —Lucile Leech was born September 9, 1888

6 Samuel Boyd Leech, the sixth child, and second son of
Samuel L. and Anne Steen Leech, was born in Egypt, three
and one-half miles northeast of Hendrysburgh, Belmont
County, Ohio, August 3, 1841 He was married at the same
place, February 28, 1867 to Miss Martha Jane Henderson
she having been born near Antrim, Guernsey County, Ohio,
April 7, 1847 Mr Leech is by occupation a traveling salesman Residence Des Moines, Iowa The following are the
children of Samuel B and Martha J Leech

I —Clyde Clifton Leech was born in Grove City Cass
County, Iowa, December 20, 1867

II —Margaret Anna Leech was born in Winterset, Madison
County, Iowa, April 14, 1869

III —Lillian May Leech was born in Winterset, Madison
County, Iowa, April 15, 1871

II' —William Frederic Leech was born in Fairview, Guernsey County, Ohio, November 12, 1875

7 James Alexander Leech the seventh child and third son of Josiah and Anne Steen Leech, was born in Belmont County, Ohio, November 25, 1843 He studied medicine, and has practiced medicine for many years He is now a prominent physician in Colorado Springs, Colorado He was married in Cambridge, Ohio, August 7, 1867, to Miss Amanda Robe, of Washington, Ohio, a daughter of William and Mary Robe They have no children Residence, Colorado Springs, Colorado

8 Joseph Arastus Leech, the eighth child and fourth son of Josiah L and Anne Steen Leech, was born in Belmont County, Ohio, in 1846, and died in 1848, when about two years old

9 Martha Anna Leech, the ninth child, the fifth and youngest daughter of Josiah L and Anne Steen Leech, was born near Fairview, Guernsey County, Ohio, May 15, 1853 She was married in Winterset, Madison County, Iowa, November 9, 1881, to George M Violet — a merchant — he having been born near Oskaloosa, Iowa, July 1 1855 Residence, Afton, Union County, Iowa The following are their children

I —Claire J Violet was born in Afton, Iowa, September 24, 1882

II —Anna L Violet was born in Afton, Iowa, June 7, 1885

VI —Thomas Steen, a son of Samuel and Mary Mayers Steen, was born in Berkeley County, Virginia He removed with his parents to their home and farm, near St Clairsville Belmont County, Ohio He was married and brought up a family of children in Belmont County O, where they continued for a long time to reside, at least up to the time of the Civil War in 1861-65

VII —Samuel Steen, a son of Samuel and Mary Mayers Steen, was born in Berkeley County, Virginia He came with his parents to their new home and farm, near St Clairsville Belmont County, Ohio, where he afterwards resided He was by occupation a blacksmith, and used to live at Martin's Ferry, Belmont County, Ohio, near to Wheeling, West Virginia During the period before the war he used to correspond with his cousin, Aaron F Steen, who at that time lived near Winchester, Adams County, Ohio He was married and brought up a family that lived in Ohio

VIII —Stephen Steen, a son of Samuel and Mary Mayers Steen, was probably born in Berkeley County, Virginia He came with his parents when they located on their new farm near St Clairsville, Belmont County, Ohio He was married, and during the later portion of his life lived in Virginia He died in old age in Berkeley County, Virginia in 1891 Stephen and Mary Steen brought up a family They had a married daughter living near Martinsburgh, Virginia, a few years ago.

IX —Robert Steen, a son of Samuel and Mary Mayers Steen, was probably born in Berkeley County, Virginia and came with his parents to their new home and farm, near St Clairsville, Belmont County, Ohio, in which county he spent the remainder of his life This Robert Steen was a grandson of the Robert Steen who was born in Ireland about 1730, and settled in Lancaster County, Pennsylvania He was married and brought up a family in Ohio He died about 1849 or 1850 His family afterwards removed to Illinois, near Macon

X —Sarah Steen, a daughter of Samuel and Mary Mayers Steen, was born in Berkeley County, Virginia, probably about 1817 (?) She resided with her parents until after their death, and then still lived in Ohio for many years She finally removed to the East and lived and died in Philadelphia, Pennsylvania She was never married

XI —Mary Ellen Steen, a daughter of Samuel and Mary Mayers Steen, was born in Berkeley County, Virginia, June 3, 1819 She was brought by her parents from Virginia to their new home, on a farm near St Clairsville, Belmont County, Ohio, where she continued to live until after the death of her parents A Rev Mr Love now owns and lives upon the farm her father used to possess and cultivate Two of her brothers, who were both single at the time, went away from their home in Ohio many years ago, and the family ceasing to hear from them, naturally supposed they had died unmarried Mary Ellen Steen was a devoted Christian, a member of Adena Presbyterian Church She lived in the blessed hope, and died a triumphant death at the home of her son, near Emerson, Jefferson County, Ohio, April 18, 1890, in the 71st year of her age. She was married near Shepherdstown, Belmont County, Ohio, December 3, 1847, to William Shields, he having been born in Delaware County, Pennsylvania, November 26, 1804. The following are their children

1 Joseph B Shields, the eldest child and only son of William and Mary Ellen Steen Shields, was born in Belmont County, Ohio August 15, 1848 — a useful Christian man, a practical farmer, and a dairyman He was married near Mount Pleasant, Jefferson County, Ohio, November 11, 1890, to Miss Virginia Elizabeth Hampton, she having been born in Somerton, Belmont County, Ohio October 22, 1857   Residence, Emerson, Jefferson County, Ohio   The following are their children

  I —Richard Henry Shields was born at Emerson, Ohio, August 17, 1891

  II —Louis Hampton Shields was born at Emerson, Ohio, August 28, 1892

  III —Mary Elizabeth Shields was born at Emerson, Ohio, September 10, 1894

  IV —Alice Margaret Shields was born at Emerson, Jefferson County, Ohio July 9, 1896

2 Martha P Shields, the second child and eldest daughter of William and Mary E Steen Shields, was born in Belmont County, Ohio, November 28, 1849, and died May 28, 1868 in the 19th year of her age

3 Margaret Shields, the third child and second daughter of William and Mary Ellen Steen Shields, was born in Belmont County, Ohio, August 26, 1851. She was married at Emerson Ohio, December 29, 1881, to Harvey Watson Graham — a farmer — he having been born at Morristown, Ohio, February 11, 1857   The following are their children

  I —William Clyde Graham was born at Uniontown, Belmont County, Ohio, September 21, 1882

  II —Bertha Belle Graham was born at Martin s Ferry, Belmont County, Ohio, May 10, 1888

4 Letitia Shields the fourth child and third daughter of William and Mary Ellen Steen Shields, was born in Belmont

County, Ohio, November 25, 1852 She was married at
Emerson, Ohio, April 17, 1873, to Leonard Payne — a
farmer — he having been born at Red Lion, York County,
Pennsylvania, March 6, 1839 The following are their children

I —Rachael Ann Payne was born at Smithfield, Jefferson
County, Ohio, April 9, 1874

II —William Leander Payne was born at St Clairsville,
Belmont County, Ohio. October 16, 1876

5 Catherine A Shields the fifth child and fourth daughter of
William and Mary Ellen Steen Shields, was born in Belmont County, Ohio, November 24, 1854

6 Emily A Shields, the sixth child and fifth daughter of William and Mary Ellen Steen Shields was born in Belmont
County, Ohio, February 19, 1857

CHAPTER II

Robert Steen, the second child and son of Robert
and Elizabeth Boyd Steen was born near Chestnut Level, in
Lancaster County Pennsylvania, about 1763 (?) He was
brought up on his father's farm and spent his whole life near the
place He was a bright, intelligent, and industrious man — a
school teacher by profession — but was a cripple, suffering from
a diseased spine He was never married, and died while he was
comparatively a young man

CHAPTER III

Mary Steen, called "Polly," the third child and eldest
daughter of Robert and Elizabeth Boyd Steen was born
near Chestnut Level in Lancaster County Pennsylvania about
1767 (?), and spent her whole life upon the farm, taking care of
her parents while they lived and afterwards making the place
her home She was never married

CHAPTER IV

———

Elizabeth Steen, called "Betsy," the fourth child and second daughter of Robert and Elizabeth Boyd Steen, was born near Chestnut Level, in Lancaster County, Pennsylvania about 1770 (?), and was brought up on her father's farm. She was never married, but resided with her parents, and with her sister took care of them so long as they lived. After her parents' death she and her sister lived together on the place, in possession of the property. She outlived her sister and brothers, and died about 1838 or 1839. After her death a letter was written to her brother, Alexander Steen, in Ohio, to come and see after the estate, but he had died a year or two previous to that time, and none of his children went back to Pennsylvania to see after their interest in the property.

———

CHAPTER V.

———

Alexander Steen, the fifth and youngest child and third son of Robert and Elizabeth Boyd Steen, was born near Chestnut Level, in Lancaster County, Pennsylvania, February 14, 1773 — (more than three years before the declaration of American independence) — and brought up on his father's farm which was not far from the Susquehanna River. In early manhood he removed to Berkeley County, Virginia, where he remained several years. He was married at Martinsburgh, Berkeley County, Virginia, February 2 1803 to Miss Agnes Nancy Faris, daughter of a prominent citizen of that place she having been born there, March 2 1777 and died at the residence of her eldest son, Aaron Faris Steen, near Youngsville Adams County, Ohio November 17, 1852 aged 75 years, 8 months, and 15 days.*

———

* "THE FARIS FAMILY"—Mr Faris whose wife's name was Nancy was the father of several children, all born at or near Martinsburgh, Berkeley County Virginia, among whom were the following
1—Aaron Faris was born about 1769 was married and brought up a family at Martinsburgh Virginia

In 1805 Alexander Steen removed with his family from Virginia and located two miles north of Flemingsburgh, Fleming

---

II —John Faris was born about 1772; was married at Martinsburgh, Virginia, removed to Flemingsburgh, Kentucky, with Alexander Steen and family, near which place he brought up a family of several children

III.—Rebecca Faris was born about 1774, was married at Martinsburgh, Virginia, to Peter Schriver, and removed to Adams County, Ohio, where they brought up a family of eight children, and where a numerous posterity remains The following are their children, all born in Adams County, Ohio

  1 John Schriver, who married Elizabeth Hannah, and had five children
      I —William Scriver
      II —John Schriver
      III —Aaron Schriver
      IV.—A daughter.
      V —A daughter.
  2 Robert Schriver, who first married Sarah Bailey, and after her death Margaret ——— To his first wife was born two children, and to his second wife three children, as follows.
      I —Joshua Schriver
      II —Rachel Schriver
      III —Thomas Schriver
      IV —Sarah Ellen Schriver
      V —Alice Schriver
  3 Eli Schriver, who was married and brought up a family
  4 Elizabeth Schriver, who married William Havens and had several children
      I —Martha Havens
      II —Anderson Havens, and other children
  5 Nancy Schriver, who married George Higginbotham and brought up a family
  6 Mahala Schriver, who married Ezra Sparks and brought up a family of nine children, as follows
      I —Solomon Sparks
      II —John Sparks.
      III —Levi Sparks
      IV —Rebecca Ann Sparks
      V.—Robert Sparks
      VI —Mary Sparks
      VII —Catherine Sparks
      VIII —Acquilla Sparks
      IX —Ezra Sparks
  7. Rebecca Ann Schriver, who married James Sparks and brought up a family
  8 Ellen Schriver, who married Joseph Bailey, to whom were born—
      I —Rachel Ellen Bailey
      II —Joshua Bailey The family moved West, and had other children.

IV.—Agnes Nancy Faris was born March 2, 1777, was married at Martinsburgh, Virginia, February 2, 1803, to Alexander Steen, formerly of Lancaster County, Pennsylvania They removed to Kentucky in 1805, and settled permanently near Winchester, Adams County, Ohio, in 1820 where they spent the remainder of their lives They had a family of eight children, whose record is given in "The Steen Family," Book One, Chapter V

County, Kentucky where he "opened out" a farm Here he built a substantial hewed log house, two stories high and comprising several good rooms In this house which was considered quite an excellent residence in those early days, he continued to reside while cultivating the farm for nearly fifteen years In the summer of 1876 the writer, accompanied by his father, visited this "old Kentucky home", was shown over the farm and through the house, the room where his father was born, in 1807, and the grounds where he had played when a child Alexander Steen while living in Kentucky, was thrown from his horse, and one of his legs was broken and it became slightly shorter than the other, making him a little lame ever afterwards He was not only a successful farmer, but a popular music teacher, and taught old-fashioned singing schools in many localities, and for many years And as music books could not easily be obtained, he *had to write them* for his pupils, and became quite remarkable for the rapidity, neatness of execution, and the skill he acquired in this regard In 1820 he removed from Kentucky with his family, and located upon a farm two miles east of Winchester, in Adams County, Ohio, where he continued to reside for several years. This farm was situated on the west side of Brush Creek and is now on the turnpike road leading from Winchester to Buck Run A school-house was built upon it a few years ago, near the iron bridge across the creek He afterwards purchased a large farm one mile northwest of the Mount Leigh Presbyterian Church (three miles from Youngsville, four miles from Winchester and about two miles from the present railway station at Seman, Adams County, Ohio), where he built a large two-story hewed log residence and spent the remainder of his life, an enterprising farmer and successful music teacher The Mount Leigh Church although a country church, was a place of religious importance in those early days where people gathered for worship from many miles around, and it still continues to be a center of usefulness, with services every Sabbath and an active membership of nearly two hundred sending forth excellent men and women into the various walks of life Alexander Steen was a man of strong character, an earnest Presbyterian, in which faith he had been brought up by his parents, in Pennsylvania, and exerted an extensive influence in the community His wife's parents were also Presbyterian and all her brothers and sisters continued to be so, except one brother, who married a lady of another denomination and united with the Methodist Episcopal Church Mr and Mrs

(4)

Steen both descended from a long line of Scotch-Irish Presbyterian ancestors, and were themselves members of the Mount Leigh Presbyterian Church for many years   Alexander Steen died at his home, near Mount Leigh, April 30, 1837, aged 64 years, 2 months, and 16 days   After his death Mrs Agnes Nancy Steen lived with her children until November 17, 1852, when she died at the residence of her eldest son, Aaron F Steen, near Youngsville, Ohio, and was buried by the side of her husband, in the Mount Leigh cemetery   To Alexander and Agnes Nancy Steen were born the following eight children   Jane, Rebecca A, Aaron F, R. Wilson, Catherine E, John W, Alexander B, and Josiah Y Steen

I —Jane Steen, the eldest child and daughter of Alexander and Agnes Nancy Steen, was born near Martinsburgh, Berkeley County, Virginia, September 19, 1803   She was brought by her parents to their home, near Flemingsburgh, Kentucky, when only two years old, where she spent fifteen years of happy girlhood school days   She removed again with her parents to Ohio, and died the next year, unmarried, at her father's residence, two miles east of Winchester, Adams County, Ohio, September 10, 1821, in the 18th year of her age   She is said to have been a beautiful and accomplished young lady, very much beloved

II —Rebecca Ann Steen the second child and daughter of Alexander and Agnes Nancy Steen, was born near Martinsburgh, Berkeley County, Virginia, November 27, 1804, and was brought in the arms of her mother, when an infant, to their home in Kentucky   She spent fifteen years of happy life upon her father's farm, near Flemingsburgh, Kentucky and in attending school, helping her mother, etc   In the summer of 1820 she removed with her parents to their home near Winchester, Adams County, Ohio, where she continued to reside   She died near Winchester, Ohio, October 15, 1837 aged 32 years, 10 months, and 18 days

Rebecca A Steen was married at the residence of her father, near Winchester, Adams County, Ohio, by Aaron Moore, J P, October 22, 1823, to Samuel Rhoades, a son of Anthony and Jennie Gillespie Rhoades — a farmer by occupation — he having been born in Pennsylvania in 1803, and died in Adams County, Ohio, in 1859, aged 56 years

To Samuel and Rebecca A Steen Rhoades were born the following seven children

1 Sarah Jane Rhoades, the eldest child and daughter of Samuel and Rebecca A Steen Rhoades, was born near Winchester, Adams County, Ohio, in 1824, and died unmarried in 1842, aged 18 years

2 Samuel David Belt Rhoades, the second child and eldest son of Samuel and Rebecca A. Steen Rhoades, was born near Winchester Adams County, Ohio, in 1826 From 1856 until his death he was quite feeble, and suffered from lung disease He traveled in the South considerably for his health, his brother, Anthony A Rhoades, accompanying and caring for him In returning from Galveston, Texas, whither they had gone and while crossing the Gulf of Mexico on their way to New Orleans the steamer on which they journeyed was caught in a terrible storm, and it was thought the vessel would be wrecked and all on board would perish In the midst of the raging storm and the great signals of distress, he died, January, 1859, in the 33d year of his age At the time of his death his brother was also very sick and unable to lift his head from his pillow The vessel at length reached New Orleans in safety and S D Belt Rhoades was buried in the potter's field two days later, at the request of his brother by the hand of strangers

3 Cynthia Ann Rhoades, the second daughter and third child of Samuel and Rebecca A Steen Rhoades, was born near Winchester Adams County, Ohio, September 22, 1828, and spent her whole life in the county She made her home a good deal of the time in the family of her uncle, Aaron F Steen Cynthia A Rhoades was married near Winchester, Ohio, in June, 1855, to Joseph K Vance, and died April 28, 1857, in the 29th year of her age Her husband afterwards died in Ripley Ohio They had no children

4 Nancy Ann Rhoades, the fourth child and third daughter of Samuel and Rebecca A Steen Rhoades, was born near Winchester, Ohio, January 19, 1832, and died near the Mount Leigh Presbyterian Church March 7, 1870, in the 39th year of her age She studied in Ohio University, Athens, Ohio but spent nearly her whole life in Adams County, Ohio Nancy A Rhoades was married about two miles from the Mount Leigh Church, at the residence of her uncle Colonel

Josiah Y Steen by the Rev Samuel Van Dyke, June 11, 1857, to Absalom Day, a son of Absalom and Elizabeth Earhart Day, who as early as the year 1800 had settled upon a farm three miles east of Williamsburgh, Clermont County, Ohio and afterwards located in Brown County, Ohio, where this Absalom Day was born December 26 1817, and died at the residence of his son, Erastus Henry Day, in Fredericktown, Madison County, Missouri, May 10, 1897, aged 79 years 4 months, and 13 days His body was tenderly laid away to rest in the Masonic Cemetery, May 12, 1897 He was a man of sterling worth, highly respected, a devout Christian, and an industrious and useful citizen To Absalom and Nancy A Rhoades Day were born the following four children

I —Icedora Day, the oldest child and daughter of Absalom and Nancy A Day was born in Mount Orab, Brown County, Ohio, July 15, 1858 After the death of her mother, in 1870, she resided for one year in the family of Mr and Mrs John T Beveridge near Buck Run, Adams County, Ohio She afterwards made her home, until 1893, in the family of her uncle, Colonel Josiah Y Steen and from 1893 until 1896 she lived at Mount Washington, near Cincinnati, Ohio She early united with the Mount Leigh Presbyterian Church, and became an active, devout, and useful member of the church, and of society in general She was married by the Rev U G Humphrey, at the residence of A C Butler, near Seman, Adams County, Ohio, March 31, 1896, to William Wiggins Whittaker, a son of John and Sarah Ann Whittaker, he having been born at South Point, Franklin County, Missouri, near the Missouri River, June 28, 1855 Mr Whittaker is a house carpenter by occupation, a devout Christian, and a member of the Presbyterian Church Residence Murphysboro Jackson County, Illinois

II —Effie Day, the second daughter of Absalom and Nancy A Day, was born near Youngsville, Adams County, Ohio, July 15, 1861 She was married at the same place by the Rev George Fulton, October 3, 1883, to Franklin LaFayette Higgins, a son of James P and Mary Higgins he having been born near West Union, Adams County, Ohio, July 13, 1859 James P Higgins, the father of Franklin

L. Higgins was born in Fayette County, Pennsylvania, and came to Adams County, Ohio, in 1837, where he was married, and has since resided upon a farm near West Union, Ohio, adjoining that upon which his son now lives Franklin L. Higgins and his family reside upon a farm two and one-half miles west of West Union, Adams County, Ohio The following are their children

1 Nellie Etta Higgins, the eldest child of Franklin L. and Effie Day Higgins was born near West Union, Ohio, January 17, 1885

2 Elvis Earl Higgins, the second child of Franklin L. and Effie Day Higgins, was born near West Union Ohio, October 27, 1889

3 Anna Marie Higgins, the third child and second daughter of Franklin L. and Effie Day Higgins, was born near West Union Ohio November 13, 1893

III —Anna Josephine Day the third daughter of Absalom and Nancy A Day, was born near Youngsville Adams County Ohio, September 24, 1863, and died in Oregon City, Oregon, March 3, 1889 aged 25 years, 5 months, and 21 days She continued to live at or near the place of her birth until the autumn of 1884, when she removed to Oregon City, Oregon, and made her home in the family of her uncle, Thomas W Rhoades, proprietor of the "Cliff House," in that city Miss A Josephine Day was married by the Rev S P Davis, pastor of the Baptist Church in Oregon City, Oregon August 11, 1886, to Hezekiah H Johnson, a son of Rev Hezekiah Johnson, a pioneer missionary in Oregon he having been born in Oregon City, July 23, 1849, and where he has ever resided In 1891 Mr Johnson was the esteemed County Clerk of Clackamas County, and a popular official Residence, Oregon City Oregon To Hezekiah H and A Josephine Day Johnson were born in Oregon City the following children

1 Violet Olive Johnson was born June 12, 1887

2 Anna Day Johnson was born October 9, 1888, and died January 16, 1889

IV —Ann Elizabeth Day the fourth daughter of Absalom and Nancy A Rhoades Day, was born near Youngsville,

Adams County, Ohio, October 4, 1866 Residence, Walnut Hills Cincinnati, Ohio

Thomas Wilson Rhoades, the fifth child and second son of Samuel and Rebecca A Steen Rhoades, was born near Winchester, Adams County, Ohio, August 28, 1833 and spent his early life in that region He was apprenticed to William Sharp, under whom he learned the brickmason's trade He early became quite proficient in his work, and molded all the bricks and assisted in building near Mount Leigh, Ohio, the large brick residence of his uncle, Aaron F Steen, in 1849, when he was only a youth of 17 years In 1850 he removed to Berlin, Sangamon County, Illinois, and two years later caught the California fever, and with many other emigrants crossed the plains, expecting to make a fortune For some time afterwards he was superintendent of mason work in the erection of some Government buildings in Los Angeles, for which he received six dollars a day After several years in California he became a traveling agent In 1857 he located in Portland, Oregon, and for about fifteen years worked there at his trade, and in Boise City, Idaho About 1875 he removed to Oregon City, and opened "The Cliff House," a hotel, of which he continued to be the genial proprietor until his death He was well known in Oregon City and throughout Clackamas County, and always had a pleasant word for everybody In 1884 he made an extensive journey in the Eastern States, visiting many relatives and friends in Ohio whom he had not seen since his boyhood days, in 1850 On returning to Oregon he brought with him his sister's daughter, Miss Anna Josephine Day, who afterwards made her home in his family He died of pneumonia after a short illness in Oregon City, February 17, 1885, aged 51 years, 5 months and 20 days Thomas W Rhoades was married in Portland, Oregon, January 1, 1861, to Miss Anna Eliza White, a daughter of Judge William L and Mary E White, she having been born in Carroll County, Missouri, January 30, 1844 Family residence, Oregon City, Oregon To Thomas W and Anna Eliza Rhoades were born the following

I—Jerome Earnest Rhoades was born in East Portland Oregon, October 23, 1861 — a clerk Residence, Oregon City, Oregon

II —James Louis Rhoades was born in Oregon City, Oregon, February 27, 1867, and died May 21, 1868

III —William Samuel Rhoades was born in Portland, Oregon, September 22, 1875 — a clerk by occupation Residence, Oregon City, Oregon

6 Anthony Alexander Rhoades, the sixth child and third son of Samuel and Rebecca Ann Steen Rhoades, was born near Winchester, Adams County, Ohio September 22, 1834, and died in Albany, Oregon, February 3, 1890 His mother died when he was a little child, only three years old, and he was brought up in the family of his uncle, Alexander B Steen near Mount Leigh, Ohio where he worked on the farm in summer and attended school in winter, until he was eighteen years of age In May, 1855, he removed from Adams County, Ohio, to Sangamon County, Illinois, where he made his home for many years In 1858 he left his regular work to travel with and take care of his brother, S D Belt Rhoades, who at that time was in very poor health, and gradually kept on growing weaker until at length he died while they were crossing the Gulf of Mexico, and in the midst of a terrible storm which took place in January, 1859. In 1862 he went to the Pacific Coast, where he spent more than three years, principally in Oregon, and returned to Illinois in the autumn of 1865, being on the stormy Atlantic on his 31st birthday From San Francisco, California, he made the trip in thirty-six days, spent two weeks in Greytown, Nicaragua, afterwards continued his journey to New York, going on board the vessel 'Ericsson," which was propelled by *hot air*, and safely reached his destination From 1865 until 1883 he resided continually in Sangamon County, Illinois, and worked at his trade — a plasterer and calciminer, then permanently removed to Albany, Oregon, where he spent the remainder of his days In 1857 he became a member of the Christian Church, or Disciples of Christ, was ordained a deacon in 1869, and continued an active worker in the Master's cause until his death He was a most agreeable companion, witty, full of jokes and always very fond of music, even in his boyhood days He possessed a rich, sweet voice, acquired great skill and was a popular music teacher and leader of the choir in the church for many years In the winter of 1889-90 he suffered from

a severe attack of la grippe, or influenza, which finally terminated in pneumonia, from which he died at his home, in Albany, Oregon, quietly passing away from earth in the full hope of a glorious immortality. Anthony A. Rhoades was married by the Rev. Perry Bennett, a Baptist minister, in Berlin, Sangamon County, Illinois, in December, 1860, to Miss Nancy A. Harmon, a daughter of Henry and Mary Harmon, of Berlin, she having been born in 1841, and died December 12, 1866 aged 25 years. Her body was laid to rest in the Island Grove cemetery. Anthony A. Rhoades was married a second time by the Rev. Charles Rowe, at Berlin, Ill., March 21, 1869, to Miss Mary Frances Yates, a daughter of Thomas and Nancy Higgins Yates she having been born in Berlin, Illinois, March 28 1838. Her father's brother, Richard Yates, was the War Governor of Illinois and United States Senator. In March, 1889, the twentieth anniversary of the married life of Anthony A. and Mary F. Rhoades was delightfully celebrated at their residence, in Albany, Oregon. Many relatives and friends of the family were gathered together, and proceeded with a most enjoyable programme. The bride and groom of twenty years expressed their satisfaction with each other, and renewed their vows of faithfulness until death. The following poem, written for the occasion by J. B. Hughes, a special friend of the family, was sung by himself and others.

TWENTY YEARS AGO

We've come to help you celebrate
Your china wedding day,
To bring remembrance of the time
Wher every heart was gay.
We will partake of pie and cake,
And spend an hour or so
To wish you joy, as others did
Just twenty years ago

You've wandered far from that dear place
Where childhood's days were spent,
Where youthful sports in early life
To bless a while were sent,
Where hearts took fire with love's desire,
Consumed and melted so,
The preacher called and made you one
Just twenty years ago

We can not be the same dear friends
Who met to bless you then,
Reflecting back your happiness
Again and yet again

You've come away, and wandered they,
   And some are sleeping low,
And all so changed you ne'er can meet
   Like twenty years ago

The wheel of time is rolling on;
   How swift the years do pass,
To change us all from youth to age,
   And reap us down at last
But happy we will try to be
   While dwelling here below,
And be as true as those you knew
   Some twenty years ago

You occupy the middle ground
   'Twixt youth and crumbling age,
The silver hairs begin to mark
   You for another stage
May purest love draw thee above,
   Nor ever cease to flow
For us now here, and those so dear
   Of twenty years ago

'Tis well to pause mid cares of life
   And cast a backward look,
And in your thoughts live o'er again
   The time thy courtship took,
To well decide for groom and bride,
   'Mongst all that each did know,
Which one to choose and not refuse,
   Some twenty years ago.

Oh, happy choice, where love directs,
   And makes the heart to move!
And you have both had time enough
   Your constancy to prove
Again we wish each china dish
   With good things may o'erflow,
And joys to bless be never less
   Than twenty years ago

Anthony A Rhoades was the father of the following children

I—Thomas Henry Rhoades, the eldest son and only child of Anthony A and Nancy A Harmon Rhoades was born in Berlin, Sangamon County, Illinois, October 8, 1861, and removed to Oregon with his father's family in 1883 He was married by the Rev Hiram P Webb, of the M E Church, in Albany, Oregon, July 29, 1886 to Miss Mary R Payne, a daughter of Nimrod P and Rosina Culver Payne, she having been born in Linn County, Oregon, October 5 1868 Residence Albany, Oregon The following are their children

1 Russell Harmon Rhoades the eldest child of Thomas
H and Mary R Rhoades, was born in Albany, Oregon,
September 12, 1887

2 Leah Rhoades, the second child, a daughter of Thomas
H and Mary R Rhoades, was born in Albany, Oregon,
July 23, 1891

3 Eugene Victor Rhoades, the third child and second
son of Thomas H and Mary R Rhoades, was born in
Albany, Oregon, February 17, 1896

II—Nellie Patti Rhoades, the second child and eldest
daughter of Anthony A Rhoades (and the first child by
his second wife Mary Frances Yates Rhoades), was born
in Berlin, Sangamon County, Illinois, June 23, 1870, and
brought by her parents to Oregon in 1883, when thirteen
years of age   She was married by the Rev James F
Stewart, of the Christian Church, at the residence of her
mother, in Albany, Oregon, March 29, 1891, to Dan
Walter Myers, a son of John W and Margaret Stratton
Myers, he having been born in Wayne County, Ohio,
July 8, 1867   Residence, Albany Oregon   The following are their children

1 Agnes Myers was born in Albany Oregon, April 2,
1892 and died April 3, 1892

2 Mary Frances Myers was born in Albany, Oregon,
November 12, 1893

3 Hallie Rhoades Myers was born in Albany, Oregon,
May 18, 1895

4 Helen Steen Myers was born in Albany, Oregon, May
18, 1895

5 Lyndon T. Myers was born in Albany, Oregon, June
16 1898

III—Phebe Rebecca Rhoades, the second daughter of
Anthony A and Mary Frances Yates Rhoades, was born
in Berlin, Sangamon County, Illinois, June 3, 1873, and
brought by her parents to Oregon in 1883, when she was
ten years old   Residence, Albany, Linn County Oregon

IV—Bessie Price Rhoades, the fourth child of A A
Rhoades, but the third child of Anthony A and Mary
Frances Yates Rhoades, was born in Berlin Sangamon
County, Illinois, October 24, 1874, and brought by her

parents to Oregon in 1883 She died in the faith of Christ at the home of her mother in Albany, Oregon, May 31, 1892, in the eighteenth year of her age

V —Richard Yates Rhoades, the fifth child of A A Rhoades, but the fourth child and only son of Anthony A and Mary Frances Yates Rhoades, was born in Berlin, Sangamon County, Illinois, and was brought by his parents to Oregon in 1883 He died a devout Christian, at the home of his mother, in Albany, Linn County, Oregon, May 29, 1897, in the twentieth year of his age

7 Aaron Martin Rhoades, the seventh child and fourth son of Samuel and Rebecca Ann Steen Rhoades, was born near Winchester, Adams County, Ohio, in October, 1837, and died in November, 1837, when only a few weeks old

III —Aaron Faris Steen, the third child and eldest son of Alexander and Agnes Nancy Faris Steen was born two miles north of Flemingsburgh, Fleming County, Kentucky August 23, 1807, and died at his home in Xenia, Ohio, February 15, 1881, aged 73 years, 5 months and 23 days He spent his happy boyhood days on the farm in that old Kentucky home,' and was brought by his parents to their new location near Winchester, Adams County, Ohio, in 1820, when thirteen years of age Here he grew to manhood, assisting his father upon the farm in summer, and attending school in winter, and when a young man taught school for a while He also devoted much attention to music, in which he became quite proficient, and very popular as an instructor During the winter months he taught many singing schools in various parts of the county, and for many years was leader of the music in the Mount Leigh Presbyterian Church His social qualities and natural genial disposition made him quite a general favorite in the society of both old and young Aaron F Steen was married at the residence of Michael Freeman, on Scioto Brush Creek, ten miles east of West Union, Adams County, Ohio, March 25, 1830, to Miss Mary Freeman, a daughter of Michael and Elizabeth Duncan Freeman she having been born in the same house in which she was married, October 7, 1810 The Rev. John Meek, who had been engaged to solemnize the marriage was unable to reach the place, because of the high waters then prevailing and the lack of bridges across the streams and Thomas Williams a Justice of the Peace, who was present as an invited guest, performed the marriage ceremony

Moses and Nancy Knight Freeman, the grandparents of Mary Freeman, were born in England married in London, and emigrated to America about 1762, and located upon a farm in Queen Anne County, in the British colony of Maryland, near the eastern shore of the Chesapeake Bay, where they brought up a family of several children

Michael and Elizabeth Duncan Freeman, the parents of the bride, were among the early settlers in the Northwest Territory, having removed from the eastern shore of Maryland and located on Blue Creek, in what is now Adams County, Ohio, in the year 1797—less than ten years after the first permanent white settlement was made in what is now the great State of Ohio   A few years later they secured a large farm, situated on both sides of Scioto Brush Creek, at the mouth of Burley's Run, where they made their permanent home   Here they built a large hewed log house, a story and a half high, with an enormous stone chimney and ample fireplace, which at that time was considered a fine residence, in which Mary Freeman was born and married   The bride's mother was a daughter of Charles and Keziah Duncan, of Queen Anne County, Maryland, who were the parents of several children, one of whom at least (Mary Duncan) was married in Maryland to John Williams, and removed in that early day to the Far West probably in the same company of immigrants with Michael and Elizabeth Duncan Freeman, but locating first in Kentucky, and afterwards coming into what is now Adams County, Ohio   After his marriage Aaron F Steen located upon a farm which he had leased for five years, situated on Brush Creek, at the mouth of Elk Run two miles east of Winchester, Ohio   Here, upon an elevation overlooking the stream, and near a fine spring, he built a comfortable log cabin and went to housekeeping   Soon afterwards he united with the Presbyterian Church at Mount Leigh, as also did his wife, she having previously been connected with the Methodist Episcopal Church at Blue Creek ever since she was thirteen years old   Both were devoted and earnest Christians, active and useful members of the church   For nearly five years Aaron F Steen successfully and profitably cultivated the farm on Brush Creek, but in the autumn of 1834, his lease having nearly expired, his father-in-law now growing old, and wishing to retire from the business, offered him favorable terms to come and take charge of his large farm He accepted the terms and soon afterwards removed with his family to the old Freeman homestead, near the headwaters of the east fork of Scioto Brush Creek, two miles above the mouth of Blue Creek and about ten miles from Rome, a village on the Ohio River This farm is located on the main road leading from West Union to Portsmouth about ten miles east of West Union and about twenty-six from Portsmouth In front of the house was a beautiful grassy lawn and further on the creek, bordered with rocky cliffs crowned with evergreen spruce and cedar trees, quite romantic From one cliff to another across the creek extended a high footbridge, with a railing on either side Along the rear of the house was a wide veranda or porch, from the north end of which was an entrance to the kitchen and dining-room and at the south end a bedroom Back of the house there was a fine orchard south of this one hundred yards was Burley's Run while just beyond was "The Ridge or Sugar Camp of many delightful associations Away to the east and across the creek were the principal agricultural lands The surrounding country was hilly almost mountainous for the hills were large, covered with finest timber and inhabited by wild beasts

Mr Steen was scarcely yet settled upon the old Freeman farm when Michael Freeman sickened and died April 14, 1835 This sad event disarranged his plans, but again terms were offered which he accepted and continued in charge of the farm for thirteen years, making farming his principal business, though he also taught many singing schools During the years of residence on Scioto Brush Creek Mr and Mrs Steen were members and regular attendants of the Presbyterian Church at West Union, ten miles away, but for their accommodation services were often held in their own house The pastor was the Rev John P Van Dyke a man of sterling worth, and faithful in doctrinal instruction The Seceders held regular services at Wait's Mill on Blue Creek once a month which they usually attended, as it was near their home the second story of the mill having been fitted up for church purposes Aaron F and Mary Steen were on September 1, 1838, regularly dismissed from the Mt Leigh Church to unite with the church in West Union, where they were duly received and continued as such until March 24, 1840, when they were again

received into the church at Mt Leigh   They were devotedly
attached to their children, and earnest in their religious instruction; daily morning and evening family worship was regularly
observed in the household   The Bible and the Shorter Cate-
chism were the text-books of study on the Sabbath, which by
them was a day devoted to religious reading and worship, and
at length it was their privilege and joy to see all their children
who lived to maturity connected with the church.

Aaron F Steen was a tall man, just six feet high with pale
blue eyes, fair skin, light hair, and beard a little sandy   He
grew up slender, but when he was older became fleshy, and
weighed over two hundred pounds.   His wife was a short,
slender little woman of dark complexion, black eyes and hair,
energetic and sprightly, like her mother, but in later years she
also became more fleshy   About 1843 Mr Steen purchased a
farm near his father's old home, on Mt Leigh, in which neighborhood all his brothers resided   This farm he leased for a
term of years to a man who built a house and stable, cleared a
few fields, cultivated the land, and put the place in good repair
This farm was situated on the main road from Winchester to
the Mt Leigh Church, three miles east of Winchester,
one mile and a half from Mt Leigh, and two miles
from Youngsville. Ohio   The Cincinnati, Portsmouth
and Virginia Railway now passes directly through it,
just back of the orchard and the barn   After having settled the
Freeman estate, on August 31, 1848, Mr Steen removed to his
new home, in the neighborhood of Mt Leigh, several wagons
being loaded with goods and a number of persons driving the
stock over the rough and hilly way, a distance of about twenty
miles   To this new home, in addition to his own family, he
brought his wife's mother* his wife's oldest sister, Nancy K
Freeman who never married, and his wife's brother's daughter, Sarah M K F Freeman, then only a little child where
they all continued to reside   Here Mrs Elizabeth Duncan
Freeman the mother of Mrs Steen died April 23 1851, aged
83 years, 7 months and 2 days   Her body was taken to the
old cemetery on Blue Creek and tenderly laid away to rest by
the side of her husband

---

* Mrs Elizabeth Duncan Freeman being in poor health, did not
come to Mount Leigh until November, 1850 after the new house was
built, in the meantime living with her son, James Freeman, on Scioto
Brush Creek near the old homestead

AARON F. STEEN,
(Born 1807; Died 1881.)

At Mt Leigh the whole family were regular attendants at the church and Sabbath-school, of which the Rev James Dunlap was pastor, and by whom all the living children were baptized in the church on Sunday morning October 2, 1848

Aaron F Steen having previously been elected, was duly ordained and installed a ruling elder of the Mt. Leigh Presbyterian Church, December 1, 1849, which office he held for many years, and frequently represented the session as a member of Chillicothe Presbytery The summer of 1849 was one of unceasing toil on the farm, and it was fortunate that the boys were large enough to render considerable assistance Mr. Steen had a peculiar tact in making even small boys useful, without overtaxing their strength, and this summer every boy had his mission to fill The bricks were made and burned principally by the boys, under the direction of William Sharp and his apprentice, Thomas W Rhoades, and late in the fall a fine, large, two-story brick residence was built and a roof put upon it The next season (1850) it was finished inside and furnished, and a large, new bank barn erected, and thus improvements were going on On this farm Mr Steen continued to reside for seventeen years, an enterprising, successful man, and an influential citizen In the summer of 1865 he sold the farm near Mt Leigh and bought a small tract of land on West Second Street adjoining the city of Xenia Ohio, to which he removed with his family, and where he spent the remaining sixteen years of his life Here himself and wife united with the First Presbyterian Church of which Rev William T Findley, D D, was pastor at that time He cultivated the little farm and with his eldest son kept a provision store in Xenia In 1874 a delightful family reunion was held in his home, near Xenia at which all his living descendants were present Excellent music enlivened the occasion, old associations were revived, and many amusing incidents connected with early life recalled An artist was present, who took a picture of the entire group including the family residence Before they separated, religious services were held, in which all heartily joined, every member of the family over ten years of age being a consistent member of the Presbyterian Church The Golden Wedding, or fiftieth anniversary of the marriage of Mr and Mrs Aaron F Steen, was duly celebrated at their residence, on Thursday, March 25, 1880 at which many friends and relatives were gathered from different counties and States, and all con-

(5)

curred in the opinion that it was one of the most delightful occasions of the kind they had ever witnessed   Something like the following order was observed   Ceremony, congratulations, historical addresses — ' The Steen Family in Europe," by Rev M D A Steen, of Ludlow, Kentucky   "The Steen Family in America ' by Prof W Freeman Steen, of Cincinnati, Ohio, "The Steen Family — Present Generation," by Dr John A Steen, of Ripley, Ohio   "Reminiscences of His Early Life," by Mr Aaron F Steen, 'Recollections of the Wedding Fifty Years Ago ' by the only guest now living Mrs Catherine E Blair, of North Liberty, Ohio   'The Characteristics of the Steen Family,' by William Ferguson, Esq, of Xenia, Ohio Letters of regret were read from Prof E W Steen, of Knoxville, Tennessee, Mr Alexander B Steen, of Winchester, Ohio, Prof Silas M Steen, of Washington C H, Ohio, and Mr William A Blair, of Eaton, Indiana   Among the presents received was an elegant gold-headed cane, from Dr John A Steen, of Ripley, Ohio

Not long after this joyful occasion Mr Steen's health began to fail, and he grew weaker until his death, which occurred at his residence on Tuesday morning, February 15, 1881, in the 74th year of his age   The funeral took place from the Presbyterian church on the Thursday following, conducted by the Rev F M Wood, and his body was lovingly laid to rest in Woodlawn cemetery, near Xenia   He was a man highly respected and much beloved by all who knew him

Mrs Mary Freeman Steen, after the death of her husband, rented the place and moved into the city, with her daughter, where they lived together until after the latter's marriage, in 1885, and for two years afterwards resided with her in Yellow Springs, Ohio   Since 1887, and until her death, she lived with her son, in Knoxville, Tennessee, and became a member of the Third (Southern) Presbyterian Church in that city   She also made extensive visits to her daughter, who at different times lived in Westboro, Massachusetts and Cincinnati, Ohio   Well does the writer remember how that when he was a child and guilty of some misdoing, she used to lead him to some quiet place alone, lovingly earnestly, and often tearfully tell him of his fault, and then kneel down with him and pray to God for pardon and His grace to make him a better boy God was pleased to bless her faithful instructions and prayers to his conversion, and the life-work of a

MRS. MARY FREEMAN STEEN.
(Born 1810: Died 1895.)

Christian minister She was a woman well known wherever she resided, and one who exerted a wide religious influence She was noted for generous hospitality, and a genial, social, and benevolent disposition, which made her always ready to make sacrifices for the good of others After an illness of about two months, she died at the residence of her son, No 19 Pearl Place Knoxville, Tennessee, at 6 30 A M, July 27, 1895, in the 85th year of her age, rejoicing in hope of a glorious immortality, leaving her children, grandchildren, and great-grandchildren to mourn her loss, but to "rise up and call her blessed " She was the last surviving member of her father's family, which came into Ohio in 1797. Her body was taken to Ohio and tenderly laid by the side of her husband, in the beautiful Woodlawn cemetery, near Xenia 'Blessed are they that do His commandments, that they may have a right to the tree of life, and may enter in through the gates into the city "

To Aaron F and Mary Freeman Steen were born the following children W Freeman, E Watson, S Martin J Truman, Moses D A , Josiah James, S Catherine, Isaac Birt, and William Wirt Steen

1 Wilson Freeman Steen, the eldest son of Aaron F and Mary Freeman Steen, was born two miles east of Winchester, Adams County, Ohio, May 11, 1831, and died in Xenia, Ohio, March 20, 1883, aged 51 years, 10 months, and 9 days. When a little child, in the autumn of 1834 or very early in the spring of 1835, he was taken by his parents to the old home of his grandfather, Michael Freeman, on Scioto Brush Creek, two miles west of Blue Creek in Jefferson Township, Adams County, Ohio, where he spent his happy boyhood days, attended school, and assisted his father upon the farm In the summer of 1848 he removed with his parents to their new home, three miles east of Winchester, on the road to the Mt Leigh Church, where he continued to work upon the farm in summer and go to school in the winter He was a regular attendant at church and Sabbath-school, a diligent student, an energetic and industrious young man He early gave his heart to Christ, and united with the Mt Leigh Presbyterian Church, in 1849, and ever afterwards maintained a devout, consistent, and useful Christian life After he became of age he spent one year in Delaware County, Indiana, where he taught school on Jake's Creek, four miles

north of Muncie, near the residence of his uncle, Isaac Freeman, with whom he boarded   In 1853 he returned to Adams County, Ohio, and engaged in teaching near the place of his birth   Like his father, grandfather, and great-grandfather Steen, he was always very fond of music, and possessed a natural talent for it, which he cultivated to the highest degree   In musical institutes, under competent leaders, and at a musical Normal school in Decatur, Ohio, under the direction of Prof Dwight H Baldwin, he was thoroughly qualified and became a popular and successful teacher of vocal and instrumental music   He taught many classes in Adams, Brown and Clermont Counties, often so many as three at different places, upon each secular day of the week, and for some time resided in Williamsburgh, Ohio   In 1860 he removed to Xenia, Ohio, and followed his chosen profession , was associated with his father in a provision store, and for a time carried on the Xenia marble works   His services were in constant demand at musical institutes, and as leader of church choirs and singing classes   In 1867 he removed to Cincinnati Ohio, and opened a store for the sale of musical instruments   also leader of the music in the First Presbyterian Church   In the summer of 1877 he removed to Ludlow Kentucky, just across the river, and himself and family united with the First Presbyterian Church there of which at that time his brother was pastor   He was ordained and installed a ruling elder in that church September 15 1878, in which position he was an efficient church officer and a very useful man   As leader of the music and teacher in the Sabbath-school his work was exceedingly profitable   W Freeman Steen was a man of sterling worth and unflinching integrity   a devout Christian for many years, having been connected with the Presbyterian churches at Mt Leigh, Xenia, Cincinnati, Ohio, and finally at Ludlow, Kentucky He was by nature possessed of a kind heart and gentle spirit , was always interested in every good work, and constantly making friends   In the autumn of 1882 failing health obliged him to cease from all business, and he returned to Xenia, Ohio, to spend his remaining days   Here he gradually grew weaker   but continued very meek, patient and uncomplaining to the last   He died March 20, 1883, in the assured hope of a blessed inheritance, and his body was laid

PROF. W. FREEMAN STEEN.
(Born 1831; Died 1883.)

away to rest in the beautiful Woodlawn cemetery, near Xenia, Ohio

Prof W Freeman Steen was married by the Rev William Fee, in Xenia, Ohio, December 25, 1862, to Miss Emma Marie Stipp, a daughter of Dr Nathan B and Eliza J Stipp, she having been born in Bellbrook, Greene County, Ohio, October 8, 1842 and died of paralysis, in Cincinnati, Ohio, October 3, 1899, aged 57 years Her body was laid beside her husband, in Xenia cemetery, October 6, 1899 To Prof W Freeman and Emma M Steen were born the following children

I —Edith Marie Steen, the eldest child and only daughter of Prof. W Freeman and Emma M Steen, was born in Xenia, Ohio, March 28, 1864 She was married in Cincinnati, Ohio, September 17, 1882 (?), by the Rev Edward Anderson (?), to Charles William Bogart, the only son of John H and Anna M Bogart, he having been born in Ludlow, Kentucky, April 20, 1864 They have resided in Cincinnati, Ohio, Ludlow Kentucky, Covington, Kentucky, Hamilton, Ohio, and Buffalo, New York Mr C William Bogart is a good musician, an excellent wood engraver, and a skillful machinist — manufacturer of gas engines Residence, Buffalo, New York The following are their children

1 Charles Franklin Bogart was born in Cincinnati, Ohio, July 12 1883

2 Edwin Richard Bogart was born in Ludlow, Kentucky, December 28, 1885

3 John Albert Bogart was born in Ludlow Kentucky, February 18, 1889

4 James Helmus Bogart was born in Ludlow, Kentucky, August 26 1891

5 Lawrence Wilson Bogart was born in Covington, Kentucky February 2 1894

6 Marine Dewey Bogart, the sixth son of C William and Edith M Bogart, was born in Hamilton Ohio, January 20, 1898

II —Ernest Linden Steen, the second child and eldest son of Prof W Freeman and Emma M Steen, was born in Xenia, Ohio, November 2, 1865 He resided with his

parents until after his father's death, and afterwards in
Cincinnati, Ohio   He died unmarried, in Cincinnati,
Ohio, July 8, 1894, aged 28 years, 8 months and 6 days

III—Clarence Freeman Steen, the third child the second
and youngest son of Prof W Freeman and Emma M
Steen, was born in Ludlow, Kentucky, February 23, 1870
After his father's death he resided with his mother until
1890, then spent four years with his uncle, Prof E W
Steen, in Knoxville, Tennessee, attending school   In 1891
he returned to Cincinnati, Ohio and resided with his
mother until her death, October 3, 1899   Clarence F
Steen is a bookbinder by trade   Residence, Toledo, Ohio

2   Eli Watson Steen, the second son of Aaron F and Mary
Freeman Steen was born at the home of his parents, on
Brush Creek, near the mouth of Elk Run, two miles east of
Winchester, Adams County, Ohio August 6, 1833   When
a very little child he was taken by his parents to the old
Freeman farm on Scioto Brush Creek, two miles west of
Blue Creek, and ten miles east of West Union Adams
County, Ohio, where his happy boyhood days were spent,
attending school and assisting his father on the farm   He
removed with his parents, August 31, 1848, when he was fifteen years old, to the farm his father had purchased, lying
on the road from Winchester to Mt Leigh, and about a mile
from the place where he was born   He and his older brother
were his father s principal assistants on the farm, which was
new and required much hard labor   They worked faithfully
during the summer and attended school in the winter   He
was a regular attendant at the Mt Leigh Presbyterian
Church and Sabbath-school for many years   early gave his
heart to Christ, and united with the church in 1849, and ever
afterwards maintained a consistent Christian life   Like his
ancestors, his father, and his brother, he delighted in music,
and had a special talent for it, which was highly cultivated
When he became of age he took a thorough course in musical studies in Normal music schools in Russellville, and in
Decatur, Ohio, under the direction of Prof Dwight H Baldwin, and became a teacher of vocal and instrumental music,
in which profession he became very proficient and quite popular   He held many classes in different parts of Adams
County, Ohio sometimes having as many as three singing

PROF. E. WATSON STEEN.

schools upon each secular day of the week, also leading the
music in the church on the Sabbath   He had a sweet voice,
was a fine singer, and to some extent a composer of music
His services were eagerly sought at musical institutes, con-
ventions, and as an instructor in Normal music classes   in
which he was very successful   After his marriage in 1855,
he located upon a farm which his father had purchased, and
which he afterwards possessed, lying on the direct road from
Winchester to Youngsville, about one and a half miles from
the latter place   and the same distance from the Mt Leigh
Presbyterian Church   In the summer of 1862 he enlisted as
a private soldier in the Union Army for the defense of his
country, in Company E, Ninety-first Regiment, Ohio Volunteer Infantry   was promoted to Second Sergeant, and on a
few occasions commanded the company   He was stationed
principally in West Virginia, and owing to failing health was
honorably discharged from the service   During his absence
in the army his own house was ransacked by the soldiers of
John Morgan in their raid through Ohio   In the summer of
1867 he sold his farm near Youngsville and Mt Leigh, and
removed to Xenia, Ohio where he continued to reside and
follow his profession for several years,   then became a traveling agent for the large music house of D H Baldwin &
Co , of Cincinnati, Ohio, being one of their most esteemed
and successful salesmen   Owing to a complete failure of
health he was compelled to retire from business for several
years, and resided with his family in Xenia, Ohio   His
health having somewhat improved, and desiring to locate in a
milder climate, in May, 1880, he removed to Knoxville Tennessee   and in connection with another gentleman opened a
music house, for the sale of music and musical instruments,
under the firm name of " Steen & Marshall " but in a year or
two dissolved partnership and continued in business by himself alone   At Xenia, Ohio, E Watson Steen and all his
family were members of the First Presbyterian Church, and
at Knoxville, Tennessee, they all united with the Third
(Southern) Presbyterian Church, of which he was elected
ordained and installed a ruling elder, which office he still
holds   After the death of his father, in 1881, he was made
executor of his estate   In 1887 his mother came to reside in
his family   where she made her home until her death in
1895 although she made extensive visits to her daughter

who lived in Westboro, Massachusetts, and in Cincinnati, Ohio Mr Steen has acquired considerable property, and resides at his pleasant home, No 19 Pearl Place, Knoxville, Tennessee

Prof E Watson Steen was married by the Rev James Dunlap, in West Union, Adams County, Ohio, October 25, 1855, to Miss Julia Emily Lilly Diboll, a daughter of Dr Victor M and Philena L Diboll, she having been born near Sardinia, Brown County, Ohio December 7, 1839, and died at her home, No 19 Pearl Place, Knoxville Tennessee, September 17, 1896, in the 57th year of her age Mrs Steen was a woman of social nature, strong attachments, and possessed of considerable musical and literary ability, and was the writer of several stories and unpublished poems Her body was interred in the Woodlawn cemetery, near Xenia, Ohio To Prof E Watson and Julia E L Steen were born the following three children

I —Laura Alice Steen, the eldest daughter of Prof E Watson and Julia E L Steen, was born at the home of her parents, on the farm near Youngsville and Mt Leigh, in Adams County, Ohio, August 18, 1856 and resided with her parents, in Adams County, and in Xenia, Ohio She early united with the First Presbyterian Church in Xenia, Ohio, of which she remained a consistent member She received a good education in the Xenia schools Like her father, she possessed fine musical talents, which were cultivated to a high degree, so that she became not only an accomplished singer, but an excellent teacher of instrumental music as well Miss L Allie Steen was a young lady of good social qualities and attractive manner, but her genial and useful career was soon cut off by that dread disease, quick consumption She died at the home of her parents, in Xenia, Ohio, June 5 1878, in the 22d year of her age and in the certain hope of a blessed immortality. The funeral took place from the Presbyterian church, and her body was laid away in Woodlawn cemetery, near Xenia, Ohio

II —Mary Estella Steen the second daughter of Prof E Watson and Julia E L Steen, was born at the home of her parents, near Mt Leigh and Youngsville Adams County, Ohio, January 13 1860, and continued to live with her parents, near Mt Leigh, and in Xenia, Ohio, until her marriage She early united with the First Presbyterian Church, in Xenia, and remained a consistent member She secured a good education in the Xenia schools, and was an interesting and accomplished young lady, possessing considerable literary talent She published several interesting original stories of high merit, one being entitled "Book Learning Versus Housekeeping" Mary E Steen was married by her uncle Rev Moses D A Steen at the Grand Hotel, Cincinnati, Ohio March 16 1880, to Earnest L Lawrence, of Xenia, Ohio They resided in Xenia, Ohio, for about five years after marriage, where Mr Lawrence was agent for the Xenia Powder Company In 1885 they removed to Chicago Illinois, where they continued to reside until her death, which took place March 19 1890, aged 30 years, 2 months and 6 days Her body was buried in Chicago To Earnest L and Mary E Lawrence were born the following children

1 Mildred Lawrence was born in Xenia, Ohio June 1, 1884

2 Meredith Fay Lawrence was born in Chicago, Illinois, November 10 1889

III—Julia Emerine Pearl Steen, the third daughter of Prof E Watson and Julia E L Steen was born in Xenia, Ohio August 8, 1871, and has resided with her parents in Xenia Ohio, and Knoxville, Tennessee She early united with the Third Presbyterian Church of Knoxville and has ever maintained a consistent Christian life She secured a good education, and has fine musical talents, which have been thoroughly cultivated, making her a very popular singer, as well as an excellent performer in public She has composed and published many pieces of music which are quite meritorious She took the first prize offered by The Atlanta Journal for the best musical composition open to musicians of several States The Knoxville and Chattanooga papers have recently spoken of her in highest terms of praise

The following is taken from The Atlanta Journal of August 4, 1894

MISS JULIA PEARL STEEN

Miss Julia Pearl Steen, of Knoxville, Tennessee, is the winner of The Journal's prize for the best musical composition Some time ago The Journal offered a prize of twenty-five dollars in cash to the musician sending in the best production A great many contributions from far and near were received, and in order that justice might be done, three distinguished musicians— Messrs J. P O'Donnelly, Fred Wedemeyer and Marion Dunwoody—were selected to pass upon the merits of the different pieces sent in After going over them all and testing their respective merits. the committee sent in the following award

' ATLANTA, GEORGIA, August 1, 1894
"To the Editor of The Journal
"After careful examination of all the manuscripts sent to The Journal, we have awarded the prize to Miss Julia Pearl Steen, of Knoxville, Tennessee deeming hers the most meritorious of all   Very respectfully,

"J P O'DONNELLY,
'FRED WEDEMEYER,
"MARION DUNWOODY,
"*Committee*

THE SWEET SINGER

Miss Steen is a young lady of more than ordinary attractions She is of medium height, and has a sweet, gentle face, brightened by a pair of soulful brown eyes Her hair is of the auburn tint and her face is one that suggests a soul full of music In writing of her singing, one who heard her said "While her voice is not so strong as some, it possesses that sweet pathos and musical articulation that reaches down after a fellow's heart-strings '

A SKETCH OF HER LIFE

Julia Pearl Steen was born in Xenia Ohio, August 8, 1871 Both her parents were of musical family, and she was reared in an atmosphere of music At a very early age she manifested a decided musical talent, and was allowed access to the piano Little by little she learned to play, under her mother's direction At the age of two years she played a little waltz At the age of five years she composed her first piece—a simple song, to the words "I live for those who love me " For several years she had access to the celebrated May Festivals in Cincinnati, which wonderfully delighted her Her appreciation of complicated harmonies and fine rendition of classic music was considered at the time remarkable in one so young When she was nine years of age her parents moved, with her, to Knoxville, Tennessee, which has since been her home At the age of fourteen she played such selections as Gottschalk's "Last Hope' also his "Trovatore, and Beethoven's 'Pathetique,' etc, pursuing her studies in Knoxville, and later in Chicago Miss Steen has a mezzo-soprano voice, sweet but not strong Her compositions number about twenty Among those best known are 'A Twilight Reverie " ' To Dreamland ' A Hammock Lullaby," "Sleepy Clovers," and an organ fantasie, entitled "Egyptian Lament " from the story of 'Ben Hur "

Miss Steen presides at the organ of the Third Presbyterian Church of Knoxville and is recognized as one of the leading organists of that city She resides with her parents at their home, "Pearl Place," North Knoxville, where she pursues her studies and entertains many musical friends. In stature she is about five feet five inches, has brown eyes, an abundant suit of auburn hair, and a clean complexion, and is popular among her many friends

THE PRIZE MUSIC

The music written by Miss Steen accompanies the song, "The Parting," written by Miss Lois Huntington.

THE PARTING

Darling, why that look of sadness?
Shadows o'ercast thy lovely brow;
In the eyes once filled with gladness
Tears of sorrow startle now!
True that to-morrow I must leave thee,
But for a little while, you see,
I'm parting, parting,
Only a little while from thee

Smile once more on me, my darling!
Dry those dear eyes now wet with tears;
That the last look that thou giv'st me,
Loving looks my heart to cheer,
Thou'rt all this whole wide world to me, dear,
Drear would it be without thy love,
Dreary, dreary,
Would be this world without thy love!

While we're absent from each other
Let this sweet comfort still be thine,
That the line of shining silver
'Round our hearts be still entwined;
And it will whisper to thee, darling,
That I am coming back to thee;
I'm coming, coming,
That I am coming back to thee!

Julia Emerine Pearl Steen was married at Knoxville, Tennessee, on Monday, December 4, 1899, to Dr Charles A. Garratt Residence, Knoxville. Tennessee.

3 Samuel Martin Steen, the third son of Aaron F and Mary Freeman Steen, was born on the old Freeman homestead, on Scioto Brush Creek, two miles above the mouth of Blue Creek, in Adams County, Ohio, July 5, 1836 Here he lived with his parents until he was twelve years of age, going to school, and assisting his father as he was able In 1848 he removed with the family to their new home, twenty miles distant, near the Mt Leigh Presbyterian Church, where he continued to work on the farm in summer and attend school in the winter, while at the same time he continued to be a regular attendant at the Mt Leigh Church and Sabbath-school Having secured a good common school education

(6)

at Mt Leigh, he afterwards attended the State Normal
School at Lebanon, Ohio, under the direction of Prof E H
Holbrook, and became a teacher   S Martin Steen was a
young man of brilliant talents, a natural mathematician,
delighting in difficult problems   He was also able in argu-
ment, and extremely fond of it   Often he would present a
proposition to his brother, or other friend, to see which side
he would take, then take the opposite side and use such
strong arguments as to compel his opponent to confess himself in the wrong   Then, after taking a good laugh, he would
take up the other side of the question, and convince him back
again that he had been right after all, and enjoy another
hearty laugh   He had the peculiar faculty of doing this
without giving offense and purely from the love of debate
He was a young man of great energy and perseverance, and
had his life been spared he would probably have made his
mark in the world   He taught quite successfully several
terms of school, the last one being at Sandy Springs, Adams
County, Ohio near the Ohio River, which closed in June,
1859   While living at Sandy Springs he united with the
Methodist Episcopal Church upon profession of faith in
Christ   Here also, while engaged in teaching, he caught a
very severe cold, which settled upon his lungs and soon
developed into quick consumption   He died at the residence
of his father, near the Mt Leigh Church with an assured
hope of a glorious immortality, October 13, 1859, aged 23
years, 3 months and 8 days   His body was lovingly laid
away to rest in the Mt Leigh cemetery

4 John Truman Steen, the fourth son of Aaron F and Mary
   Freeman Steen, was born on the old Freeman homestead, on
   Scioto Brush Creek, in Jefferson Township, Adams County,
   Ohio, May 18, 1838   His earliest associations were connected with the home of his mother's parents, who came from
   Maryland to that locality in 1797 and where his mother was
   born and brought up   This old homestead was located ten
   miles east of West Union, and about the same distance northwest of Rome a village on the Ohio River   When a little
   child he went to school on Blue Creek, two and one-fourth
   miles away   Near the mouth of this beautiful stream there
   was a junction of the roads leading to Portsmouth, Rome,
   and West Union , also a country store, a post-office, a blacksmith shop, etc , where the principal trading and business of

the locality was done In 1848, when ten years of age, he
was taken by his parents to their new home, on the farm his
father had purchased, three miles from Winchester, Ohio,
on the road to the Mt Leigh Church, where he grew up to
manhood Here in the Mt Leigh school he secured a good
common school education He afterwards attended the
State Normal School at Lebanon, Ohio, under the superin-
tendency of Prof E H Holbrook, and qualified himself for a
teacher, in which profession he was especially successful.
He taught quite a number of schools, the last being at Harsha s Mills, about four miles from his father's home He
was exceedingly fond of music, and is said to have had the
finest and most natural talent for it of any member of the
family His social qualities were also of a very high order,
and hence his company was sought and enjoyed by all his
acquaintances J Truman Steen united with the Mt Leigh
Presbyterian Church June 9, 1858, on profession of faith in
Christ, and continued to be an earnest, devout and useful
Christian While engaged in teaching at Harsha s Mills,
Adams County, Ohio, he caught a severe cold, which devel-
oped into consumption He died at the residence of his
father, June 25, 1862 aged 24 years, 1 month and 7 days
He was universally beloved, and his death greatly lamented
His body was tenderly laid away to rest in the cemetery at
Mt Leigh

5 Moses Duncan Alexander Steen, the fifth son of Aaron F
and Mary Freeman Steen, was born at the old Freeman
homestead, on Scioto Brush Creek, ten miles east of West
Union, and two miles west of Blue Creek, in Adams County,
Ohio, April 24, 1841 His earliest recollections were of the
old home, where his mother was born and brought up — the
orchard, the creek, the rocky cliffs and cedar trees, the high
bridge the sugar camp, the old church, the graveyard, and
the surrounding hills The death of his little brother, in the
autumn of 1844 was never effaced from his memory His
first day at school on Blue Creek remains as a vivid picture,
one brother holding each hand as they walked along until
they came to Smalley's store, where they bought a
"primer" full of bright pictures and proceeded to the school-
house, where the teacher took him on her lap, the school
exhibition the next winter, at which he recited "Twinkle,
twinkle, little star" and the long Sabbath services of the

Seceders at Wait's Mill, have never been forgotten   In 1848, when he was seven years old, the family removed to their new home, near the Mt Leigh Presbyterian Church, in which he was baptized by the Rev James Dunlap, October 2, 1848, and grew up to manhood on his father's farm   He was a regular attendant at the Mt Leigh Church, Sabbath-school and district school, while every Sabbath afternoon was devoted by his parents to the religious instruction of their children   Moses D A Steen united with the Mt Leigh Presbyterian Church on profession of faith in Christ, June 8, 1858, and began a course of study in North Liberty Academy   He afterwards spent three years in Salem Academy, then under the direction of Rev James A. I. Lowes, D.D., one year in Hanover College, at Hanover, Indiana, and completed the classical course in Miami University, Oxford, Ohio, from which he was graduated, receiving the degree of B A June 27, 1866   He entered the United Presbyterian Theological Seminary, at Xenia, Ohio, September 1, 1886, and remained one term   He afterwards attended the Presbyterian Theological Seminary of the Northwest, at Chicago, Illinois, from which he was graduated April 1, 1869, having spent the autumn session of 1868 in Princeton Theological Seminary, at Princeton, New Jersey   He was licensed to preach the Gospel by the Old School Presbytery of Chillicothe, in Hillsboro, Ohio, April 8, 1868, and spent the summer vacation in preaching at Mt Sterling and Sharpsburgh, Kentucky   Immediately after graduating from the Theological Seminary, in April, 1869, he took charge of the church at Worthington, near Columbus, Ohio, and the next year accepted an invitation to the church in Vevay, Indiana, and was ordained to the full work of the ministry in that church by the Presbytery of New Albany, September 8, 1870   In January, 1872, he accepted a call to the pastorate of the church at Solon, near Cleveland, Ohio, which, in April, 1873, he resigned to accept a call to the church at Conneautville, Pennsylvania   On Monday, June 1, 1874, a terrible conflagration swept away a large part of the village, leaving many without homes and seriously affecting the work of the church   In December of that year Mr Steen resigned the pastorate and took charge of the church in Waterford, Erie County, Pennsylvania   In May, 1875, he accepted a call to the First Presbyterian Church of Ludlow, Kentucky, opposite Cincinnati, Ohio, where he remained six years and three months. Through his patient, faithful and persistent labors a heavy and pressing mortgage debt was removed, and the church placed upon a substantial basis of prosperity. In the summer of 1877, while in charge of this church, he made an extensive tour through Europe, traveling leisurely throughout Ireland, Scotland, England, Holland, Belgium, Germany, Switzerland and France, and returned to his work with renewed vigor. August 19, 1881, he resigned his charge at Ludlow, Kentucky, and accepted an invitation to the church at Pleasant Ridge, near Walnut Hills, a suburb of Cincinnati, Ohio, where he remained for a year. His wife being in feeble health at the time, they determined to seek a change of climate, and he accepted an invitation to Davisville, California, where he entered upon the work with encouraging prospects, in September, 1882, but a few months later returned to the East. In the summer of 1883 he supplied the churches of Troy and Edwardsville Illinois, and in the fall accepted an invitation to Tabernacle Presbyterian Church, Gunnison, Colorado entering upon his work there the first Sabbath in October, 1883 and had a prosperous year. October 1, 1884, he accepted an invitation to the church at Black Hawk, Colorado, but owing to the high altitude, which affected her heart, Mrs Steen could not live there and by physicians' advice the next summer they came to the Pacific Coast, reaching Portland, Oregon, July 1, 1885, spent one Sabbath at Albany, Oregon, preached two months in the First Church of Tacoma, Washington, and supplied the church at Snohomish, Washington, for one year, the church doubling its membership during that time. July 1, 1886 Mr Steen accepted an invitation to the Presbyterian Church of Woodbridge, California, to begin his labors September 1, at which time he accordingly removed to Woodbridge, California, was afterwards called to the pastorate, and still continues in charge of the church.

Moses D A Steen and his wife, since coming to the West, in 1883, have devoted their leisure hours in special courses of study together, and have received diplomas, or certificates of graduation, from the Chautauqua Literary and Scientific Circle at Monterey, California, in 1889, and afterwards the Guild of the Seven Seals, which is the highest rank obtainable   They also completed the seven years' course of Bible study in the Philadelphia Bible Correspondence School, receiving their diplomas in 1890   In connection with his work in Woodbridge, California, after some months of preliminary services, Mr Steen, on September 29, 1889, organized a church at Clements, fourteen miles east, where no church organization of any kind had before existed, and supplied it with preaching at regular intervals for several years With a membership of only nine persons, he was instrumental in building and dedicating, without debt, on this mission field a beautiful and substantial church edifice, worth $5,000

Moses D A Steen has been frequently called to conduct memorial services and act as chaplain and orator on public occasions   He has also published several sermons, essays, and contributed articles   In 1888 he was invited by the faculty to preach the annual sermon at San Joaquin Valley College, which was received with favor, and a few days later at the annual session of the Board of Trustees they conferred upon him the honorary degree of Doctor of Divinity   In 1889 the University of Wooster, Ohio, conferred upon him the degree of Doctor of Philosophy, upon examination "The Wooster Quarterly," in speaking of it, says

The degree was conferred on thesis and examination in Course A   The examination covered the course as published in 1887, and was superintended and certified by President D A Mobley, of San Joaquin College, Woodbridge   It was taken in ten sittings of two hours and a half each, the questions being given out in sections, and the examination papers consisted of seventy-six large and carefully written pages   .   Many of our readers will remember the sermon by Dr Steen, which appeared in the Pulpit Supplement to the Quarterly   He is well known in California as an able and earnest preacher of the Word, and has been placed in honorable position by the Synod of the Pacific as a member of the Permanent Committee on Education

The twenty-fifth anniversary of the marriage of Rev Dr. and Mrs. M D A Steen was duly celebrated June 22, 1895, under the auspices of the King's Daughters   Many invitations had been sent out, the church profusely decorated, and as the wedding march was played the procession entered, headed by the King's Daughters and six little girls, all dressed in white, and bearing flowers   The Rev D A Mobley, D D, ex-President of S J V College, performed an appropriate ceremony, and brief addresses were made by

MRS. MARY FOSTER STEEN.

representatives of the church, the King's Daughters, several ministers and others. Congratulations, a happy reunion, and a banquet followed Among the many greetings received was the following little poem, written for the occasion by the Rev. James S McDonald, D D , formerly superintendent of Home Missions in California

> Never did bells with sweeter tune
> Laden the fragrant air of June,
> And fill your hearts with such delight
> And lure you to a path so bright,
> As on the day when your new life
> Began as happy man and wife
> The music of that joyful day
> Has gained in sweetness all your way.
>
> Discordant strains have never come
> To mar the peace of your dear home,
> Where lovers' hearts do not grow old,
> Their early love will not grow cold.
> There is a joy love only knows,
> That you may keep till life shall close,
> When all your goodness shall increase
> In God's eternal home of peace

Dr Steen has frequently been chosen Moderator of the Presbytery with which he has been connected. From 1887 until 1893 he was Permanent Clerk, and since 1893 has been the Stated Clerk and Treasurer of the Presbytery of Stockton, which comprises a territory as large as the State of Ohio He was chosen Commissioner to the Presbyterian General Assemblies which met in Madison, Wisconsin, in 1880; Omaha, Nebraska, in 1887, and Saratoga Springs, New York, in 1894 In 1895 he was elected by the General Assembly at Pittsburgh, Pennsylvania , a delegate to "General Council of Alliance of the Reformed Churches throughout the World Holding the Presbyterian System," to meet in Glasgow, Scotland, in June, 1896 On this journey he was accompanied by his wife, and after the Council they extended their visit to many places of interest in British and Continental Europe, returning to America via the Northern route, through the Gulf and River St Lawrence, to Quebec, Montreal, the Thousand Islands, Kingston and Toronto, Canada He has traveled quite extensively in the United States, Canada and Mexico Including missionary work in the West with other journeys, he has visited every State and Territory in the American Union, except Alaska, and preached the Gospel in many of them, sometimes in the forest, in frontier settlements, in log cabins, and school-houses, on river and ocean steamers, among Indians, Mexicans and all classes and conditions of people — rich and poor, learned and illiterate   Residence, Woodbridge, California

Moses D A Steen was married by the Rev William R. Parsons, at Worthington, Ohio, near Columbus. June 22, 1870, to Miss Mary Foster, a daughter of Archibald and Harriet Foster, formerly of Sugar Creek, Venango County, Pennsylvania, she having been born at Sugar Creek, Pennsylvania, July 21, 1843, and united with the Presbyterian Church at that place June 8, 1858, the same day that her husband joined the church in Ohio   She has ever been a true helpmeet to her husband in his sacred profession, cultivated, amiable, and devout   Since 1887 she has been the Stockton Presbyterial Secretary of the Woman's Occidental Board of Foreign Missions   The bride's father was a son of John Foster, who was born in County Armagh, Ireland, June 23 1768, came to America when about twenty years of age, married Rebecca Lee in 1796, in Centre County, Pennsylvania, where they resided until 1797 when he removed to Venango County, and located upon a farm at Sugar Creek Pennsylvania   Mary Foster's mother was a daughter of John and Isabella McQuaid, a granddaughter of William and Elizabeth Duffield and a great-granddaughter of Philip and Jane Armstrong Duffield, who owned real estate near Ballynahinch in County Down Ireland   William Duffield was the eldest child and only son of Philip and Jane Armstrong Duffield was born in Ireland about 1744, came to America in 1770 was married in Mifflin County, Pennsylvania, in 1776 to Elizabeth Hasson, by whom he had seven children   Isabella Duffield was the sixth child of William and Elizabeth Hasson Duffield, and was born in Centre County, Pennsylvania, November 15, 1790 was brought to Venango County, in 1800, was married by Abram Selders in Franklin, Pennsylvania, September 8, 1808 to John McQuaid, by whom she had six children   Harriet C. McQuaid, the second child and eldest daughter of John and Isabella Duffield McQuaid, was born in Venango County, Pennsylvania November 5, 1811   was married by the Rev. Thomas Anderson at Sugar Creek, Pennsylvania, April 19, 1832, to Archibald Foster, he having been born at Sugar

LULU GRACE STEEN.

Creek, Pennsylvania, November 7, 1804, by whom she had twelve children, Mary Foster being the eighth child and fifth daughter   To Moses D A and Mary Foster Steen was born one child, as follows

I.—Lulu Grace Steen was born in Conneautville, Crawford County, Pennsylvania, July 4, 1873, and died in Ludlow, Kentucky, July 3, 1876   On her third birthday her body was tenderly laid away to rest in the Woodlawn cemetery, near Xenia, Ohio   She was a general favorite, the joy of the household, a remarkably bright and interesting child, affectionate, obedient, patient, yet full of life and enthusiasm   She was intelligent beyond her years, and devotional to an eminent degree   She delighted in family worship, and often in her play would sit down and act as though she were reading, then close the book, kneel down by a chair, cover her face with her hands, and reverently say   ' God bless Lulu and make her a good girl ; God bless papa and make him a good man ; God bless mamma and make her a good lady   Amen "

6 Josiah James Steen, the sixth son of Aaron F and Mary Freeman Steen, was born at the old Freeman homestead, on Scioto Brush Creek, near Blue Creek, Adams County, Ohio, February 25, 1844, and died at the same place September 8, 1844, aged 8 months and 13 days   'A sweet little bud taken from the earth to bloom in heaven "

7 Sarah Catherine Steen, called "Kate," the seventh child and only daughter of Aaron F. and Mary Freeman Steen, was born at the home of her parents, three miles east of Winchester, Adams County, Ohio, April 1, 1853, where her happy childhood days were spent   She attended the public school, the church, and Sabbath-school at Mt Leigh when she was still a child   She removed with her parents to their new home, at Xenia, Ohio, in the summer of 1865, when she was twelve years of age, and in early life united with the First Presbyterian Church of that place, and of which she was a useful member   At Xenia she received a good education in the common schools, and was graduated from the High School in 1872   Like her father and elder brothers, she was possessed of unusually fine musical talents, which she delighted to cultivate and exercise, and under the continuous instruction of her brother, Prof E. W Steen, she soon

acquired a cultivated voice, skill in execution, and became an accomplished teacher of vocal and instrumental music In 1879 she taught music in Clarksville, Tenn After the death of her father, in 1881, she, with her mother, removed to the center of the city of Xenia, where they lived together, and she gave music lessons to many private pupils. In 1883 she accepted the position of teacher of vocal music and voice culture in Antioch College, at Yellow Springs, Ohio, but still making her home with her mother in Xenia, and traveling back and forth by rail until January 1, 1886, when they removed to Yellow Springs, Ohio.

Sarah Catherine (Kate) Steen was married by the Rev. John S Axtell at Xenia, Ohio, December 24, 1885, to the Rev. Elijah Alfred Coil, a son of Jesse A and Lydia Coil, he having been born May 2, 1858, and brought up on his father's farm, near Delphos, Allen County, Ohio His mother died when he was a little child only five years old He attended the public school in the neighborhood in which he was brought up, and secured his higher education at Antioch College, Yellow Springs, Ohio Here, as his music teacher, he became acquainted with his future wife. The Rev E Alfred Coil received a call to the Christian Church in Yellow Springs, Ohio, which he accepted, entered upon his work September 1, 1885, and continued in charge for two years September 1, 1887, he received and accepted a call to the First Unitarian Church at Westboro, Massachusetts, and continued in charge four years He removed to Cincinnati, Ohio, September 1, 1891, and became pastor of the Unity Church of that city and remained four years Again, September 1, 1895, he received and accepted a call to the First Unitarian Church of Marietta Ohio and removed with his family to that place, and still continues pastor of that church To the Rev E Alfred and Kate Steen Coil have been born the following children

I —Emery Wilbur Coil, the eldest child of Rev E Alfred and Kate Steen Coil, was born in Westboro, Massachusetts, September 28, 1888

II —Harold Coil, the second child and son of Rev E Alfred and Kate Steen Coil, was born in Westboro, Massachusetts, May 1, 1891.

III —Alfreda Coil, the third child and eldest daughter of

MRS. KATE STEEN COIL.

Rev E Alfred and Kate Steen Coil, was born in Cincinnati, Ohio, June 15, 1892

IV—Marion Coil, the fourth child and third son of Rev E Alfred and Kate Steen Coil, was born in Marietta, Ohio, November 30, 1895

8. Isaac Birt Steen, the eighth child and seventh son of Aaron F and Mary Freeman Steen, was born at the home of his parents, three miles east of Winchester, Adams County, Ohio, June 8, 1856, and died June 16, 1856, aged 8 days. The body was laid away to rest in the Mt Leigh cemetery.

9. William Wirt Steen, the ninth child and eighth son of Aaron F and Mary Freeman Steen, was born three miles east of Winchester, Adams County, Ohio, June 8, 1856, and died at the same place June 26, 1856, aged 18 days The body was laid away to rest in the Mt Leigh cemetery, by the side of his little twin brother

IV—Robert Wilson Steen, the fourth child and second son of Alexander and Agnes Nancy Faris Steen, was born two miles north of Flemingsburgh, Kentucky, May 24, 1809 and died suddenly of heart failure at his residence, two miles east of Winchester, Ohio, November 11, 1873, aged 64 years, 5 months and 18 days He was brought with his parents, when they removed from Kentucky, in 1820, and located on a farm two miles east of Winchester, Adams County, Ohio Here he was carefully and religiously brought up, working on the farm in summer and attending school in winter. At that time Ohio was a new country, and labor of every kind had to be done without machinery, so that much hard work was necessary in clearing the fields, putting in and gathering the grain, in which he faithfully assisted his father until he grew to manhood After he became a man he purchased a farm near his father's residence, located on Brush Creek, at the mouth of Elk Run, where he continued to reside all his life, a practical and successful farmer. R. Wilson Steen was married by John Treber, J P, at the residence of the bride's parents, near Dunkinsville, Adams County, Ohio, September 13, 1832, to Miss Louisa Chambers, a daughter of Elijah and Ann Wilcox Chambers, formerly from near Baltimore, Maryland, she having been born near Baltimore, Maryland, April 21, 1809, and died at the residence of her son, in Washington C. H, Fayette County, Ohio,

(7)

on Good Friday, April 15, 1892, in the 83d year of her age
On the following Sunday — Easter Day — her body was tenderly laid away by the side of her husband, in the Mt. Leigh
cemetery R Wilson Steen and his wife were for many years
members of the Mt Leigh Presbyterian Church. To them
were born nine children, as follows

1 Aaron Marshall Steen, the eldest son of R Wilson and
Louisa C Steen, was born at the home of his parents, two
miles east of Winchester, Adams County, Ohio, July 1, 1833,
and died near New Market Highland County, Ohio, February 3, 1891. aged 57 years, 7 months and 2 days His body
was laid away to rest in the Mt Leigh cemetery.

A Marshall Steen grew up to manhood upon his father's
farm, attending school in winter, and was by occupation a
farmer all his life He resided in Adams County, Ohio, near
his father's residence until 1865, when he removed to Mercer
County, Illinois, and located upon a farm near Aledo, where
he continued to live for several years, then settled upon his
own farm near Millersburgh, in the same county, where he
remained a number of years In 1884 he returned to Ohio
and resided near New Market, Highland County, until his
death

A Marshall Steen was married by the Rev Nathaniel
Williams at the residence of the bride's parents, near Mt
Leigh Presbyterian Church, September 4, 1856, to Miss
Mary Ellen Dunlap, a daughter of Andrew and Jemima
Robey Dunlap, she having been born April 24, 1838. Her
father, Andrew Dunlap, was born in Fayette County, Pennsylvania, June 10, 1796, and her mother, Jemima Robey
Dunlap, was born in Monongalia County, West Virginia,
December 24, 1808 Mrs Mary E Dunlap Steen was
married a second time, August 12, 1896, to William Pinkerton, who is a brother of her brother Hiram Dunlap's wife
Residence, Viola, Illinois To A Marshall and Mary E
Steen were born the following eight children

1 —Stephen Cary Steen, the eldest son of A Marshall and
Mary E Steen, was born near Winchester, Ohio, August
23, 1857, and was taken by his parents to Illinois in February, 1865, and lived in Mercer County and assisted his
father upon a farm until he grew up to manhood In the
summer of 1882 he removed from Illinois to Lenox, Tay-

lor County, Iowa, where he remained one year, then to San Buena Ventura, Ventura County, California, where he resided two years In 1885 he removed to Colfax, Whitman County, Washington, where for three years he kept a livery stable, and since that time has followed the occupation of a farmer S Cary Steen was married by the Rev G. M. Tuttle, in Winfield, Henry County, Iowa, February 9, 1882, to Miss Justine Melvina Hale, a daughter of James Porter and Louisa Mariah Hale, she having been born in Winfield, Iowa, March 15, 1858 Residence, Colfax, Whitman County, Washington. To S Cary and Justine M Steen were born the following children.

1 Loren Areton Steen was born in Lenox, Iowa, August 8, 1883

2 Myrtle Florence Steen was born in Colfax, Washington, July 5, 1886, and died the same day

3 Gertrude Clarence Steen was born in Colfax, Washington, July 5, 1886, and died the same day

4 Ivy Faunetta Steen was born in Colfax, Washington, February 13, 1889

5 —————— Steen, a daughter, was born in Colfax, Washington

6 —————— Steen, a daughter, was born in Colfax, Washington

II —Albert Newton Steen, the second son of A Marshall and Mary E. Steen, was born near Winchester, Ohio, July 21, 1859 He was brought to Illinois by his parents in February, 1865, and continued to live with them upon the farm He died near Millersburgh, Mercer County, Illinois, March 9, 1880 aged 20 years, 7 months and 16 days

III —Elsiena Victoria Steen, the third child and eldest daughter of A Marshall and Mary E Steen, was born near Winchester, Adams County, Ohio, March 12, 1861 She lived with her parents in Ohio until she was four years old, and was brought up on her father's farm, in Mercer County, Illinois, where she was educated in the common schools She was married by the Rev George M Morey, at the residence of her parents, near Millersburgh, Mercer County, Illinois, December 29, 1880, to William Martin Bean, a son of Marshall and Hannah Jane Bean, he having

been born in Greenville, Mercer County, Pennsylvania,
September 6, 1858 — a farmer They resided for several
years near Millersburgh, Illinois, and then moved to
Nebraska and located on a farm near David City Residence, David City, Nebraska To them were born the
following children:

1. Maude Alberta Bean was born near Millersburgh, Illinois, October 20, 1881

2 Mary Leona Bean was born near Millersburgh, Illinois,
August 6, 1883

3 Ada Minerva Bean was born near Millersburgh, Illinois, March 11, 1885

4. Ruby Pearl Bean was born near Millersburgh, Illinois,
February 24, 1887

5 Julius Caesar Bean was born near David City,
Nebraska, October 7, 1888, and died at the same place
August 5, 1890

6. Fred Ritchie Bean was born near David . City,
Nebraska, November 5, 1893

IV.—Emily Ellen Steen, the fourth child and second daughter of A Marshall and Mary E Steen, was born near Winchester, Adams County, Ohio, April 22, 1863 She was
brought to Illinois by her parents in February, 1865, and
resided with them upon a farm in Mercer County, until
her marriage She was educated in the common schools ;
was a very amiable young lady, and early became a devout
Christian and faithful member of the M E Church in
Millersburgh, Illinois She was married by her pastor,
the Rev William T Kerr, at Pomeroy, Mercer County,
Illinois, February 10 1885 to Thomas Leroy Duncan, a
son of James M and Margaret Duncan, of Millersburgh,
Illinois, he having been born June 14, 1862 — a telegraph
operator After marriage they lived two years in Corning,
Iowa, three years in Horace, Kansas, several years in
Osceola, Iowa, and Murray, Iowa Residence, Murray,
Iowa To them were born the following

1 Lela Myrtle Duncan was born in Prescott, Adams
County, Iowa, June 11, 1888

2 Harold Steen Duncan was born in Murray, Clarke
County, Iowa, June 23, 1899

V —Andrew Wilson Steen, the fifth child and third son of A Marshall and Mary E Steen, was born near Winchester, Adams County, Ohio, January 1, 1865, and in February, 1865, brought by his parents to their new home in Illinois. He grew up to manhood upon his father's farm, in Mercer County, near Mi'lersburgh, Illinois, where he attended school   In 1882, when 17 years old, he removed to the West with his eldest brother, and lived one year in Iowa, two years in Ventura County, California, and since 1885, in the State of Washington   For some time he resided in Colfax, and afterwards in Pullman, Whitman County, Washington — a railroad man   He was married by the Rev S W Walters, in Pullman, Washington, August 4, 1895, to Miss Lizzie Carlson, a daughter of Charles and Anna Carlson, she having been born April 21, 1871   Residence, Pullman, Washington.

VI —Leora Steen, called 'Ora," the sixth child and third daughter of A Marshall and Mary E Steen, was born near Aledo, Mercer County, Illinois, March 28, 1867   She grew to womanhood upon her father's farm, near Millersburgh, Illinois   She was married in Piper City, Ford County, Illinois, by John R Lewis, Esq, November 14, 1888, to Elbridge Clyde Thornhill a son of Barney and Mary Ann Gibson Thornhill, he having been born in Westboro, Clinton County, Ohio February 14, 1865   He is now engaged in buying stock, and Mrs Ora Steen Thornhill keeps a millinery and notion store   Residence, Joy, Mercer County, Illinois

VII —Mary Isabella Steen, the seventh child and fourth daughter of A Marshall and Mary E Steen, was born near Aledo, Illinois, April 12, 1869   She was brought up on her father's farm, in Mercer County Illinois, and attended school in Millersburgh   She was married near Millersburgh, Illinois, February 23, 1888, to George F Bailey a son of John and Martha Bailey he having been born in Scotland County Missouri, August 3, 1859 — a railroad fireman   Residence, Monmouth, Illinois   To them were born the following children

   1 Albert Clarence Bailey was born at Keithsburgh, Mercer County, Illinois, January 6, 1891

2 Leora Wahretta Bailey was born near New Boston, Mercer County, Illinois, December 16, 1893

VIII —John Ritchie Steen, the eighth child, the fourth and youngest son of A Marshall and Mary E Steen, was born near Millersburgh, Mercer County, Illinois, August 6, 1876, where he spent his early days upon his father's farm and attended school in Millersburgh From 1891 until 1896 he resided with his mother, at Seaton, Mercer County Illinois He is by occupation a farmer   J Ritchie Steen was married by the Rev William S Davis, D D , in Aledo, Illinois, on Thursday, September 24, 1896, to Miss Della Elberta May Moore, a daughter of George and Henrietta F. Moore, she having been born in New Boston, Mercer County, Illinois, April 25, 1878. Residence, Viola, Mercer County, Illinois

2 Nancy Ann Steen, the second child and only daughter of R. Wilson and Louisa C Steen, was born at the home of her parents, on Brush Creek, near the mouth of Elk Run, two miles east of Winchester, Adams County Ohio, November 6, 1834, and was brought up on her father's farm, and attended school in the neighborhood N Ann Steen was married at the residence of her parents, near Winchester, Ohio by the Rev James Dunlap, December 25, 1851, to Silas Holmes Sharp, a son of Samuel Sharp, who was born in Virginia, and Margaret Holmes Sharp, who was born in Adams County Ohio, he having been born in Highland County, Ohio, September 4, 1831 — a carpenter and builder, a member of the Christian Church Residence, Winchester, Adams County, Ohio To Silas H and N Ann Steen Sharp were born the following nine children

I —Albert Newton Sharp was born near Youngsville, Adams County, Ohio January 4, 1853, and died on the morning of July 6, 1860

II —Emma Belle Sharp was born near Youngsville, Ohio, July 28, 1854, and was brought up in the home of her parents She died near Cynthiana, Pike County, Ohio, May 10, 1881 Emma B Sharp was married December 19, 1875, to James Madison Penn, a son of Stephen and Mary Penn, he having been born near Cynthiana, Ohio, and where he and his wife resided until her death   To them were born the following children:

1 Edward Penn was born near Cynthiana, Ohio, in 1877.

2 Cary I. Penn was born near Cynthiana, Ohio, in 1880, and died in 1882

III —Eva Josephine Sharp was born near Youngsville, Ohio, ———— 23, 1856, and died in the evening of July 6, 1860, the same day her brother died

IV.—Elsie Jane Sharp was born near Youngsville, Ohio, January 1, 1859, and died July 22, 1860

V —Luelia Ann Sharp was born near Youngsville, Ohio, November 5, 1860, and brought up in her father's family She was married by the Rev Mr. Lowe, of the M E. Church, at the residence of her parents, September 18, 1878 to Daniel A Fulton, a son of James and Isabella Fulton, he having been born in Russellville, Brown County, Ohio, November 5, 1854 — a farmer   After their marriage they lived in Ohio three years, then removed to Doniphan County, Kansas, where they remained until 1891, when they located near Horton, Brown County, Kansas, where they still reside   To Daniel A and Luella A Fulton were born the following children

1 Robert Fulton was born in Winchester, Ohio, April 10, 1880

2 Anna Belle Fulton was born in Winchester, Ohio, May 27 1882, and was married in Horton, Kansas June 1, 1898, to Ray Hetherington   To them was born

a James Hetherington was born near Horton Kansas, December 15, 1899

3 Roy Fulton was born near Severance, Doniphan County, Kansas, October 30, 1884

4 Mary Pearl Fulton was born near Severance Doniphan County, Kansas, October 30, 1887

5 Margaret Fulton was born near Horton, Brown County, Kansas, in March, 1893.

VI —James Lovel Sharp the sixth child and second son of Silas H and N Ann Steen Sharp, was born in Adams County, Ohio, January 6, 1863, and brought up in the

home of his parents   He was married by the Rev N
Bradford, at the residence of the bride's parents, near
Winchester, Ohio, August 25, 1887, to Anna Viola
Swearingen a daughter of Benjamin K and Jane M.
Swearingen, she having been born in Adams County,
Ohio, April 9, 1869   Residence, Winchester, Ohio   The
following are the children of James L and Anna V Sharp:

1 Benjamin Sharp was born near Winchester, Ohio,
June 6, 1888.

2 Coleman S Sharp was born near Winchester, Ohio,
July 24, 1890

3 Frank Sharp was born near Winchester, Ohio December 23, 1892

4 Wiley Sharp was born near Winchester, Adams County,
Ohio, December 25, 1894

VII —Mary Inez Sharp, the seventh child and fifth daughter
of Silas H and N Ann Steen Sharp, was born in Adams
County, Ohio, February 24, 1865, and died in Chicago,
Illinois, January 28, 1897, in the 32d year of her age —
shot and instantly killed   She was married by the Rev
George M Fulton at the residence of her parents, in Winchester, Ohio, September 19, 1883, to Andrew Coleman
Denning, a son of Washington and Mary Denning, he
having been born in Adams County, Ohio, February 4,
1860 — a liveryman   Residence, Hastings, Nebraska
To Andrew C and M Inez Denning were born the following children

1 William Edmond Denning was born in Winchester,
Ohio, July 22, 1884

2 Silas Earl Denning was born in Winchester, Ohio,
April 23 1886

VIII —Austie Fleming Sharp, the eighth child and sixth
daughter of Silas H and N Ann Steen Sharp was born
in Brown County, Ohio December 24, 1866, and brought
up in her father's family   She was married by the Rev.
Mr. Denman, at the residence of her parents, in Winchester, Ohio March 10, 1885, to Charles H Wood, a son of
Thomas H and Eliza McGovie Wood, he having been
born in Brown County, Ohio, December 1, 1863   Resi-

dence, Winchester, Ohio To Charles H and Austie F Wood were born the following children

1 Samuel Frederick Wood was born in Winchester, Ohio, January 14, 1886

2 Ethel Pearl Wood was born in New Vienna, Clinton County, Ohio, June 2, 1888.

3 Mary Anna Wood was born in Winchester, Ohio, June 5, 1890

4 Irmel Wood was born in Winchester, Ohio, October 30, 1893

5 Rena Wood was born in Winchester, Ohio, August 16, 1896

6 Hildred Wood was born in Winchester, Ohio, October 17, 1898

IX —Margaret McCormick Sharp, the ninth child and seventh daughter of Silas H and N Ann Steen Sharp, was born near Winchester, Adams County, Ohio, August 24, 1869, and brought up in her father's family. She died in Athens, Ohio, July 1, 1894, in the 25th year of her age. She was married by the Rev Thomas S Park, at the residence of her parents, in Winchester, Ohio, June 16, 1887, to Edward Fisher Wheatley, a son of John and Margaret Wheatley, he having been born in Newtown, Hamilton County, Ohio, November 19, 1865 — occupation, an undertaker Residence, Lynchburgh, Highland County, Ohio To Edward F and Margaret M Wheatley the following child was born

1 Silas Joseph Wheatley was born in Lynchburgh, Ohio, February 5, 1891

3 John Chambers Steen, the third child and second son of R Wilson and Louisa C Steen, was born at the home of his parents, on Brush Creek, two miles east of Winchester, Adams County, Ohio, November 26, 1836, and brought up on his father's farm, and in the winter attended school in the neighborhood In March, 1858, he removed to Illinois and worked a while near Galesburgh, then went to Sunbeam, Mercer County, where he remained until January, 1861, when he returned to Ohio He remained in Adams County, Ohio, until March 1863, when he again removed to Illinois and

located upon a farm near Wenona, Marshall County, where he continued until 1865   He is a successful and prosperous farmer, having cultivated and resided on farms in Knox County, Marshall County, Livingston County, and Ford County, Illinois   In early life he became a devout Christian, and has been a useful citizen   John C Steen was married by the Rev Nathaniel Williams, at the residence of the bride's parents, three miles east of Winchester, Ohio, October 2, 1861, to Miss Mary Elizabeth Ramsey, a daughter of James and Susan Ramsey, she having been born in Adams County, Ohio, April 4, 1843, and died near Wenona, Marshall County, Illinois, May 31, 1865, aged 22 years, 1 month and 27 days   John C Steen was married a second time by the Rev Mr Collins, at Memphis, Missouri, January 5, 1867, to Miss Elizabeth Alice Moore, a daughter of William and Margaret Moore, she having been born in Adams County, Ohio, April 13, 1849 — a member of the M E Church. Residence, Paxton, Ford County, Illinois. The following are the children of John C Steen·

I —William Steen, the eldest son of John C and Mary E. Ramsey Steen, was born near Winchester, Adams County, Ohio, August 4, 1862, and grew up to manhood in his father's family on farms in Illinois   In 1890 he removed to Kansas and engaged in farming near Latham, in Butler County, but afterwards returned to Illinois, and is engaged in farming near Lostant, La Salle County, Illinois   He was married by the Rev. Perry Hoag, at Wenona, Marshall County, Illinois, September 21, 1887, to Miss Minnie Webber, a daughter of John Henry and Phoebe Francis Webber formerly of New York, she having been born in Illinois October 7, 1867   To William and Minnie W Steen were born the following children

   1 Elmer Steen was born in Livingston County, Illinois, February 5, 1889

   2 John Milton Steen was born near Lostant, La Salle County, Illinois, July 12 1896
      Residence, Lostant, Illinois

II —Effie Anna Steen, the second child, a daughter of John C and Mary E Ramsey Steen, was born near Wenona, Marshall County, Illinois, April 29, 1864, and was brought

up in Illinois She was married by the Rev Perry Hoag,
at the residence of her grandfather, James Ramsey, near
Ancona, Livingston County, Illinois, February 26, 1885,
to Curtis Gotchell, a son of John and Anna Storer Gotchell,
formerly of Pennsylvania, he having been born near Mans-
field, Ohio, December 21, 1860 — an engineer, now
engaged in farming. Residence, near Cheney, Lancaster
County, Nebraska The following are their children

1 James Francis Gotchell was born near Cheney,
Nebraska, November 22, 1886

2 Clarence Victor Gotchell was born near Cheney,
Nebraska, June 5, 1891

III —Richard Avis Steen, the third child and second son of
John C Steen, the eldest child by his second wife, Elizabeth
A Moore Steen, was born near Chatsworth, Livingston
County, Illinois, June 26 1869, and brought up on his
father's farm. He taught school for two years, studied
in the Northwestern University, in Evanston, Illinois, and
afterwards with the law firm of James, French & Samuels,
in Chicago He was admitted to the bar in March, 1895
— an attorney-at-law Residence, Chicago, Illinois

IV —Charles Wilson Steen, the fourth child of John C
Steen, the second son by his second wife, Elizabeth A
Moore Steen, was born near Chatsworth, Illinois, February 24 1873, and died near Piper City, Illinois, December
26, 1874

V.—Emma Louisa Steen, the fifth child and second daughter
of John C Steen the third child and eldest daughter by
his second wife, Elizabeth A Moore Steen, was born near
Piper City, Ford County, Illinois, January 30, 1875, and
died August 7, 1895, in the 21st year of her age

VI —Clara Ruby Steen, the sixth child and third daughter of
John C Steen, the fourth child and second daughter by his
second wife, Elizabeth A Moore Steen, was born near
Piper City, Illinois, August 4, 1878, and was brought up
in the family of her parents Residence, Paxton, Ford
County, Illinois

4 Reuben Russell Steen, the fourth child and third son of R
Wilson and Louisa C Steen, was born at the home of his

parents, on Brush Creek two miles east of Winchester, Ohio, September 18, 1838   He resided with his parents until he was grown, working upon the farm, and in winter attending school   After becoming of age, he engaged in farming for himself in Adams County, Ohio, for more than twenty-five years, several of which were spent near North Liberty   In March, 1887, R Russell Steen removed with his family and purchased a farm near Anthony, Harper County, Kansas, upon which he permanently located, and where he still resides   While residing in Ohio R Russell Steen and his wife and family were devout members of the Presbyterian Church, but since removing to Kansas they have connected themselves with the Cumberland Presbyterian Church near their home   R Russell Steen was married by the Rev Nathaniel Williams, at the residence of the bride's parents, on Elk Run, one mile east of Winchester, Ohio, October 18, 1860, to Miss Sarah Ann Swearingen, a daughter of Allen Swearingen, who was born in Fayette County, Pennsylvania October 4, 1810, removed to Ohio in 1832, and was married to Mary Ann Denney, November 26, 1835, who was born in Brown County, August 7 1816   Sarah Ann Swearingen, who was married to R Russell Steen, was born near Winchester, Adams County, Ohio January 14 1841   Residence, near Anthony, Harper County, Kansas   To R Russell and Sarah A Steen were born the following five children

I —Susannah Elva Steen, the eldest child and daughter of R Russell and Sarah A Steen, was born near Winchester, Ohio, July 28, 1861   She was married by the Rev Moses D A Steen at the residence of her parents near North Liberty, Ohio, December 22, 1880, to William McNeeley Blake, a son of Nicholas and Esther Blake, he having been born near North Liberty, Adams County, Ohio, December 25, 1856   William M. Blake resided in North Liberty, Ohio, engaged in the manufacture of flour until 1885, when he sold his mill and removed to a farm near Anthony, Kansas   In the fall of 1892, having purchased one hundred and sixty acres of land near Bluff City, in Harper County, Kansas, he brought his family to it, where they still reside   He has been very prosperous and successful in business, and acquired considerable property   To Wilham M and S Elva Steen Blake have been born the following children·

1 Howard Truman Blake was born in North Liberty, Adams County, Ohio, August 25, 1882

2. Inez Virgil Blake was born five miles southwest of Anthony, Harper County, Kansas, May 22, 1886   Residence, near Bluff City, Kansas

II —Allen Wilson Steen, the second child and eldest son of R Russell and Sarah A Steen, was born near Winchester, Ohio, March 8, 1864, and brought up in his father's family. About 1885 he removed to Kansas, and located upon a farm near Anthony, where he remained for several years. About 1894 he removed to Grant County, Oklahoma Territory, where he secured a farm of his own, which he cultivated, and also has charge of a store   He was married by the Rev John Martin, at the residence of the bride's parents, near North Liberty, Adams County, Ohio, August 6, 1885, to Miss Emma Cora Kirk, a daughter of John Henry and Almira Kirk, she having been born in Chattanooga, Tennessee, February 20, 1867   Residence, Wakita, Oklahoma Territory   To Allen W and E Cora Steen were born the following children.

1 Mecia Laura Steen, the eldest child, was born near Anthony, Kansas, May 3 1886

2 Charles Moses Steen, the second child and only son, was born near Anthony, Kansas, January 28, 1888

3 Anna May Steen, the third child and second daughter, was born near Anthony, Kansas, October 24, 1890

4 Blanche Steen was born near Anthony, Kansas, May 1, 1893

5 ——

III —Lyman Edward Steen the third child and second son of R. Russell and Sarah A Steen, was born near Winchester Adams County, Ohio, March 18, 1866, and brought up in his father's family   He was a farmer for a number of years, but is now in business in Anthony, Kansas   L. Edward Steen was married by the Rev Thomas B Greenlee, near Anthony, Harper County, Kansas, January 8, 1890, to Miss Mary Olive Lewis a daughter of Elisha and

Rachel Lewis, she having been born in Belmont County,
Ohio, March 18, 1870 Residence, Anthony, Kansas
To L Edward and M Olive Steen were born the following
children

1 Ersie Leona Steen was born at Anthony, Kansas, June ,
13, 1891

2 Mabel Edith Steen was born at Anthony, Kansas, September 14, 1892

3 Lena Steen was born at Anthony, Kansas, September
1, 1894   •

4 Fred Lewis Steen was born at Anthony Kansas, October 8, 1896

IV —Mary Anna Steen, the fourth child and second daughter of R Russell and Sarah A Steen, was born near Winchester Adams County, Ohio, October 26, 1868, and died
near New Vienna Clinton County, Ohio, January 19, 1873,
aged 4 years, 2 months and 24 days The body was laid
away to rest in the Winchester cemetery

V —Sarah Eleanor Steen, the fifth child and third daughter
of R Russell and Sarah A Steen, was born near North
Liberty, Adams County, Ohio, March 16, 1874, and was
brought to Kansas by her parents when she was thirteen
years of age. Sadie E Steen was married by the Rev
Charles B Parkhurst, at the residence of her parents, near
Anthony, Kansas, November 26, 1890, to George William
Halcomb, a son of Warren and Nancy Margaret Halcomb
he having been born in Simpson County, Kentucky, September 25, 1865 — a farmer. He resided for a few years
in Harper County, Kansas, and about 1894 removed to
Oklahoma Territory, where he secured a farm of his own
Residence, near Pond Creek, Grant County, Oklahoma
Territory To George W and Sadie E Halcomb were
born the following children

1 Hazel Halcomb was born near Anthony, Kansas, October 30, 1891, and died June 20, 1893, aged 1 year, 8
months and 21 days

2 Vira May Halcomb was born near Anthony, Kansas,
April 6, 1893

3 Lulu Irene Halcomb was born near Anthony, Kansas, November 3, 1894

4 Elva Halcomb was born near Pond Creek, Oklahoma Territory, May 1, 1896, and died August 4, 1896, aged 3 months and 3 days   She was buried by the side of her sister Hazel, in Harper County, Kansas

5. Ray Steen Halcomb was born near Pond Creek, Oklahoma Territory, February 14, 1899

5 Robert Wilson Fleming Steen, the fifth child and fourth son of R Wilson and Louisa C Steen, was born at the home of his parents, on Brush Creek, two miles east of Winchester, Ohio, November 23, 1840, and brought up on his father's farm. In 1859 he entered North Liberty Academy, where he continued for a while   For some years he was a salesman in the general store of Dixon & Wilkins, in Winchester, Ohio   He afterwards became a merchant in Winchester, Ohio, Ripley, Ohio, and about 1873 removed to Ottawa, Franklin County, Kansas, where he conducted a mercantile business until 1895, when he removed to Kansas City, Missouri   Robert W. F. Steen was married by the Rev Granville Moody in Ripley, Brown County, Ohio, November 12, 1868, to Miss Inez Williams, a daughter of Edward E and Eliza E Wilkins, she having been born in Winchester, Ohio, October 9, 1849   To them have been born the following children

I —Ida Marie Steen, the eldest daughter of Robert W. F and Inez Steen, was born in Mason County, Kentucky, September 25, 1869, and died in Ottawa, Kansas, July 26, 1879, in the tenth year of her age

II —Louisa Edith Steen, the second daughter of Robert W. F and Inez Steen, was born in Ripley, Brown County, Ohio, November 4, 1871. She was graduated from the high school, Ottawa, Kansas, May 26, 1892, and died April 7, 1897, in the 25th year of her age.

III —Columbia Wilkins Steen, the third daughter of Robert W F and Inez Steen, was born in Miami County, Kansas, September 23, 1873   She was graduated from the high school, Ottawa, Kansas, May 26, 1892

IV —Infant son of Robert W. F and Inez Steen was born

in Ottawa, Franklin County Kansas, October 6, 1877, and died October 7, 1877, aged one day

V —Robert Wilson Steen, the fifth child and second son of Robert W F and Inez Steen, was born in Ottawa, Franklin County, Kansas, November 26, 1878, where he was brought up and educated

6 Stephen Perry Steen the sixth child and fifth son of R. Wilson and Louisa C Steen, was born on Brush Creek, at the home of his parents, two miles east of Winchester, Ohio, March 27, 1843 and died August 18, 1845, aged 2 years, 4 months and 21 days

7 Josiah Rufus Steen, the seventh child and sixth son of R Wilson and Louisa C Steen, was born at the home of his parents, on Brush Creek, near the mouth of Elk Run, two miles east of Winchester, Ohio, July 29, 1845 and brought up on his father s farm   He has devoted himself largely to raising fine stock, especially to the raising and training of fine horses   He has resided in various localities in Adams, Fayette and Highland Counties, Ohio   J Rufus Steen was married by the Rev I H DeBruin, at the residence of the bride's parents, near Youngsville, Adams County, Ohio, December 19, 1872, to Miss Sarah Emily Young, a daughter of Alfred Young, who was born in Loudoun County, Virginia, and Elizabeth Patton Young, who was born in Highland County, Ohio, she having been born near Youngsville, Ohio, January 20 1855   Residence, Hillsboro, Highland County, Ohio   To them have been born the following children

I —Elijah Steen, the eldest son of J Rufus and Sadie E Steen, was born near Youngsville, Ohio, March 8, 1874, and brought up in his father s family — a dry goods salesman   Residence Wilmington, Ohio.

II —Charles Steen, the second son of J Rufus and Sadie E Steen, was born in Washington C H , Fayette County, Ohio, November 21 1875, and died there July 2, 1876, aged 7 months and 11 days

III —Lulu Steen, the third child and eldest daughter of J. Rufus Steen and Sadie E Steen, was born in North Liberty, Adams County Ohio, April 15, 1880, and died October 7, 1880, aged 5 months and 22 days

IV —Ione Steen, the fourth child and second daughter of J Rufus and Sadie E Steen, was born in Hillsboro, Ohio, October 20, 1882, and died there July 1, 1883, aged 8 months and 11 days

V —George Alfred Steen, the fifth child and third son of J. Rufus and Sadie E Steen, was born in Hillsboro, Ohio. January 8, 1884 Residence, Hillsboro, Ohio

VI —Bessie Steen, or Elizabeth, the sixth child and third daughter of J Rufus and Sadie E Steen, was born in Hillsboro, Ohio, September 14, 1885 Residence, Hillsboro Ohio

VII —Infant son of J Rufus and Sadie E Steen was born in Hillsboro, Ohio, August 19, 1887, and died September 14, 1887, aged 24 days.

8 Alpheus Steen, the eighth child and seventh son of R Wilson and Louisa C Steen, was born at the home of his parents, on Brush Creek, two miles east of Winchester, Ohio November 29, 1848, and brought up on his father's farm He was married by the Rev Mr. Zink, of the M E. Church, in Winchester, Ohio, February 28, 1871, to Miss Hester Margaret Phibbs, a daughter of William and Ann Phibbs, she having been born in Winchester, Ohio, December 6, 1847 Residence, New Vienna Ohio The following are their children

I —Exie Maude Steen, the eldest daughter of Alpheus and Hester M Steen, was born in Winchester, Ohio, February 22, 1872, and brought up in her father's family She united with the Presbyterian Church in 1891, and has maintained a consistent Christian life She was married by the Rev. Joseph Wright, in New Vienna Ohio, November 16, 1892, to Jesse Bertsell Gardner — a railroad employee — a son of Rozzell and Katherine Gardner he having been born in May Hill, Clinton County, Ohio January 31, 1870 Residence, Chillicothe, Ohio To them have been born the following children·

1. Elizabeth Geraldine Gardner, the eldest child of Jesse B and F Maude Gardner was born in Chillicothe, Ohio, October 26, 1893

(8)

2. Wilder Bowers Gardner, the second child and eldest
son of Jesse B and E Maude Gardner, was born in
Chillicothe, O , May 18, 1896

II.—Inez Pearl Steen, the second daughter of Alpheus and
Hester M Steen, was born in Greenfield, Highland
County, Ohio, December 22, 1875, and brought up in her
father's family. Residence, New Vienna, Ohio

III —Annie Louisa Steen, the third daughter of Alpheus and
Hester M Steen, was born in Winchester, Ohio, September 29, 1878   Residence, New Vienna, Ohio

IV —William Wilson Steen, the fourth child and eldest son
of Alpheus and Hester M Steen, was born in North Liberty, Ohio, June 21, 1881   Residence, New Vienna, Ohio

V —David Phibbs Steen, the fifth child and second son of
Alpheus and Hester M Steen, was born in Winchester,
Ohio, January 17, 1884   Residence, New Vienna, Ohio.

VI —Hezekiah Pennington Malone Steen, the sixth child
and third son of Alpheus and Hester M Steen, was born
in New Vienna, Clinton County, Ohio, December 3, 1888
Residence, New Vienna, Ohio.

9. Elijah Steen, the ninth child and eighth son of R Wilson
and Louisa C. Steen, was born at the home of his parents,
on Brush Creek, near the mouth of Elk Run, two miles east
of Winchester, Adams County, Ohio, January 2, 1854, and
brought up on his father's farm. Here he lived and labored
until after his father's death, then removed with his mother to
Youngsville, Ohio, where he resided several years   He afterwards located in Washington C H , Fayette County, Ohio,
and is by occupation a trainer of fine horses   He was married by the Rev Jonathan Stewart, at the residence of the
bride's parents, near Youngsville, Ohio, September 22, 1874,
to Miss Ruth Rector, a daughter of Samuel Y and Barbara
Ann Rector, formerly of Loudoun County, Virginia, she
having been born near Youngsville, Adams County, Ohio,
May 25, 1857   Residence, Washington C H , Ohio   To
them were born the following children

I —Jennie Pearl Steen, the eldest daughter of Elijah and
Ruth R. Steen, was born in Youngsville, Ohio, October 3,
1875, and brought up in her father's family   She was married by the Rev Mr Dixon, in Washington C. H , Ohio,

February 3, 1893, to Thomas Munford Hazelwood — a tailor — a son of John Absalom and Isabella Ann Hazelwood, formerly of Lexington, Virginia, he having been born in Botetourt County, Virginia, October 6, 1866 Residence, Washington C. H., Ohio To them were born the following children

    1 Clara Juanita Hazelwood was born in Washington C H , Ohio, March 3, 1894

    2 Ruth Isabella Hazelwood was born in Washington C H , Ohio, September 22, 1896

II —Myrtle Romane Steen, the second daughter of Elijah and Ruth R Steen, was born in Youngsville, Ohio, October 19, 1877

III —Jessie Lee Steen, the third daughter of Elijah and Ruth R Steen, was born in Youngsville, Ohio, May 15, 1881

IV —Samuel Wilson Steen, the fourth child and eldest son of Elijah and Ruth R. Steen, was born in Hillsboro, Highland County, Ohio, May 28, 1883

V —Frank Carpenter Steen, the fifth child and second son of Elijah and Ruth R Steen, was born in Washington C. H , Fayette County, Ohio, August 19, 1887

VI —Clarence Hector Steen, the sixth child and third son of Elijah and Ruth R Steen, was born in Washington C H , Ohio, March 2, 1891, and died the same day

VII —Rector Linnwood Steen, the seventh child and fourth son of Elijah and Ruth R Steen, was born in Washington C H., Ohio, November 17, 1892

VIII —Elijah Earl Steen, the eighth child and fifth son of Elijah and Ruth R Steen, was born in Washington C H , Ohio, January 23, 1895

IX —Paulina Elizabeth Steen, the ninth child and fourth daughter of Elijah and Ruth R Steen, was born in Washington C H , Ohio, March 9, 1897

V —Catherine Elizabeth Steen, the fifth child and third daughter of Alexander and Agnes Nancy Faris Steen, was born at the home of her parents, on a farm, two miles north of Flemingsburgh, Fleming County, Kentucky March 11, 1810, and died in North Liberty, Adams County, Ohio, December 25, 1880 aged 79 years, 9 months and 14 days She was brought from

Kentucky by her parents when a child of nine years to their
new home, on Brush Creek, two miles east of Winchester,
Adams County, Ohio, in 1820, where she grew to womanhood.
She was married by Aaron Moore J P , at the residence of her
parents, two miles east of Winchester, Ohio, June 24, 1830, to
William Lord Blair, he having been born near Jonesboro, Ten-
nessee, December 25, 1803, and died in North Liberty, Ohio,
September 8, 1870, in the 77th year of his age   William Lard
Blair was the son of William Blair, Sr , who was born in Ire-
land, February 1, 1762 and married to Margaret Wallace in
Jonesboro, Tennessee, in the autumn of 1794, she having been
born in Jonesboro Washington County, Tennessee, November
4, 1774   Mr William Blair, Sr , died in Adams County, Ohio,
July 26, 1850, aged 88 years, 5 months and 25 days   His wife,
Mrs Margaret Wilson Blair, died in Adams County, Ohio,
January 4, 1820, aged 45 years and 2 months.   They were the
parents of a large family of children, who have left a numerous
posterity   William L and Catherine E Steen Blair, called
"Kitty," were both earnest and devout Christians, and for
many years members of the Mt. Leigh Presbyterian Church
They brought up their children in the fear of the Lord, to
whose service all were early consecrated   William L Blair
was an early and strong advocate of the abolition of human
slavery, and a ruling elder in the Presbyterian Church from
1851 until his death   William L and Catherine E Blair spent
the greater portion of their lives in Adams County, Ohio   Mr
Blair was by occupation a farmer, and at different times lived in
several different places in the county and followed different
occupations   In 1850, during the summer, he removed to
Morgan County, Illinois, where he cultivated a farm for one
year, but owing to severe and protracted sickness in the family
he returned to Ohio   For some time he was proprietor of a
hotel in Mt Orab, Brown County, Ohio, then kept a country
store and post-office at Mt Leigh, Ohio , afterwards removed
to Russellville, Ohio, and finally to North Liberty, Ohio where
he spent the remaining years of his life   William L. and
Catherine E Blair were the parents of the following thirteen
children

1   Rebecca Ann Blair, the eldest child and daughter of William
    L 'and Catherine E Blair, was born near Winchester, Ohio,
    May 12, 1831, and died the same day

2 William Alexander Blair, the second child and eldest son of
William L. and Catherine E. Blair was born near Winchester, Ohio, and brought up in his father's family. He is a
man of devout spirit and earnest Christian life, and for many
years a member of the Mt. Leigh Presbyterian Church.
After removing to Indiana he united with the Presbyterian
Church in Muncie, and brought up his family in the fear of
the Lord. He was married by the Rev. Nathaniel Williams
at the residence of William Davis, two miles east of Winchester, Ohio, April 12, 1855, to Miss Mary Ellen Bloom, a
daughter of John and Jane Bloom, she having been born in
Adams County, Indiana, July 5, 1835, and died at their home,
three miles east of Winchester, Adams County, Ohio July 5,
1856, aged 21 years. W. Alexander Blair was married a
second time by the Rev. Nathaniel Williams, at the residence
of his uncle Aaron F. Steen, near Mt. Leigh Ohio, December 24, 1857, to Miss Sarah Moore Freeman, a daughter of
Isaac and Jemima Freeman, she having been born on Scioto
Brush Creek, in Adams County, Ohio, November 16, 1823,
and died at their home in Eaton, Delaware County, Indiana,
June 15, 1878, aged 54 years, 8 months and 1 day. W.
Alexander Blair was married a third time by the Rev. Augustus Taylor, at the residence of the bride's parents, near
Manchester, Adams County, Ohio, January 27, 1879, to Miss
Jennie McKee, a daughter of Peter and Rachel McKee, she
having been born in Adams County, Ohio, November 16,
1852. Residence, Muncie, Delaware County, Indiana. To
W. Alexander Blair and his first wife there are no children.
To W. Alexander Blair and his second wife were born three
children. To W. Alexander Blair and his third wife were
born three children.

1 —Dora Ette Blair, the eldest child of William Alexander
  Blair and the first daughter by his second wife, Sarah M.
  Freeman Blair, was born near Winchester, Ohio, October
  29, 1858. In 1863 she was taken by her parents to their
  new home in Selma, Delaware County, Indiana, where
  she was brought up. She was married by the Rev. O. M.
  Todd, at the residence of her parents, in Eaton, Delaware
  County, Indiana, August 19, 1875, to Zechariah Young,
  a son of Enoch and Catherine Ann Young, he having been
  born in Delaware County, Indiana, May 6, 1851 — a gen-

eral merchant   Residence, Eaton, Indiana   To them
were born the following children

1 Theodore Ovid Young was born at Eaton, Indiana,
March 3, 1877, and died April 3, 1877, aged one month

2 Ralph Blair Young was born at Eaton Indiana, February 23, 1891, and died June 9, 1891, aged 3 months and
14 days

3 Mary Eve Young was born at Eaton, Indiana July 9,
1892, and resides with her parents

II —Austie Ellen Blair, the second daughter of W. Alexander and Sarah M Blair, was born near Winchester,
Ohio, February 19, 1860, and brought to Selma, Delaware
County Indiana, by her parents in the autumn of 1863,
where she was brought up and lived a devout Christian
life   She died in Milroy, Rush County, Indiana, September 4 1883, aged 23 years, 6 months and 14 days   Austie
E. Blair was married by the Rev. Thomas Sells, of the
M E Church, in April, 1882, to James L Walters, a son
of Jacob Walters, he having been born in Delaware
County Indiana, and died in Eaton, Indiana, December
18, 1882   No children

III —Ora Maud Blair, the third daughter of W Alexander
and Sarah M Blair, was born in Selma, Delaware County,
Indiana, November 7, 1868, and brought up in her father's
family   She was married at the residence of her father, in
Muncie, Indiana, ——, to Irving Buchtel Allen, a son of
Wilber Romenzo and Cynthia Allen, he having been born
at South Bend, Indiana, March 27, 1867   Occupation,
tinner, slater, etc   Residence, Hartford City, Indiana
To Irving B and Ora Maud Allen were born the following children

1 Bernice Allen was born in Hartford City, Indiana, September 14, 1893

2 Katherine Allen was born in Hartford City, Indiana
May 7, 1897

IV —Edith Beatrice Blair, the fourth child of W Alexander
Blair and the eldest by his third wife, Jennie McKee Blair,
was born in Eaton, Indiana, April 21, 1880   Residence,
Muncie, Indiana

V —Ethel Cleora Blair, the fifth daughter of W Alexander Blair, and the second daughter by his third wife, Jennie McKee Blair, was born in Eaton, Delaware County, Indiana, July 17 1881. Residence, Muncie, Indiana

VI —Frank Paul Blair the sixth child and only son of W Alexander Blair, and the third child by his third wife, Jennie McKee Blair, was born in Milroy, Rush County, Indiana, May 17, 1885 Residence, Muncie, Indiana

3 Josiah Whitfield Blair, the third child and second son of William L and Catherine E. Blair, was born near Winchester, Ohio, June 13, 1833, and died of cholera in Montgomery County, Illinois, August 22, 1851, aged 18 years, 2 months and 9 days

4 Nancy Jane Blair the fourth child and second daughter of William L and Catherine E Blair, was born near Winchester, Ohio, December 8, 1834, and died in Adams County, Ohio, July 5, 1841, aged 5 years, 7 months and 28 days

5. Martha Ann Blair, the fifth child and third daughter of William L and Catherine E Blair, was born near Winchester, Ohio, April 16, 1837, and died at her home, on Buck Run, Adams County, Ohio, August 18, 1859, aged 22 years, 4 months and 2 days She was married by the Rev Samuel Van Dyke, at the residence of her parents, near the forks of Brush Creek, four miles east by north from Winchester, Ohio, January 24, 1856, to Samuel McCoy Alexander a son of Isaiah and Sarah McCoy Alexander, he having been born two miles east of Winchester, Ohio, at the home of his parents, which was the farm first occupied by Alexander Steen and family, when they came into Ohio in 1820 Samuel McCoy Alexander was born July 19, 1835 — a farmer To Samuel M and Martha A Alexander was born one child

I —James Emery Alexander was born at the home of his parents, on Buck Run, about six miles northeast of Winchester, Ohio, August 27, 1858 — a farmer He was married by the Rev J W Clice, at Hillsboro, Ohio, December 28, 1887, to Miss Rebecca Webster, a daughter of John and Susannah Webster, she having been born near Lynchburgh, Highland County, Ohio, August 1, 1868 Her father was born May 3, 1834, and her mother May 29, 1831, and resided near Fairfax, Highland County,

Ohio   To Emery and Rebecca W Alexander were born the following children

1 Edna May Alexander was born December 9, 1888.

2 Virgie Lillian Alexander was born January 19, 1890

3 John Truman Alexander was born September 17, 1891

4 Vernon Lloyd Alexander was born September 23, 1894

6 Aaron Wallace Blair, the sixth child and third son of William L and Catherine E Blair, was born near Winchester, Ohio, November 13, 1838, and died in Mt Orab, Brown County, Ohio, December 29, 1856, aged 18 years, 1 month and 16 days

7 Marion Ellen Blair, the seventh child and fourth daughter of William L and Catherine E Blair, was born near Winchester, Ohio, February 17, 1841, and brought up in her father's family   She died from paralysis at Metropolis, Illinois, February 19, 1900, aged 59 years and 2 days   She was married by the Rev Emile Grand-Guard, at the residence of her parents, near Russellville, Brown County, Ohio, February 15, 1866, to William Martin, a son of Isaac and Amanda Martin, he having been born near Youngsville and Mt Leigh, Adams County, Ohio, January 27, 1842, brought up on his father's farm, and attended the Mt Leigh school. The next year after their marriage, in April, 1867, they removed from Ohio and located upon a farm which had previously been entered from the government, near Metropolis, Massac County, Illinois, where they continued to live for more than twenty-five years   William Martin enlisted as a soldier in Battery F First Regiment Ohio Light Artillery, May 1, 1861, and served his country faithfully until the close of the Civil War   He was honorably discharged at Camp Denison, near Cincinnati, Ohio, July 22, 1865   After settling upon his farm, near Metropolis, Illinois, Mr Martin taught school for about ten years and six months, and was also engaged as a surveyor and civil engineer   In April 1892, William Martin and his wife gave the farm into the charge of their son and removed into Metropolis City, where Mr Martin became city civil engineer and is a prosperous man   All the family are devout Christians and members of the Methodist Episcopal Church in Metropolis City   Resi-

dence, Metropolis City, Illinois   To them were born two children, as follows

I —Annie Marie Martin, the eldest child of William and M Ellen Martin, was born near Metropolis, Illinois, June 19, 1867   Resides with her father, in Metropolis City, Massac County, Illinois

II.—William Isaac Martin, the second child of William and M. Ellen Martin was born near Metropolis, Illinois, and brought up on his father's farm   He early united with the M E Church, and was an earnest Christian   He died in the triumphs of faith September 21, 1895, and his body was laid away to rest in the Masonic cemetery in Metropolis City   He was married October 19, 1893, to Miss Emma Owens, to whom was born one child, as follows·

  1 Cecil Blair Martin, a son of William Isaac and Emma Owens Martin, was born near Metropolis City, Illinois, August 29, 1894, and died May 18, 1895, aged 8 months and 20 days

8 George Washington Blair, the eighth child and fourth son of William L and Catherine E Blair, was born near Winchester, Ohio, February 15, 1843, and died in Linwood, near Cincinnati, Ohio, April 6, 1890, aged 47 years, 1 month and 20 days   His body was taken to the Mt Leigh cemetery for interment   George W Blair was brought up in his father's family and lived at home until the breaking out of the Civil War, attended the Mt Leigh public school, and became a member of the Presbyterian Church in 1858   In August, 1861, he enlisted in Battery F, First Regiment Ohio Volunteer Light Artillery, at Camp Denison, Ohio   He was bugler in the battery, and together with his brother, James F Blair, served his country faithfully throughout the entire war   He re-enlisted among the veterans, January 4, 1864, for three years more, or during the war, and after its close was honorably discharged at Camp Denison, Ohio, July 22, 1865   In the battle of Chickamauga he was slightly wounded by a piece of shell   After the close of the war he followed the jeweler's trade and resided in Manchester, Ohio, Maysville, Kentucky, Clinton, Illinois, and several other places   He

was married by the Rev Joseph West at the residence of the
bride's parents, in Russellville, Ohio, October 24, 1867, to
Miss Ora Ann Wilkins, a daughter of Samuel and Susan
Edwards Wilkins, she having been born near Decatur,
Brown County, Ohio, June 16, 1846, and died in Knoxville,
Tennessee, June 13 1887, aged 41 years   To them were
born the following children

 I —Edward Wilkins Blair, the eldest son of George W and
  Ora A Blair, was born in Manchester, Ohio, December
  7, 1868 and grew up in his father's family   He was hotel
  clerk in Cincinnati, Ohio, where he died, October 31
  1895, aged 26 years, 10 months and 7 days.   His body
  was taken to Mt Leigh cemetery for interment, November
  3, 1895

 II —Wilber Rocha Blair, the second son of George W and
  Ora A Blair, was born in Clinton, Illinois, May 11, 1872
  and brought up in the home of his parents   He is by
  occupation a merchant   Residence, Blaine, Tennessee.

9 James Faris Blair, the ninth child and fifth son of William
L and Catherine E Blair, was born near Winchester, Ohio,
July 21, 1844, and died in Linwood, Cincinnati, Ohio, on
Friday, February 2, 1894, in the 50th year of his age   His
body was interred at Mt Washington cemetery on Sunday,
February 4, 1894   He was brought up in his father's family, and lived at home until the breaking out of the Civil
War   In youth he attended the public school at Mt Leigh
and Brush Creek, and also the Presbyterian Church, of
which he early became a consistent member   When only a
little more than seventeen years old, October 1, 1861, he
enlisted in Battery F. First Regiment Ohio Volunteer Light
Artillery, at Camp Denison, Ohio   He afterwards re-enlisted
among the veterans and served as a brave and faithful private soldier until the War of the Rebellion was at an end
The battery to which he belonged was composed of six guns,
and was principally in the Army of the Cumberland, under
Generals Buell, Rosecrans, Halleck and Grant, with Generals
Crittenden and Thomas as corps commanders, and Generals
Hazen and Granger in command of the brigade   In the
battle of Stone River James F Blair had a horse killed
under him, which fell on his left leg, but without serious

GEORGE W. BLAIR.
(Born 1843; Died 1890.)

injury, while at the same time three minnie balls passed
through his clothing In the battle of Chickamauga his
horse was shot through the neck, and his hat knocked off
and torn to pieces with the fragment of a shell, and in the
battle of Decatur, Alabama, his horse was shot and severely
wounded   George W and James F Blair were together in
sixteen heavy engagements, including Perryville, Kentucky,
Stone River Chickamauga, Lookout Mountain, Mission
Ridge, etc, but a kind providence permitted them to return
home in safety Victory having been achieved, they were
honorably discharged from the service at Camp Denison,
Ohio, July 22 1865 After the close of the war James F.
Blair devoted himself to the study of medicine, and was
graduated from Louisville Medical College February 26,
1876 The same summer he began a successful practice at
Marshall, Highland County, Ohio, where he remained until
February 1, 1886, when he removed to Linwood, Ohio, a
suburb of Cincinnati where he built up an extensive practice
and continued to reside until his death   At the organization
of Calvary Presbyterian Church, at Linwood, April 21, 1887,
he was elected, ordained and installed a ruling elder, which
office he held as long as he lived   He was a good man, a
devout Christian, much beloved, and exerted a wide religious
influence Dr James F Blair was married by the Rev
Peter P Wohr, at the residence of the bride's parents, in
Marshall, Highland County Ohio, April 11, 1878, to Miss
Laura Elizabeth Hughes, a daughter of John Love and
Elizabeth Carlisle Hughes, she having been born in Highland
County, Ohio, July 12, 1855 Family residence, Linwood
Cincinnati, Ohio   To them were born the following chil-
dren

I —Mirpha Gertrude Blair, the eldest child and only daughter of Dr. James F and Laura E Blair, was born in Marshall, Highland County, Ohio, February 28, 1879, and
brought up in the home of her parents   She was graduated with honor from Glendale Female College, June 4,
1896, taking the English salutatory and free scholarship
at Wellesley College. Residence, Linwood, Cincinnati,
Ohio

II —Faris Morell Blair, the second child and only son of
Dr James F. and Laura E Blair, was born in Marshall,

Ohio, December 5, 1880, and brought up in the home of his parents — a student   Residence, Linwood, Cincinnati, Ohio

10   John Wilson Blair, the tenth child and sixth son of William and Catherine E Blair, was born near Decatur, Brown County, Ohio, February 8, 1846, and brought up in his father's family   He began the study of dentistry with Dr John C Allen, at Ripley, Ohio, April 9, 1866, where he remained three and a half years   He opened an office for himself in Manchester, Ohio, October 1, 1869, where he remained seven years, then removed to Ripley, Ohio, October 1, 1876, where he remained in practice for a little more than four years.   He located permanently in Winchester, Adams County, Ohio, January 1, 1881, where he has ever since continued in the successful practice of dentistry   For many years he has been a member and is now a ruling elder in the Presbyterian Church in Winchester   Dr. John W Blair was married by the Rev James E Williamson, at the residence of the bride's parents, in Winchester, Ohio, July 12, 1881, to Miss Nancy Ellen Plummer, a daughter of Moses and Minerva Jane Plummer, she having been born near Winchester, Ohio, December 25, 1857, and died January 6, 1890, in the 33d year of her age   He was married a second time by the Rev Thomas S Park, in Sardinia, Brown County, Ohio, December 24, 1890, to Miss Nerva Belle Bingaman a daughter of George and Minerva Ross Bingaman, she having been born at Bingaman Place, Brown County, Ohio, June 21, 1862   Family residence, Winchester, Ohio   To Dr. John W. Blair the following children were born

I —William Leslie Blair, the eldest child and only son of Dr J W Blair, the only child by his first wife, Nancy E Plummer Blair, was born in Winchester, Ohio, April 7, 1882   Residence, Winchester, Ohio

II —Laura Etta Blair, the second child and only daughter of Dr J W Blair, and the only child by his second wife, Nerva Belle Bingaman Blair, was born in Winchester Ohio, October 18, 1891, and resides there with her parents

11. Robert Belt Blair, the eleventh child and seventh son of William L. and Catherine E. Blair, was born near Winchester, Ohio, August 29, 1847, and brought up in his father's family. Although very young, while living in Brown County, Ohio, he enlisted in the army at Cincinnati, Ohio, February 22, 1863, and served his country in the Civil War in Company H, Fifth Regiment Ohio Volunteer Cavalry. After the close of the war he followed the occupation of a farmer. Since 1892 he has been afflicted with paralysis of the lower limbs, which renders him unable for any business. R. Belt Blair was married by the Rev. Thomas Slater, in Highland County, Ohio, June 19, 1875, to Miss Exira Ann Penn, a daughter of Stephen and Mary Penn, she having been born near Cynthiana, Pike County, Ohio, November 24, 1847. Residence, near Cynthiana, Ohio. To them were born the following children:

I.—Frank Penn Blair, the eldest son of R. Belt and Exira A. Blair, was born near Cynthiana, Ohio, August 14, 1876.

II.—Herman Alexander Blair, the second son of R. Belt and Exira A. Blair, was born near Cynthiana, Ohio, January 25, 1881.

12. Thomas Alfred Blair, the twelfth child and eighth son of William L. and Catherine E. Blair, was born near Winchester, Ohio, March 22, 1849, and died of cholera in Montgomery County, Illinois, August 14, 1851, aged 2 years, 4 months and 23 days.

13. Mary Catherine Blair, the thirteenth child and fifth daughter of William Lard and Catherine Elizabeth Steen Blair, was born in Morgan County, Illinois, February 16, 1851, and brought up in the home of her parents. She was married by the Rev. John E. Carson, at the residence of her mother, in North Liberty (Cherry Fork Post-office), Adams County, Ohio, September 25, 1876, to Hiram Smith Kennett — by occupation a traveling salesman, and a son of George Kennett, he having been born near Russellville, Brown County, Ohio, January 16, 1851, and died in Portsmouth, Scioto County, Ohio, January 1, 1886, in the 35th year of his age. Since her marriage, M. Catherine Blair Kennett, called "Kit," or Kate, has lived five years in Milroy, Indiana, fourteen years in Portsmouth, Ohio, and from 1897 to 1899 in

Columbus, Ohio   Residence, Hartford City, Indiana   To them were born the following children

I —Earnest Budmon Kennett, the eldest child and only son of H Smith and M Kate Kennett, was born in North Liberty, Ohio, December 13, 1877, and died in Portsmouth, Ohio, January 23, 1897, aged 19 years, 1 month and 10 days.

II —Nellie Grace Kennett, the second child and only daughter of H Smith and M Kate Kennett, was born in Portsmouth, Ohio, March 24 1883   Residence, Hartford City, Indiana

VI.—John Work Steen, the sixth child and third son of Alexander and Agnes Nancy Faris Steen, was born on the farm, two miles north of Flemingsburgh, Fleming County, Kentucky, May 5, 1813, and brought by his parents to Adams County, Ohio, in 1820   Here he grew up to manhood in the very neighborhood in which he spent his life, working upon his .ather's farm in summer and attending school in the winter. He was a successful farmer and lived on the old homestead, which, after his father's death, he owned   It was located four miles east of Winchester, Adams County, Ohio, and less than a mile north of the Mt Leigh Presbyterian Church   At this place he died, after a lingering illness, January 20. 1882, aged 68 years, 3 months and 15 days   In early life he united with the Mt Leigh Presbyterian Church, and was ever afterwards an active and exemplary Christian man   He was ordained and installed a ruling elder of this church October 9, 1847, which office he continued to hold until his death, always enjoying the fraternal confidence and affection of his brethren   He was a man of sweet disposition. gentle manners and unselfish nature — a bright example   of the reality and power of the religion which he professed   He died as he had lived, in the full hope of a blessed immortality. and longing to be "with Christ, which is far better"   He brought up his family in the fear of the Lord, and all were brought into full membership of the same church with himself   John W Steen was married by the Rev John Graham, at the residence of the bride's parents, on Buck Run Adams County, Ohio, June 3, 1841, to Miss Nancy Ewing Campbell, a daughter of James and Elizabeth Campbell, she having been born on Buck Run. Ohio, December 22, 1819, and died on the old Steen family homestead, near Mt Leigh Presbyterian Church, where she had lived so long, May 26, 1887, in the 68th year of her age To John W and Nancy E Steen were born on the old Grandfather Steen homestead, near Mt Leigh, Ohio, the following children

1 Elizabeth Jane Steen the eldest daughter of John W and Nancy E. Steen, was born near Mt Leigh Ohio, April 8, 1842, and died at her home, near Tranquility, Adams County, Ohio, October 8, 1874, aged 32 years and 6 months She was married at the residence of her parents by the Rev John Gilmore, a United Presbyterian clergyman, February 8, 1866, to John A McCreight, a farmer, living near Tranquility, Ohio, a son of David and Rebecca McCreight, he having been born near Tranquility, Ohio, November 8, 1838 Family residence, Tranquility Ohio To them were born the following children

I —Louis Love McCreight the eldest child of John A and Elizabeth Jane McCreight was born near Tranquility, Ohio, November 24, 1886 and brought up in his father's family — principal of the schools Residence, Gridley, McLean County Illinois

II —Emma Alice McCreight the second child and only daughter of John A and Elizabeth Jane McCreight, was born near Tranquility, Ohio, July 29 1868 and died February 1 1891 aged 22 years 6 months and 2 days

III —Orwin Steele McCreight, the third child and second son of John A and Elizabeth Jane McCreight, and a twin brother of the preceding, was born near Tranquility, Ohio, July 29 1868, and brought up in his father's family Residence Tranquility, Ohio

2 Albertine Steen, the second daughter of John W and Nancy E Steen, was born on the old Steen homestead, near Mt Leigh, Adams County, Ohio, October 15 1843 and brought up in her father's family She was married at the residence of her parents by the Rev M Keck, a Methodist minister September 18, 1867 to Robert Miller Butler a son of Daniel and Jane Butler he having been born May 10 1845 Mr Butler is a blacksmith by trade and has resided in several different localities For several years they lived

in Grafton, West Virginia   He is now a merchant, dealing in farm implements and machinery.   They have no children   Residence Sabina, Clinton County, Ohio

3 Sarah Adaline Steen, the third daughter of John W and Nancy E Steen, was born on the old Steen family homestead, near Mt Leigh, Adams County, Ohio, July 20, 1846, and died in Ottawa, Franklin County, Kansas, rejoicing in Christ, December 26, 1898 aged 52 years, 5 months and 6 days   She was married by the Rev David Van Dyke, at the residence of her parents, July 20, 1869, to John Albert Frow — merchant salesman — a son of John and Susan Frow, he having been born in Winchester, Adams County, Ohio, November 5, 1845   After their marriage they continued to reside in Winchester for fifteen years, and in 1884 removed to Ottawa, Kansas, where he still remains a merchant salesman and bookkeeper   Family residence, Ottawa, Kansas   To them were born the following children

I —Lydia Gertrude Frow, the eldest daughter of J Albert and Sallie A Frow was born in Winchester, Ohio, October 16 1871   Residence Ottawa, Kansas

II —Eunice Ewing Frow, the second daughter of J. Albert and Sallie A Frow, was born in Winchester, Ohio, January 7, 1875   Residence, Ottawa, Kansas

III —Susan Faris Frow, the third daughter of J Albert and Sallie A Frow, was born in Winchester, Ohio, December 16, 1878   Residence, Ottawa, Kansas

4 Samuel Wilson Steen, the fourth child and only son of John W and Nancy E Steen, was born at the old Steen family residence, where his father and grandfather Steen lived and died, May 3, 1848   He grew up in his father's family, working on the farm in summer and attending school in winter   He continued to live in the neighborhood and cultivate a farm near Irvington, Adams County, Ohio, until 1893 when he removed to Kansas and located upon a farm near Ottawa   Samuel W Steen was married by the Rev. John Stewart, a United Presbyterian clergyman, at the residence of the bride's parents, near Youngsville, Adams County, Ohio October 24 1872 to Miss Regina Williams, a daughter of John and Mary Williams, she having been born in Adams

County, Ohio, May 20, 1852   Residence, near Ottawa,
Kansas   To them were born the following children

I —William Orlando Steen, the eldest son of Samuel W. and
Regina Steen, was born near Youngsville, Ohio, October
5, 1873   Residence, Ottawa, Kansas

II —Frank Work Steen, the second son of Samuel W and
Regina Steen, was born near Youngsville, Ohio, March 5,
1874   Residence, Ottawa, Kansas

III —Clyde Glasgow Steen, the third and youngest son of
Samuel W and Regina Steen, was born near Youngsville,
Ohio, September 8, 1878, and died October 6, 1878, aged
nearly one month

5 Ann America Steen, the fifth child and fourth daughter of
John W and Nancy E Steen, was born on the old Steen
family homestead, in Adams County, Ohio, near the Mt
Leigh Presbyterian Church, April 29, 1851   She resided
with her parents until after their death, and afterwards in the
old home until 1891, when the place was sold.   She removed
with her sisters, Alice J and Nannie E Steen, to Ottawa,
Kansas, in the fall of 1891, and established and carried on
dressmaking   After a few years she removed to Emporia,
Kansas, and continued in the business   Residence,
Emporia, Kansas

6 Alice Josephine Steen, the sixth child and fifth daughter of
John W and Nancy E Steen, was born on the old Steen
homestead, four miles east of Winchester, Ohio, May 27,
1853   She was brought up on the old home farm, and lived
with her parents until after their death   In 1891 she removed
with her sisters Ann America and Nannie E Steen, to
Ottawa, Kansas, and afterwards to Emporia, where they are
engaged in dressmaking   Residence, Emporia, Kansas

7 Nancy Ellen Steen, the seventh child and sixth daughter
of John W and Nancy E Steen, was born on the old Steen
homestead, near the Mt Leigh Presbyterian Church in
Adams County, Ohio, August 29, 1856, and resided there
until after the death of her parents   In 1891 she removed
with her sisters Ann America and Alice J Steen, to Ottawa
Kansas and afterwards to Emporia, where she was associated with them in dressmaking   She died in Emporia

Kansas, August 5, 1898, in the full hope of a blessed immortality aged 41 years, 11 months and 4 days

8 Margaret Catherine Steen, called "Maggie," the eighth child , and seventh daughter of John W and Nancy E Steen, was born on the old Steen family homestead, four miles east of Winchester and near the Mt Leigh Presbyterian Church, in Adams County, Ohio, October 31, 1858, where she was brought up and resided   She was married at the same place by the Rev William A Anderson, a United Presbyterian clergyman, October 3, 1889, to Matthew Allen Palmer, a son of William and Jane Palmer, he having been born about six miles east of Winchester, near the Calvary Methodist Protestant Church, in Adams County Ohio, June 3, 1865 After her marriage Maggie C. Steen Palmer resided on the old Steen homestead with her husband and unmarried sisters for two years. Mr Palmer having charge of the farm   After the sale of the old homestead and property in 1891, they removed to Illinois, and Mr Palmer cultivated a farm near Aledo, in Mercer County   They afterwards located near Reading, in Lyons County, Kansas, and finally settled upon a farm near Emporia, Kansas   Residence, Emporia, Kansas To them was born the following child

I—Mildred Viola Palmer, daughter of Matthew A and Maggie C Palmer, was born near Reading, Lyons County, Kansas, December 24, 1895

VII —Alexander Boyd Steen, the seventh child and fourth son of Alexander and Agnes Nancy Fairs Steen, and a twin brother of John Work Steen, was born at the home of his parents, on a farm two miles north of Flemingsburg, Kentucky, May 5, 1813, and died at his residence, three miles east of Winchester Ohio in the early morning of March 8, 1895 aged 81 years 10 months and 3 days   His body was lovingly laid away to rest the next day in the cemetery at Mt Leigh, near which place he had resided for almost seventy-five years   He was brought by his parents into Ohio in 1820, and ever afterwards lived in the vicinity of his father's first settlement in Ohio three miles east of Winchester as a practical and successful farmer Alexander B Steen was a child of the covenant, and descended from a long line of staunch Scotch-Irish Presbyterian ancestors, who had endured persecutions and suffered imprisonment for the sake of their religious faith   He was a most saintly man, 'greatly beloved" by all who knew him, and his gentleness of manner, sweet devotion, and absorbing zeal reminded one of our ideal good old Apostle John   He occupied comparatively an humble sphere, and was very unpretentious, but no man in all that region of country exerted a wider religious influence than he   In private conversation his spiritual insight and heavenly-mindedness was a real uplift to the soul   His faith in God's Word was unbounded, and the divine promises were living realities   He was no mere idle dreamer, thinking only of the future glory, but insisted upon the faithful performance of the practical duties of to-day   He was not a learned man, but yet was more familiar with the English Bible than many professors of theology ; and would quote from memory the chapter and verse to substantiate his position on any subject of conversation. ' It says" was a satisfactory answer to him on any subject, and an end to all controversy   He was frequently called to positions in the church, but always humbly declined, thinking he could serve God more acceptably in a private station   By a fall some years before his death he was severely injured in the hips, which largely confined him to the house This he afterwards spoke of as a special blessing of providence, inasmuch as it gave him a better opportunity to study the Scriptures   He brought up his family of eight children in the fear of the Lord, and it was his privilege and great joy to see them all brought into the Christian fold, members of the same church with which he was connected for more than fifty years Three of his brothers and four of his sons have been ruling elders in the Presbyterian Church   Alexander B Steen was married by the Rev Robert Steward, near Harshasville, Adams County, Ohio to Miss Nancy Jane McClure, a daughter of Michael and Elizabeth McClure, she having been born in Hillsboro, Highland County, Ohio, September 11, 1821, and died March 18, 1893, aged 71 years, 5 months and 7 days   To Alexander B and Nancy J Steen were born the following children:

1 Mary Jane Steen, the eldest child and only daughter of Alexander B and Nancy J Steen, was born on the old Grandfather Steen homestead, near the Mt Leigh Presbyterian Church, in Adams County, Ohio February 26, 1839, where she spent her childhood and attended school   She early united with the Mt Leigh Church and grew up to be a

young lady of winning manners, kindly heart, devout spirit
and intelligent interest in everything good   She died at the
home of her parents, on Brush Creek, about four miles northeast of Winchester, Ohio January 27, 1857, aged 17 years 10
months and 25 days much beloved by those who knew her

2 John Alexander Steen, the second child and eldest son of
Alexander B and Nancy Jane Steen, was born on the old
Grandfather Steen homestead, near Mt Leigh Presbyterian
Church, in Adams County, Ohio, March 26, 1841   Here
he spent his early days, working upon the farm in summer
and attending the Mt Leigh school in winter   About 1855
he removed with his parents to their new home and farm
on Brush Creek, about two miles away, where he continued
to live until he became of age.   With several other young
friends and relatives he united with the Mt Leigh Presbyterian Church, June 9, 1858, and has ever maintained a consistent Christian character   He enlisted in the army at Winchester, Ohio, August 1, 1862, in Company I, Ninety-first
Regiment Ohio. Volunteer Infantry, and served his country
faithfully until the close of the war, when he was honorably
discharged   After the war he studied dentistry under Dr
John N. McClung of Cincinnati Ohio, and practiced his
profession with good success in North Liberty, Ohio, until
November 13, 1875, when he removed to Ripley, Ohio, where
he still carries on an extensive and profitable business   Here
he united with the First Presbyterian Church, of which he is
a useful and influential member   He is a genial, kind-
hearted man, always has a pleasant word for every one, is
widely known, and wins hosts of friends wherever he goes
Dr John A Steen was married by the Rev James R. Gibson,
at the residence of the bride's parents, near Eckmansville,
Adams County, Ohio, December 29, 1869 to Miss Jennie M
Reighley, a daughter of Henry and Nancy G Ramsey Reighley, she having been born at Siglersville, Mifflin County,
Pennsylvania, October 16, 1844, and died in their pleasant
home in Ripley, Ohio, January 3, 1895, aged 50 years, 2
months and 18 days   She was a most amiable, devout and
useful woman, in the family the church, and community, and
brought up her children in the fear of the Lord   Dr John
A. Steen was married a second time in Manchester Ohio,
March 17 1897 to Miss Sarah Lawwill, a daughter of John

Dr John A. Steen.

K. and Amanda N. Lawwill, she having been born in Brown County, Ohio. Residence, Ripley, Ohio. The following are his children:

I.—Minnie Maud Steen, the eldest child of Dr. John A. and Jennie M. Steen, was born in North Liberty (Cherry Fork Post-office), Adams County, Ohio, January 27, 1871, and was brought up in Ripley, Brown County, Ohio. Here she was graduated from the high school, and afterwards received her higher and musical education at Oxford College. She was married by the Rev. Joseph W. Torrence, D.D., in the First Presbyterian Church, Ripley, Ohio, March 26, 1891, to Howard Charles Green, a son of Henry Duncan and Mary Ann Green, he having been born in New Richmond, Clermont County, Ohio, October 28, 1863. Residence, 708 Sixtieth Street, Englewood, Chicago, Illinois. To them were born the following children:
1. Caden Rae Green, the eldest son of Howard C. and Minnie M. Green, was born in Chicago, Illinois, December 18, 1891, and died March 7, 1899, in the eighth year of his age.
2. Charles Howard Green, the second son of Howard C. and Minnie M. Green, was born in Ripley, Ohio, February 23, 1893.

II.—Lulu Edna Steen, the second daughter of Dr. John A. and Jennie M. Steen, was born in North Liberty, Ohio, August 8, 1874, and brought up in Ripley, Ohio, in the home of her parents. She was graduated from the high school in Ripley, Ohio, May 20, 1892. She was married by the Rev. Eberle W. Thompson, at the residence of her father, in Ripley, Ohio, July 16, 1896, to Espy Edwin Higgins, a son of Henry T. and Lue Higgins, he having been born in West Union, Ohio, December 28, 1873 — a traveling salesman. Residence, Denver, Colorado. To them was born the following:
1. Martha Steen Higgins was born in Denver, Colorado, February 16, 1899.

III.—Harry Watson Steen, the third child and only son of Dr. John A. and Jennie M. Steen, was born in Ripley, Brown County, Ohio, November 15, 1877, where he was brought up and educated. He was graduated from the

Ohio Dental College Cincinnati, Ohio, May 10 1900
Residence, Ripley, Ohio

II—Merta Steen. the fourth child and third daughter of Dr
John A and Jennie M Steen, was born in Ripley, Ohio,
November 22, 1880 where she was brought up and edu-
cated   Residence, Chicago, Illinois

I —John Alexander Steen, Jr, the fifth child and second
son of Dr John A Steen, the eldest child by his second
wife, Sarah L Steen was born in Ripley, Ohio, May 18,
1899

3 James Faris Steen, the third child and second son of Alexander B and Nancy Jane Steen, was born on the old Grandfather Steen homestead, near the Mt Leigh Presbyterian
Church, in Adams County, Ohio, July 14, 1843   He was
brought up on his father's farm, and attended school in the
neighborhood   He early united with the Mt Leigh Presbyterian Church, and maintained a consistent Christian life
Being a loyal patriot, he enlisted in the Union Army at Winchester, Ohio, August 1, 1862, when 19 years of age, in
Company I, Ninety-first Regiment Ohio Volunteer Infantry
He served his country faithfully until his death, September
19, 1864, when he fell in battle, at Winchester, Virginia aged
21 years, 2 months and 5 days

4 William Chester Steen, the fourth child and third son of
Alexander B and Nancy Jane Steen, was born on the old
Grandfather Steen homestead near the Mt Leigh Presbyterian Church, in Adams County, Ohio, August 30, 1845,
and brought up in his father's family   In his youth he
worked on the farm in summer and attended school in winter, and obtained a good common school education   He was
for several years a teacher, but finally purchased a farm and
became a successful farmer   In April, 1862, he united with
the Mt Leigh Presbyterian Church, and in March 1877, was
ordained a ruling elder   In 1890 he sold his farm near Mt
Leigh and removed to Iowa and rented a farm near Tingley,
but after three years he returned to Ohio again and purchased his father's farm, three miles east of Winchester, on
the road to Buck Run   Here he remained until the autumn
of 1898, when he sold his farm and in 1899 removed to Winchester Ohio, and became an agent for the sale of farm

implements W Chester Steen was married by the Rev
John Gilmour, a United Presbyterian clergyman, near Tran-
quility, Ohio October 6, 1868, to Miss Anna Dora
McCreight a daughter of Alexander and Rebecca
McCreight, she having been born near Tranquility, Ohio
May 2, 1852 Residence, Winchester, Ohio To them were
born the following children

I —Cora Olive Steen, the eldest child of W. Chester and A
   Dora Steen was born three miles east of Winchester,
   Ohio October 10, 1869, and brought up in her father's
   family She was married by the Rev Joseph McNab a
   United Presbyterian clergyman, near Tingley, Ringgold
   County, Iowa, December 24 1891, to Byron J Stevenson,
   a son of Andrew and Mary C Stevenson, he having been
   born in Reynoldsburg, Licking County, Ohio, December
   24, 1866 — a farmer Residence, Tingley, Iowa To
   them were born the following children·

   1 Anna Cornelia Stevenson was born near Tingley, Iowa
      November 24, 1893

   2 John Corwin Stevenson was born near Tingley Iowa,
      January 1, 1895

   3 Beulah May Stevenson was born near Tingley, Iowa
      February 13, 1896

   4 Orville Gilbert Stevenson was born in April 1898, and
      died August 6, 1899, aged 1 year and 3 months

II —James Truman Steen the second child and eldest son
   of W Chester and A Dora Steen, was born near Winchester, Ohio, October 17, 1871 and brought up on his father's
   farm He was married by the Rev James L McWilliams,
   at the residence of the bride's mother, near the Calvary
   M P Church September 9 1896, to Jennie Lynn Stroup,
   a daughter of Peter and Ann Kennedy Stroup, who were
   formerly from Mifflin County, Pennsylvania, she having
   been born in Adams County, Ohio, October 29, 1874
   Residence six miles east of Winchester Ohio To them
   was born one child

   1 —Florence Steen daughter of J Truman and Jennie L
      Steen, was born February 5, 1899

III —Otto Lee Steen, the third child and second son of W

Chester and A Dora Steen was born near Winchester, Ohio, December 12, 1874, and brought up on his father's farm — a teacher. Residence, Winchester, Ohio

IV —Clara Ida Steen, the fourth child and second daughter of W Chester and A Dora Steen, was born near Winchester, Ohio, January 14, 1878 and brought up in her father's family Residence, Winchester, Ohio

V —Warren Luther Steen, the fifth child and third son of W Chester and A Dora Steen, was born near Winchester, Ohio, December 14, 1881, and brought up in his father's family Residence, Winchester, Ohio

VI —Ohn Kerr Steen, the sixth child and fourth son of W Chester and A Dora Steen, was born near Winchester, Ohio, December 1885

VII —Lillie Mabel Steen, the seventh and youngest child, the third daughter of W Chester and A Dora Steen, was born near Winchester, Ohio, June 20, 1890, and resides with her parents

5 Samuel Steward Steen, the fifth child and fourth son of Alexander B and Nancy Jane Steen, was born on the old Grandfather Steen farm, near Mt Leigh Ohio, November 15, 1847, and was brought up on his father's farm   He early united with the Mt Leigh Presbyterian Church and has ever maintained a consistent Christian life. S Steward Steen was married by the Rev John Carson, near West Union, Adams County, Ohio July 4, 1872, to Miss Mollie E McCreight, a daughter of William K. and Mary McCreight, she having been born near Tranquility, Ohio, April 10, 1847, and died at their home, near Winchester, Ohio, January 11, 1877, in the 30th year of her age   There were no children to this marriage   S Steward Steen was married a second time by the Rev Walter Mitchell, in Winchester, Ohio, March 14, 1882, to Miss Estella Miller, a daughter of Robert Allen and Martha E Miller (who was a daughter of Wallace Blair), she, Estella Miller, having been born in Carlisle, Brown County, Ohio February 22, 1858, and died in Manchester, Ohio, on Sunday, February 12, 1899 in the 41st year of her age   S Steward Steen continued to reside on his farm, three miles east of Winchester, Ohio, until the autumn of 1894, when he sold the place and removed to Winchester, Ohio,

PROF. SILAS M. STEEN.
(Born 1849; Died 1892.)

and the next year (1895) to Manchester, Adams County,
Ohio Residence Manchester Ohio To S Steward and
Estella Steen were born three miles east of Winchester,
Ohio, the following children

I —Mattie Lee Steen was born December 22, 1882.

II —Lizzie May Steen was born September 15, 1886

III —Nola Jeannette Steen was born July 11 1891

6 Silas McClure Steen the sixth child and fifth son of Alexander B and Nancy Jane Steen was born on the old Grandfather Steen homestead, near Mt Leigh, Ohio, December
14. 1849. and died in his own home near Duarte, Los
Angeles County, California September 6 1892, aged 42
years 9 months and 8 days He was brought up on his
father's farm, in Adams County Ohio where he attended
the public schools in the neighborhood and obtained a good
common school education He early united with the Mt
Leigh Presbyterian Church, and was ever a consistent member He possessed fine musical talents and pursued a full
course of study in the College of Music He was recognized
as a fine singer a successful music teacher, as well as a popular leader of music in churches Prof Silas M Steen was
for several years a traveling salesman for the large music
house of D H Baldwin & Co Cincinnati, Ohio, and opened
branch houses in Washington C H, Ohio, and St Joseph.
Missouri He was also for several years the manager of the
Piano and Organ Department in the music house of Root &
Co Chicago, Illinois In 1887 owing to failing health, he
removed to California and opened a music house in Los
Angeles, and was quite successful in business He resided
in Alhambra In 1888 he was elected and ordained a ruling
elder of the Presbyterian Church of Alhambra, California
and the same season chosen to represent the Session in the
Synod of the Pacific, which met in Pasadena In 1890, by
the advice of his physician, he sold out his music business
and purchased a fruit farm at Duarte, upon which he continued to reside until his death While living in Duarte he
was a member and ruling elder of the Presbyterian Church
of Monrovia two miles away He was universally beloved
a man of fine social qualities and keen business sagacity
Prof Silas M Steen was married by the Rev Moses D A
Steen near Worthington Franklin County, Ohio, May 6,

1873, to Miss Harriet Foster, a daughter of Archibald and Harriet C Foster, she having been born near Sugar Creek, Venango County, Pennsylvania, February 7, 1850, and died at her residence in Alhambra, California, November 25, 1899, aged 49 years 9 months and 18 days Her funeral took place from the Presbyterian Church of which she was long a devout and consistent member, on Sunday, November 26, 1899 Her body was tenderly laid to rest beside her husband, in the beautiful Alhambra cemetery Family residence, Alhambra, California To them were born the following children

I —Dwight Baldwin Steen the eldest son of Silas M and Harriet Steen, was born in Washington C H, Fayette County, Ohio, July 22, 1875, and brought up in his father's family He was graduated from the Los Angeles High School in 1895, and studied medicine in Los Angeles Medical College Dwight B Steen was married by the Rev Vaclave Bazata in Alhambra, California, December 22, 1897, to Miss Elsie Buckwell, she having been born in England, and removed to California in 1892 Residence Alhambra, California

II —Carl Foster Alexander Steen the second son of Silas M and Harriet Steen was born in St Joseph, Missouri, June 16, 1879, and resided with his parents until after his father's death In 1894 he returned to Ohio Residence, Worthington, Ohio

III —Earl Lucien Steen, the third son of Silas M and Harriet Steen was born in Chicago, Illinois, June 23, 1882 Residence, Los Angeles, California

II —Ralph Washington Steen, the fourth son of Silas M and Harriet Steen was born in Alhambra, California October 27, 1888 Residence, North Ontario, California

7 Josiah Colter Steen, the seventh child and sixth son of Alexander B and Nancy Jane Steen, was born on his father's farm, four miles east of Winchester, Ohio, November 11 1852, where he grew up to manhood and obtained his education in the public schools of the neighborhood He early united with the Mt Leigh Presbyterian Church, and has ever maintained a devout Christian character He is now a ruling elder in the Fourth Presbyterian Church, Dayton, Ohio of which all his family are members For several

years after his majority he was a successful music teacher, afterwards engaged in the sale of musical instruments for the firm of D H Baldwin & Co, of Cincinnati, Ohio, and for two years for W F Steen, of the same city   J Colter Steen began the study of dentistry in 1881 with his brother, Dr Marion W Steen, of Augusta, Kentucky, where he continued one year, then spent two years with his older brother Dr John A Steen, of Ripley Ohio   In 1884 he opened a dental office in Georgetown, Ohio, where he continued four years   During his stay in Georgetown he attended the Louisville Dental College, from which he was graduated June 14, 1887   In 1888 he removed to Dayton, Ohio, where he still continues in the successful practice of dentistry   Dr J Colter Steen was married by the Rev William I Fee in Felicity, Clermont County, Ohio, March 25, 1874, to Miss Mary Ida Fee, a daughter of Thomas D and Manoiah Fee, she having been born in Felicity, Ohio, March 25, 1856 Residence, Dayton, Ohio   To them were born the following children

I —Lulu Fee Steen, the eldest daughter of Dr J Colter and Mollie I Steen, was born in Felicity Ohio, July 6, 1877, brought up and educated in Dayton, Ohio, where she still resides

II —Mamie Steen, the second daughter of Dr J Colter and Mollie I Steen, was born in Felicity, Ohio, January 13, 1879, and brought up and educated in Dayton, Ohio, where she still resides

3 Marion Washington Steen, the eighth child and youngest son of Alexander B and Nancy Jane Steen, was born on his father's farm, near the forks of Brush Creek, four miles northeast of Winchester Adams County Ohio and two miles from the Mt Leigh Presbyterian Church, January 27, 1855, where he grew up to manhood and obtained a good common school education   He began the study of dentistry September 19 1874, under the instruction of his brother Dr John A Steen, then of North Liberty, Adams County, Ohio, and after fourteen months' apprenticeship began practice for himself in North Liberty   He removed to Augusta Kentucky, April 15, 1878 and opened a dental office where he has continued ever since   After nine years of successful practice in Augusta, where he had built up an extensive
(10)

business, he entered the Louisville College of Dentistry, at
Louisville, Kentucky, spent one term, and was graduated
therefrom June 14, 1887   Dr Marion W Steen is now a
a ruling elder and an influential member of the First Presbyterian Church in Augusta Kentucky   He was married by
the Rev John N McClung, at the residence of the bride's
parents, near North Liberty, Adams County, Ohio, to Miss
Sarah Emma Patton, a daughter of John Elder and Sarah
Ann Patton, she having been born near North Liberty,
Ohio. (Cherry Fork Post-office,) July 16, 1857   Residence,
Augusta, Kentucky   To them were born the following
children

   I —Charles Guy Steen, the eldest son of Dr Marion W and
S Emma Steen, was born in North Liberty, Adams
County, Ohio April 7, 1877, and brought up in his father's
family   He was educated in Central University, Richmond, Kentucky, and was graduated from the Ohio Dental College, Cincinnati, Ohio, in 1899   He has opened a
dental office in Ashland, Kentucky, and is doing a good
business   Residence, Ashland, Kentucky

   II —Wilbur Armstrong Steen, the second son of Dr Marion
W and S Emma Steen, was born in Augusta, Kentucky,
November 11, 1892, and resides there with his parents

VIII —Josiah Yates Steen, the eighth child, the fifth and youngest son of Alexander and Agnes Nancy Faris Steen was born
on a farm at the home of his parents, two miles north of
Flemingsburgh, Fleming County, Kentucky, February 14,
1816, and died, after a brief but severe attack of pneumonia, at
his own residence, upon his farm, two miles northwest of the
Mt Leigh Presbyterian Church and three miles east of
Winchester, Adams County, Ohio, January 19 1877, aged 60
years, 11 months and 5 days   He was brought by his parents
from Kentucky to Adams County, Ohio when a child of four
years   Here he grew up to manhood working upon his
father's farm in summer and attending school in winter, and
thus secured the ordinary common school education of the
times   Like his father and eldest brother, he was exceedingly
fond of music devoted much time and attention to it, became
quite skilled in the art, and like them taught many music
classes during the winter months, while at the same time he

was a practical and successful farmer all his life. In those
early days all men between the ages of 21 and 45 years were
required by law to form military companies in township and
county organizations, and at the appointed times assemble and
exercise in military tactics. An annual general muster of all
the companies in the county was held for drill, parade, and
often sham battles were fought. In these matters Josiah Y.
Steen became somewhat prominent, was chosen Lieutenant,
and afterwards Captain, Major, and finally rose to Lieutenant
Colonel of the county militia. Hence he afterwards bore the
title of Colonel Steen. He early united with the Mt. Leigh
Presbyterian Church, and was ordained a ruling elder in 1851,
which office he continued to hold with great acceptance until
the time of his death, a period of about twenty-six years. He
was a man of great activity and energy, firm in his convictions,
and a strong advocate of anti-slavery sentiments long before
the Civil War. Col. Josiah Y. Steen was married by the Rev.
Samuel Steele, D.D., in Highland County, Ohio, at the residence of the bride's parents, near Marshall, November 9, 1837,
to Rebecca Colter Weare, a daughter of James C. and Nellie
Colter Weare, she having been born in Highland County,
Ohio, November 28, 1817, and died at the residence of her
son-in-law, John T. Beveridge, six miles northeast of Winchester, Ohio, November 2, 1895, aged 77 years, 11 months
and 4 days. To Col. Josiah Y. and Rebecca C. Steen were
born the following children:

1. Eliza Ellen Steen, the eldest daughter of Col. Josiah Y. and
   Rebecca C. Steen, was born at the home of her parents, near
   the forks of Brush Creek, three and a half miles east of
   Winchester, Ohio, and two miles northwest of the Mt. Leigh
   Presbyterian Church. March 10, 1843. She possessed a
   kind heart, pleasing manners, and fine social qualities, which
   made her a general favorite. She early united with the Mt.
   Leigh Presbyterian Church, and has maintained an earnest
   and devout spirit, exerting a wide religious influence. Eliza
   E. Steen was married by the Rev. Victor M. King, at the
   residence of her parents, December 30, 1862, to John
   Thomas Beveridge, a son of Samuel R. and Harriet C. Beveridge, he having been born on his father's farm, six miles
   northeast of Winchester, Ohio, near the Calvary M. P.
   Church, April 3, 1839. In his earlier life Mr. Beveridge fol-

lowed the profession of a school teacher, but for many years
he has been a successful and prosperous farmer   He now
resides upon his own farm, near Calvary Methodist Protestant Church, six miles from Winchester, Ohio   He is a
useful Christian man, and with his wife is regularly at the
services of the Mt Leigh Presbyterian Church   His post-
office address is Buck Run, Adams County, Ohio   To them
were born the following children

I —Charles William Beveridge, the eldest son of John T
and Eliza E Steen Beveridge, was born near Sugar Tree
Ridge Highland County, Ohio, April 3 1864, and brought
up in the home of his parents   Having secured a good
common school education, he afterwards attended the
National Normal School at Lebanon, Ohio, and qualified
himself for the profession of a teacher, in which, during his
life, he was quite successful   Charles W Beveridge early
became a member of the Mt Leigh Presbyterian Church,
was a young man of sweet disposition, devout piety, and
exerted a good influence   He died at the residence of his
parents, near the Calvary M P Church, July 20, 1888, in
the 25th year of his age

II —John Harrie Beveridge the second and youngest son of
John T and Eliza E Steen Beveridge, was born near
Sugar Tree Ridge Highland County, Ohio January 21,
1869, and brought up on the farm   Under his father's
care he secured a good common school education, and
taught in various district schools   He afterwards attended
the Business College at Delaware Ohio, from which he
was graduated September 25, 1889, then entered the
National Normal University at Lebanon Ohio, and was
graduated from the scientific course, March 25, 1892   The
following summer he aided in conducting a summer school
in Hillsboro, Ohio, and while there was elected superintendent of the public schools at Glidden, Iowa where he
continued three years with good success and increase of
salary each year   In 1895 he secured a certificate from
the Iowa State Board of Examiners with an average grade
of 95 per cent   In the autumn of 1895 he entered the
Junior Class in Ohio University from which he was graduated June 16, 1897   The following summer he conducted
a summer school at North Liberty Ohio, and in Septem-

MRS. ELIZA STEEN BEVERIDGE.
MRS. KATE STEEN BLAIR.

ber of the same year returned to Glidden, Iowa, as superintendent of the public schools and instructor in the college there   Prof J Harrie Beveridge was married by the
Rev Fred J. Tower, at Glidden, Iowa, July 7. 1897, to
Miss Florence Margaret Haselton, a daughter of Hon
Harvey Barden and Jane Gibson Haselton she having
been born in White Rock Township, Ogle County. Illinois, April 7, 1874, and was by profession a teacher   Both
husband and wife are devout and earnest Christians and
members of the Presbyterian Church   Residence, Glidden, Iowa   To them was born one child, as follows·

   1 Lenora Lodema Beveridge, a daughter of J Harrie and
     Florence M Beveridge, was born in Glidden, Iowa,
     April 18 1898

2 Nancy Catherine Steen, the second daughter of Col Josiah
Y and Rebecca C Steen, and a twin sister of Eliza E Steen,
was born at the home of her parents, near the forks of Brush
Creek three and a half miles east of Winchester, Ohio, and
two miles northwest of the Mt Leigh Presbyterian Church,
March 10, 1843 where she spent her happy girlhood days
She early united with the Mt Leigh Presbyterian Church, of
which she was a faithful and useful member   N Catherine
Steen, called "Kate," was married by the Rev David Van
Dyke, at the home of her parents, on her 27th birthday,
March 10, 1870, to James Alfred Blair, a son of James and
Margaret Blair, he having been born in Stockwell, Indiana,
February 25, 1841, and died in Hillsboro, Highland County,
Ohio, February 1, 1897, in the 56th year of his age   James
A Blair was a prosperous farmer, and for several years a
ruling elder in the Mt Leigh Presbyterian Church   He
spent the most of his life in Adams County, Ohio, and for
several years preceding his death on Buck Run, near Campbell's Mill   In the autumn of 1896, on account of poor
health, he removed with his family to Hillsboro, Ohio, where
he continued until his death   Family residence, Hillsboro,
Ohio. To James A and N Kate Blair were born five children, all of whom, parents and children, were members in
full communion with the Mt Leigh Presbyterian Church,
but they are now scattered

1—Orsin Steen Blair, the eldest son of James A and N
   Kate Steen Blair, was born in Stockwell, Tippecanoe

County, Indiana, January 18, 1871 — a druggist   He was
married by the Rev Robert A Watson, in North Liberty,
Adams County, Ohio, September 12, 1894, to Miss Nora
Belle Widney, a daughter of John and Susan Kaufman
Widney, she having been born in Black Jack, Douglas
County, Kansas, April 10, 1873   Residence, Dayton,
Ohio   .

II —Elta May Blair, the second child and eldest daughter
of James A and N Kate Steen Blair, was born near
Winchester, Ohio, December 2, 1872, and brought up in
her father's family   She was married by the Rev William
J McSurely, D D , in Hillsboro, Ohio, June 2, 1897, to
Almanza Kirker McCreight, a son of David Steele and
Matilda Snedigar McCreight, he having been born near
Tranquility, Adams County, Ohio, December 19, 1870
Mr A Kirker McCreight is a millwright by occupation,
and superintendent of a mill.   Residence, Richmond,
Indiana   To them the following child was born

 1 Verl Dean McCreight, a son of A Kirker and Elta
 May McCreight, was born in Richmond, Indiana,
 August 7, 1898

III —William Ariel Blair, the third child and second son of
James A. and N Kate Steen Blair, was born near Winchester, Ohio, January 3, 1875, and brought up on the
farm   W Ariel Blair was a student of North Liberty
Academy and Ada Normal University, and is a teacher
by profession, an instructor in Glidden College Iowa
Residence, Hillsboro, Ohio

IV —Lora Pearl Blair, the fourth child and second daughter
of James A and N Kate Steen Blair, was born near Winchester, Ohio, December 25, 1875   Residence, Hillsboro, Ohio

V —Margaret Reba Ellen Blair, the third daughter, the
fifth and youngest child of James A and N Kate Steen
Blair, was born near Winchester, Ohio, January 10, 1880,
and died October 2, 1882, aged 2 years, 8 months and 22
days   Her body was interred in the Mt Leigh cemetery

3 James Boyd Steen, the third child and only son of Col
Josiah Y. and Rebecca C Steen, was born at the home of his
parents, near the forks of Brush Creek, three and a half

miles east of Winchester, Ohio, and two miles northwest of
the Mt Leigh Presbyterian Church, May 15, 1845 Here,
upon the farm he grew to manhood, assisting his father in
summer and attending school in winter   He early united
with the Mt Leigh Presbyterian Church, of which he is still
a consistent and useful member   He resided at the forks of
Brush Creek, near his father s home, for a number of years
and assisted him in the work on the farm   Since his father's
death in 1877, he has lived at the old home and cultivated
the farm, which he now owns   His post-office address is
Winchester, Adams County, Ohio   J Boyd Steen was married by the Rev Mr Howe at the residence of the bride s
parents, near Tranquility, Ohio, September 27, 1870, to
Anna Elizabeth Lovett, a daughter of Joseph T and Margaret Ann Lovett, she having been born near Tranquility,
Ohio September 27 1845, and died at their own home July
6 1877, aged 31 years, 8 months and 9 days   J Boyd Steen
was married a second time by the Rev Mr Smith, at the
residence of John T Beveridge near Buck Run, Ohio September 28, 1898, to Mrs Vianna Victoria Lewis of Newport,
Ohio a daughter of John Wilson and Sarah Catherine
Rogers who reside near Newport, Adams County, Ohio
and a widow of Vernon D Lewis she having been born in
Adams County, Ohio March 26, 1863, and married to Ver
non Douglas Lewis September 29, 1881, who died January
15 1888   Residence, three and a half miles east of Winchester, Ohio   The following are the children of J Boyd
Steen

1 —Herbert Othello Steen the eldest son of J Boyd and
Anna E Steen, was born at the home of his parents, three
and one-half miles east of Winchester Ohio, September
21, 1871   He lived in his father's home until 1893, when
he removed to Princeville Illinois, where he remained two
years, and then returned to Ohio, and is engaged in farm
ing H Othello Steen was married by the father of the
bride, the Rev James McNelm, at his home near Dunkinsville, Adams County, Ohio, August 28, 1895, to Minnie Florence McNelm, whose mother's maiden name was
Anne McCleran, she having been born near Dunkinsville Ohio, April 12, 1868   Residence, Seman Ohio

II —Joseph Orris Steen the second son of J Boyd and
Anna E Steen, was born at the home of his parents, April
9, 1873, and brought up on the farm   He is by occupa-
tion a farmer   J Orris Steen was married by the Rev.
J W Shumaker, at his residence in West Union, Ohio, to
Jessie Ida Neal, a daughter of John Randolph and Emma
Jane Neal   Residence forks of Brush Creek, three and a
half miles east of Winchester, Ohio

III —James Earnest Steen, the third son of J Boyd and
Anna E Steen was born at the home of his parents, at
the forks of Brush Creek, August 30, 1874, and brought
up on the farm   He is by occupation a farmer   Residence, three and one-half miles east of Winchester, Ohio

IV —Minor Yates Steen, the fourth and youngest son of J
Boyd and Anna E Steen, was born at the family residence,
at the forks of Brush Creek, three and one-half miles east
of Winchester, Ohio, January 19, 1877, on the day of his
grandfather's death   He lived for some years in the home
of his uncle, John T Beveridge, and for a while with his
Grandfather Lovett, near Newport, Ohio   He is now
(1900) a teacher of penmanship in a College at Dallas,
Texas

V —Infant daughter, the fifth child and only daughter of J
Boyd Steen, the only child of his second wife, Vianna D
Lewis Steen was born at the family home, east of Win-
chester, Ohio, March 4, 1900, and died the same day

4   Sarah Emeline Steen, called ' Emma," the fourth child, the
third and youngest daughter of Col Josiah Y and Rebecca
C Steen, was born at the home of her parents, near the
forks of Brush Creek, three and a half miles east of Winchester, Ohio and two miles northwest of the Mt Leigh
Presbyterian Church, November 19, 1847, where she spent
her youthful days   She was educated in the common
schools of the neighborhood   She early united with the
church and has lived a devout, noble, and useful Christian
life.   She was kind-hearted, generous, energetic, sprightly
in her disposition, and has always had many friends   S
Emma Steen was married by the Rev David Van Dyke, at
the residence of her parents November 1, 1870, to Henry
Harrison Redkey a son of John and Rachel Redkey, he
having been born near Marshall, Highland County, Ohio,

MRS. EMMA STEEN REDKEY.

March 1, 1839 — a farmer. Henry H. Redkey enlisted as a soldier in the Union Army at Sugar Tree Ridge, Ohio, August 10, 1862, in Company I, Eighty-ninth Regiment Ohio Volunteer Infantry, and held the office of Sergeant, serving his country faithfully until the close of the war. He was captured by the enemy in the battle of Chickamauga, Georgia, September 20, 1863, and held a prisoner in Richmond, Virginia; Danville, Virginia, and Andersonville, Georgia, for nineteen months, during which he suffered greatly until the war was at an end. He was honorably discharged from the service at Camp Chase, near Columbus, Ohio, June 8, 1865. Henry H. Redkey, ever since his marriage, in 1870, has resided upon his own farm, near Sugar Tree Ridge, Highland County, Ohio, a devout Christian, a prosperous farmer, and a man of influence, who has twice been elected to represent his county in the Ohio State Legislature. His post-office address is Sugar Tree Ridge, Ohio. To them were born the following children:

1.—Cora Edith Redkey, the eldest child of Hon. Henry H. and S. Emma Steen Redkey, was born near Sugar Tree Ridge, Ohio, November 20, 1871, where she was brought up. She was married by the Rev. W. J. Baker, at the home of her parents, October 15, 1890, to Frank Homer Hetherington, a son of George and Keziah Hetherington, he having been born in Sugar Tree Ridge, Ohio, October 2, 1867, and died in Hillsboro, Ohio, October 2, 1897, aged 30 years. Frank H. Hetherington was a merchant, residing for several years in Sugar Tree Ridge, and afterwards removed to Hillsboro, Ohio, where Mrs. Cora E. Hetherington still resides with her family. To Frank H. and Cora E. Hetherington were born in Sugar Tree Ridge, Ohio, the following children:

1. Infant son was born August 9, 1891, and died the same day.

2. Ruby Lilian Hetherington was born September 3, 1892.

3. Henry Edwin Hetherington was born September 27, 1894.

4. Roger Earl Hetherington was born September 28, 1896

II —Edwin Stanley Redkey, the second child and eldest son of Hon Henry H and S Emma Steen Redkey, was born at the home of his parents, near Sugar Tree Ridge Ohio, January 13 1877, and brought up on the farm Residence, near Sugar Tree Ridge, Ohio

III —Nellie Blanche Redkey, the third child and second daughter of Hon Henry H and S Emma Steen Redkey, was born at the home of her parents, near Sugar Tree Ridge, Ohio, November 8, 1878, and brought up in her father's family, where she still resides (1900) — a music teacher by profession

IV —Harry Starling Redkey, the fourth child and second son of Hon Henry H and S Emma Steen Redkey, was born at the home of his parents, near Sugar Tree Ridge, Ohio June 11, 1880, and brought up on his father's farm — now a student at Valparaiso, Indiana (1900) Residence, near Sugar Tree Ridge, Ohio

V —Mary Lilian Redkey, the third daughter, the fifth and youngest child of Hon Henry H. and S Emma Steen Redkey, was born on her father's farm, near Sugar Tree Ridge, Ohio April 10, 1886 and still resides there with her parents

BOOK TWO.

DESCENDANTS OF JAMES STEEN

James Steen was born in Ireland, probably near a place called "The Vow," in County Antrim, Province of Ulster, about 1734, and came into the British Colonies in America about 1755. He finally settled in Union District, South Carolina, where he married a Miss Bogard and brought up his family. He was a soldier in the Revolutionary War and was killed in the battle of King's Mountain, October 7, 1780.

James Steen was of Scotch-Irish descent, but was born in Ireland, and with the multitude of immigrants came into the British Colonies in America near the middle of the Eighteenth Century, along with his brothers and perhaps his father's family. They landed in New York but soon afterwards made their way into Pennsylvania, where they all continued to reside for a while. James Steen was probably a son of Richard Steen (?), whose ancestors came into Ireland with Oliver Cromwell about 1649, and settled first in Kalinski County Down and afterwards located in County Antrim, where they had lived for several generations. They probably lived on the old "Green Hill farm" near a place called "The Vow" which is located about eight Irish miles from Coleraine near the banks of the River Bann, in County Antrim, and Province of Ulster. The writer visited the

(159)

place in 1896 and found there an old lady whose mother was a
Steen, and her son John Steen Martin, who now cultivates the
old farm. There is an old cemetery near the river, and
an old mill site, a few old houses, and a school, which
we visited, but there is no post-office. In the cemetery
there is the grave of John Steen, who was born in 1755 and
died February 14, 1818, and Catherine Steen, his wife who was
bo n in 1749 and died November 9 1829, aged 80 years. The
following familiar names also appear on tombstones at that
place. John Boyd, died January 2, 1859, Elizabeth Boyd, died
April 14. 1862 aged 67 years, and several others of the same
name. who were probably from the same ancestral family as
Elizabeth Boyd, who married Robert Steen and brought up her
family in Lancaster County Pennsylvania. James Steen was
born in Ireland about 1734 (?), came to America with his brothers, other relatives and perhaps his father's family about 1755 (?)
After a temporary residence in Pennsylvania he removed to the
South, and located permanently in Union District, South Carolina. He was a man of great energy, a staunch Presbyterian in
faith, and an enthusiastic patriot. At the breaking out of the
Revolutionary War he joined the Colonial Army as a soldier
and was killed in the battle of King s Mountain, October 7 1780
while fighting bravely in defense of his country. The writer
remembers that when he was a mere child he heard his father tell
about his grandfather Robert Steen s brother, who went into
South Carolina and became a soldier in the Revolutionary War.
There is no good reason to doubt that Robert Steen of Lancaster County Pennsylvania, and James Steen, of Union District, South Carolina, were full brothers. James Steen was married in South Carolina to a Miss Bogard about 1770 by whom
he became the paternal ancestor of a large branch of the Steen
family residing in the Southern States. To James Steen and his
wife were born the following children. Richard Sarah,
James (?), and William Steen (?)

CHAPTER I

Richard Steen the son of James Steen and his wife (formerly a Miss Bogard), was born in Union District South Carolina, June 2, 1772 and was married in the same locality to Nancy McDonald whose parents emigrated from Scotland and located in South Carolina   Richard and Nancy M Steen continued to reside in South Carolina until about the year 1806, when they removed to the State of Indiana and located upon a farm in Knox County, thirteen miles from Vincennes or St Vincent as it was then called, where they remained until death   Richard Steen died November 17 1859, aged 87 years 5 months and 15 days To Richard and Nancy M Steen were born eleven children who lived to mature years

I—James Steen, the eldest son of Richard and Nancy M Steen, and a grandson of the James Steen who came from Ireland and was killed in the battle of King's Mountain was born in Union District South Carolina July 26, 1793, and brought to Indiana by his parents when he was about thirteen years old He was married in Knox County Indiana August 14 1817 to Mary Dunn   To them were born eight children as follows

 1 Richard Ervin Steen, the eldest son of James and Mary Dunn Steen, was born in Knox County Indiana May 31 1818, and brought up on the farm   He was a devoted Christian, and for many years a ruling elder of the Presbyterian Church of Wheatland, Indiana   He gave the land upon which the church was built   He died at his home in Wheatland Indiana, November 27, 1877 in the 60th year of his age   Richard Ervin Steen was married in Knox County, Indiana April 11 1852 to Sarah Steffy, she having been born in Wythe County, Virginia in May 1824 and now resides in the family residence in Wheatland Indiana No children

 2 Samuel N Steen, the second son of James and Mary Dunn Steen, was born in Knox County Indiana, October 30 1819 and died June 27, 1829, in the 10th year of his age

 3 Angeline Steen, the third child and eldest daughter of James
    (11)

and Mary Dunn Steen, was born in Knox County, Indiana, April 30, 1822, and died December 10, 1822, aged 7 months and 10 days

4 Nancy J Steen, the fourth child and second daughter of James and Mary Dunn Steen, was born in Knox County, Indiana September 9, 1823, and was married to Alfred Wallace   To them were born six children, as follows Residence Wheatland, Indiana.

I —Mary Wallace, who married Lee Chambers

II.—Helen Wallace, who married Martin Pitman

III — —— Wallace, who married Winnie Keith

IV —Lottie Wallace, who married William Gilmore

V —Charles Wallace, who married a Miss Bicknell

VI—Martin Wallace, who married a Miss Freeman

5 Joseph W Steen, the fifth child and third son of James and Mary Dunn Steen was born in Knox County, Indiana, August 20, 1826, and married Martha Nicholson   To them were born seven children   Residence, Wheatland, Indiana

I —Laura Steen

II —Charles Steen

III.—Richard Steen, and four others, now dead

6 John A Steen, the sixth child and fourth son of James and Mary Dunn Steen, was born in Knox County, Indiana, November 30, 1828, and died September 12, 1875, in the 47th year of his age   He was married to Mary Leap   To them were born seven children

7 Leah E Steen, the seventh child and third daughter of James and Mary Dunn Steen, was born in Knox County, Indiana, October 10, 1831, and married W C White   To them were born the following children

I —India White, who married Thomas A Green

II —Elizabeth White, who married James Steen a cousin of Richard E Steen

8 Mary Ellen Steen, the eighth child and fourth daughter of James and Mary Dunn Steen, was born in Knox County, Indiana July 1 1834, and died April 30, 1877 in the 43d year of her age   She was married to James Prather by whom she had two children

I —Louisa Prather, who died in infancy

II —Amanda Prather, who married Joseph Dunn, and died

II —John Steen, the second son of Richard and Nancy McDonald Steen, was born in Union District, South Carolina, November 12, 1797, and brought to Indiana by his parents in 1806, where he resided until his death, July 3, 1852, in the 55th year of his age   He was married in Knox County, Indiana, April 18, 1820, to Ruth Robinson she having been born in North Carolina, and died at the family residence in Knox County, Indiana, July 1, 1851   There were several intermarriages between the Steens and the Robinsons   Elender Steen married Harmon Robinson and three of her brothers married three of his sisters   The older Robinsons were originally Quakers, but Harmon Robinson became an elder in the Presbyterian Church and all the younger Robinsons held to the doctrines and practices of the Presbyterian Church   To John and Ruth Robinson Steen were born seven children

1 Nancy Ann Steen the eldest daughter of John and Ruth R Steen, was born in Knox County, Indiana, March 11, 1821, and died July 21 1852, aged 31 years, 4 months and 10 days   She was married November 26, 1846, to W P. Long by whom she had two children who lived to mature age

I —Harriet Almira Long was born September 24 1848, and was married July 6, 1886 to Albert P DuBuler

II —John Steen Long, son of W P and Nancy Ann Steen Long was born in Knox County, Indiana November 9 1850 and was married in May 1878 to Mary E DuKate, and died January 19, 1888 in the 38th year of his age   To them were born two children, as follows

1 Grace DuKate Long was born March 10, 1879

2 Anna Temple Long was born February 6, 1881

2 Naomi Steen, the second daughter of John and Ruth R Steen, was born in Knox County, Indiana November 4, 1823   She was married September 21, 1853 to John L Cox by whom she had six children as follows

I —Enoch Steen Cox was born April 26, 1856

II —James Lane Cox was born October 9, 1857

III —Richard Cox was born September 8 1859

IV.—Logan Cox was born February 14, 1861

V—Naomi Cox was born May 26, 1865

VI.—Caroline Cox was born October 21, 1867

3 Caroline Steen, the third daughter of John and Ruth R Steen, was born in Knox County, Indiana November 23, 1825, was never married She resided at the old family residence near Wheatland, Indiana, until her death, about 1893

4 Infant son of John and Ruth R Steen was born near Wheatland Indiana, and died when a few months old

5 Infant son of John and Ruth R Steen was born near Wheatland Indiana, and died in infancy

6 Melissa Ellen Steen, the sixth child and fourth daughter of John and Ruth R Steen, was born near Wheatland, Knox County, Indiana, January 8, 1830 She was married April 21, 1868, to Eli H Dunn, and died November 20, 1887, aged 57 years, 6 months and 29 days To Eli H and Melissa Ellen Steen Dunn were born two children, as follows

I—Ruth Caroline Dunn was born October 29 1870

II—John Eli Dunn was born August 31, 1872

7 Enoch Richard Steen, the seventh child and only son of John and Ruth R Steen, was born near Wheatland Knox County, Indiana, March 29 1836, and died April 10, 1881, aged 45 years and 11 days He was married September 29 1868, to Sarah E Wallace, who died April 23, 1874 To them were born three children

I—Eleanor Ruth Steen, the eldest daughter of Enoch Richard and Sarah E Steen, was born near Wheatland, Knox County, Indiana, July 23 1869, and died in Bicknell, Knox County, Indiana June 16, 1895, in the 26th year of her age Her body was interred at Wheatland, Indiana She was married in Wheatland, Indiana August 22, 1894, to William Voorhes Troth, he having been born in Vandalia, Owen County, Indiana March 20, 1869 No children

II—Hannah May Steen, the second daughter of Enoch Richard and Sarah E Steen, was born in Wheatland Knox County Indiana May 6, 1871 She was married at the same place May 18, 1892 to Charles Nicholson he having been born in Wheatland, Indiana January 9

1864 Residence, Wheatland, Indiana To them were born the following children.

   1 Lois Steen Nicholson was born April 28 1894

   2 Ruth Nicholson was born November 26, 1895

III —Earl Richard Steen, the third child and only son of Enoch Richard and Sarah E Steen, was born in Wheatland, Knox County, Indiana August 7, 1873, where he was brought up and educated He pursued a course of medical studies in Rush Medical College, Chicago Illinois from which he was graduated in 1899 — a physician Residence Wheatland Indiana

III —Mary Steen the third child and only daughter of Richard and Nancy McDonald Steen and a granddaughter of the James Steen who came from Ireland, and was killed in the battle of Kings Mountain, was born near Vincennes, Knox County, Indiana January 1, 1807 and died in April, 1841 in the 35th year of her age She was married October 25, 1825 to James Dunn, who died in April 1869 To them were born the following eight children

   1 Samuel W. Dunn was born in Knox County Indiana, August 30, 1827 and died March 1 1875 in the 48th year of his age He was married in 1860 to Phoebe J Merrifield To them were born five children

   2 Richard H. Dunn the second son of James and Mary Steen Dunn was born February 19 1829 and died October 8, 1868 in the 40th year of his age He was married March 12 1856 to Eliza Williams a daughter of James Williams, To them were born five children

   3 John A Dunn, the third son of James and Mary Steen Dunn was born March 7 1830, and was married March 8, 1855, to Elizabeth Young

   4 Nancy M Dunn the fourth child and eldest daughter of James and Mary Steen Dunn was born in Knox County Indiana, March 14, 1832

   5 James S Dunn, the fifth child and fourth son of James and Mary Steen Dunn was born December 30, 1833 and married October 9 1872, to Ruth M Robinson

   6 Anna E Dunn, the sixth child and second daughter of

James and Mary Steen Dunn, was born in Knox County,
Indiana, November 25, 1835, and died December 23, 1837

7 William H. Dunn the seventh child and fifth son of James
and Mary Steen Dunn, was born in Knox County, Indiana,
June 2, 1837. He was killed in the battle of Gettysburgh,
Pennsylvania, July 2, 1863, aged 26 years and 1 month

8 Francis M Dunn, the eighth child, the fifth and youngest
son of James and Mary Steen Dunn, was born in Knox
County, Indiana, February 2, 1839 He was married in
1860 to Christina Hollingsworth, and has since died

IV —Samuel Steen, the fourth child and third son of Richard
and Nancy McDonald Steen, was born near Vincennes Knox
County, Indiana, about 1810 He was married to Mary
Robinson, and brought up a family of children

V —William Gregory Steen, the fifth child and fourth son of
Richard and Nancy McDonald Steen, and a grandson of the
James Steen who was killed in the Revolutionary War, at the
battle of King's Mountain, was born near Wheatland, Knox
County, Indiana, March 16, 1813, and died in Salem, Oregon,
September 27, 1883, in the 71st year of his age He continued
to reside in Knox County, Indiana, until 1843, when at the age
of 30 years he removed with his family to Sullivan County,
Indiana, where he remained one year In 1844 he removed
again to Marion, Grant County, Indiana, where he continued
for eight years In March, 1852, he emigrated with his family
to the far Northwest, and settled permanently in Salem,
Marion County, Oregon, where he continued to reside until
his death He was by occupation a carpenter and house-
builder William G Steen was married in Knox County,
Indiana, April 4, 1832, to Naomi Robinson, who survived him
nearly five years, and died in Salem, Oregon, July 21, 1888
To them were born ten children, as follows

1 Clanton Enoch Steen, the eldest son of William G and
Naomi R Steen, was born in Wheatland, Indiana December 5, 1832 and died in Salem Oregon, August 25, 1880, in
the 48th year of his age

2 Lodeena Brittain Steen the second child and eldest daughter of William G and Naomi R Steen, was born in Wheatland, Indiana, November 5, 1834, and died in Whitman

County, Washington, May 1, 1883, in her 50th year She was married in Salem, Oregon, in 1854, to William Morgan, by whom she had three children She was married a second time in Walla Walla, Washington, July 27, 1867, to Joel Anderson Kirby, he having been born in Jennings County, Indiana, August 28, 1836, and now resides in Olympia, Washington

I —George Washington Morgan, the eldest son of William and Lodeena Steen Morgan, was born about 1855 Residence, Earl, Lincoln County, Washington

II —William Harrison Morgan, the second son of William and Lodeena Steen Morgan, was born about 1858

III —Benjamin Franklin Morgan, the third son of William and Lodeena Steen Morgan, was born about 1860

IV.—Walter Henry Kirby, the first child of Joel A Kirby, the second husband of Lodeena Steen Kirby, but her fourth child, was born in Yamhill County, Oregon, May 27, 1868 Residence, Olympia, Washington

V.—Mary Lucretia Kirby, the eldest daughter of Joel A. and Lodeena Steen Kirby, was born in Yamhill County, Oregon, June 17, 1870 She was married in Colfax, Washington, December 12, 1889, to Frank M Stason Residence, Colfax, Washington.

VI —Naomi E Kirby, the second daughter of Joel A and Lodeena Steen Kirby, was born in Yamhill County, Oregon, June 22, 1873, and died in Umatilla County, Oregon, September 29, 1875, aged 2 years, three months and 7 days.

VII —Joel Milton Kirby, the fourth child of Joel A and Lodeena Steen Kirby, but the seventh and youngest child of the latter, was born in Umatilla County, Oregon, September 18, 1875 Residence, Olympia, Washington

3 William Milton Steen, the third child and second son of William G and Naomi R Steen, was born in Knox County, Indiana, January 17, 1837 and brought up in his father's family He was educated in Willamette University, owned a large farm, and was a member of the State Legislature He was married in Marion County, Oregon, February 3, 1867, to Narvesta Ann McAlpin, she having been born in Andrew County, Missouri, January 22, 1848 Hon Wil-

ham M Steen died near Weston, Oregon, January 30, 1895, aged 58 years and 13 days Family residence, Walla Walla, Washington To the Hon William M and Narvesta A. Steen were born, in Umatilla County, Oregon, the following nine children

I —Frank Baker Steen was born June 28, 1869 He was married in Umatilla County, Oregon, October 28, 1891, to Cora May Andross, she having been born in Rice County, Minnesota, April 26, 1870

II —Claude Walter Steen was born April 23, 1871.

III —Bertha Steen was born March 8, 1875, and died October 27, 1875, aged 7 months and 19 days.

IV —William Hershell Steen was born August 17, 1877

V —Jessie May Steen was born August 24, 1879

VI —Ralph Perry Steen was born July 31, 1883

VII —Louie Steen was born August 27, 1885, and died February 17, 1886 aged 5 months and 21 days

VIII —Grant Steen—

IX —Grace Steen—
    twin children of the Hon William M and Narvesta A Steen, were born July 24, 1887

4 Richard Perry Steen, the fourth child and third son of William G and Naomi R Steen, was born in Wheatland, Knox County, Indiana, February 29, 1840 He was brought by his parents to Salem, Oregon, when 12 years of age In July 1861, he removed to Walla Walla County, Washington Territory, and the next year visited the Auburn mines In 1874 he removed to Columbus County, Washington Territory, where he continued to reside for seven years He was a member of the Oregon State Grange in 1875, was elected sheriff of Columbia County, Washington Territory, in 1876, and re-elected in 1878 He was a member of the first City Council, and president of the first fire company in Dayton, Washington Territory In 1881 he was elected a Representative to the Territorial Legislature from Columbia County, Washington Territory He removed to Garfield County, Washington Territory, in 1883 and engaged in sheep raising until 1887, and in 1888 removed again to Lewiston, Idaho Territory Richard Perry Steen is a Democrat in politics, and a member of F

Hon. William M. Steen.
(Born 1837; Died 1895.)

and A. M and A O U W Lodges, in Pomeroy, Washington He was married by the Rev Cushing Eells, one of the early Presbyterian missionaries to the West. June 18, 1863, to Elizabeth Ann Teel, she having been born in McHenry County, Illinois, April 1, 1845 Residence Waha, Nes Perces County, Idaho To the Hon Richard Perry and Elizabeth Ann Steen were born eight children, as follows

I —Euretta Arminta Steen was born in Walla Walla, Washington Territory March 30, 1865 Residence, Waha, Idaho

II —Infant daughter was born and died in Walla Walla Washington Territory, in 1867

III —Infant son was born and died in Walla Walla, Washington Territory, in 1868

IV —Ulysses Leroy Steen was born in Walla Walla, Washington Territory, December 20, 1868, and died March 28, 1869

V —Richard Robinson Steen was born in Walla Walla, Washington Territory, January 14, 1869 Residence, Waha, Idaho

VI —Mary Naomi Steen was born in Walla Walla, Washington Territory, January 8, 1871 Residence, Waha, Idaho

VII —John Byron Steen was born in Walla Walla, Washington Territory November 7, 1873, and died of scarlet fever in Dayton, Washington Territory, April 7, 1879, aged 5 years and 5 months

VIII —Luella May Steen, the youngest child of Hon Richard P and Elizabeth A Steen, was born in Dayton, Washington Territory, January 20, 1879 Residence, Waha Nes Perces County, Idaho

5 Naomi Lucretia Steen, the fifth child and second daughter of William G and Naomi R Steen, was born in Wheatland, Knox County Indiana, May 19 1843, and died in Salem, Oregon, August 1 1862 aged 19 years, 2 months and 18 days

6 Abner Marion Steen the sixth child and fourth son of William G and Naomi R Steen, was born in Wheatland, Indiana, May 19 1843, a twin brother of the preceding He was brought by his parents to Salem, Oregon when nine

years old   He is by occupation a house carpenter   Abner
Marion Steen was married in Marion County Oregon, January 24, 1872 to Emma Phoebe Leabs, she having been
born in Marion County, Oregon February 22, 1854   No
children   Residence, Salem, Oregon

7 Nancy Ann Steen, the seventh child and third daughter of
   William G and Naomi R Steen, was born in Marion, Grant
   County, Indiana, September 8 1846, and brought by her
   parents to Salem Oregon, in 1852 where she was brought
   up   She was married in Salem, Oregon, November 27,
   1870, to Joseph Tate Halfpenny, having been born in
   Ottawa, Canada, about 1840 and died in McMinnville Ore-
   gon, February 10, 1876   No children by this marriage
   Nancy A Steen Halfpenny was married a second time in
   Dayton, Columbia County Washington Territory April
   25, 1880, to John Henry Kennedy, M D who graduated in
   medicine in 1871 he having been born in Wapello County,
   Iowa, April 1, 1850 To them were born three children
   Residence, Dayton, Washington

   I—Faith Goldie Kennedy, the eldest daughter of Dr J H
      and Nancy A Steen Kennedy, was born in Dayton, Wash-
      ington Territory, February 11, 1881

   II—Hope Ruby Kennedy, the second daughter of Dr J H
      and Nancy A Steen Kennedy, was born in Dayton Wash-
      ington Territory April 3 1884

   III—Bliss Emerald Kennedy the third child and only son
      of Dr J H and Nancy A Steen Kennedy was born in
      Spokane Falls Washington Territory, August 19, 1888

8 Mary Ellen Steen the eighth child and fourth daughter of
   William G and Naomi R Steen, was born in Marion Grant
   County Indiana, January 25, 1849, and died in Nebraska,
   near the North Fork of Loup River while her parents were
   on the journey to Oregon, June 8 1852, aged 3 years, 4
   months and 14 days

9 John Estes Steen the ninth child and fifth son of William
   G and Naomi R Steen, was born in Marion, Grant County
   Indiana, September 12 1851, and brought by his parents
   to Oregon the next year   He resided with his parents until
   he was grown and became a farmer by occupation   He
   was married in Columbia County Washington Territory
   April 14, 1879 to Celeste Isabel Miller, a granddaughter of

RICHARD STEEN.
(Born 1817; Died ———.)

Hon E Ping, she having been born in Dayton Washington
Territory, January 24, 1862 To them were born three
children. Residence, Murray Shoshone County, Idaho

I —Alice Celeste Steen the eldest daughter of John E and
Celeste I Steen, was born near Pomeroy, Garfield County
Washington Territory, February 14, 1881

II —Sarah Ethel Steen, the second daughter of John E and
Celeste I Steen, was born near Pomeroy, Washington
Territory August 26, 1882

III —John Leroy Steen, the third child and only son of
John E and Celeste I Steen, was born near Pomeroy,
Washington Territory, April 6, 1884

10 Louisa Jane Steen, the tenth child and fifth daughter of
William Gregory and Naomi Robinson Steen was born in
Salem Oregon, where she was brought up She was mar-
ried in Salem, Oregon, October 24, 1875, to John Amos Flor-
ence, a farmer and stock-raiser, he having been born in
Chariton County, Missouri, December 12, 1838 To them
were born six children Residence, Creston Lincoln
County, Washington

I —Jessie Maud Florence, the eldest daughter of John A
and Louisa J Steen Florence, was born in Salem, Oregon,
August 20, 1876

II —Eugene Albert Florence, the second child and eldest
son of John A and Louisa J Steen Florence, was born
in Umatilla County, Oregon, January 24, 1879

III —Infant son of John A and Louisa J Steen Florence
was born in Whitman County, Washington Territory, January 20, 1884, and died the next day

IV —Daisy Blanche Florence, the fourth child and second
daughter of John A and Louisa I Steen Florence was
born in Whitman County, Washington Territory March
27, 1885

V —Cleveland Florence—

VI —Carlisle Florence—
twin children of John A and Louisa J Steen Florence
were born in Lincoln County, Washington Territory,
June 22, 1890 Residence, Creston Lincoln County
Washington

VI.—Richard Steen, the sixth child and youngest son of Richard and Nancy McDonald Steen, a grandson of the James Steen who came from Ireland, located in Union District South Carolina, and was killed in the battle of King's Mountain was born in Wheatland, Knox County, Indiana, February 22, 1817, where he grew up to manhood, an honored and respected citizen, and followed the occupation of a farmer. He was married near Wheatland Indiana, to Eliza Van Arsdale, where they resided until their death, several years ago. No children.

CHAPTER II

Sarah Steen was a daughter of the James Steen who came from Ireland, located in Union District, South Carolina, entered the Colonial Army and was killed in the battle of King's Mountain, October 7, 1780. She was born in Union District, South Carolina about December, 1773, in which locality she was brought up and resided until her death, which took place December 23, 1851, aged about 78 years. She possessed considerable property, and was married, about 1794, to a gentleman whose name is not certainly known, the record having been lost. He was probably a first or second cousin, bearing the name of Steen. It is certainly known that after her marriage she retained the name of Steen; that her husband had the full charge of her affairs, and that her children all bore the name of Steen. To them were born the following six children.

I.—Gideon Steen, the eldest son of —— and Sarah Steen was born near Unionville, Union District, South Carolina, March 5, 1796, and died on his own estate, near Santuck, Union County, South Carolina March 26 1855, in the 60th year of his age. His boyhood days were spent upon the farm where he rapidly developed his mind, as well as his body. His school advantages were limited but his handsome appearance, industry, energy, manly character and graceful manners rendered him quite a general favorite. He was married near Union C. H. Union County, South Carolina, November 10, 1813, to

Naomi Townsend, a beautiful and accomplished young lady. Not long after their marriage they removed to the Indiana Territory, expecting to make that their future home, but the failure of his wife's health soon caused him to return with her to his old home, in his native State, where they continued to live happily and prosperously until her death May 13 1851. With his noted energy and industry, Gideon Steen rapidly accumulated property, and became one of the largest land owners and slave-holders in the district. He brought up a large family of children, and as soon as they married off he settled upon them each one valuable lands and several slaves. He had no political aspirations, but took great interest in the organized militia and was the Colonel of a regiment for many years. He is reported to have been a model Christian man, a pillar in the Presbyterian Church, a philanthropist universally respected and honored for his sterling worth. To himself and wife were born the following thirteen children

1 Mary Steen the eldest daughter of Col Gideon and Naomi Townsend Steen, was born near Santuck, Union District, South Carolina, June 12, 1817, and brought up in her father's home. She was married in the winter of 1838 to John Keasler. They resided in Union District, South Carolina. To them was born one child, as follows

   I—Mary Jane Keasler who lived in Union District South Carolina

2 Louisa Steen, the second daughter of Col Gideon and Naomi T Steen, was born near Santuck Union District South Carolina November 15 1818 and brought up in the home of her parents. She was married in the autumn of 1837 to James Rochester. Residence, Unionville, South Carolina

3 Sarah Ann Steen the third daughter of Col Gideon and Naomi T Steen, was born near Santuck, Union District South Carolina, March 12 1820 and brought up at the home of her parents. She was married in January, —— to John Crocker

4 Jane Steen, the fourth daughter of Col Gideon and Naomi T Steen, was born at the home of her parents near Santuck South Carolina, December 10, 1821, where she was brought up. She was married in the autumn of 1839 to James Keasler

(12)

5 William Steen, the fifth child and eldest son of Col Gideon and Naomi T Steen, was born at the home of his parents, near Santuck, South Carolina, April 29, 1823 and died in Lowndes County, Mississippi, December 1, 1888 in the 66th year of his age   He was a successful and prosperous farmer   He was married in Union District, South Carolina, December 16, 1857, to Sarah Palmer, a daughter of Ellis and Nancy Palmer, she having been born January 15, 1828   Family residence, Steenston, Mississippi   To them was born one child

I—Marion Lillian Steen, a daughter of William and Sarah Palmer Steen, was born in Union District, South Carolina, September 13, 1855   She was married in Carrollton, Alabama, March 2, 1875 to F M Bell, by whom she had eight children, as follows

1 Sarah M Bell
2 Anna Maud Bell
3 William Marvin Bell
4 Charles Gideon Bell
5 Cora Lillian Bell
6 Minta Frances Bell
7 Joseph Steen Bell
8 Kate Morris Bell

6 Frances E Steen, the sixth child and fifth daughter of Col Gideon and Naomi T Steen, was born near Santuck, South Carolina, December 6 1824   She was married in 1846 to John Taylor   Residence Unionville, South Carolina

7 John Steen, the seventh child and second son of Col Gideon and Naomi T Steen, was born in Union District, South Carolina, June 23, 1827

8 Thomas Steen the eighth child and third son of Col Gideon and Naomi T Steen was born near Santuck, South Carolina, December 10 1828, and was brought up on his father's farm   He was married in Union District, South Carolina, December 12 1852, to Nancy Gregory   They keep a boarding house   Residence Pacolet, Spartansburgh County South Carolina   To them were born thirteen children, as follows

I—John Steen, the eldest son of Thomas and Nancy G Steen, was born January 4, 1854

MRS. ELIZABETH STEEN GOSSETT.
(Born 1833; Died 1869.)

II.—Leonora Steen the second child and eldest daughter of Thomas and Nancy G Steen, was born June 23, 1855

III.—Infant daughter of Thomas and Nancy G Steen a twin sister of the preceding, was born June 23, 1855, and died the same day

II.—William Steen, the fourth child and second son of Thomas and Nancy G Steen, was born June 26, 1857

V.—Mary Steen, the fifth child and third daughter of Thomas and Nancy G Steen, was born June 26, 1857, a twin sister of the preceding

VI.—Gideon Steen—

VII.—Naomi Steen—

twin children of Thomas and Nancy G Steen were born July 19 1859

VIII.—George Steen the eighth child and fourth son of Thomas and Nancy G Steen was born June 30 1861

IX.—Virginia Steen, the ninth child and fifth daughter of Thomas and Nancy G Steen, was born January 27, 1865

X.—James Steen the tenth child and fifth son of Thomas and Nancy G Steen was born August 22 1866

XI.—Nancy Steen, called "Nannie," the eleventh child and sixth daughter of Thomas and Nancy G Steen, was born March 26, 1869

XII.—Ida Steen, the twelfth child and seventh daughter of Thomas and Nancy G Steen, was born February 20, 1872

XIII.—Eva Steen, the thirteenth child of Thomas and Nancy G Steen, the eighth and youngest daughter, was born July 3, 1873

9. Nancy Steen the ninth child and sixth daughter of Col Gideon and Naomi T Steen, was born near Santuck Union District, South Carolina, May 30, 1830, and brought up in her father's family She was married April 10, 1849, to William Gregory — a farmer — who joined the army in 1861, and was killed in battle during the war To them were born six children three sons and three daughters as follows Residence, Unionville, South Carolina

I.—S J Gregory was born September 24, 1851

II—B. G Gregory—

III—C C Gregory—

twin children, were born March 2, 1854

IV—William B Gregory was born June 15, 1856

V—M E Gregory was born May 13, 1858

VI—V T Gregory was born June 13, 1861

10 George Steen, the tenth child and fourth son of Col Gideon and Naomi T Steen was born in Union District, South Carolina, September 26 1831

11 Elizabeth Steen the eleventh child and seventh daughter of Col Gideon and Naomi T Steen was born near Santuck, Union District, South Carolina, January 26 1833, and died August 20 1869 aged 36 years, 6 months and 25 days She was married at the residence of her parents, near Santuck South Carolina, August 29, 1854, to Pleasant Tollerson Gossett, a son of John and Katherine Gossett, he having been born in Spartansburgh District South Carolina, August 24, 1826, and died in 1870 To them were born, in Spartansburgh District, South Carolina, nine children, as follows

I—Martha Jane Gossett, the eldest daughter of Pleasant T and Elizabeth Steen Gossett, was born July 3, 1855, and died April 2 1879 aged 23 years, 8 months and 29 days She was married December 21 1873, to Richmond W Stone, by whom she had three children, as follows

   1 Elizabeth Stone was born December 7, 1874

   2 John Arthur Stone was born October 7, 1877

   3 Katherine Stone was born March 27 1879

II—Nancy Zipora Gossett, the second daughter of Pleasant T and Elizabeth Steen Gossett was born June 24, 1856 She was married April 26 1874 to John M Kirby, of Pacolet Mills, by whom she had six children, as follows

   1 Hiram Washington Kirby was born September 20, 1875.

   2 Victor Hamilton Kirby was born May 8, 1877

   3 Walter Edgar Kirby was born June 9 1879

   4 Giles Evan Kirby was born September 13 1880

   5 John Earl Kirby was born April 4, 1882

JAMES P. GOSSETT.

o Martha Elizabeth Kirby was born March 26 1884

III —Emma Elizabeth Gossett, the third daughter of Pleasant T and Elizabeth Steen Gossett, was born September 2, 1857 and died June 15, 1858, aged 9 months and 13 days

II —John Gideon Gossett, the fourth child and eldest son of Pleasant T and Elizabeth Steen Gossett was born February 3 1859 He was married August 12 1882, to Susanna Kirby, of Pacolet Mills To them were born four children as follows Residence, Pacolet, South Carolina

1 James Lloyd Gossett—

2 William Floyd Gossett—

twin children, were born September 2, 1883

3 Lillie May Gossett was born December 31 1888

4 Jesse Gideon Gossett was born February 6, 1891

V —James Pleasant Gossett, the fifth child and second son of Pleasant T and Elizabeth Steen Gossett was born September 23 1860 He is now a prosperous merchant and business man, residing in Williamston, South Carolina and a member of the Board of Directors of Williamston Female College He has recently built himself an elegant home in Williamston The following sketch was written by Professor John G Clinkscales of Clemson College South Carolina December 14, 1891

James P Gossett was born in Rich Hill Spartansburgh County, South Carolina September 23 1860 In 1869 he had the great misfortune to lose his mother and in 1870 his father died The orphan boy lived among relatives in Spartansburgh County until he was fifteen years old, when he started out in the world poor and uneducated to battle for himself No boy ever had gloomier prospects but it is just to young Gossett to say that no boy battled harder for success than he At the end of three years he saved $100 He was poor but proud and ambitious, and determined to put that $100 where it would yield the largest dividend The youth was thoughtful, affable and bright, and had seen enough of the world to convince him that a man without an education must expect a rough time of it in this world So he determined without hesitation to put his first earnings into his head He bought his own provisions and hired his cooking done With this start he began the work of educating himself matriculating in the Pacolet High School, then under the management of Prof L B Haynes Renting a few acres of land young Gossett put every spare moment into his cotton patch and by sheer force of will and indomitable energy he succeeded in supplementing his original

$100 Thus he went on for three years, overcoming every
difficulty and removing every obstacle, at the same time
winning the confidence and admiration of his neighbors
and associates The writer of this sketch was one of young
Gossett's last teachers It gives him peculiar pleasure to testify
to the dauntless courage and unmistakable manhood of the boy
who was not born to *down*, but who struck the world squarely
in the face, until abundant success has crowned his efforts I
stand with hat off in the presence of the man who knows no
defeat, but whom a high sense of honor and unflinching courage
led on to "confidence and competence," two things to be desired
by all noble-minded men At the end of three years young
Gossett applied to the County Examining Board of Spartansburgh County for a license to teach He won a first-grade certificate and taught a school three months, to the entire satisfaction of patrons and school authorities At the end of that
time he accepted a clerkship in the store of Rogers & Clinkscales, at Williamston, Anderson County, South Carolina Here
he soon became very popular as a salesman and as a young man
of sterling worth After two years he obtained a better position
and better salary at Greenville, South Carolina, in the wholesale
and retail hardware establishment of Wilkins, Poe & Co In
this larger field young Gossett soon made for himself an enviable
reputation Step by step he arose in the mercantile world, until
he is the owner of a large and successful shoestore in Anderson,
South Carolina, and traveling agent, or salesman for the Bay
State Shoe and Leather Company, of New York, one of the
largest establishments of the kind in the Union Mr Gossett
now commands a fine salary, has accumulated considerable
property, and is a popular and prominent citizen While at
Williamston he met and wed Miss Sallie Brown, eldest daughter
of Dr B F Brown, the leading physician of that town The
Browns are ranked among the first families in the up-country,
and Miss Sallie, the accomplished young lady whose hand
Mr Gossett won, holds two diplomas from the Williamston
Female College the first female college in the State in point
of scholarship and general excellence Besides fighting his own
battles successfully Mr Gossett has helped his younger brothers
up the ascent of life's hill In the midst of his prosperity he
is never unmindful of the interests of those whom he loves,
or of any young man struggling hard against the tide of life

James P Gossett was married in Williamston, South
Carolina, November 20 1883 to Miss Sallie A Brown
a daughter of Dr B F Brown To them have been born
the following seven children Residence, ' The Oaks "
Williamston South Carolina.

1 Benjamin Brown Gossett was born August 8 1884

2 Sarah Elizabeth Gossett was born January 15, 1886

3 James Pleasant Gossett, Jr , was born March 1. 1888

4 Ralph Gossett was born January 10, 1890

5 Mabel Gossett was born November 22, 1892

Thomas H. Gossett.

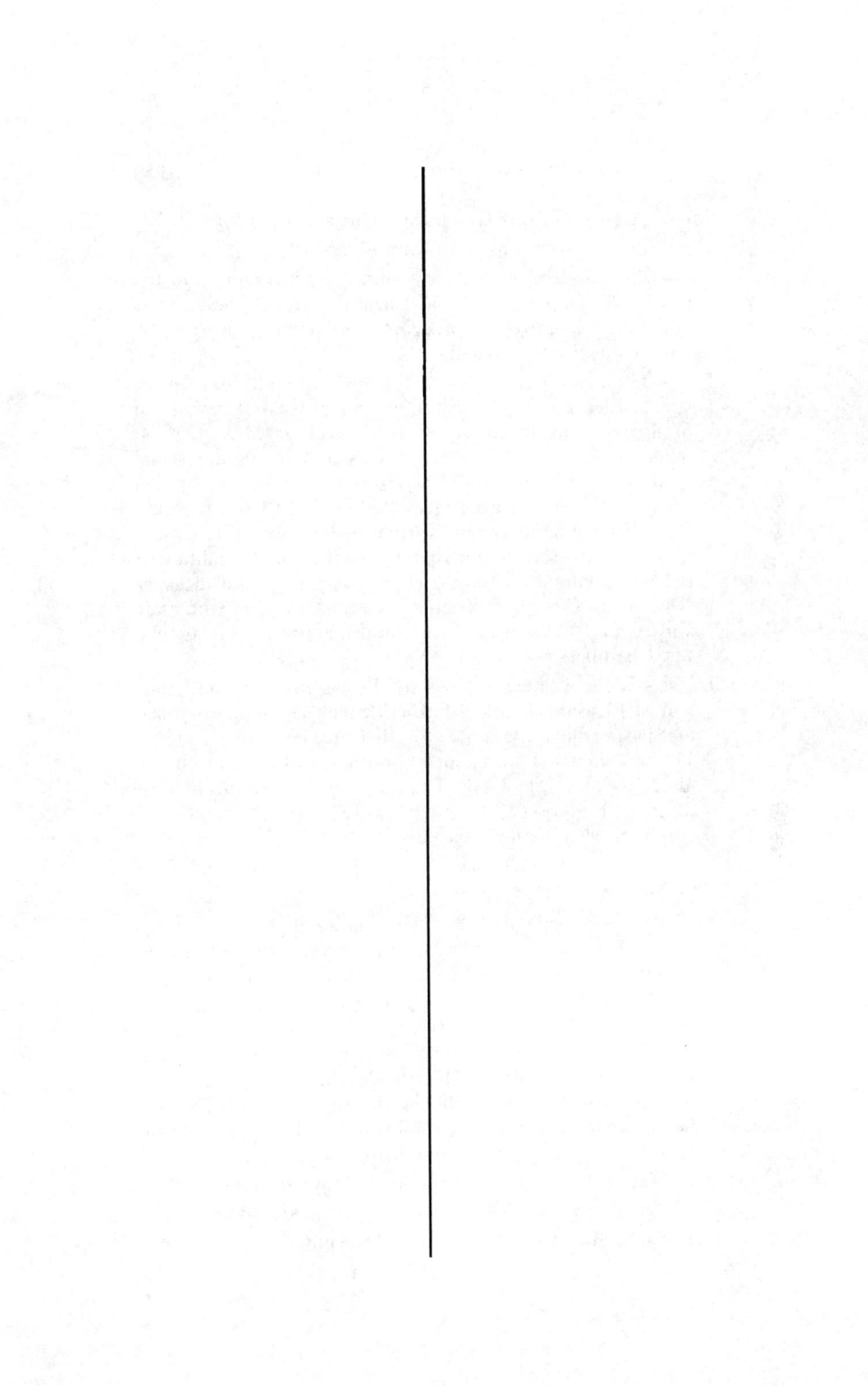

6. Margery Gossett was born February 13, 1895

7. Edith Gossett was born August 26 1896

II—William George Beaty Gossett, the sixth child and the third son of Pleasant T and Elizabeth Steen Gossett, was born May 18, 1863 — a prosperous merchant Residence, Anderson South Carolina

III—Thomas Henry Gossett the seventh child and fourth son of Pleasant T and Elizabeth Steen Gossett was born in Spartansburgh County South Carolina May 5 1865 where he was brought up He is a man of fine social qualities and keen business sagacity and has prospered greatly His great-great-grandfather, John Gossett, came from France, and was of Norman origin, and the present family of Gossetts seem to possess the good qualities of the Huguenots Thomas H Gossett is in business in New York City, with John H Graham & Co wholesale and retail dealers in hardware, and manufacturers agents 113 Chambers Street, New York New York

IIII—Edgar Converse Gossett, the eighth child and fifth son of Pleasant T and Elizabeth Steen Gossett was born in Spartansburgh County South Carolina, April 2 1867 He was married in Pacolet, South Carolina, March 20 1887, to Miss Mary M Thomas she having been born August 13, 1869 To them were born the following children Residence Spartansburgh South Carolina

1 Clyde B Gossett was born April 1 1891, and died April 25, 1891

2 Ernest F Gossett was born May 20, 1892

3 Pearl Eunice Gossett was born May 20, 1892 and died June 12 1892 The two last named were twins

IX—Edward Bobo Gossett the ninth child and sixth son of Pleasant T and Elizabeth Steen Gossett, a twin brother of Edgar Converse Gossett was born April 2 1867 He was married at Pacolet South Carolina April 24, 1887 to Miss Nancy Ann Smith she having been born December 4, 1867 To them the following children were born Residence, Anderson South Carolina

1 Claude Young Gossett was born May 20 1888

2 Anna Virginia Gossett was born May 16 1890

3 Sallie Shea Gossett was born December 4 1892

12 Margaret Steen the twelfth child and eighth daughter of Col Gideon and Naomi T Steen was born near Santuck Union District South Carolina, April 3, 1835   She was married in the summer of 1851 to William Stewart

13 Naomi Steen the thirteenth child and ninth daughter of Col Gideon and Naomi Townsend Steen, was born near Santuck Union District, South Carolina, January 12, 1839 where she was brought up   She was married at the same place to James Kirling   Residence, Pacolet South Carolina

I—Nnah Steen a daughter of ———— and Sarah Steen, (a granddaughter of the James Steen who came from Ireland and was killed in the battle of King s Mountain, and a sister of Col Gideon Steen,) was born in Union District, South Carolina December 24, 1798   She was married to William Hewitt by whom she had three children, all born in Union District, South Carolina
1 Sarah Hewitt
2 Ashley Hewitt
3 Ruth Hewitt

II—Jane Steen, the third child and second daughter of ———— and Sarah Steen, a sister of Col Gideon Steen was born near Santuck, Union District, South Carolina January 14, 1801   She was married at the same place to Abraham Stowers or Stours   They removed to Alabama, where they brought up a family of children

V—John Campbell Steen the fourth child and second son of ———— and Sarah Steen (a brother of Col Gideon Steen, and a grandson of the James Steen who was killed in the battle of King s Mountain, South Carolina October 7, 1780,) was born in Union District South Carolina near Santuck April 15, 1805, and died near Washington, Daviess County, Indiana December 5 1878, aged 73 years 7 months and 20 days   He was married near Union South Carolina March 28 1828, to Phebe Gregory who died near Washington Indiana October 5 1850   In the year 1837 John C Steen removed from South Carolina with his family and located upon a farm near Washington Daviess County, Indiana, where they spent the remainder of their lives   To them were born the following five children

1 Isaac Jefferson Steen, the eldest son of John C and Phœbe G Steen was born near Union South Carolina, November 13, 1829 — a farmer He was married in Daviess County Indiana, December 27, 1849, to Sarah Jane Sholtz, who died near Glendale Indiana September 4, 1869 To them were born nine children, as follows

 I — John Franklin Steen the eldest son of Isaac J and Sarah J Steen was born in Daviess County Indiana, November 2 1850 He was married May 7 1873, to Mary Catherine Lock she having been born in Indianapolis, Indiana November 26 1854 To them were born ten children, six boys and four girls, as follows

  1 Ashbury Jefferson Steen was born March 17 1874

  2 Armata Zeno Steen was born June 9, 1877

  3 Ellis Morton Steen was born May 26 1879

  4 Lettie E Steen was born March 30 1881, and died December 15 1881

  5 John Ellsworth Steen was born December 14, 1882

  6 Robert Oglesby Steen was born March 27 1885

  7 Mary Etta Steen was born October 20 1887

  8 Nellie Glen Steen was born December 27 1889, and died October 26 1896

  9 Orion Arvilla Steen was born November 10 1892

  10 Edison McKinley Steen was born July 14, 1896

 II — James Richard Steen the second son of Isaac J and Sarah J Steen, was born in Daviess County Indiana July 31, 1852 Residence, Glendale, Indiana

 III — Thomas M Steen the third son of Isaac J and Sarah J Steen, was born in Daviess County Indiana, October 11 1854 and died September 21 1856

 II — Mary Ann Steen the fourth child and eldest daughter of Isaac J and Sarah J Steen, was born in Daviess County Indiana September 22, 1856, and died, unmarried March 25, 1885 aged 28 years 6 months and 3 days

 V — Lucy Angeline Steen the fifth child and second daughter of Isaac J and Sarah J Steen was born in Daviess County Indiana November 27 1858 She was married to John C Harrell, by whom she had ten children five boys and five girls   Family residence, Glendale, Indiana

VI—Tabitha Ellen Steen, the sixth child and third daughter of Isaac J and Sarah J Steen   was born in Daviess County, Indiana, November 25, 1860   She was married, and resides at Hyatt, Daviess County, Indiana

VII—William Warner Steen, the seventh child and fourth son of Isaac J and Sarah J Steen, was born in Daviess County, Indiana, January 23, 1863   He was married, and resides at Ivy, Pike County, Indiana

VIII—Charles Ellsworth Steen, the eighth child and fifth son of Isaac J and Sarah J Steen was born in Daviess County, Indiana March 25 1863   Residence in Oregon

IX—Emma Glen Steen the ninth child and fourth daughter of Isaac J and Sarah J Steen, was born in Daviess County Indiana, April 20, 1868   She was married, and resides at Plainville, Indiana

2 Martha Jane Steen the second child and eldest daughter of John Campbell and Phœbe Steen was born near Union, South Carolina, June 5 1832 and was brought to Indiana by her parents in 1837   She was married near Glendale, Indiana, February 22, 1852, to Richard M Clark, and died near Glendale, Indiana, February 3 1861 aged 28 years, 7 months and 29 days   To them were born four children as follows

I—Sarah Elizabeth Clark was born in Daviess County Indiana, in 1854   She was married, in June 1875 to James W Mattingly, a teacher, by whom she had two children

   1 John R Mattingly was born March 4, 1879

   2 Henry B Mattingly was born July 25, 1892

II—Ritter Clark the second child of Richard M and Martha J Steen Clark, was born in 1855 and died

III—Lettie Ellen Clark, the third child of Richard M and Martha J Steen Clark, was born in 1857   Residence, Glendale Indiana

IV—Emma Jane Clark, the fourth child of Richard M and Martha J Steen Clark, was born in 1859, and died

3 Benjamin Watts Steen, the third child and second son of
John Campbell and Phœbe Gregory Steen, was born near
Union, South Carolina, January 4, 1834, and brought by his
parents to Indiana in 1837   He was married in Daviess
County, Indiana, January 25, 1855, to Martha R Colbert,
she having been born in Daviess County, Indiana, January
18, 1834   To them were born two children   Residence,
Glendale, Indiana

   I—Oliver Byron Steen, the eldest child of Benjamin W and
   Martha R Steen, was born in Daviess County, Indiana
   November 7, 1856   He was married at Alfordsville,
   Indiana, October 8, 1878 to Emma Bartl   He was mar-
   ried a second time, December 5, 1881, to Elizabeth
   Traylor of Pike County, Indiana   He was married a
   third time, June 12, 1890 to Maud Emily Yeager, of
   Missouri

     1 Emma Bartl Steen the eldest child of O B Steen, and
     the only child by his first wife, was born August 26,
     1879   Residence, Indianapolis, Indiana

     2 Leona Steen the second child of O B Steen, and the
     only child by his second wife, was born ———   Resi-
     dence, Washington, Indiana

     3 Rozilla Steen, the third child of O B Steen and the
     eldest by his third wife, was born January 8, 1893,
     and died July 2, 1893

     1 Byron Steen the fourth child of O B Steen and the
     second by his third wife, was born November 16 1894

   II—Luella Steen a daughter of Benjamin W and Martha
   R Steen was born in Daviess County Indiana December
   19, 1872   She was married June 30, 1892, to Spencer
   Ashbury Ward, a merchant, and a native of Daviess
   County Indiana   To them was born the following
   Residence Washington, Indiana

     1 Ernest Steen Ward was born in Washington Indiana
     December 14, 1895

4 Sarah Elizabeth Steen, the fourth child and second daughter
of John C and Phœbe G Steen, was born near Union, in
Union District South Carolina, December 5, 1835   She
was brought by her parents to Indiana when she was a very
small child, and brought up on her father's farm   She was
  (13)

married near Washington Daviess County, Indiana. March
15, 1855, to Captain John W. Clark She died in Daviess
County, Indiana, December 5, 1859 aged 24 years To
them was born one son

I—Benjamin Watts Clark was born near Washington,
Indiana. December 3, 1855, and was married, September
15, 1895, to Mrs Elmira E Jones

5 Lettie Ellen Steen, the fifth child and third daughter of
John Campbell and Phœbe Gregory Steen, was born near
Washington, Daviess County, Indiana, August 14, 1840,
and was brought up on the farm She was married, February 19 1857 to James R Arthur, a prosperous and influential citizen of the county, who began life a poor man, but
has accumulated a good deal of property To them were
born fourteen children Residence, Glendale Indiana

I—John Franklin Arthur was born October 24, 1857,—a
teacher He was married September 14, 1880 to Clara
Emma McCafferty Residence, Washington Indiana

II—Nancy Ann Arthur was born August 12, 1859 She
was married, November 27, 1881 to McLoid Washington
Chappell of Pike County, Indiana Residence, Minden,
Nebraska

III—Charles Watts Arthur was born February 26 1861.
Residence, Briggs, Idaho

IV—Sarah Belle Arthur was born February 12, 1862, and
died January 16 1868

V—Laura Jane Arthur was born August 12, 1863 She
was married August 29 1886, to Douglas Hooker Ricks,
a farmer Residence, Glendale, Indiana

VI—William Arthur was born March 22, 1865 — a farmer
He was married September 12, 1886, to Clara Belle Lett,
of Daviess County Indiana Residence, near Glendale,
Indiana

VII—Phœbe Angeline Arthur was born April 11, 1867
She was married November 11, 1889 to James Blanken-
ship Meade a farmer Residence near Glendale, Indiana

VIII—Emma Naomi Arthur was born December 19 1868
and died November 16, 1870

IX—Elijah Arthur was born July 31, 1870, a student for the ministry in the Cumberland Presbyterian Church at Franklin Indiana

X—Hamilton Arthur was born July 20 1872 a student in Indianapolis Medical College

XI—Martin Luther Arthur was born August 18, 1876, a student in Indianapolis Medical College

XII—Nora Maud Arthur was born June 27, 1879   Residence near Glendale, Indiana

XIII—Martha Rozilla Arthur was born August 14, 1881, Residence, near Glendale, Indiana

XII —Austin Owen Arthur was born August 18, 1883. Residence, near Glendale, Indiana

John Campbell Steen the fourth child and second son of ———— and Sarah Steen was married a second time, in March, 1851, to Angeline B Hollingsworth she having been born in Indiana April 11 1824 and died January 21, 1882 To this marriage were born six children

6 Nancy Naomi Steen the sixth child of John Campbell Steen, and the eldest by his second wife Angeline Hollingsworth was born near Washington Indiana, December 8, 1853 and died at Brownwood Missouri March 4, 1896 She was married in Daviess County, Indiana, August 5, 1875, to George C Harrell, he having been born August 9 1856 Residence, Campbell Missouri   To George C and Nancy Naomi Steen Harrell were born the following nine children

I—Bertie Sebastian Harrell was born October 29, 1876

II—Jesse Campbell Harrell was born July 21 1878

III—Austin Eathie Harrell was born October 11 1879

IV—Ezra Jacob Harrell was born February 25, 1881

I —Josephine Merdora Harrell was born May 23 1883

VI—Edith Lucy Harrell was born January 23 1885

VII—Benjamin Watts Harrell was born January 29, 1888

VIII—Ada Nellie Harrell was born December 8 1889

IX—Frank Otis Harrell was born February 19, 1893.

7 Eliza Ann Steen, the seventh child of John Campbell Steen, and the second by his second wife, Angeline B Hollingsworth Steen, was born near Washington Indiana September

6, 1855   She was married at the same place January 8, 1874,
to William P Lownsdale, he having been born May 12, 1850
To them were born nine children   Residence, Campbell,
Missouri

I —Ella Lownsdale was born October 22, 1874   She was
married April 9, 1893, to James Currie, he having been
born January 14, 1869   To them

    1 Robert Currie was born January 13 1894

II —John Ray Lownsdale was born April 6, 1876

III —Perry Thomas Lownsdale was born October 4, 1878

IV —Elijah Ellis Lownsdale was born June 30, 1881

V —Frank Philip Lownsdale was born October 1, 1883

VI —Edgar Lownsdale was born October 28 1886

VII —Oscar Ellsworth Lownsdale was born September 25,
1888

VIII —Henry Arthur Lownsdale was born September 23,
1891

IX —Sarah Catherine Lownsdale was born November 14,
1893

8. Lucinda Frances Steen, the eighth child of John C Steen
and the third by his second wife Angeline B Steen, was
born near Washington, Indiana, December 26 1859, and
died unmarried in Campbell, Missouri, January 18, 1890 in
the thirty-first year of her age

9 Melissa May Steen the ninth child of John C Steen, and
the fourth by his second wife, Angeline B Steen, was born
near Washington, Daviess County, Indiana, August 16, 1862
She was married in Campbell Missouri September 5 1883
to John Ezra Ricks he having been born in Daviess County
Indiana, September 24 1861   To them were born six children   Residence, Campbell, Missouri

I —Phœbe Gertrude Ricks was born in Campbell Missouri
July 12, 1884

II —Henry Hooker Ricks was born February 12, 1886

III —Thomas Otto Ricks was born October 28, 1887, and
died June 12 1889

IV —Millie Agnes Ricks was born January 22, 1890

V —Claude Earl Ricks was born October 20, 1891

REV. HENRY W. STEEN.

VI.—Ora Redman Ricks was born in Campbell, Missouri, May 16 1893

10 William Sherman Steen, the tenth child of John C Steen, but the fifth by his second wife, Angeline B Steen, was born near Washington, Daviess County, Indiana, July 31, 1864, and died unmarried, near Glendale, Indiana, January 18, 1890, aged 25 years, 5 months and 18 days

11 Henry Wylie Steen the eleventh child of John C Steen, and the sixth by his second wife Angeline B Steen, was born near Washington, Daviess County, Indiana, January 23, 1867 and brought up on his father's farm In 1887 he entered the Normal College at Mitchell, Indiana and in 1888 the Cumberland University, at Lebanon, Tennessee, where he continued two years He was ordained to the ministry of the Gospel by the Presbytery of Morgan, of the Cumberland Presbyterian Church, at Huntingsburgh, Dubois County, Indiana April 11 1891, and had charge of the Ellettsville and Harrodsburgh congregations from April, 1890, to August, 1894, when he removed to Franklin Indiana, and took charge of the Shiloh Cumberland Presbyterian Church, near Franklin, while he prosecuted his studies in Franklin College Since 1897 he has been pastor at Carroll, Indiana, and Stated Clerk of the Presbytery Rev Henry W Steen was married at Ellettsville, Monroe County, Indiana, August 1, 1894, to Lora May Benzel, she having been born April 15, 1875 ' To them was born one child

I—Wylie Frederick Steen son of Rev Henry W and Lora M Steen, was born in Franklin, Indiana, April 1, 1896

V—Thomas Jefferson Steen, the fifth child and third son of —— and Sarah Steen (a brother of Col Gideon Steen and John Campbell Steen, and a grandson of the James Steen who came from Ireland and was killed in battle at King's Mountain, South Carolina, October 7, 1780.) was born in Union District, South Carolina August 31 1812 He removed to Chickasaw County, Mississippi, in 1852, where he died January 14, 1886, in the 74th year of his age He was married in Union District, South Carolina, July 31, 1832, to Eleanor Cunningham To them were born seven children, all in Union District, South Carolina

1 James Harvey Steen the eldest son of Thomas J and Eleanor C Steen, was born July 17, 1833 and died September 15, 1834

2 Mary Jane Steen, the second child and eldest daughter of Thomas J and Eleanor C Steen, was born December 25, 1834, and died February 25, 1857, aged 22 years and 2 months She was married in Chickasaw County, Mississippi, January 3, 1856, to Benjamin Francis McIntosh, he having been born about 1831, and was killed in Georgia during the Civil War To them was born one child, as follows

I —John McIntosh was born February 7, 1857, and died September 27, 1857, aged 7 months and 20 days

3 John Cunningham Steen, the third child and second son of Thomas J and Eleanor C Steen, was born March 20, 1836, and died September 26 1855, aged 19 years 6 months and 6 days

4 William Thomas Steen, the fourth child and third son of Thomas Jefferson and Eleanor Cunningham Steen, was born February 4, 1838 He has followed the occupation of a farmer and miller, and resided for many years with his family near Houlka, Chickasaw County, Mississippi He was married in Chickasaw County Mississippi October 7 1858, to Elizabeth Frances Craig, she having been born December 14, 1835 The whole family are devout Christians and earnest Presbyterians Residence, near Houlka, Mississippi To William T and Elizabeth F Steen were born five children, as follows

I —Mary Catherine Steen, the eldest daughter of William T and Elizabeth F Steen, was born in Houlka, Chickasaw County, Mississippi October 10, 1860, and still resides with her parents

II —George Howe Steen the second child and eldest son of William T and Elizabeth F Steen was born in Houlka, Chickasaw County, Mississippi, August 10 1864 and was graduated from the Southwestern University at Clarksville Tennessee, in 1887 He also completed the divinity course in the same University in 1887 He was licensed to preach the Gospel by the Presbytery of Chickasaw, August 5 1887, and ordained to the full work of the ministry in the Southern Presbyterian Church by the Presby-

REV. GEORGE H. STEEN, D.D.

tery of Tombeckbee, and installed pastor of the Okolona
Church October 20 1887   In connection with this charge
he acted as stated supply of the West Point and Buena
Vista Churches from 1887 to 1889   From 1889 to 1892 he
was stated supply at Tupelo, Unity and Providence
Churches from 1892 to 1893 of the Church of Aberdeen
Mississippi, from 1893 to 1894 of the church of Arkadel-
phia, Arkansas   In 1894 he became pastor of the church
at Pontotoc Mississippi where he continued one year and
then accepted a call to the pastorate of the church at
Marion, Alabama where he remained from 1896 to 1899
In 1893 he also served as an evangelist for the Synod of
Memphis, and in 1899 was chosen evangelist for the Presbytery of South Alabama   He was called to the Presbyterian Church in Longview, Texas in 1899, where he now
resides   In 1900 Rutherford College, North Carolina
gave him the degree of Doctor of Divinity   Rev George
H Steen was married by the Rev S C Caldwell, in Memphis Tennessee October 25, 1887 to Carrie Brown Hunt
a daughter of William H and Annie B Hunt, she having
been born in Grenada, Mississippi June 8, 1863   To them
were born five children as follows   Residence, Longview, Texas

1   Carrie Brown Steen was born near Houlka Mississippi
    October 18, 1888

2   George Waddell Steen was born in Tupelo, Mississippi
    January 4, 1891

3   Annie Frances Steen was born in Pontotoc, Mississippi
    June 12, 1893

4   William Hunt Steen was born in Marion, Alabama
    June 13 1896

5   Mary Evelyn Steen was born in Marion Alabama,
    December 8, 1898

III—James Neely Steen the third child and second son of
    William T and Elizabeth F Steen was born near Houlka,
    Chickasaw County Mississippi July 14, 1866, and died
    August 28 1866, aged 1 month and 14 days

IV—Annie Belle Steen, the fourth child and second daugh-
    ter of William T and Elizabeth F Steen, was born near
    Houlka, Chickasaw County, Mississippi, January 7, 1868

and brought up in the home of her parents   Residence
Houlka Mississippi

    V—Eleanor Pulcheria Steen, the fifth and youngest child of
William T and Elizabeth F Steen, was born near Houlka,
Chickasaw County. Mississippi October 6, 1875   She still
resides with her parents at Houlka, Mississippi.

5 George Howe Steen, the fifth child and fourth son of
Thomas Jefferson and Eleanor Cunningham Steen, was born
in Union District South Carolina December 29 1839, and
brought up in his father s family   He was never married
He joined the Confederate Army and was fatally wounded
in the second battle of Manassas Junction, Virginia, August
28, 1862 from the effects of which he died the next day, aged
22 years and 8 months

6 Ann Catherine Steen, the sixth child and second daughter of
Thomas Jefferson and Eleanor Cunningham Steen, was born
in Union District South Carolina July 7, 1842 and died in
Chickasaw County Mississippi July 7, 1892, aged 50 years
She was married in Chickasaw County, Mississippi April
10, 1866, to Robert Bankhead Marion, he having been born
January 26, 1837   To them were born twelve children
Residence, Houlka. Mississippi

    I—Mary Jane Marion was born in Chickasaw County, Mis-
sissippi July 2, 1867, and was married December 9, 1885
to Robert Martin Hulsell, by whom she had two children
    1 Annie Tarethea Hulsell was born September 25, 1886
    2 India Elma Hulsell was born December 1, 1889

    II—Hattie Alema Marion, the second daughter of Robert B
and Ann C. Steen Marion, was born in Chickasaw County,
Mississippi, June 29, 1868, and was married November 30,
1887 to William Hance Harris

    III—Frances Rosella Marion was born October 25 1869
and died August 20 1884

    IV—Neely Howe Marion the fourth child and eldest son
of Robert B and Ann C Steen Marion, was born February 13, 1871

    V—Mattie Lulu Marion was born April 8 1872.

    VI—Thomas Bankhead Marion was born October 11, 1873

    VII—James West Marion was born February 19, 1875

VIII—Nannie Kate Marion was born June 11, 1876, and died February 15 1878

IX—Maggie Alberta Marion was born March 15, 1878

X—William Robert Marion was born December 23 1879

XI—Bessie Lee Marion was born September 15 1881

XII—John Cunningham Marion was born October 21 1883 and died August 20 1884, aged 9 months and 29 days

7 Amanda Harriet Steen the seventh child and third daughter of Thomas Jefferson and Eleanor Cunningham Steen was born in Union District South Carolina August 28 1845 She was married in Chickasaw County Mississippi, December 22 1869, to Francis Taylor Marion he having been born November 9, 1846 To them were born twelve children, and all who lived to maturity professed their faith in Christ and united with the Presbyterian Church Residence, Houlka, Chickasaw County Mississippi

I—Ida Ann Marion was born October 9 1870, and died October 19 1886 aged 16 years and 10 days

II—Mary Melvina Marion was born December 11, 1871

III—Thomas David Marion was born March 19, 1873

IV—Janet Eugenia Marion was born September 4 1874

V—William Patrick Marion was born February 16 1876

VI—James Harvey Marion was born December 21, 1877

VII—John Alexander Marion was born August 26 1879

VIII—George McNeely Marion was born January 18, 1881

IX—Robert Newton Marion was born December 6, 1882

X—Nellie Rose Marion was born January 2, 1885

XI—Caroline Frances Marion was born April 7, 1887

VII—Edward Smith Marion was born September 24 1888

VI—Eleanor Steen the sixth child and third daughter of —— and Sarah Steen, (a full sister of Col Gideon Steen, and a granddaughter of the James Steen who came from Ireland located in South Carolina, and was killed in the battle of King's Mountain) was born near Santuck, Union District South Carolina October 8, 1814 and died in her youth unmarried

VII —James William Steen the seventh child and fourth son of —— and Sarah Steen (and a grandson of the James Steen who came from Ireland, located in South Carolina, and was killed in the battle of King's Mountain,) was born near Santuck, Union District, South Carolina, October 2 1816   He was never married   He joined the United States Army at the time of the war with Mexico   He was wounded in the battle at the capture of the City of Mexico, from the effects of which he died, October 10, 1847, aged 31 years and 8 days

CHAPTER III

James Steen (a son of the James Steen (?) who was born in County Antrim, Ireland, came to America, and finally located in Union District South Carolina was killed in the Revolutionary War at the battle of King s Mountain, October 7 1780,) was born in Union District, South Carolina (?), and settled permanently in Chesterfield District South Carolina   He was a prosperous farmer, and his descendants were a race of thrifty farmers   He was married to Jane Graham by whom he had at least two sons — Thomas Steen and Elisha Steen   And one great-granddaughter writes that in addition to these he had three others, named William Steen, John Green Steen, and Susan Steen — all born in Chesterfield District South Carolina   Of these children of James and Jane Graham Steen we have the following record

I —Thomas Steen was born in Ireland or in Chesterfield District, South Carolina (?) and died in 1830   He was married to Elizabeth Hollifield a daughter of Jacob Hollifield, by whom he had five children, as follows

1   Mary Steen, who was married to a Mr Joplin
2   Ellery Steen
3   James Steen
4   Wilson Steen, who served in the Confederate Army resided at Filler's Ferry, Kershaw County, South Carolina for many years and died in 1897   He was married and brought up a family of several children

I.—Henry Steen, the eldest son of Wilson Steen, was born in 1841, was a Confederate soldier in the Civil War under Captain Lucas, in the Seventh South Carolina Battalion Infantry. He was with the army (Gen. Joseph E. Johnston, commanding,) at the surrender near Greensboro, North Carolina. He attended the general reunion of Confederate soldiers in Charleston, South Carolina, in May, 1899; met his old Captain Lucas and Lieutenant Gurdun there, and "had a glorious time." Henry Steen was married and has brought up a family of eight children. Residence, Newman, Chesterfield County, South Carolina.

1. Randolph Steen, who was married to ———.
2. Jesse Steen, who was married to ———.
3. Emma Steen.
4. Elias Steen.
5. Una Steen.
6. Joseph Steen.
7. William Steen.
8. Muldrow Steen.

5. Joseph Steen, the fifth child and fourth son of Thomas Steen and Elizabeth Hollifield Steen, was born in Chesterfield District, South Carolina, about 1813, and died suddenly of heart disease July 21, 1861. He was married about 1841 to Elizabeth Ann Taylor, she having been born in Anson County, North Carolina, September 13, 1824. Residence, McCaskill, Chesterfield County, South Carolina. To Joseph and Elizabeth A. Steen were born the following children:

I.—Sarah Elizabeth Steen was born in Chesterfield District, South Carolina, April 18, 1844. She was married to Robert Lee Taylor, he having been born in Chesterfield District, South Carolina, August 28, 1836. To Robert L. and Sarah E. Steen Taylor were born nine children, as follows. Residence, Colbert, Indian Territory.

1. Daniel Smiley Taylor was born March 18, 1867.
2. Robert Ady Lee Taylor was born November 11, 1870.
3. William Duffey Taylor was born February 26, 1873.
4. John H. Taylor—
5. James Benjamin Taylor—
   twin children, were born April 1, 1875.

6 Peter Taylor was born November 28 1877

7 Minnie Lenora Taylor was born December 25, 1880

8 Fannie Belle Taylor was born January 20, 1883

9 Thomas Jefferson Taylor was born October, 1891

II —William Thomas Steen, the second child and eldest son of Joseph and Elizabeth A Steen, was born in Chesterfield District South Carolina September 28, 1845 He was married in Anson County, North Carolina, May 28, 1868 to Eliza F Musk, she having been born November 16 1848, and died December 9, 1877, aged 29 years and 25 days To them were born four children William Thomas Steen was married a second time, May 8, 1879, to Margaret Catherine Hendrix To them were born four children Residence, Gift, Alcorn County Mississippi

1 —William John Washington Steen, son of William T and Eliza F Steen was born December 30 1870

2 Susan Levisa Steen, daughter of William T and Eliza F Steen, was born October 11, 1872

3 Mary Elizabeth Steen daughter of William T and Eliza F Steen, was born — —

4 Joseph Thomas Edmund Steen, son of William T and Eliza F Steen was born February 21 1875

5 James Clay Sanford Steen, son of William Thomas and Margaret Catherine Steen, was born November 23, 1880

6 Samuel Jefferson Hendrix Steen, son of William T and Margaret C Steen, was born April 5 1886

7 Shelley May Steen, daughter of William T and Margaret C Steen was born March 18 1888

8 Emma Catherine Lillian Steen, daughter of William Thomas and Margaret Catherine Steen, was born September 25, 1890

III —Louisa Jane Steen, the third child and second daughter of Joseph and Elizabeth A Steen, was born in Chesterfield District, South Carolina, in 1847 She was married to William High of North Carolina Residence, near Jefferson Post-office Chesterfield County South Carolina

IV.—James Washington Steen, the fourth child and second son of Joseph and Elizabeth A. Steen, was born in Chesterfield District, South Carolina, November 28, 1848. He was married in Union County, North Carolina, December 9, 1866, to Nancy Elvina Kiker, she having been born in Union County, North Carolina, November 18, 1848. To them were born four children. Residence, Elmwood, North Carolina.

1. Mary J. V. Steen, the eldest daughter of James W. and Nancy E. Steen, was born October 30, 1867. She was married April 12, 1885, to Moses Waller, by whom she had one child.

   a. Darwood T. Waller was born March 17, 1890.

2. Susan Cora Steen, the second daughter of James W. and Nancy E. Steen, was born January 5, 1869.

3. Selone L. Steen, the third daughter of James W. and Nancy E. Steen, was born February 7, 1870. She was married May 27, 1888, to J. E. Wilhelm, by whom she had one child.

   a. Horace C. Wilhelm was born August 15, 1890.

4. Margaret Elvina Steen, the fourth daughter of James W. and Nancy E. Steen, was born January 19, 1874.

V.—Mary Frances Steen, the fifth child and third daughter of Joseph and Elizabeth A. Steen, was born in Chesterfield District, South Carolina, March 5, 1849. She was married in Alcorn County, Mississippi, October 20, 1876, to Gen. Taylor Smith, he having been born in Desoto, Mississippi, February 16, 1850. To them were born six children, as follows. Residence, Gift, Alcorn County, Mississippi.

1. Joseph Edmund Smith was born January 16, 1877.

2. Sarah Ann Onia Smith was born October 11, 1879.

3. William Thomas Smith was born September 14, 1881.

4. Susan Jennette Smith was born January 27, 1883.

5. Jesse Sanford Smith was born February 7, 1885.

6. Ernest Cleveland Smith was born August 16, 1890.

VI.—Edmund Daniel Steen, the sixth child and third son of Joseph and Elizabeth A. Steen, was born in Chesterfield District, South Carolina, in 1852. He was married and

(14)

removed to Texas — a farmer Residence, near Denison, Texas

VII—Susan Adeline Steen, the seventh child and fourth daughter of Joseph and Elizabeth A Steen, was born in Chesterfield District, South Carolina, November 4 1855. She was married April 17, 1872, to William Chapman Stanley, by whom she had seven children Residence Mt Croghan, Chesterfield County, South Carolina

VIII—Laura Ellen Steen, the eighth child and fifth daughter of Joseph and Elizabeth A Steen, was born in Anson County, North Carolina, February 3, 1857 She was married by the Rev W H Moore, in Chesterfield County, South Carolina, November 16, 1882, to Augustus Sullivan — a farmer — he having been born in Chesterfield District, South Carolina, February 12, 1853 [Previous to 1868 all the divisions in South Carolina were called "Districts," but since that date the name of Counties" has been given them, as in other States] To Augustus and Laura Ellen Steen Sullivan was born one child Residence, near McCaskill, Chesterfield County, South Carolina

1 Leonidas Charles Sullivan was born in Chesterfield County, South Carolina June 26, 1887

IX—Emeline Amanda Steen, the ninth child and sixth daughter of Joseph and Elizabeth A Steen, was born in 1859 She was married to Zach Beecham Residence, Oak Forest, Iredell County, North Carolina The following members of the Steen family reside at Mt Croghan, Chesterfield County, South Carolina William Steen, Jackson Steen, Nancy Gibson, Polly Jordan, and John Steen

I—Elisha Steen a son of the James Steen who lived in Chesterfield District South Carolina, and possibly a grandson of the James Steen that was killed in the battle of King's Mountain during the Revolutionary War (?), was born in Chesterfield District, South Carolina

BOOK THREE.

DESCENDANTS OF WILLIAM STEEN

William Steen was born in Ireland about 1738, came to the British Colonies in America, and after a time located in Union District, South Carolina He was a soldier in the Revolutionary War, and was wounded in the battle of King's Mountain October 7, 1780 He was married about 1772 to Nancy Lusk and brought up a family of eleven children in Union District, South Carolina

---

William Steen was born in Ireland and came to the British Colonies in America near the middle of the eighteenth century and eventually located in South Carolina, near the Great Broad River He was a farmer by occupation, a soldier in the Revolutionary War, and was wounded and taken prisoner in the battle of King's Mountain, October 7, 1780 He was soon afterwards rescued from the British by a band of American soldiers, among whom was Jacob Neely, whose granddaughter, Margaret Ann Neely, afterwards married his grandson, Carroll Jeffries Steen in Rankin County, Mississippi The following report was sent to the writer by one of his descendants When William Steen was wounded, his wife and three children were in a fort for safety, sixty miles away One of the children had just died, and at that time lay a corpse As soon as Mrs. Steen heard of the calamity she procured a horse, and leaving her dead child with her friends, proceeded at once in great haste to her husband   It was late in the afternoon, and she had to travel all alone along the dreary road that sad and gloomy night, and did not reach his side till after daylight the next morning.   This brave and heroic act shines in the family until this day as characteristic of them   They are not only politically but religiously enthusiastic and patriotic Mrs Steen was a very energetic and intelligent woman, and lived to be eighty-eight years of age   She used to relate to her grandchildren many interesting accounts of the trials and hardships of those early struggles and conflicts during the Revolutionary War. One of her grandchildren writes·   "She was as true a Christian as the world affords "   Several years after the close of the Revolutionary War William Steen started to remove with his family from South Carolina to Mississippi, stopping for a time in Carroll County, Tennessee, where he was taken sick and died   Not long after his death his wife and all her children, except three, resumed their journey and went on to Lawrence County, Mississippi, where they afterwards resided   After their father's death John Steen returned to South Carolina, Sarah Steen married Thompson Enochs and remained in Tennessee, and Jane Steen married Levi Noble and removed to Texas.   Five of the children of William Steen were among the early settlers and influential citizens of Rankin County, Mississippi   All were farmers, and brought up large families.   One son located in Holmes County Mississippi, and another near Hazlehurst, Copiah County, Mississippi.   This large family of William Steen has left a numerous posterity   One of the grandsons writes concerning his own family as follows   "We have ten children, and thirty-seven grandchildren.   My father had cousins in Alabama   There is a large number of Steens in Chickasaw County, Mississippi, and a number of Steens were in Knox County, Indiana, fifty years ago cousins to my father   I think it would be a difficult task to count the descendants of the original Steens who came into this country from Ireland   I am almost inclined to think that they are like the descendants of Abraham for multitude   They are also remarkable for strong constitutions   I have never heard of a consumptive or dyspeptic one   I think we should justly be proud of the name of Steen   I have never known one who failed to pay his honest debts   They are remarkable for reverence, hospitality, charity, and industry, and among this large number I have never known or heard a breath of suspicion in regard to their moral character "

Captain Isaac V Enochs, of Terry, Mississippi, another grandson of William Steen, in 1893, wrote as follows. "I have some reputation for an extraordinary memory I certainly feel surprised at the distinctness with which memory photographs my old grandmother, as she and my mother coddled together over their domestic work, and grandmother, with her quaint Gaelic expressions and brogue, recounted to my mother the history that I now see reached back into the centuries. I can even see myself as I lay around with my heels up and drank down the curiosity — feeling such stimulating draughts — as she told of the Trans-Atlantic history of her old uncles, and great-uncles and aunts As I remember, the Steens and Lusks were pure Orange Irish and Presbyterians, while their English cousins, the Hayes, were Welsh My Grandfather Steen was wealthy when he was married I have often seen a little unique trunk, or strong box, covered with ox hide, holding something over a gallon, which he placed in his wife's keeping, filled with English guineas, but the old stronghold impressed my young imagination with the 'what might have been ' When the Revolutionary War had closed, and grandpa was dead, his property was reduced to the ownership of one negro woman 'Milly,' which grandfather had purchased in my mother's name, the evening after he had accidentally clipped off the fingers of her right hand with a broad-axe And just here hangs an example of Irish generosity, in this, that this woman and her progeny were passed back into the estate Thus it happened that the number of her children corresponded with the number of grandma's children, so that each had a negro to begin life with, and they all, except Uncle Thompson and Aunt Sallie Enochs, afterwards became thrifty slave-owners A history of the Steens without their connection with the Enochs would be like a three-wheeled wagon The old families were related through the Hays, or Hayes I am not sure about the orthography My Grandmother Steen's mother was a Hays. My Grandmother Enochs' mother was a Hays, she and grandfather being related, I don't know how, through the Hays It is the General Jackson Hays Gen Harry Hays, of New Orleans, and his still more celebrated brother, Jack Hays, who killed on the streets of San Francisco its then marshal, were grandsons of my grandmother's brother This was the connecting link between the old Steens and Enochs, or Enos, as it was in old German, or more recent English history   My great-grandfather, Enoch Gabriel Enos, was a round-headed Welshman, and a follower of Cromwell   He made himself too conspicuous — a well-known family trait   And right here let me compare the distinguishing characteristics of the connecting families   The Enochs are willful, aggressive, while the Steens are won'tful, cautiously stubborn   It has been said of your correspondent that he has all the aggressiveness of the Enochs and the stubbornness of the Steens, minus their caution   In the decapitation of Charles II, and after the fall of his great leader, my grandfather, Gabriel Enochs smuggled his way with the Hays (who were British sailors) across the Atlantic and hid himself away in the mountains of Southwest Virginia and North Carolina till the Revolutionary War was well under way   My grandfather and grandmother Steen came from Ireland, and lived near the line of North and South Carolina   Thither my great-grandfather went when he dared, and the two related families were raised up together   And when the young State of Tennessee began to come into notice, both families migrated thither, except the eldest son of each, and were raised up in the shadow of the Hermitage, each feeling proud of the blood of its hero and central figure   I remember with zest the accounts my father and uncles used to give of their fun with the Crocketts, and the pride they had in the denouement of the only break that ever existed in a lifelong relation between the Crocketts and our family   There were so many more of our folks than of the Crocketts, the whole trouble was to be settled by Uncle Thompson Enochs and David Crockett knocking it out in a single fight, but when 'Bill' Crockett saw that Uncle Thompson was getting the best of it, he brought on an additional scrimmage with my father   Of course, they used to tell us the Crocketts got the worst of it   I have never heard the Crockett version of the affair   This I know, however, that the old men shed sincere tears when David Crockett fell at the Alamo   When grandpa had been gone to the war nearly two years, getting a furlough to return, he was shot through the body when within two miles of home   The Tory neighbors, knowing the sorrow that was already in that home, placed him upon a litter and took him to his already distressed family   'Polly' was dead and laid upon the cooling board   'Can a mother forget her offspring?'   I have heard grandmother say   'Yes, when I saw the greater sorrow, it was now 4 P M — I caught up Polly's body and laid it upon a clothes shelf in the back room   The next morning, at 9 o'clock, I wanted clothes that were upon that shelf, and found my dead child that I had forgotten till then   Grandpa survived the wounds, but was never well   Grandma kept as a memento — and I have seen the red bandana kerchief that she and her Tory neighbors, without a doctor, drew through his body, in accordance with the vulgar idea of the surgery of that period   Silas Steen, the youngest son, died in 1857, aged about 56 years, which would indicate that grandpa lived into the present century"   Captain Enochs concludes a communication of many pages as follows   "One more morsel I will give you in pride, and I can say just pride   Five weeks ago I spent a Sunday and night with my afflicted double cousin, Carroll J Steen, who has recently lost the wife of his youth   'Cousin Isaac,' said he, 'I regard our family, taken as a whole, as a wonder   You and I can trace them over a century, count them by name by the hundreds, and yet not one of them ever came in contact with the laws of his country for a mean thing   No woman ever failed to make a good wife, and not a breath of suspicion ever marred her good name, and while none have reached extraordinary wealth, all have been good livers'   But you are tired, so is my hand.

"Terry, Mississippi   ISAAC V ENOCHS"

William Steen was married in South Carolina, near the Great Broad River, about 1772, to Nancy Lusk, she having been born in Ireland and died in Mississippi   To them were born eleven children, all born and brought up in South Carolina   Their names were   John Mary called 'Polly", James, Sarah, called "Sally", Nathaniel, Elias, Robert, William, Mary (2d), called "Polly", Jane, and Silas

---

CHAPTER I

John Steen, the eldest son of William and Nancy Lusk Steen, was born in South Carolina, near the Great Broad River, about 1774   He was an industrious and prosperous farmer, and made his home in South Carolina until his death   He was married in

South Carolina to a Miss Jeffries, who came from Virginia into that State They were the parents of eight children, two sons and six daughters, as follows·

I—William Steen, a son of the John Steen who married a Miss Jeffries, was born in South Carolina, and brought up on his father's farm He was married to a Miss Lusk, a kinsgirl, and a protege of his father They removed to Mississippi, where they brought up their family At the time of his death, in 1860, or 1861, he was a wealthy cotton planter in La Fayette County, Mississippi One of his daughters married Dr Wright, who died in Water Valley, Mississippi, in 1893, said to have been the wealthiest man in North Mississippi In 1893 Dr. Wright had three sons, two of whom were in Birmingham, Alabama, where he had large investments, and one daughter in school

II—Eliza Steen, a daughter of John Steen who married a Miss Jeffries, was born in South Carolina and brought up in her father's home She was married to Archibald Stratton, who drowned himself — family taint of insanity

III—Dorcas Steen, a daughter of John Steen who married a Miss Jeffries, was born in South Carolina She was married to a Mr Dean, and removed to Texas.

IV—Sarah Steen, a daughter of John Steen who married Miss Jeffries, was born in South Carolina, in 1819 She was married to a Mr. Pearce, and lives in Rankin County, Mississippi They have two sons, who are thrifty men

V.—Lucretia Steen, a daughter of John Steen who married Miss Jeffries, was born in South Carolina She was married to a Mr Harrison, and lives in Texas.

VI—Cyrena Steen, a daughter of John Steen who married Miss Jeffries, was born in South Carolina She was married to a Mr Dear, and lives in Texas

VII—Mary Ann Steen, called "Polly," a daughter of John Steen who married Miss Jeffries, was born in South Carolina She was married to a Mr Lane, and has two children living in Texas

1 Steen Lane
2 Merritt Lane

VIII—John Vance Steen, the eighth and youngest child of John Steen who married Miss Jeffries, and a grandson of William and Nancy Lusk Steen, was born near the Great Broad River, in South Carolina. April 29, 1811   He was a moderately successful merchant for fifty-five years, and afterwards retired to his small farm   He was a devoted Christian and member of the Baptist Church   He wrote his family history in 1891 John V Steen was married in Greensboro, Mississippi, August 23, 1843, to Elizabeth ————, and brought up a family of children, whom he has educated and taught to succeed

1 Lorenzo Asa Steen, the eldest son of John Vance and Elizabeth Steen, was born in Greensboro, Mississippi, January 29, 1851, and died February 26, 1863, aged 12 years

2 John Vance Steen, Jr, the second son of John Vance and Elizabeth Steen, was born in Greensboro, Mississippi, February 6, 1853

3 Inez Loraine Steen, the third child and eldest daughter of John V and Elizabeth Steen, was born in Greensboro, Mississippi, May 28. 1855, and died November 20, 1855

4 Clarence Vance Steen, the fourth child and third son of John V. and Elizabeth Steen, was born in Greensboro, Mississippi, September 23, 1856 and died May 11, 1875, in the 19th year of his age.

5 Loraine Heman Steen, the fifth child and fourth son of John V and Elizabeth Steen, was born in Greensboro, Mississippi, April 29, 1862

6 Eoline Magnolia Steen, the sixth child and second daughter of John Vance and Elizabeth Steen, was born in Greensboro, Mississippi, November 20, 1864, and died September 22, ——

CHAPTER II.

Mary Steen, called Polly," the second child and eldest daughter of William and Nancy Lusk Steen, was born in South Carolina, near the Great Broad River, about 1776, and died about 1778, during the Revolutionary War, when her father was very severely wounded

CHAPTER III

James Steen, the third child and second son of William and
Nancy Lusk Steen, was born near the Great Broad River, in
Union District, South Carolina, October 29, 1781   He was married February 5 1809, to Sarah Collins, she having been born
November 1, 1788   About 1814 they removed to Mississippi, and
were among the first settlers in Lawrence County, where they
brought up their family and acquired considerable property   It
is said that when he died, in 1843 or 1844 James Steen was the
largest slave-owner in his county   To James and Sarah Steen
were born eleven children, as follows

I —Melissa Steen, the eldest daughter of James and Sarah Steen,
was born in Union District, South Carolina, March 22, 1810
She was married in Lawrence County, Mississippi, to Samuel
Prestridge, and brought up a family
  1 Major James Prestridge, of Memphis, Tennessee, is one of
their children

II —Necysia Steen the second daughter of James and Sarah
Steen, was born in Union District, South Carolina, October
11, 1811   She was married in Lawrence County, Mississippi,
to Fleet Cooper

III —Perimela Steen, the third daughter of James and Sarah
Steen, was born in Union District, South Carolina, August 13,
1813   She was married in Lawrence County, Mississippi, first
to G C Maxwell, and again to William Brewer

IV —Cynthia Steen, the fourth daughter of James and Sarah
Steen, was born in Lawrence County, Mississippi, February 5,
1816   She was married first to D D Cummings and a second
time to T W Wilson

V —Miles Charles Steen, the fifth child and eldest son of James
and Sarah Steen, was born in Lawrence County, Mississippi,
October 7, 1817   He was married about 1839 to Louvice
Prestridge, to whom were born three children   She died in
1844   He was married a second time to a Miss Johnson, to
whom were born also three children   Miles C Steen died in
Arkansas in 1861   He was the father of six children, as follows

1. Melvina Steen, daughter of M. C. and L. P. Steen, was born about 1840, and died.

2. Infant son of M. C. and L. P. Steen was born about 1841, and died.

3. James Steen, the third child of M. C. and L. P. Steen, was born in Lawrence County, Mississippi, April 9, 1843—a farmer. He was married in Rockport, Mississippi, January 11, 1871, to Nancy Josephine Nix, she having been born in Copiah County, Mississippi, March 29, 1852. To them were born in Simpson County, Mississippi, the following children. Residence, Rockport, Mississippi.

  I.—Miles C. Steen was born February 6, 1874.

  II.—Ella J. Steen was born November 28, 1875.

  III.—Samuel J. Steen was born June 1, 1878.

  IV.—Alice M. Steen was born August 11, 1880.

  V.—Estes Steen was born December 19, 1881.

  VI.—Hattie E. Steen was born June 19, 1885.

  VII.—John Steen was born November 27, 1886.

  VIII.—Silas F. Steen was born February 5, 1888.

  IX.—Lee Devon Steen was born May 5, 1892.

4. F. E. M. Steen, the fourth child of Miles C. Steen and the eldest by his second wife, was born about 1854.

5. A. J. Steen was born about 1858.

6. Silas A. Steen was born about 1860.

VI.—Nellie C. Steen, the sixth child and fifth daughter of James and Sarah Steen, was born in Lawrence County, Mississippi, May 9, 1819. She was married to T. W. Wilson.

VII.—Nancy Jane Steen, the seventh child and sixth daughter of James and Sarah Steen, was born in Lawrence County, Mississippi, April 11, 1821. She was married to Addison Whitworth.

VIII.—Clarke C. Steen, the eighth child and second son of James and Sarah Steen, was born in Lawrence County, Mississippi, March 5, 1823, and died April 6, 1823.

IX.—Sarah Ann Steen, the ninth child and seventh daughter of James and Sarah Steen, was born in Lawrence County, Mississippi, June 17, 1824. She was married to W. S. Mullen.

X —John Augustus Steen the tenth child and third son of James and Sarah Steen, was born in Lawrence County, Mississippi. December 15, 1826   He was married to Patience Mullen

XI —William Davis Steen, the eleventh child and fourth son of James and Sarah Steen, was born in Lawrence County, Mississippi, May 27, 1829   He was married December 27. 1855, to Elizabeth Prestridge, she having been born April 2, 1837   To them were born five children

1   John Watson Steen, the eldest son of William D. and Elizabeth P Steen, was born January 3, 1858   He was married March 4, 1891, to India Anna Janes, she having been born December 6, 1869   Residence, Monticello, Mississippi

I —Pleasant LaFayette Steen, son of John W and India A. Steen, was born February 28, 1892

2   Silas William Steen, the second son of William D and Elizabeth P Steen, was born March 10, 1860   Residence, Monticello, Mississippi

3   Robert Steen the third son of William D and Elizabeth P Steen, was born March 7, 1862   He was married March 5, 1885, to Elizabeth Herrington, she having been born November 16, 1867   To them were born the following children   Residence, Monticello, Mississippi

I —Ada Steen was born April 25, 1886

II —Lorena Steen was born January 26, 1889

III —Victoria Steen was born October 14, 1890

IV —Alice Steen was born February 24, 1892

4   Emma Steen the fourth child and eldest daughter of William D and Elizabeth P Steen, was born November 28, 1863   She was married December 24, 1888, to Napoleon Hubbard Maxwell, he having been born March 5, 1861   To them was born one child

I —Elizabeth D Maxwell was born November 2, 1889

5   Elizabeth Steen, the second daughter and youngest child of William D and Elizabeth P Steen, was born September 3, 1865   Residence, Monticello Mississippi

CHAPTER IV

Sarah Steen called ' Sallie," a daughter of William and Nancy Lusk Steen, was born near the Great Broad River, in South Carolina, in 1783, and removed with her parents to Tennessee when that young State began to come into prominence   She was married in Tennessee to Thompson Enochs a son of Enoch and Lydia Enochs, and continued to reside in Carroll County, Tennessee   Sarah Steen Enochs was the mother of twelve children, and has left a numerous posterity   One of her children was Miles Enochs who married and had one child, named Francis Enochs, who never married, and died in 1867, worth over $120,-000   Edgar Enochs, who lives in Benela, Calhoun County, Mississippi, strongly resembles the old Steen family   He was a Mexican War veteran, was for many years the sheriff of that county, was twice a member of the Mississippi Legislature, was a Major in the Fourth Mississippi Regiment in the Civil War, and has a large family   Two sons of Sarah Steen Enochs still reside in Carroll County, Tennessee — Gabriel and Isaac Enochs and one son of the latter, Dr William Enochs, is a popular physician in Jackson, Tennessee

CHAPTER V.

Nathaniel Steen, son of William and Nancy Lusk Steen, was born in South Carolina, near the Great Broad River, about 1786 He was married and removed from Lawrence to Madison County, Mississippi, where he died   He had two sons, and at last accounts a granddaughter of his, Mrs Ella McWright, was living at Glenmora, Louisiana

I.—Thomas Jefferson Steen a son of Nathaniel Steen, and a grandson of William and Nancy Lusk Steen was born and lived in Mississippi   During the Civil War he became a Major General in the Western Division of the Confederate Army.

The old people used to say that when he was a boy, no more three breakneck boys ever lived than he and his two cousins William C Enochs and Levi Noble, who also became a Major General in the Trans-Mississippi Department of the Western Army of the Confederate States   There was no form of break-neck fun that these boys would not undertake   Captain Enochs writes as follows

"Imagine Uncle Robert s butting ram, well trained by them! Sunday morning comes · lots are cast as to who shall have the post of honor, when the ram is to get the worst of it My mother's rice pot is stolen out of the kitchen for a helmet, and the trap is set for his royal sheepship, who is cautiously driven into the snare   The fortunate champion is squatted on all fours, with the pot well wadded with moss, where it pressed upon the hero's shoulders   The plot thickens, and the pro-pitious moment comes   Ram-y sees something worth butting Bim! ! Aunt Polly's rice pot is in a hundred pieces, and a limber champion in the lane , but his head was too hard for the pot, or the ram's horns   Life comes back into him, and two wars since then have found him in the thickest of the fight, and nine years have been added to his allotted time "

II —Nathan Steen, a son of Nathaniel Steen, was born and brought up in Mississippi and was said to have been killed by a negro

CHAPTER VI

Elias Steen, son of William and Nancy Lusk Steen was born in South Carolina, near the Great Broad River, March 3, 1779, and died in Rankin County, Mississippi, February 13, 1847, in the 68th year of his age   He removed with the rest of his father's family into Tennessee, and thence on to Rankin County Missis-sippi, about 1814, when about thirty-five years of age   He was married in Lawrence County, Mississippi, February 18, 1818, to Elizabeth Smith, she having been born May 11, 1801, and died in Rankin County, Mississippi, December 14, 1864, in the 64th year of her age   To them were born eleven children, as follows

I —Isaac Steen, the eldest son of Elias and Elizabeth Steen was born in Rankin County Mississippi, January 15, 1819 He was a Captain in the Confederate Army during the Civil War, and afterwards a thrifty farmer in the Guadalupe Valley, in Texas He was married to a Miss Rucker, and is said to have an interesting family

II —William Steen the second son of Isaac and Elizabeth Steen, was born in Rankin County, Mississippi, April 20, 1821 He was married to Martha Dear. Both are dead, but they have one son, a prosperous farmer, now living in Simpson County, Mississippi

III —Melissa Steen, the third child and eldest daughter of Elias and Elizabeth Steen, was born in Rankin County Mississippi, January 22, 1823

IV —Nancy Jane Steen, the fourth child and second daughter of Elias and Elizabeth Steen, was born in Rankin County, Mississippi, May 24, 1825

V —Nathaniel H Steen, the fifth child and third son of Elias and Elizabeth Steen, was born in Rankin County, Mississippi, August 14, 1827 He was married to Elizabeth Pringle To them were born two daughters

  1 Mrs Ward Russell

  2 Mrs Nevil Smith, who has one son

VI —Eliza Louisa Steen, the sixth child and third daughter of Elias and Elizabeth Steen was born in Rankin County, Mississippi, November 7, 1829

VII —Isam R Steen the seventh child and fourth son of Elias and Elizabeth Steen, was born in Rankin County, Mississippi, December 13, 1831

VIII —Asenith Steen, the eighth child and fourth daughter of Elias and Elizabeth Steen, was born in Rankin County, Mississippi, December 13 1834 She was married to William P Dear, and has a large family still living in Rankin County, Mississippi

IX —Mary Ann Steen, the ninth child and fifth daughter of Elias and Elizabeth Steen, was born in Rankin County, Mississippi, February 9, 1837 She was married to a Mr Byrd — a farmer — living in Simpson County, Mississippi.

X —Elias Estes Steen, the tenth child and fifth son of Elias and
Elizabeth Steen, was born in Rankin County, Mississippi,
December 27, 1839   He was married to a Miss Scarborough,
went to Texas, and died there, leaving four children, two of
whom are dead

XI —Silas V. Steen, the eleventh child and sixth son of Elias and
Elizabeth Steen, was born in Rankin County, Mississippi,
November 23, 1842

CHAPTER VII

Robert Steen, a son of William and Nancy Lusk Steen, was
born in South Carolina, near the Great Broad River, about 1781
He removed with his parents into Carroll County, Tennessee,
and from thence to Rankin County, Mississippi, where he spent
the remainder of his life   He was for many years, and until his
death, sheriff of Rankin County, Mississippi   He was married to
Malony Hollingsworth   To them were born several children,
whose names are given   but not in the order of birth, for that is
unknown to the writer

I —Lucietia Steen, who married Vincent Harrison   They lived
together several years, and died in Freestone County, Texas
Their children reside in Texas
  1 George Harrison lives in Cotton Gin, Texas
  2 Mary Harrison, who married Dr John Headley, and lives in
Cotton Gin, Texas
  3. Amanda Harrison, who married John Hallan, and died

II —Cyrena Eleanor Steen was born in Rankin County, Mississippi, November 18 1833, and died in Stay, Louisiana, May 22
1898, in the 65th year of her age   She was married in Rankin
County, Mississippi, November 21, 1850, to Capt Darling
Pinkney Morris — a farmer — he having been born in Lawrence County, Mississippi, March 9, 1829   In 1857 they
removed to Winn Parish, Louisiana, where they afterwards
resided, and where Mr Morris still (1900) resides at Stay,
Louisiana   To them were born eight children, as follows

1 Silas Lawrence Morris, the eldest child of Capt. Darling P
and Cyrena E Steen Morris was born in Rankin County,
Mississippi, July 31, 1854, and brought up in Winn Parish,
Louisiana, to which place his parents had removed in 1857
In 1876 he entered Mississippi College, afterwards attended
Soule's Business College, in New Orleans, and in 1878
removed to Texas He was converted at the age of sixteen
years, and ordained a Baptist clergyman before he reached
his majority In 1881 he entered the Senior class in Waco
University, deferred his graduation but was unanimously
elected an alumnus He was pastor of a Baptist church in
Louisiana before he came to Texas He served the churches
of Cow Bayou, Beulah, New Zion, and in 1882 became pastor of the church in Marlin, Texas The next year he was
appointed financial agent of Waco University, and secured
an endowment of $60,000 He was for a time editor of ' The
Home and Sunday School,' a religious newspaper In 1886
he purchased "The Guardian," a Baptist monthly magazine,
which he still continues to edit and publish, at Waco, Texas,
being ably assisted in the work by his accomplished wife
Rev. Silas L Morris was married in 1879 to Mary J Davis,
of Robertson County, Texas, who died soon afterwards He
was married a second time April 30, 1885, to Hallie Byrd
Burleson, only daughter of the Rev Dr Rufus C and
Georgia Burleson, she having been born in Waco, Texas
September 3, 1865 She was graduated from Waco University in 1883, of which institution her father is now (1900) and
has been since 1861, its honored President Residence,
Waco, Texas To the Rev Silas L. and Hallie B Morris
were born four children, two of whom died in infancy
Those now living are as follows

I —Georgia Lene Morris was born in Waco, Texas, February 28, 1886

II —Silas Lawrence Morris Jr , was born in Waco, Texas,
April 24, 1889

2 Margaret Ellen Morris the second child and eldest daughter of Capt Darling P and Cyrena E Steen Morris was
born in Rankin County, Mississippi, December 15, 1856, and
died in Winn Parish, Louisiana September 10 1860, in the
fourth year of her age

(15)

3 Nathan David Morris, the third child and second son of
Capt Darling P and Cyrena E Steen Morris, was born in
Winn Parish, Louisiana, August 7, 1859 He was married
in Grant Parish, Louisiana, September 14, 1879, to Margaret S Storks, she having been born in Grant Parish, Louisiana, August 8, 1862   Residence, Zion, Winn Parish,
Louisiana To them were born the following seven children·

I —Silas Nathan Morris was born September 4, 1880

II —Margaret D. Morris was born July 12, 1883

III —William Burleson Morris was born February 25, 1886

IV —David Pinkney Morris was born September 2, 1889

V —George Storks Morris was born June 26, 1892

VI —Nancy Ann Morris was born July 5, 1895

VII —Mary Ola Morris was born July 27, 1899

4 Rebecca Ida Morris, the fourth child and second daughter
of Capt Darling P and Cyrena E Steen Morris, was born
in Winn Parish, Louisiana, April 23, 1861   She was married
to Thomas Washington Barton, in 1881, he having been
born in 1859 and died December 28, 1887, aged 28 years
To this marriage were born five children   Mrs Rebecca
Ida Barton was married a second time in 1889 to Thomas
Graham Bell, he having been born November 6, 1862   Residence, Stay, Louisiana   The following are the children of
Mrs R Ida Bell

I —Benjamin Pinkney Barton was born March 6, 1883

II. —Earley Materson Barton was born April 17, 1884

III —D Thomas Barton was born April 17, 1884

IV —William Carroll Barton was born February 13, 1886

V —Silas Edward Barton was born March 4, 1888

VI —John Graham Bell was born July 27, 1890

VII —Houston Steen Bell was born March 7, 1892.

VIII —Darling Baldridge Bell was born April 15, 1893

IX —Margaret Elizabeth Bell was born December 18, 1894

X —Kate Bell was born September 18, 1896

XI —Milton Morris Bell was born February 18, 1898, and
died October 1, 1898

XII —Drew Oscar Bell was born August 1, 1899

5 William Morris, the fifth child and third son of Capt Darling
   P and Cyrena E Steen Morris, was born August 22 1865, in
   Winn Parish, Louisiana, and died in Waco, Texas, March 13,
   1886, in the 21st year of his age

6 Houston Steen Morris, the sixth child and fourth son of
   Capt Darling P and Cyrena E Steen Morris, was born in
   Winn Parish, Louisiana, in 1868   He was married in Grant
   Parish, Louisiana, January 13, 1895, to Amanda Antoinette
   Tony   Residence, Flagon, Louisiana   To H Steen and
   Amanda H Morris were born the following children

   I —Era Lucile Morris was born October 17, 1895 and died
      June 30, 1896

   II —William Lee Morris was born January 13, 1898, and
      died January 18, 1899

   III —Eva Eugenia Morris was born August 28, 1899

7 Julia Ann Cyrena Morris, the seventh child and third daughter of Capt Darling P and Cyrena E Steen Morris, was
   born in Winn Parish, Louisiana, August 15, 1871.   She was
   married at Stay, Louisiana, January 24 1900, to Elisha S
   Murrell, he having been born in Grant Parish, Louisiana,
   January 13, 1873   He was brought up on his father's farm,
   became a clerk and bookkeeper, and is now a prosperous
   business man, and the postmaster at Flagon, Grant Parish,
   Louisiana

8 Darling O Morris the eighth child, the fifth and youngest
   son of Capt Darling P and Cyrena Eleanor Steen Morris,
   was born in Winn Parish, Louisiana, February 9, 1873   He
   was married November 22, 1894, to Arlevia Walker, she
   having been born April 25, 1878   Residence, Stay, Winn
   Parish, Louisiana   To them were born the following children

   I —Henry Etter Morris was born October 18, 1895

   II —Ruthy Gertrude Morris was born November 11, 1896,
      and died July 3, 1897

   III —Bonnie Rene Morris was born November 21, 1897

   IV —Huey Houston Morris was born July 18 1899

III —Emma Steen, a daughter of Robert Steen, was married to
   Robert Stratton   They have two children living in Johnston
   County, Texas

1 Robert Stratton
2 Emma Stratton Tilletson

IV.—Sarah Steen, a daughter of Robert Steen, married a Mr
Pierce, and died   They have one son
1 Bradford Pierce, who lives at Steen's Creek, Mississippi

V.—Dorcas Hollingsworth Steen, a daughter of Robert Steen,
was born April 22, 1822   She was married to Thomas Hamilton Deen, August 25, 1846, and died   Mr Deen lives in Hamilton, Texas   The following are the children of Thomas H
and Dorcas H Steen Deen
1 Malona Deen was born July 5, 1847, and died April 18, 1867,
in the 20th year of her age
2 Elizabeth Deen was born April 22, 1849, and died October
5, 1876, in the 28th year of her age
3 Araminta Deen was born October 5, 1851, and died October
26, 1868, aged 17 years and 21 days
4. William Redwine Deen was born September 23, 1853, and
died December 4, 1857, in the 5th year of his age
5 Alice Solome Deen was born January 19, 1857, and died
December 11, 1857, aged nearly eleven months
6 Frederick Pierce Deen was born March 26, 1859   Residence Pottsville, Hamilton County, Texas

VI.—Silas Lusk Steen, a son of Robert Steen, married Margaret
Butler, and was sheriff of Rankin County, Mississippi, after
his father   They had seven children, only three of whom are
now living.
1 Susan E Steen who married a Mr Pierce, and lives at
Steen's Creek, Mississippi
2 Sarah Pierce Steen, who married a Mr Dun, and lives at
Glenmora, Louisiana
3 Silas Wright Steen, who lives at Rayne Station, Louisiana

VII.—Mary Jane Steen, a daughter of Robert Steen married
Hansford Lane, and lived and died at Steen's Creek, Mississippi

VIII—Isaac Hollingsworth Steen, a son of Robert Steen, was
born in Rankin County, Mississippi, May 5, 1826, and died in
Hamilton, Texas February 21, 1881, in the 55th year of his
age   He was a man of influence, and County Clerk of Hamilton County, Texas, from 1862, until his death, in 1881, except
two years   He was married, about 1854, to Frances A. F.
Anderson, who died soon afterwards   He was married a second time in Freestone County, Texas, to Amanda Elizabeth
Lewis, who died November 16, 1891   To them were born the
following ten children

1   Silas Lusk Steen, the eldest son of Isaac H and Amanda E.
    Steen, was born in Freestone County, Texas, March 10,
    1856, and died in infancy

2   Lewis Vincent Steen, the second son of Isaac H   and
    Amanda E Steen, was born in Freestone County, Texas,
    February 8, 1858 — a farmer   He was married in Hico,
    Hamilton County, Texas, in September, 1880, to Emma
    Alford   Residence Hamilton, Texas   To them were born,
    in Hamilton, Texas, the following children

    I —Ida Elona Steen was born in 1881, and died in infancy

    II —Percy Valcour Steen was born in 1884

    III —Amanda Steen was born about 1886, and died in
        infancy

    IV —Lydia Steen was born about 1888

    V —Nellie Eleanor Steen was born about 1890

    VI —Robert Owen Steen was born about 1892

    VII —Louis Vincent Steen was born about 1894

3   Thomas Pierce Steen the third son of Isaac H and Amanda
    E Steen, was born in Limestone County, Texas, March 2,
    1860 — a clerk   He was married in Hamilton County,
    Texas, September 1, 1881, to Annie Elizabeth Grigsby
    Residence, Pottsville, Texas   To them were born the fol-
    lowing children

    I —Carl T Steen was born July 7, 1882

    II.—Festus A Steen was born December 28, 1884

    III —Homer Steen was born December 29, 1889

    IV —Minnie Ruth Steen was born May 8, 1893

    V —Lottie Fola Steen was born June 26, 1895

4 John Virgil Steen, the fourth son of Isaac H and Amanda
   E Steen, was born in Hamilton County, Texas, March 6,
   1863   He was married at Babb's Bridge, Louisiana, January
   5, 1890, to Ida Lillian Dun   Residence, Glenmora, Louisiana   To them were born the following children

   I —Wiley Hollingsworth Steen was born in Hamilton,
   Texas, March 24, 1891

   II —Calvin Pierce Steen was born in Hamilton, Texas, January 21, 1893

   III —William Oliver Steen was born in Hamilton, Texas,
   September 26, 1894, and died in Glenmora, Louisiana,
   January 21, 1897

   IV —Minnie Annan Steen was born in Glenmora, Louisiana,
   September 1, 1897

5 Malony Jane Steen, the fifth child and eldest daughter of
   Isaac A and Amanda E Steen was born in Hamilton
   County, Texas, November 5, 1865   She was married in
   August, 1885, at Hico Texas, to John H Taylor, a mer-
   chant   Residence Hamilton Texas   To them were born,
   in Hamilton, Texas, the following children

   I —Jessie Lee Taylor was born October 20. 1886

   II —Minnie Eleanor Taylor was born January 30, 1889

   III —Alice Etoile Taylor was born August 17, 1891

   IV —W F Taylor was born December 15, 1897

6 Minnie Aurelia Steen, the sixth child and second daughter
   of Isaac H and Amanda E Steen, was born in Hamilton,
   Texas, December 24, 1868   She was married at the same
   place in July, 1880 to James R Miller — a clerk   To them
   were born the following children, the first four at Gentry's
   Mill, Texas. and the last one at Hamilton, Texas, where they
   all now reside

   I —Robert Benard Miller was born July 12, 1890

   II —Warner Steen Miller was born May 25, 1892, and died
   October 30, 1898

   III —Rodger Henderson Miller was born May 7, 1894

   IV —Malony Margaret Miller was born June 7, 1896

   I' —Andrew Miller was born February 5, 1899

7 William Morris Steen, the seventh child and fifth son of Isaac H and Amanda E Steen, was born in Hamilton Texas December 21, 1871 — a cattle man Residence Endee, New Mexico

8 Robert Lot Steen, the eighth child and sixth son of Isaac H. and Amanda E Steen, was born in Hamilton, Texas November 1, 1874 — a saddler Residence, Hamilton, Texas

9 Isaac Mills Steen, the ninth child and seventh son of Isaac H and Amanda E Steen, was born in Hamilton Texas May 18, 1877 He was married at Gentry's Mill, Texas, in September, 1898, to Ora Kendall To them was born the following

I.—Charles Edwin Steen was born July 20, 1899

10 Charles Rupert Steen the tenth child and eighth son of Isaac II and Amanda E Steen, was born in Hamilton, Texas, March 9, 1880 Residence, Hamilton, Texas

CHAPTER VIII

William Steen, a son of William and Nancy Lusk Steen, was born in South Carolina, near the Great Broad River, and near the line between North and South Carolina, in February, 1783 He was a farmer by occupation He removed with his father's family first to Carroll County, Tennessee, where his father died Afterwards, with his mother and all her children, except three, he went into Lawrence County, Mississippi, and not long afterwards settled in Rankin County, Mississippi, among its early inhabitants William Steen was married in Carroll County, Tennessee, in 1811, to Mary R Enochs, a daughter of Enoch and Lydia Enochs she having been born in 1792, and died in Rankin County, Mississippi, August 19, 1846 After the death of his wife, William Steen and all his children then living, married and unmarried, nine in number, started, October 30, 1846, to remove to DeWitt County, Texas He was taken sick on the way, and died soon after reaching Texas, at the residence of his brother-

in-law, Levi Noble, in Nacogdoches C H   He was buried in the
old North Churchyard, about four miles from Nacogdoches
Two of his sons afterwards returned to Rankin County, Mississippi, where they continued to live   William and Mary R Steen
were earnest and devout Christians, and brought up their family
in the fear of the Lord   To them were born, in Rankin County,
Mississippi fourteen children, as follows

I —Cyrena Steen, the eldest daughter, was born February 10.
1812, and died September 30, 1824, in the 13th year of her age.

II —Asanath Steen, the second daughter of William and Mary R.
Steen, was born February 11, 1814   She was married in 1838
to Elisha Stephens, and brought up a large family of children
One son, James Stephens, died in the hospital at Nashville,
Tennessee, in 1862   Family residence, Cairo, Texas

III —Miles Steen, the third child and eldest son of William and
Mary R Steen, was born August 26, 1815, and died August
21, 1834, in the 19th year of his age

IV —Carroll Jeffries Steen, the fourth child and second son of
William and Mary R Steen, was born November 29, 1816 and
died from pneumonia at his residence, near Cato Rankin
County, Mississippi, January 2 1897 aged 80 years, 3 months
and 4 days   He was a prosperous farmer, an earnest Christian, and an influential citizen   He was married at the residence of the bride's parents, six miles east of Jackson, Mississippi, October 8 1846, to Margaret Ann Neely a daughter of
Thomas and Katherine Neely, she having been born at Silver
Creek, Simpson County, Mississippi, February 5, 1826, and
died at their home, near Cato Mississippi, November 28, 1892,
in the 67th year of her age   She was a devoted Christian a
granddaughter of Jacob Neely a soldier in the Revolutionary
War who was slightly wounded in the battle of King's Mountain, October 7, 1780, and assisted in the rescue of William
Steen, who had been captured by the British   To Carroll J
and Margaret A Steen were born the following ten children

1 Mary Catherine Steen, the eldest daughter was born in
Rankin County Mississippi, March 9, 1850   She was married at the same place by the Rev Loder Price, August 5,
1869 to Jeremiah Porter Russell, a prosperous farmer, he

having been born in Rankin County, Mississippi April 25, 1839 To them were born thirteen children, as follows:

I —Infant daughter—

II —Infant daughter—

twin children, born July 22 1870, and died

III —Carroll Steen Russell was born November 28, 1871, and died

IV —Charles Enoch Russell was born November 28, 1873

V —Margaret Rachel Russell was born October 4, 1875

VI —Mary Bertha Russell was born April 20 1877

VII —Sarah Catherine Russell was born October 24, 1878

VIII —Jeremiah Porter Russell was born April 20, 1880

IX —Lora Lee Russell was born March 4, 1882

X —Kathleen Russell was born December 17, 1874

XI —Myrtle Anne Russell was born April 29, 1887

XII —Wallace Gallow Russell was born April 23 1889

XIII. —Thomas Jeffries Russell was born May 6, 1891

2 Sarah Cathleen Steen, the second daughter of Carroll J and Margaret A Steen, was born in Rankin County, Mississippi, October 14, 1851 She was married by the Rev Daniel Giddens, November 24, 1870 to Christopher Columbus Russell, an industrious and successful farmer, he having been born seven miles east of Brandon Rankin County, Mississippi, December 5, 1846 To them were born the following five children, all born in the same house

I —Robert Edmund Lee Russell was born January 9, 1872

II —Christopher Columbus Russell was born November 30 1873

III —Maud Ethleen Russell was born March 29 1877

IV —Carroll Steen Russell was born June 20 1879

V —John Clarence Russell was born July 26, 1882

3 Narcissa Jane Steen, the third daughter of Carroll J and Margaret A Steen, was born March 31, 1853 She was married by the Rev R W Hall, October 8, 1872 to Alexander Price, he having been born in Cumberland County, North Carolina March 20, 1841 To them were born,

twelve miles south of Brandon, Rankin County, Mississippi, the following nine children

I —Henry Thomas Price was born June 30, 1873, and died March 30, 1875

II —James Jeffries Price was born November 18, 1874, and died November 7, 1878

III —Percy Alexander Price was born August 30, 1876

IV —Robert Harris Price was born September 19, 1878

V —Andrew Jerome Price was born January 10, 1881

VI —Margaret Annie Price was born November 10, 1882

VII —Rosa Lee Price was born January 14, 1885

VIII —Florence Jackson Price was born April 3, 1887

IX —Carricles Price was born May 27, 1889

4 Rosa Ann Steen, the fourth daughter of Carroll J and Margaret A Steen, was born July 23, 1855 She was married by the Rev R W Hall, October 8, 1873, to Absalom May — a farmer — he having been born in Simpson County Mississippi, February 3, 1850 and died at his home October 11, 1888, in the 39th year of his age To Absalom and Rosa Ann Steen May were born the following eight children, all born in the same house, ten miles south of Brandon, Rankin County, Mississippi

I—Carroll Benton May—

II —James Neely May—

  twin children, were born September 4, 1874

III —Jeremiah Russell May was born August 12, 1876

IV —Ximena May was born January 10, 1878

V —Edna May was born July 18, 1879

VI —Enoch Absalom May was born August 23, 1881

VII —Rena May was born October 27, 1883

VIII —Margaret May was born July 23, 1888

5 Virginia Adaline Steen, the fifth daughter of Carroll J and Margaret A Steen, was born May 25, 1857 She was married by the Rev R W Hall, February 6, 1878 to Hugh Alonzo Walker, a prosperous farmer, he having been born near Silver Creek, Simpson County, Mississippi, October 25, 1857 To them one child was born, in 1879, and died in infancy, without a name They then adopted Jane Cun-

ningham, who was born in 1879, a daughter of John and Jane Cunningham, who came from Ireland, and whose mother died when she was nine days old John Cunningham, the child's father, now lives in Texas He knew many of the Steens in Ireland before he came to this country The residence of Mr and Mrs Hugh A Walker is near Mount Zion, Simpson County, Mississippi

6 Martha Ethleen Steen, the sixth daughter of Carroll J and Margaret A Steen, was born October 8, 1859 She was married by the Rev P H Bilbro, February 6, 1883 to James Osborn Trawick, a farmer, a son of Osborn and Mary Trawick, ne having been born near Pelahatchee, Rankin County, Mississippi February 22, 1861 To them were born the following four children

I—Mary Trawick was born near Cato, Rankin County, Mississippi, February 1, 1884

II—Margaret Pearce Trawick was born near Linwood, Rankin County, Mississippi, August 10, 1885

III—Rosabel Trawick was born near Linwood, Rankin County, Mississippi, December 19, 1886

IV—Mittie Elizabeth Agleen Trawick was born near Linwood, Rankin County, Mississippi, July 1, 1890

7 Margaret Jackson Steen, the seventh daughter of Carroll J and Margaret A Steen, was born September 10, 1861, and died July 24 1863

8 Ximena Steen, the eighth daughter of Carroll J and Margaret A Steen was born in Rankin County, Mississippi, May 22, 1863, and died November 8, 1888, in the 26th year of her age She was a devout, faithful and useful Christian, having united with the Baptist Church at the age of sixteen years She was married by the Rev J P Hemley, March 19, 1885, to the Rev James Rhesa Johnston, a Baptist clergyman, he having been born in Simpson County, Mississippi, December 22, 1858 To them was born one child, as follows·

I—George Carroll Johnston was born at the residence of his grandfather, Carroll J. Steen near Cato, and twelve miles south of Brandon, Rankin County, Mississippi, January 26, 1886

9 Annie Lee Steen, the ninth daughter of Carroll J and Margaret A Steen, was born in Rankin County, Mississippi, June 7, 1865 She was married by her brother-in-law, the Rev James R Johnston, October 4 1888, to the Rev Joseph Edwin Barnett. a Baptist clergyman, he having been born in Rankin County Mississippi April 24, 1864 To them were born the following children

I —Louise Powell Barnett was born in Tate County, Mississippi, July 19, 1889

II —Annie Steen Barnett was born in Arkabutla. Tate County, Mississippi, September 8 1890

10 William Thomas Enoch Steen, the tenth and youngest child and the only son of Carroll Jeffries and Margaret Ann Neely Steen, was born near Cato, Rankin County, Mississippi, twelve miles south of Brandon, November 3 1871 — a farmer Residence, near Cato, Mississippi

V —Campbell Steen. the fifth child and third son of William and Mary R Steen, was born April 18, 1818, and died December 16, 1841, in the 24th year of his age

VI —Sarah Ann Steen, the sixth child and third daughter of William and Mary R Steen, was born April 28 1820 She was married in 1842 to Joseph Stephens. and brought up a large family They were prosperous and well-to-do people Residence. Gonzales Texas

VII —Nancy Agnes Steen, the seventh child and fourth daughter of William and Mary R Steen, was born in Rankin County, Mississippi, December 16, 1822 She was married in 1846, to Alexander Stephens, and brought up a large family of children.

VIII —Narcissa Steen, the eight child and fifth daughter of William and Mary R Steen, was born in Rankin County, Mississippi, January 15, 1824 She was married in De Witt County, Texas, August 7, 1851, to John Henry Stephens a wholesale dealer in beef and cattle Residence, Kansas City, Missouri To them were born the following children

1 Mary Eliza Stephens was born January 11 1853

2 Susannah Stephens was born May 26, 1854

3 Josephine Stephens was born July 16 1861 Residence, Kansas City, Missouri

IX.—John Remley Steen, the ninth child and fourth son of William and Mary R Steen, was born in Rankin County, Mississippi, October 30 1825, and removed to Texas in 1846, when he was 21 years of age   He is now a prosperous farmer, residing near Hockheim, De Witt County, Texas   He was married in Gonzales County Texas, April 14, 1850, to Mahala Burkett To them were born thirteen children, as follows

1 James Polk Steen, the eldest son of John R and Mahala Steen was born in Gonzales County, Texas, February 9, 1851.

2 Mary Virginia Steen, the second child and eldest daughter of John R and Mahala Steen, was born in Gonzales County, Texas June 15, 1852   She was married August 15, 1869 to Dr Charles Champion, and after his death, to a Mr Williams   She is the mother of three children, as follows Residence, Hockheim, De Witt County, Texas

I—Ulpian Steen Champion was born August 25, 1872

II—Spurgeon Williams was born August 28, 1878

III—Josephine Boardman Williams was born June 1 1880

3 Martha Adaline Steen, the third child and second daughter of John R and Mahala Steen, was born in Gonzales County, Texas, October 27 1853   She was married at the same place November 5, 1883, to F L Haynes   Residence, Hockheim, Texas   To them were born the following children

I—John Franklin Haynes was born near Hockheim Texas August 14, 1885, and died September 10, 1889

II—Samuel Parnassus Haynes was born October 1, 1888

4 Margaret Ann Steen, the fourth child and third daughter of John R and Mahala Steen, was born in Gonzales County Texas October 27, 1855   She was married August 16 1874 to Hiram G Brown, a traveling salesman for the Virginia Tobacco Company, he having been born in Rankin County, Mississippi August 4, 1853   Residence, Hye, Blanco County, Texas   To them were born the following six children

I—Mahala Ophelia Brown was born February 6 1876

II—George Redman Brown was born March 12, 1878, and died March 24, 1880

III —Beulah Belle Brown was born February 21, 1881

IV —Hiram Eugene Brown was born June 29, 1883

V —Edna Pearl Brown was born April 12, 1886

VI —John Steen Brown was born June 17, 1889

5 Sarah Boardman Steen the fifth child and fourth daughter of John R and Mahala Steen, was born in Gonzales County, Texas, April 29, 1857   She was married January 11, 1876, to L B Brown   Residence, near Hockheim, Texas

6 William David Steen, the sixth child and second son of John R and Mahala Steen was born in Gonzales County, Texas November 8, 1859   He was married in the same county February 18, 1884, to Louisa Cunningham, to whom three children were born   Residence, near Hockheim Texas

I.—Minnie May Steen, daughter of William D and Louisa Steen, was born December 25, 1884

II —Sidney David Steen, the second child and eldest son of William D and Louisa Steen, was born January 28, 1891

III —Clyde Clement Steen, the third child and second son of William D and Louisa Steen, was born December 19, 1891

7 Josephine Antoinette Steen, the seventh child and fifth daughter of John R and Mahala Steen, was born in Gonzales County, Texas March 30, 1861   She was married in the same place, February 6 1878, to J B North   Residence, Hockheim, Texas

8 John Henry Steen the eighth child and third son of John R and Mahala Steen, was born December 24 1862   He was married in Gonzales County, Texas, February 18, 1885, to Letitia Hock   Residence, Hockheim, Texas   To John H and Letitia Steen were born six children, as follows

I —Arthur Eugene Steen was born November 10, 1883

II —Claude Campbell Steen was born November 24, 1886, and died February 15, 1889

III —Sarah Boardman Steen was born September 20, 1888

IV —Margaret Elizabeth Steen was born April 5, 1890

V —Hiram Steen was born October 2 1891

VI —Cora May Steen was born January 8, 1893

9 Mahala Ophelia Steen, the ninth child and sixth daughter of
   John R and Mahala Steen, was born December 19, 1864
   She was married in Gonzales County, Texas, November 22,
   1888, to L A Johnston, Residence, Hockheim, Texas

10 Robert Enoch Steen, the tenth child and fourth son of
    John R and Mahala Steen, was born in Gonzales County,
    Texas August 26, 1867   Residence, Hockheim, Texas

11 Narcissa Champion Steen, the eleventh child and seventh
    daughter of John R and Mahala Steen, was born in Gon-
    zales County, Texas, February 11 1870

12 Benjamin Bartholomew Steen, the twelfth child and fifth
    son of John R and Mahala Steen, was born in Gonzales
    County, Texas December 21 1872   Residence, Hockheim
    Texas

13 Walter Eugene Steen, the thirteenth child and youngest
    son of John R and Mahala Steen, a grandson of William
    and Mary R Steen, and a great-grandson of William and
    Nancy Lusk Steen, was born in Gonzales County, Texas
    July 2, 1874   Residence, Hockheim, Texas

X —Irene Steen, the tenth child and sixth daughter of William
   and Mary R Steen, was born in Rankin County, Mississippi,
   March 18, 1827, and died April 15, 1834, aged 7 years and 28
   days

XI —William Steen, the eleventh child and fifth son of William
    and Mary R Steen and a grandson of William and Nancy
    Lusk Steen, was born in Rankin County, Mississippi, Novem-
    ber 25, 1829, and died in Gonzales County, Texas in 1862, in
    the 33d year of his age   In 1846, when 17 years old, he
    removed with his father's family to Texas, and resided near
    Gonzales until his death   He was by occupation a farmer
    He was married in Texas to a Miss Lusk, a distant relative,
    and brought up a family   One son survives

1 Henry Steen, a son of William and ——— Lusk Steen, was
   born in Gonzales County, Texas, and now resides in the
   northern part of the State

XII —Mary Steen, called "Polly," the twelfth child and seventh
    daughter of William and Mary R Steen was born in Rankin
    County, Mississippi, June 13, 1831 and died in Texas, unmar-
    ried, about June, 1852, aged 21 years

XIII —James Wiley Steen, the thirteenth child and sixth son of
William and Mary R Steen, was born in Rankin County,
Mississippi, January 8 1833, and removed to Texas with his
father's family in 1846 He was a farmer by occupation, residing near Gonzales Texas He was married in Texas, June 21,
1855, to Mrs Fannie E Stephens, the widow of Elisha Stephens After her death he was married a second time December 22, 1885, to Mrs Julia Brantly James W Steen died near
Gonzales, Texas August 18, 1889, aged 56 years, 7 months and
10 days To James W and Fannie E Steen, his first wife,
were born four children, as follows

1 Henrietta Ophelia Steen was born April 2, 1856
2 James Henry Steen, the second child and only son of James
   W and Fannie E Steen, was born near Gonzales, Texas,
   February 1, 1859
3 Mary Susannah Steen, the third child and second daughter
   of James W and Fannie E Steen, was born June 10, 1861
4 Cora Belle Steen, the fourth child and third daughter of
   James W and Fannie E Steen, was born April 25, 1865
   Residence, Gonzales, Texas

XIV —Enoch Miles Steen, the fourteenth child and seventh
son of William and Mary R Enochs Steen, was born in Rankin County, Mississippi, December 4, 1835, and removed to
Texas with his father's family in 1846, when only eleven years
of age He was married in Gonzales Texas, February 27,
1868, to Arabella Stephens To them were born three children, as follows

1 Virginia Alberta Steen, the eldest child of E Miles and
   Arabella Steen was born December 27, 1868
2 William Carter Steen was born November 7, 1877
3 Dana Lena Steen was born May 29, 1884 Residence, Gonzales, Texas

CHAPTER IX

Mary Steen a daughter of William and Nancy Lusk Steen,
was the second child bearing that name in the family The oldest daughter having died in infancy, the same name was given to

the ninth child, and both were called Polly. This Polly Steen was born in 1792, near the Great Broad River, in South Carolina. She came with her parents and the family into Carroll County, Tennessee, where she was married in 1812 to John Rumley Enochs, a son of Enoch and Lydia Enochs, of South Carolina. The Enochs and Steen families were related through the Hayes, the General Jackson family of Hayes. The grandmother Enochs was a Hayes, and the grandmother Steen was a Hayes, and the related families were brought up together in the same locality in South Carolina. They came together into Tennessee and several marriages between them brought them into the closest intimacy. Within a month of Mary Steen's marriage her husband was in the saddle with General Jackson, hastening to the relief of Fort Mims, and when they met again she had her eldest daughter in her arms. John Rumley and Mary Steen Enochs were the parents of eleven children all born in Carroll County, Tennessee.

I.—Asanath Enochs, the eldest daughter of John R. and Mary Steen Enochs was born in 1813. She was married to William Haley and had two sons, both farmers, and one daughter. All are dead but the daughter has one son and two daughters living.

II.—William Carroll Enochs, the second child and eldest son of John R. and Mary Steen Enochs was born January 8, 1815 and still lives at Steen's Creek, Mississippi. He was twice married. His son, Hon. J. R. Enochs, has two full sisters and there is quite a houseful of boys. The second wife had two boys and a girl. One of the boys is a Methodist minister and the other a member of Enochs' Milling Company.

III.—Vernetta Enochs, the third child and second daughter of John R. and Mary Steen Enochs, was born in 1819. She was married to John Hector and had one son, Frank Hector, and two daughters, Mrs. Wilson, of Memphis, and Mrs. Berry.

IV.—Nancy Jane Enochs, the fourth child and third daughter of John R. and Mary Steen Enochs, was born in 1819. She was married to J. B. Lewis, and has two sons, one of whom is a Methodist preacher in Texas, and two daughters, one of whom is married to a Baptist clergyman.

V.—Enoch A. Enochs, the fifth child and second son of John R.

(16)

and Mary Steen Enochs. was born in 1821   He was married and had nine children, all daughters

VI—Mary Ann Enochs, the sixth child and fourth daughter of John R and Mary Steen Enochs, was born in 1827   She was married to T M Wansley and had two sons, but all are now dead

VII—Eliza Enochs, the seventh child and fifth daughter of John R and Mary Steen Enochs, was born in 1828   She was married to Jesse Norwood, and has one son in Texas; and three married and two single daughters still living

VIII—John Enochs, the eighth child and third son of John R and Mary Steen Enochs, was born in 1824   He was married to a Miss Black, a sister of the Rev Dr Black of Macon, Georgia   He had eight sons and one daughter   His sons are lumbermen, and accounted among the best business men of the State

IX—Isaac V Enochs, the ninth child and fourth son of John R and Mary Steen Enochs, was born in 1829   He served in the Confederate Army during the Civil War   He was married and had seven children the four eldest dying young   One daughter married a prominent lawyer in Biloxi, Mississippi   A son, Isaac V. Enochs. Jr , is in business with his father, shippers of fruit and vegetables, and also proprietors of a cotton and stock farm   Byrd Enochs, the youngest son of Capt Isaac V Enochs, was born in 1871, and was still in school in 1893   The family residence is at Terry Mississippi

X—Julia A Enochs, the tenth child and sixth daughter of John R and Mary Steen Enochs, was born in 1833   She was married to Jefferson Wansley, but is now a widow living in Texas, with three sons and one daughter

XI—James B Enochs, the eleventh child and fifth son of John R and Mary Steen Enochs, was born in 1835   He was a captain in the Confederate Army during the Civil War   He was married and had nine children, five daughters and four sons   The four eldest are successful teachers, one in Texas, one in Indian Territory, and two in Gallman, Copiah County, Mississippi

CHAPTER X

———

Jane Steen, the tenth child of William and Nancy Lusk Steen was born in South Carolina, near the Great Broad River, and not far from the North Carolina State line, about 1795 She came with her parents, and the whole family, except her eldest brother, John Steen, who remained in South Carolina, into Tennessee She was married in Carroll County, Tennessee, about 1830, to Levi Noble, and removed to Texas, where they brought up a family of six children, near Nacogdoches C H , Nacogdoches County, Texas Her brother, William Steen, died at their residence in 1846, soon after he reached the State and was buried in the old North Church cemetery four miles away Levi Noble and his family afterwards removed to San Augustine County, where they lived a while, and then again removed to Kaufman County, Texas, where both Mr and Mrs Noble died To them were born six children, and the two older ones both gained distinction and a high rank in the Western Department of the Confederate Army during the Civil War

I —Jamison Noble, the eldest son of Levi and Jane Steen Noble, became a Major General in the Confederate Army

II —Levi Noble, the second son of Levi and Jane Steen Noble, attained the rank of Brigadier General in the Confederate service

III —S E Noble, another son of Levi and Jane Steen Noble, is now living at Omen, Smith County, Texas

The names of the other three children were not given to the writer

————

CHAPTER XI

———

Silas Steen the eleventh and youngest child of William and Nancy Lusk Steen, was born in Union District, South Carolina, near the Great Broad River, about 1790, or 1800, and died at Steen's Creek, in Rankin County, Mississippi, October 24 1858

His father started to remove with his family from South Carolina to Mississippi, but remained a while in Carroll County, Tennessee, where he sickened and died   After his father's death Silas Steen removed with his mother and her large family of children to Lawrence County Mississippi, about 1814 or 1815 and not long afterwards settled permanently at Steen's Creek, in Rankin County, Mississippi.   The Steen family was among the very early settlers in the county, and had a large influence in moulding the character of the people   In 1846 Silas Steen and family together with his brothers and their families, removed to Texas, but not long afterwards he and his brother, William Steen, and their families, returned to Rankin County, Mississippi, where they continued to reside until their death   Silas Steen was a large land owner in the vicinity of Steen's Creek, a well-to-do and prosperous farmer while he lived   He was married in Rankin County, Mississippi, April 23, 1826, to Hannah Meyers, she having been born in Union County, Mississippi, July 2, 1805, and died at their home, near Steen's Creek, August 2, 1857, aged 52 years and 1 month   To Silas and Hannah Meyers Steen were born ten children, as follows, all born near Steen's Creek Mississippi

I —Elias Estes Steen, the eldest son of Silas and Hannah Meyers Steen, was born March 27, 1827, and died July 8, 1863, aged 36 years, 3 months and 12 days   During his life he was a prosperous farmer   He was married in Rankin County, Mississippi, in 1855, to Ruthy Adaline Bunch   To them were born the following four children

 1 John Meyers Steen, the eldest son of Elias Estes and Ruthy A Steen, was born in Rankin County, Mississippi, April 18, 1857   He was educated at Oxford, Mississippi, in the University of Mississippi, and is now a successful attorney-at-law   Residence, Memphis, Tennessee

 2 Edwin Silas Steen, the second son of Elias Estes and Ruthy A Steen was born in Rankin County, Mississippi April 23, 1858   He was married September 13, 1888, to ————

 3 Ella Steen, the third child and only daughter of Elias Estes and Ruthy A Steen, was born in Rankin County, Mississippi, in 1859, and died ————

 4 William David Steen, the fourth child and third son of

Elias Estes and Ruthy A Steen, was born in Rankin County, Mississippi, in 1860. He was married April 3 1889, to
————————.

II —John Meyers Steen the second son of Silas and Hannah M Steen, was born October 26, 1828, and died August 13, 1841 aged 12 years 9 months and 16 days.

III —Frances Amanda Steen, the third child and eldest daughter of Silas and Hannah M Steen, was born May 6 1830, and died August 13, 1841, aged 11 years, 3 months and 7 days

IV —Ellen Lucretia Steen, the fourth child and second daughter of Silas and Hannah M Steen, was born near Steen's Creek, Rankin County, Mississippi, July 11, 1832, and died June 1, 1853, aged 20 years, 10 months and 11 days She was married about 1850 to Dr Thomas Jefferson Haley, by whom she had one child, as follows

   I Austin Iayne Haley, son of Dr T J and Ellen L Steen Haley, was born near Steen's Creek, Rankin County, Mississippi, December 9, 1851 — a dealer in stocks and patents He was married in Waco, Texas, November 2, 1880, to Sallie Terry McKee To them were born the following children Residence, Dallas, Texas

     I.—Murray McKee Haley was born in Waco, Texas, January 13. 1882, and died May 29, 1882, aged 4 months and 16 days.

     II —Harold McKee Haley was born in Dallas Texas. August 25, 1884

     III —Earl Lighthall Haley was born in Alameda, California, May 25, 1891

V —James Emerson Steen, the fifth child and third son of Silas and Hannah M Steen, was born February 1, 1838, and died April 10, 1855, aged 17 years, 2 months and 10 days

VI —William Gwin Steen the sixth child and fourth son of Silas and Hannah M Steen, was born near Steen's Creek, Rankin County, Mississippi, April 12, 1839 — a prosperous farmer He was married by the Rev Jesse Woodall, near Monterey, Rankin County, Mississippi February 11, 1864, to Sarah Elizabeth Sutton, a daughter of Major B F and Louisa Sutton, she having been born near Monterey, Mississippi, July 9, 1845, and died at their home, at Steen's Creek, Mississippi,

July 3, 1890 in the 45th year of her age   To them were born
the following ten children, the first four at the residence of their
grandfather, Major B F Sutton, near Monterey, and the other
six at their home at Steen's Creek   William G Steen was married a second time, December 7, 1899, to a devout and earnest
Christian woman, whose maiden name was Ann Mary Man-
gum   She had twice been left a widow, and died June 15,
1900, aged 53 years   W G Steen is now clerk of the Circuit
Court of Rankin County   Residence, Brandon Mississippi

1 Louisa Emmogene Steen, the eldest daughter of William G
   and Louisa S Steen, was born December 2, 1864   She was
   married May 24 1885, to H H Ellzey

2 Florence Albertha Steen, the second daughter of William G
   and Louisa S Steen, was born June 11, 1867   She was married July 14, 1886, to Elisha Lawley

3 Hannie Belle Steen, the third daughter of William G and
   Louisa S Steen, was born January 11 1869   She was married April 12, 1888, to David L Sistrunk

4 Elizabeth Shepard Steen, the fourth daughter of William G
   and Louisa S Steen, was born at the home of Major B F
   Sutton, near Monterey, Mississippi, November 28, 1870

5. Margaret Steen, called "Margie," the fifth daughter of William G and Louisa S Steen, was born at the home of her
   parents, near Steen's Creek, Mississippi, March 20, 1873
   She was married September 16, 1889, to Joseph F Sistrunk

6 Silas Sutton Steen, the sixth child and eldest son of William
   G and Louisa S Steen, was born November 23, 1875

7 William Gwin Steen, Jr , the seventh child and second son
   of William G and Louisa S Steen was born April 30, 1878

8 Eunice Graves Steen, the eighth child and sixth daughter of
   William G and Louisa S Steen was born July 23, 1882

9 Sallie Colon Steen, the ninth child and seventh daughter of
   William G and Louisa S Steen was born February 24,
   1885

10 Kate Levis Steen, the tenth child and eighth daughter of
   William Gwin and Louisa Sutton Steen, was born at the
   home of her parents, near Steen's Creek, Mississippi, December 16, 1887.

VII.—Emeline Hankins Steen, the seventh child and third daughter of Silas and Hannah M Steen, was born in Rankin County, Mississippi, April 15, 1842 She was married November 18, 1858, to Jonathan A Holcomb — a farmer, he having been born December 12, 1833, and died near Gatesville, Coryell County, Texas April 3, 1893, in the 60th year of his age They had no children After the death of her husband, Mrs Emeline H Steen Holcomb continued to reside near Gatesville, Texas, until her death, in 1894 Both were devout Christians and members of the Baptist Church

VIII.—Washington Webster Steen, the eighth child and fifth son of Silas and Hannah M Steen, was born May 14, 1844 — a prosperous farmer He was married by the Rev Daniel Giddens, in Rankin County, Mississippi, September 23, 1866, to Mary Esther Barnes, a daughter of Abram and Ann Elizabeth Barnes, she having been born near Columbia, Marion County, Mississippi, January 5, 1845 To them were born nine children, all born at their home, near Steen's Creek, Rankin County, Mississippi

1 Estes Barnes Steen, the eldest son of Washington W and Mary E Steen, was born August 12 1867

2 Susan Elizabeth Steen, the second child and eldest daughter of W W and Mary E Steen, was born October 2, 1869 She was married near Steen's Creek, Mississippi, December 27, 1888, to Robert Slay They reside near Hazelhurst, Copiah County, Mississippi To them one child was born
I—Anna Belle Slay, daughter of Robert and Susan E Steen Slay, was born May 25, 1890 Residence, Hazelhurst, Mississippi.

3 Silas Victor Steen, the third child and second son of W W. and Mary E Steen, was born December 1, 1872

4 James William Steen, the fourth child and third son of W W and Mary E Steen, was born January 8, 1874

5 Robert Lee Steen, the fifth child and fourth son of W W and Mary E Steen, was born August 6, 1876

6 John Henry Steen, the sixth child and fifth son of W W and Mary E Steen was born October 8, 1878

7. Ella Jane Steen the seventh child and second daughter of W W and Mary E Steen was born January 28, 1881

8. Mary Agnes Steen, the eighth child and third daughter of W. W. and Mary E. Steen, was born July 23, 1883.

9. Anna Washington Steen, the ninth child and fourth daughter of Washington Webster and Mary Esther Barnes Steen, was born July 20, 1886.

IX.—Sarah Mary Jane Steen, the ninth child and fourth daughter of Silas and Hannah M. Steen, was born May 16, 1846. She was married, November 24, 1864, to Augustus La Fayette Dear, who died July 24, 1893. The family residence is at Steen's Creek, Mississippi. To Augustus L. and Sarah Mary Jane Steen Dear were born the following nine children, all born near Steen's Creek, Mississippi.

1. Anna Judson Dear was born October 4, 1865. She was married, August 31, 1885, to L. M. Rogers.

2. Sarah Barton Dear was born May 24, 1867. She was married October 28, 1891, to Anderson Moore.

3. John I. Dear was born February 21, 1869, and died April 21, 1879, aged 10 years and 2 months.

4. Susan Emma Dear was born May 6, 1871.

5. Mary Ella Dear was born May 4, 1873.

6 Henry White Dear was born February 13, 1875.

7. Ida Leteola Dear was born February 19, 1879.

8. Augustus La Fayette Dear, Jr., was born October 18, 1884, and died June 25, 1885, aged 8 months and 7 days.

9. Myrtle Mitford Dear was born January 21, 1887. Residence, Steen's Creek, Mississippi.

X.—Susan Reber Steen, the tenth and youngest child, the fifth daughter of Silas and Hannah Meyers Steen, was born July 12, 1849, and died September 11, 1869, in the 21st year of her age. She was married March 28, 1868, to John James Jones. To them was born one child, as follows:

1. Silas Abner Jones was born near Steen's Creek, Rankin County, Mississippi, September 1, 1869. Residence, Los Angeles, California.

BOOK FOUR.

DESCENDANTS OF MATTHEW STEEN

Matthew Steen was born in Ireland in 1755, and early came to the British Colonies in America   He located first in Philadelphia, Pennsylvania, where, about 1774, he was married to Jane Taylor   In 1780 he removed with his family to Washington County, Pennsylvania, where his children grew to maturity, and where he died, April 23, 1835, aged 80 years

Matthew Steen was born in the north of Ireland in 1755, probably in County Antrim, and early removed to the British Colonies in America, locating at first in Philadelphia, Pennsylvania, where he spent several years   He removed to Washington County, Pennsylvania, about 1780, where he spent the remainder of his life, and died there April 23, 1835, aged 80 years   He was married in Philadelphia, Pennsylvania, about 1774, to Jane Taylor, she having been born in 1756, and died January 4, 1842, aged 86 years   To Matthew and Jane Taylor Steen were born the following five children   Esther, Matthew Taylor, John, Joseph, and Margaret Steen

CHAPTER I

Esther Steen, the eldest child, a daughter of Matthew and Jane Taylor Steen, was born in Philadelphia, Pennsylvania, June 11, 1775 She was married to a Mr Wood They had no children

CHAPTER II

Matthew Taylor Steen, the second child and eldest son of Matthew and Jane Taylor Steen was born in Philadelphia, Pennsylvania, November 6 1776, and died in New Castle, Pennsylvania, in 1851, aged 75 years He was married in Washington County, Pennsylvania about 1803, to Mary Mitchell, called "Polly," she having been born in Lancaster County, Pennsylvania, September 15, 1784, and died in Beaver Pennsylvania, September 13 1841, aged almost 57 years To Matthew Taylor and Mary Mitchell Steen were born seven children, as follows

I —Juliet Steen, the eldest child, a daughter of Matthew Taylor and Mary Mitchell Steen, was born in Beaver, Pennsylvania, about 1804, and died in infancy when about six months old

II —Mary Steen, the second daughter of Matthew Taylor and Mary Mitchell Steen, was born in Beaver, Pennsylvania, July 25, 1806 and died in the same locality in 1880, in the 74th year of her age She was married in Bezetha, Trumbull County, Ohio, in 1834, to James Parks — a shoemaker, he having been born in Beaver County, Pennsylvania, in 1805, where he continued to reside until his death, in 1883, in the 78th year of his age To James and Mary Steen Parks were born the following five children

1 Mary Jane Parks was born in Beaver County, Pennsylvania, February 2, 1835, and died June 28 1893, aged 58 years, 4 months and 26 days

2 Sarah Ann Parks was born in Beaver County, Pennsylvania, December 21 1838, and died in 1861, in the 23d year of her age

3 Samuel Taylor Parks was born in Beaver County, Pennsylvania, May 8, 1851. He was married to Nancy Lindsay. To them one child was born, as follows

1—Kate Parks, a daughter of Samuel T. and Nancy L. Parks was born about 1872. Residence Oil City, Pennsylvania

4 John Mitchell Parks was born in Beaver County, Pennsylvania, about 1854. He removed to the West

5 Isaac Newton Parks was born in Beaver County, Pennsylvania, in June, 1857. He was married, and has two sons living in Beaver Pennsylvania

III—Matthew Mitchell Steen, the third child and eldest son of Matthew Taylor and Mary Mitchell Steen, was born in Beaver Beaver County, Pennsylvania, February 6, 1809, and died near Green Top, Schuyler County, Missouri, March 15 1889, in the 81st year of his age. He removed from Pennsylvania to Missouri, about 1835, and located upon a farm near Green Top, Schuyler County, where he remained until his death. He was a carpenter by trade, and a soldier in the Union Army during the Civil War. M. Mitchell Steen was married near Lowell, Ohio, September 23, 1830 to Mary Buchanan, a daughter of Walter and Mary Walker Buchanan, she having been born July 18, 1805, and died at their home, near Green Top Schuyler County, Missouri November 6 1851 in the 50th year of her age. M. Mitchell Steen, his wife, and all his children were devout members of Cumberland Presbyterian Church and his descendants are nearly all members of the same church, while those who are dead have died in the faith and hope of the Gospel. To M. Mitchell and Mary Buchanan Steen were born a family of seven children, all of whom were religious, industrious, social, and full of innocent little jokes. They were brought up in Schuyler County, Missouri, and their names were as follows

1 Mary Steen, the eldest daughter of M. Mitchell and Mary B. Steen, was born June 29, 1831, and died April 1 1833, in the 2d year of her age

2 Matthew Taylor Steen, the second child and eldest son of M. Mitchell and Mary B. Steen, was born near Cleveland, Ohio June 26, 1833, and died in Putnam County, Missouri, February 3, 1894, in the 61st year of his age. M. Taylor Steen was a carpenter by trade, a soldier in the Union Army

during the Civil War, serving as First Lieutenant in Company D, Missouri Cavalry He was married in La Grange, Lewis County, Missouri, April 14, 1853, to Arminda Colbert, she having been born in Indiana, September 14, 1835 They lived near Martinstown, Putnam County, Missouri, where they brought up a family of nine children M. Taylor Steen was a ruling elder in the Cumberland Presbyterian Church for more than 23 years, and of which church the whole family were members To M Taylor and Arminda Colbert Steen were born the following children

I —Mary Louisa Steen, the eldest daughter of M Taylor and Arminda C Steen, was born January 13, 1854, and died February 23 1854

II —John Mitchell Steen, the second child and eldest son of M. Taylor and Arminda C Steen, was born September 13, 1855 — a farmer He was married April 4, 1875, to Kittie Ostrum To them have been born the following six children

   1 Vada Steen was born December 17, 1879

   2 Alpha Steen was born February 10, 1883

   3 Matthew Steen was born August 12, 1885

   4 Ola Steen was born January 17 1888, and died December 15, 1889

   5 Elvis Steen was born September 1, 1891

   6 Guerney Steen was born June 27, 1894

III —Matthew Marion Steen, the third child and second son of Matthew Taylor and Arminda Corbet Steen, was born in Putnam County, Missouri, November 30, 1857 and died February 25 1894 — a farmer by occupation He was married September 8, 1877, to Cora Alice Ostrum To them were born the following five children

   1 Iva Steen was born July 20, 1879

   2 Infant son was born and died October 2, 1881

   3 Nora Steen was born January 17, 1883, and died June 13, 1884

   4 Wilbur Steen was born June 21, 1885

   5 Flora Steen was born March 22, 1891

IV —Joseph Warren Steen, the fourth child and third son of M Taylor and Arminda C Steen, was born in Putnam

County, October 10 1860, and died March 26, 1861, aged 5 months and 16 days.

I —Gilbert William Steen, the fifth child and fourth son of M Taylor and Arminda C Steen was born in Putnam County, Missouri, January 22, 1865, and died November 2, 1885, in the 21st year of his age

VI —Anna Jane Steen, the sixth child and second daughter of Matthew Taylor and Arminda Colbert Steen, was born in Putnam County Missouri, October 12, 1868 — a teacher She resides with her mother and brother Alfred, near Martinstown, Missouri

VII —Sarah Eveline Steen the seventh child and third daughter of M Taylor and Arminda C Steen, was born in Putnam County, Missouri, November 12, 1870, and died April 4, 1899, aged 28 years, 4 months and 22 days She was married October 8, 1892, to Thomas F Martin To them were born two children Family residence, Martinstown, Missouri

1 Harvey Martin was born September 1, 1893

2 Ruby Frances Martin was born January 27, 1895

VIII —Arminda Frances Steen, the eighth child and fourth daughter of M Taylor and Arminda C Steen, was born in Putnam County, Missouri, May 27, 1873, and died September 1, 1899, in the 17th year of her age

IX —Alfred Jarratt Steen, the ninth child and fifth son of M Taylor and Arminda C Steen, was born in Putnam County, Missouri, August 13, 1875 — a farmer He conducts the old home farm and his mother and sister Anna J Steen, live with him Residence, near Martinstown Missouri

3 Walter B Steen, the third child and second son of M Mitchell and Mary B Steen, was born in Ohio, August 17 1835 and died February 1, 1837, aged 1 year, 5 months and 16 days

4 Sarah Steen, the fifth child and second daughter of M Mitchell and Mary B Steen was born in Pennsylvania, February 24, 1838 She was married near Green Top Schuyler County, Missouri, February 23 1854, to John Henry Sebree — a farmer he having been born March 24, 1835 Resi-

dence, near Green Top, Missouri To them were born the following eleven children

I —William Andrew Sebree was born July 30, 1855

II —Uriah Mitchell Sebree was born March 26, 1857

III —Mary Elizabeth Sebree was born May 8, 1859, and died

IV —George Washington Sebree was born February 22, 1861, and died

V —John Edwin Sebree was born July 30, 1862

VI —Henry Gilbert Sebree was born July 15, 1866

VII —Maud Melissa Sebree was born November 29, 1868

VIII —Julia Annie Sebree was born January 5, 1871

IX —Letitia Jane Sebree was born October 19, 1873

X —Sarah Sebree was born October 2, 1878, and died

XI —Charles Wilbur Sebree was born July 25, 1882

5 John Walker Steen, the fifth child and third son of M Mitchell and Mary B Steen, was born in Ohio, March 15, 1840, and died in Missouri January 23, 1892 in the 52d year of his age He was a farmer by occupation He was married in November, 1861 to Mary Snedigar she having been born in Pike County, Missouri February 24, 1839, and died in Putnam County, Missouri September 30, 1893, in the 55th year of her age To them were born six children, as follows

I — Narcissa Steen, the eldest daughter of John W and Mary Snedigar Steen, was born in Putnam County, Missouri, August 30, 1862 She was married October 24, 1880, to John William Benson, he having been born in Illinois, February 17, 1858, and died in Putnam County, Missouri, September 5, 1893, in the 36th year of his age Family residence, Martinstown, Missouri To them were born five children as follows

1 Harvey Aura Benson was born September 18 1881

2 Dora Edith Benson was born December 10 1882

3 Eva Belle Benson was born October 31, 1886 and died August 9, 1889 in the 3d year of her age

4 Noah Victor Benson was born July 10, 1891

5 Nora Victoria Benson was born July 10, 1891 The two last-named were twins

II—John Wesley Steen the second child and eldest son of John W and Mary S Steen, was born in Putnam County, Missouri, November 30, 1865 He was married July 3, 1894 to Mrs Margaret Ann Lippe, she having been born March 10, 1862 Residence, near Martinstown, Missouri

III—Luella Abigail Steen, the third child and second daughter of John W and Mary S Steen, was born in Putnam County, Missouri, August 4, 1868, and died April 22, 1891, in the 24th year of her age

II—Warren Monroe Steen, the fourth child and second son of John W and Mary S Steen, was born in Putnam County, Missouri, October 13, 1871, and died December 23, 1872

IV—Mary Elta Steen, the fifth child and third daughter of John W and Mary S Steen, was born in Putnam County, Missouri, October 20, 1873 She was married February 3 1889, to Timothy Hutson Cooley, he having been born February 14, 1867 Their post-office address is Low Ground, Putnam County Missouri To them were born the following three children

   1 Charles Virgil Cooley was born February 28 1890

   2 Willis Franklin Cooley was born October 23, 1891

   3 Nona Victor Cooley was born October 21 1893

VI—Willis Orley Steen, the sixth child and third son of John W and Mary S Steen, was born in Putnam County, Missouri, September 29, 1882

6 Isaac Buchanan Steen, the sixth child and fourth son of M Mitchell and Mary B Steen, was born in Missouri, June 12, 1844, and died March 14, 1852, in the eighth year of his age

7 Gilbert Steen, the seventh child and fifth son of Matthew Mitchell and Mary Buchanan Steen, was born in Missouri, September 22, 1846 and died February 16, 1875, in the 29th year of his age He was a prosperous farmer, and a soldier in the Union Army during the Civil War He was married in 1866 to Cassandra Collier To them were born four children Family residence, Kirksville, Adair County Missouri

I—Albeon Steen the eldest son of Gilbert and Cassandra

Steen, was born November 21, 1867   He was married
May 5, 1888, to Pearl Myers

II —Emma Steen, the second child and eldest daughter of
Gilbert and Cassandra Steen, was born August 17, 1869 —
a teacher

III —Carrie Annie Steen the third child and second daughter of Gilbert and Cassandra Steen, was born April 1, 1871
She was for some time a teacher. She was married in
1894

IV —John Matthew Steen, the fourth child and second son
of Gilbert and Cassandra Steen, was born in 1874, and
died in 1877 or 1878

IV —John Taylor Steen the fourth child and second son of Matthew Taylor and Mary Mitchell Steen was born in Beaver,
Beaver County Pennsylvania, June 9, 1811   He was married
in Pennsylvania, April 4, 1839, to Nancy Crawford   He died
suddenly of heart trouble, in New Sharon, Mahaska County,
Iowa, December 8, 1855 in the 45th year of his age   He was a
man of sterling worth, a devout Christian, and a prosperous
farmer   He removed from Pennsylvania in 1848, and located
on a farm near New Sharon, Mahaska County, Iowa, where he
continued until his death   To J Taylor and Nancy Crawford
Steen were born six children, as follows

1 David Steen, the eldest son of J Taylor and Nancy Crawford Steen, was born in Beaver County, Pennsylvania, September 26, 1840   He was brought by his parents to their
new home in Iowa when a small boy and brought up on his
father's farm   He was married in New Sharon, Mahaska
County, Iowa January 9, 1884, to Josie Battey, she having
been born in Marshall County, Iowa, October 18, 1856
Residence, Taintor, Iowa   His mother, Nancy C Steen,
lives with them   To David and Josie B Steen were born
three children, as follows

I —Alpha C Steen was born July 27, 1886

II —Arthur D Steen was born April 22, 1890, and died
May 12, 1891

III —Alice Steen was born July 25, 1891

2 Mary Steen, the second child and eldest daughter of J Taylor and Nancy C Steen, was born in Beaver County Pennsylvania, January 31, 1842, and brought to Iowa by her par-

ents when a child She was married to Thomas Catterson.
Residence, Taintor, Mahaska County, Iowa

3. Robert Steen, the third child and second son of J Taylor
and Nancy Crawford Steen, was born in Beaver County,
Pennsylvania, February 14, 1844 He was brought by his
parents to Iowa when a child, and died at his residence, near
Kirkman, Shelby County, Iowa, July 15, 1895, aged 51 years,
5 months and 1 day He was married in Powesheik County,
Iowa, February 19, 1869 to Sarah Ann McDowell, she having been born in Powesheik County, Iowa, June 10, 1850
Family residence, Kirkman, Shelby County, Iowa To
Robert and Sarah Ann Steen were born nine children, as
follows

I —Viola A Steen was born March 7, 1870, and died

II —Reuben A Steen was born March 24, 1872

III —Mattie L Steen was born October 8, 1874 She was
married to T H Potter

IV.—Lucinda Steen was born May 10, 1877

V —Charlotte Steen was born February 20, 1880

VI —Janette Steen was born May 8, 1882.

VII —Emma E Steen was born September 19, 1894

VIII —Mabel Steen was born October 14, 1886

IX —Clara Steen was born August 13, 1889

4 James F Steen, the fourth child and third son of J Taylor
and Nancy Crawford Steen, was born in Beaver County,
Pennsylvania, January 25, 1846 Residence, Taintor, Iowa.

5 Jonathan Steen, the fifth child and fourth son of J Taylor
and Nancy Crawford Steen, was born October 9, 1848, and
died in Mahaska County, Iowa, April 26, 1855, in the 7th
year of his age

6 John M Steen, the sixth child and fifth son of J Taylor and
Nancy C Steen, was born in Iowa, October 27, 1850 Residence, ————, Powesheik County, Iowa

V —Harriet Steen, the fifth child and third daughter of Matthew
Taylor and Mary Mitchell Steen was born in Darlington,
Beaver County, Pennsylvania April 30, 1814 She was mar-
ried in Beaver County, Pennsylvania, November 23, 1837, to
John Mitchell, he having been born June 26 1812 They
removed to Iowa in comparatively early life, and located near
    (17)

New Sharon, Mahaska County, Iowa, where Harriet Steen
Mitchell died, June 9, 1872, in the 69th year of her age, and in
the full communion of the Presbyterian Church. To John and
Harriet Steen Mitchell were born seven children, as follows:

1. Martin Mitchell was born February 2, 1839 He was married October 11, 1859, to Catherine Mossman. To them
were born two children

   I—Nettie Jane Mitchell was born August 7, 1860.

   II—Della Frances Mitchell was born April 3, 1874

2 Nancy Ann Mitchell, the second child and eldest daughter
of John and Harriet Steen Mitchell, was born December 9,
1840 She was married September 25, 1861, to Amos Bartlett Residence, Searsborough, Iowa To them was born
one child.

   I—J Martin Bartlett was born September 22, 1865

3 Mary Jane Mitchell, the third child and second daughter of
John and Harriet Steen Mitchell, was born January 18, 1843.
Residence, Harlan, Shelby County, Iowa

4. Smith Mitchell, the fourth child and second son of John and
Harriet Steen Mitchell, was born July 22, 1845.

5. Harriet Minerva Mitchell, the fifth child and third daughter
of John and Harriet Steen Mitchell, was born August 31,
1847. Residence, New Sharon, Iowa

6 Juliet Mitchell, the sixth child and fourth daughter of John
and Harriet Steen Mitchell, was born April 7, 1850 Residence, Alva, Nebraska

7 John Curtis Mitchell, the seventh child and third son of
John and Harriet Steen Mitchell, was born July 6, 1852.
Residence, Kansas City, Missouri

VI —Juliet Steen, the sixth child and fourth daughter of Matthew
Taylor and Mary Mitchell Steen (the second daughter of the
same name, the former having died in infancy), was born in
Darlington, Beaver County, Pennsylvania, May 2, 1817, and
died near Des Moines, Iowa, August 24, 1861, in the 44th year
of her age She was married in Beaver County, Pennsylvania,
November 3, 1836, to William Madden, who died in Franklin,
Pennsylvania, January 6, 1851. To them were born six chil-
dren Juliet Steen Madden was married a second time to
Stewart Robinson, by whom she had two children

1. Mary Ann Madden, the eldest daughter of William and Juliet Steen Madden, was born in 1837, and died August 7, 1849, aged 12 years

2 Lucy Jane Madden, the second daughter of William and Juliet Steen Madden, was born December 22, 1838

3 Martha Elizabeth Madden, the third daughter of William and Juliet Steen Madden, was born May 11, 1842 She was married to a Mr Barlow, who held a position of trust in the Iowa State Penitentiary.

4 Philander White Madden, the fourth child and only son of William and Juliet Steen Madden, was born February 4, 1845. He was Warden of the State Penitentiary at Anamosa, Iowa.

5 Juliet Caroline Madden, the fifth child and fourth daughter of William and Juliet Steen Madden, was born October 17, 1847, and died August 5, 1848, aged 9 months and 19 days.

6 Harriet Madden, the sixth child and fifth daughter of William and Harriet Steen Madden, was born September 16, 1849.

7 Sarah Frances Robinson, the eldest child by the second marriage of Juliet Steen Madden to Stewart Robinson, was born May 21, 1855, and died in 1890, aged 45 years.

8 Nevada Robinson, the second daughter by the second marriage of Juliet Steen Madden to Stewart Robinson was born July 11, 1858

VII —Jane Steen, the seventh child and fifth daughter of Matthew Taylor and Mary Mitchell Steen, was born in Darlington, Beaver County, Pennsylvania, September 5, 1819 She was married at the same place, July 15, 1839, to William Lindsey, who died May 4, 1882 Mrs Jane Steen Lindsey now (1900) resides at 1210 Chestnut Street, Franklin, Pennsylvania To William and Jane Steen Lindsey were born the following eight children

1 Lucy Lindsey was born in Darlington, Pennsylvania, November 14, 1840, and died in Youngstown, Ohio, July 14, 1842

2 Julia Lindsey was born in Youngstown, Ohio, November 14, 1843 Residence, Franklin, Pennsylvania

3 Almedia Lindsey was born in New Castle, Pennsylvania, August 11, 1846 She was married in Franklin, Pennsylvania, August 9, 1873 to Thomas R Mahan They have no children Residence, Denver, Colorado

4 Harriet Jane Lindsey was born in Franklin Pennsylvania, March 14 1849 She was married at the same place, December 19, 1878, to Ezekiel Franks, ot Condit, Ohio They have no children Residence, Franklin, Pennsylvania

5 Mary Abigail Lindsey was born in Franklin, Pennsylvania, October 9, 1851, and died April 6 1864 in the 13th year of her age

6 Olive Deborah Lindsey, the sixth daughter of William and Jane Steen Lindsey, was born in Franklin, Pennsylvania, March 27, 1854 She was married in Franklin, Pennsylvania, September 24, 1873, to Reed W Myers, of Youngstown, Ohio, he having been born at Prospect, Butler County, Pennsylvania, October 18 1847 Residence, Beaver Falls, Pennsylvania To them were born two children, as follows

I —Charles Edgar Myers was born in Tionesta, Forest County, Pennsylvania, October 14, 1874

II —Mary Steen Myers was born in Clear Lake, Polk County, Wisconsin, December 25, 1880

7 Willard Wallace Lindsey, the seventh child and eldest son of William and Jane Steen Lindsey, was born in Franklin, Pennsylvania, September 25 1859 He was married in Franklin, Pennsylvania, November 11, 1880, to Anna J ———— Residence, New Brighton, Pennsylvania To them was born one son

I —Alson Lindsey was born in New Brighton, Pennsylvania, December 16, 1886

8 Orville Edgar Lindsey, the youngest child of William and Jane Steen Lindsey, was born in Franklin, Pennsylvania, December 4, 1862 He was married in New Brighton Pennsylvania, January 5 1883 to Nora Moltei, she having been born in New Brighton, Pennsylvania, September 20, 1864 Residence, New Brighton, Pennsylvania To them was born one son

I —Walter Scott Lindsey was born in New Brighton, Pennsylvania, June 22, 1884.

CHAPTER III

John Steen, the third child and second son of Matthew and
Jane Taylor Steen, was born in Philadelphia, Pennsylvania,
December 30, 1778, and died at the residence of his son, Capt
Hugh B Steen, in New Castle, Lawrence County, Pennsylvania,
July 10, 1859, in the 81st year of his age   His body was tenderly
laid away to rest in Greenwood cemetery, New Castle, Pennsylvania   John Steen was brought by his parents from Philadelphia,
about 1780, to their new home, in Washington County Pennsylvania, where he was brought up   He was married in Washington County, Pennsylvania, about 1800, to Ann Cummins McDole,
who was born in Westmoreland County, Pennsylvania, by whom
he had seven children   He resided in Washington County a
few years after his marriage, and about 1804 removed with his
family to Beaver County, Pennsylvania, and permanently located
near Bridgewater   He served during the War of 1812, was
enlisted for five years, and completed his term of service at the
Arsenal, near Pittsburgh, Pennsylvania   He was a Sergeant in
Biddle's Corps of Artillery, which fact is shown from his land
warrant   He was also for many years a ruling elder in the United
Presbyterian Church, and a Justice of the Peace for the borough
of Bridgewater, Pennsylvania   After the death of his first wife
John Steen was married a second time to Catherine Barnes, who
was born in Ireland, by whom he had five children, making twelve
children in all, as follows

1 —Matthew Steen, the eldest son of John Steen and his first wife,
formerly Ann Cummins McDole, was born in Poland Township,
Mahoning County, Ohio, January 8, 1801, and died in Newport,
Lawrence County, Pennsylvania, in January, 1854, aged 53
years   Matthew Steen was a successful physician, and practiced medicine in Ohio and in Pennsylvania   He was married
in Poland Township, Mahoning County, Ohio in 1820 to
Elizabeth Galbraith, she having been born at that place in May,
1797, and died at the residence of her son, Capt Erasmus D.
Steen, in Danville Illinois, January 15, 1883, in the 86th year
of her age   To Dr Matthew and Elizabeth Galbraith Steen
were born the following eight children

1. Mary W Steen, the eldest daughter of Dr. Matthew and

Elizabeth G Steen, was born in Crawford County, Pennsylvania, in May, 1822   She was married in Butler County, Pennsylvania, about 1843 to Dr Clement Pearson, and died in Warren County, Illinois, November 13, 1854. in the 36th year of her age   Dr. Pearson, her husband, died in 1877. They were the parents of three children, all of whom are now dead

2   Samuel G Steen, the second child and eldest son of Dr Matthew and Elizabeth G. Steen, was born in Crawford County, Pennsylvania, in 1824   He was a physician and surgeon, and went to the Mexican War as Assistant Surgeon in Captain Washington's Light Artillery   He died in 1847 in the city of Saltillo, Mexico, from the effects of wounds received in battle   His body was brought home and buried with great military honors in New Castle, Pennsylvania

3   Ann M Steen, the third child and second daughter of Dr. Matthew and Elizabeth G Steen, was born in Crawford County, Pennsylvania, in 1826   She was married in Butler County, Pennsylvania, about 1846, to Michael Alford, by whom she had eight children, who are mostly living in the vicinity of Pittsburgh, Pennsylvania   She died in Centralia, Illinois, in 1863, aged about 37 years

4   John A Steen, the fourth child and second son of Dr. Matthew and Elizabeth G Steen, was born in Crawford County, Pennsylvania, in 1828   He left home about 1850, when he was 22 years of age   He was clerk on a steamboat on the Ohio River.   About 1858 he started to go to California, and was met by a friend, who told his brother of it   He was never heard of afterwards   It was reported that the whole party was murdered by Indians but it was not certainly known whether this was true or not

5   Margaret M Steen, the fifth child and third daughter of Dr Matthew and Elizabeth G Steen, was born in Crawford County, Pennsylvania, in 1830   She was married in Butler County, Pennsylvania, about 1849, to John Brant, who became a soldier in the Civil War   He was Captain in a Pennsylvania Regiment, and was killed in the battle of Fredericksburgh, Virginia, in 1863   His wife died from grief about six months later   To John and Margaret Steen Brant were born three children, two sons and one daughter.   The daughter was married and lived in Mercer County, Pennsyl-

CAPTAIN E. D. STEEN.

vania, where she died, leaving one daughter, now a grown
woman   The two sons live in Bluffton, Indiana, are prosperous, well-to-do people, and influential citizens

6 James S. Steen, the sixth child and third son of Dr Matthew
and Elizabeth G Steen, was born in Crawford County Pennsylvania, November 13, 1832   He was a soldier in the Civil
War, belonging to the Fourteenth Illinois Cavalry, and was
killed in battle at Knoxville, Tennessee, February 29, 1864
James S Steen was married in Butler County, Pennsylvania,
January 4, 1855, to Josephine Ramsey, by whom he had two
children

I —A son, who died when about four years old

II —A daughter, who was married to Charles Renner and
now lives near Ellis, in Peru South America, Mr Renner
being engaged in the oil business there

7 Erasmus Darwin Steen, the seventh child and fourth son
of Dr Matthew and Elizabeth G Steen, was born in Crawford County, Pennsylvania, October 1 1835   In 1861 he
enlisted as a soldier in the Union Army at Shelbyville, Illinois   He was Captain of Company ——, One Hundred and
Fifteenth Regiment of Illinois Volunteer Infantry, and served
his country faithfully all through the war   Out of
the eight children of his father's family he is the
only one now living, and he came very near being
left on a Southern battle-field   He writes "I have
no startling statements to make in relation to my
father's family, but one thing I can assure you of, and that is,
that in looking the matter up you will find no record of any
of the family in any of the penitentiaries of the country "
Erasmus Darwin Steen was married in Warren County,
Illinois, November 15, 1855, to Martha Fair, she having been
born in Meigs County, Ohio, March 21, 1836   Residence,
3528 Lake Avenue, Chicago, Illinois   To Capt E D and
Martha F Steen were born five children, four of whom still
survive, as follows

I —Ernest P Steen, the eldest son of Capt E. D and
Martha F Steen, was born in Warren County Illinois,
August 16, 1856   He was married in Danville, Illinois,
March, 1883, to Jennie Payton   They have no children
Ernest P Steen is the only grandchild of Dr Matthew

Steen that bears the name of Steen   Residence, No 7035
Wentworth Avenue, Chicago, Illinois.

II—Mary M Steen, a daughter of Capt E D and Martha
F Steen, was born in Shelbyville, Illinois, August 9, 1861
She was married in Danville, Illinois, in October, 1887, to
Morton W Thompson, Esq, an attorney-at-law and judge
of the County Court, Vermilion County, Illinois   Resi-
dence, Danville, Illinois.

III—Nellie F Steen, a daughter of Capt E D and Martha
F Steen, was born in Shelbyville, February 7, 1866   She
resides with her parents, in Chicago — an invalid

IV—Laura F Steen, a daughter of Capt E D and Martha
F Steen, was born in Shelbyville, Illinois, August 5, 1867.
She was married in Danville, Illinois, May 12, 1882, to W.
S Robb, of Danville, who died in 1893   To them were
born two children, a son and a daughter, the delight of
their mother, and the joy of their grandparents, who all
live together in Chicago, at 3528 Lake Avenue

8 Daniel R Steen, the eighth child and fifth son of Dr Matthew and Elizabeth Galbraith Steen, was born in Beaver
County, Pennsylvania in August, 1838   He enlisted in the
Union Army in April, 1861, served his country faithfully
in over thirty battle-fields, until the end of the war   He contracted a severe cold at Louisville, Kentucky, when he was
mustered out of the service, and died in three weeks after
reaching his home, at Shelbyville, Illinois

II—Ann Cummins Steen, the second child and eldest daughter
of John and Ann Cummins McDole Steen, was born in Cannonsburgh Washington County, Pennsylvania, November 19,
1802, and died in December, 1879, aged 77 years   She was
married in St Clairsville, Ohio, January 2, 1827, to Michael
McHugh, he having been born in County Longford, town of
Granait, Ireland, and died in Rainsboro, Highland County,
Ohio, December 4, 1854   They continued to reside in St
Clairsville, Ohio for a number of years   To Michael and Ann
Cummins Steen McHugh were born the following seven chil-
dren

1 Bridget McHugh, the eldest daughter, was born May 31,
1828, and died near Rainsboro, Ohio, May 28, 1888, aged
60 years   She was married to Jonathan Davis, who died

near Rainsboro, Ohio, in 1875 To them were born the following six children:

I.—Sarah A Davis

II—Jane Davis, who married a Mr. McCord, and lives in Cincinnati, Ohio

III—Edward Davis

IV—Amanda Davis

V.—Zail Davis

VI—Ella Davis, who married a Mr DeWitte, and lives in Greenfield, Ohio, where she brought up a family

2. Jane McHugh, the second daughter of Michael and Ann C. Steen McHugh, was born in Ohio She was married to Edward Roberts October 15, 1860, and died in triumphant Christian faith, March 15, 1900, in Rainsboro, Ohio Her husband, Edward Roberts, died in New Antioch, Ohio, in 1861 To Edward and Jane McHugh Roberts was born one son, as follows

I—Edward McHugh Roberts now principal of the public schools of Centerfield, Ohio He is married and has two children, as follows

1 Marie Roberts

2 Harry Roberts

3 Elizabeth McHugh, the third daughter of Michael and Ann C Steen McHugh, was born in Guernsey County, Ohio, July 12, 1835 She was married at Rainsboro, Ohio, to Thomas Scarratt, in 1860, and died in Rainsboro, Highland County, Ohio, in 1864 Her husband, Thomas Scarratt, survived her many years, and died in Greenfield, Ohio about 1894 To them were born two children, as follows

I—Clara Scarratt, who married William Browning Residence, Rainsboro Ohio

II.—Laura Scarratt, who married a Mr. Zimmerman, lives in Kansas, and has several children

4 Ann McHugh, a daughter of Michael and Ann Cummins Steen McHugh, was born in Muskingum County, Ohio, May 31, 1831 Residence, Rainsboro, Highland County, Ohio

5. Edward McHugh, the only son of Michael and Ann Cummins Steen McHugh, was born in Miami County, Ohio,

September 25, 1838   He was ordained an elder in the M E.
Church at Oxford, Butler County, Ohio, by Bishop Matthew
Simpson, September 9, 1860   He has been a minister of the
M E Church in Cincinnati Conference for forty years.
He has been connected with several churches in Cincinnati,
and his pastorate in that city has extended over sixteen
years   He is now (1900) pastor of the York Street M E
Church, and has recently received a large accession to his
church   He was married, May 25, 1858, to Anna E Lieurance, who took an active part in the Woman's Crusade in
1872, and died in Georgetown, Ohio, November 11, 1879
Rev. Edward McHugh was married a second time, September 25, 1889, to Mary F Shafor, who still survives   Residence, Cincinnati, Ohio   To the Rev. Edward and Anna E
Lieurance McHugh were born six children, as follows

I —Ida Noble McHugh was born in Sugar Tree Ridge,
   Highland County, Ohio, May 25, 1859   She was married
   to Rev F M Kirgan, now (1900) pastor of Fairmount M
   E Church, Cincinnati, Ohio. To them were born two
   children, as follows
   1 Edna R Kirgan
   2 Bertha Kirgan
II —Anna Cora McHugh was born in Sharonville, Hamilton
   County, Ohio, April 13, 1861   She was married to Wil-
   liam H Remley who, for twenty years past, has been
   connected with the public schools in Cincinnati, Ohio.
   He is now (1900) principal of the Twenty-eighth District
   School, Cincinnati, Ohio   Residence, Elmwood Place,
   Hamilton County, Ohio   To them were born two children, as follows:
   1 Ralph McHugh Remley
   2 Sarah Helen Remley.
III —Mary Emily McHugh, the third daughter of Rev
   Edward and Anna E Lieurance McHugh, was born in
   Felicity, Clermont County, Ohio, March 11, 1864, and
   died September 5, 1865, aged 1 year, 5 months and 15
   days
IV —Edward Rees McHugh, the fourth child and eldest
   son of Rev Edward and Anna E Lieurance McHugh,
   was born in New Richmond, Clermont County, Ohio,
   January 30, 1866   He was married to Bertha William-

REV. EDWARD McHUGH.

son Residence. Charlestown, Illinois To Edward R and Bertha McHugh were born the following three children:

1 Anna Marie McHugh

2 Augustine Edward McHugh.

3 Amos Lieurance McHugh.

V —Frank Owrey McHugh, the fifth child and second son of Rev Edward and Anna E Lieurance McHugh, was born in East Liberty, Logan County, Ohio, April 25, 1868, and married Florence Moss, of Elmwood Place, Ohio Residence, Cincinnati, Ohio

VI —Carey Weakly McHugh, the sixth and youngest child, the third son of Rev Edward and Anna E Lieurance McHugh, was born in Waynesville, Warren County, Ohio, November 4, 1870 He is in the employ of the Kimball Piano Company Residence, Washington, D. C

6. Ellen McHugh, a daughter of Michael and Ann Cummins Steen McHugh, was born March 12, 1844. Residence. Greenfield, Ohio.

7 Lottie McHugh the seventh child, the sixth and youngest daughter of Michael and Ann Cummins Steen McHugh, was born in Highland County, Ohio, and died at Marshall, Missouri, April 30, 1899 She was married to William Thornton, who died in Marshall. Missouri, in the year 1889 To them were born two children, as follows:

I —Edward Thornton Residence, Marshall, Missouri.

II —Anna Marie Thornton, deceased

III —Jane Taylor Steen, the third child and second daughter of John Steen by his first wife — formerly Miss Ann Cummins McDole — was born in Washington County, Pennsylvania, February 17, 1805, and died in Hazel Dell, Lawrence County, Pennsylvania, July 28 1890, aged 85 years, 5 months and 11 days She was married in Hartstown, Crawford County, Pennsylvania, June 25, 1825, to George Owrey, one of the first settlers, he having been born in Adamsville, Crawford County, Pennsylvania, September 15, 1802, and died in Hazel Dell, Pennsylvania, October 22 1873, aged 71 years, 1 month and 7 days To them were born the following eight children, all born in Adamsville. Crawford County, Pennsylvania

1. Mary Ann Owrey, the eldest child, was born ——— 2, 1826 She was twice married, first in Newport, January 19, 1843, to John Gow, he having been born in Scotland, by

whom she had two children   She was married a second
time, about 1850, to a Mr Nye, by whom she had nine
children   The following are her children in the order of
birth

I —John Gow was born in New Castle, Lawrence County,
Pennsylvania, about 1844, and died in Dennison, Ohio,
about 1882, aged 38 years, 5 months and 11 days   He was
an engineer on the Pan-handle Railroad   He was married, and has a grandchild now living

II —Isabel Gow was born about 1846, was married, and died
in Virginia, aged 38 years

III.—Perinna Nye—

IV —Dan Nye—

twin children, born about 1851, and died when two weeks
old

V —George A Nye was born March 5, 1853   He was married to Rebecca Duncan by whom he had four children

VI —Nathaniel Nye was born December 6, 1854   He was
married to Maria Fowler

VII.—Margaret J. Nye was born February 15, 1857   She
was married to M Main, by whom she had one child.

VIII —Alvin L Nye was born March 4, 1859   He was married to Florence Marshall, by whom he had two children

IX —James M Nye was born July 24, 1861, and died ———.

X —Thomas Nye was born May 18 1866   He was married
to Carrie Carnwick, by whom he had four children

XI —Martin Nye was born about 1868   He was married to M Newton, by whom he had six children.

Mrs Mary Ann Nye now has two great-grandchildren,
one by the name of Gow, and the other by the name of
Nye   She resides at Hazel Dell, Pennsylvania

2 John H Owrey, the second child and eldest son of George
and Jane T Steen Owrey, was born July 13, 1828   He was
married in 1850, and died in Hazel Dell, Pennsylvania,
March 25, 1871, in the 43d year of his age

3 Isabel J Owrey, the third child and second daughter of
George and Jane T Steen Owrey, was born December 28,
1830   She was married in New Castle Pennsylvania,
December 25, 1848, to John Frazier, and died in Allegheny

City, Pennsylvania, February 28, 1871, aged 40 years and 2 months.

4 James M Owrey, the fourth child and second son of George and Jane T Steen Owrey, was born August 16, 1836 He enlisted in the army, in Company A, Seventy-sixth Regiment, Pennsylvania Volunteer Infantry, October 1, 1861, was promoted to First Sergeant November 23, 1863, and was honorably discharged October 1, 1864, having faithfully served his country three years He was married in New Castle, Pennsylvania, September 23 1858, to Lizzie Watson, and died in Beaver Falls, Pennsylvania, March 31 1878, aged 41 years 7 months and 15 days

5 Martin Van Buren Owrey, the fifth child and third son of George and Jane T Steen Owrey, was born ———— 13, 1840 He enlisted in the army May 1, 1862 He spent most of his time in the United States service as a nurse in the hospital in Virginia He was married in New Castle, Pennsylvania, July 18, 1857, to Rachel Mick

6 Maggie J Owrey, the sixth child and third daughter of George and Jane T Steen Owrey, was born March 31, 1841 She was married in New Castle Pennsylvania, July 7, 1857, to Philo D Garrett, and died in Beaver Falls, Beaver County, Pennsylvania

7 Hettie D Owrey, the seventh child and fourth daughter of George and Jane T Steen Owrey, was born April 1, 1844 She was married in Ohio, November 26, 1869, to Edward Mahan, and died in Pittsburgh, Pennsylvania November 8, 1877 aged 33 years, 7 months and 7 days

8 Cassie C Owrey the eighth child and fifth daughter of George and Jane T Steen Owrey was born August 6 1846, and died September 28, 1847

IV.—John Cummins Steen, the fourth child and second son of John Steen by his first wife, Ann Cummins McDole, was born in Beaver, Beaver County, Pennsylvania, January 31, 1807, and died unmarried in 1833, aged 26 years

V —Margaret Steen, the fifth child and third daughter of John Steen and his first wife, Ann Cummins McDole, was born in Beaver, Beaver County, Pennsylvania, January 17 1809, and died in youth, unmarried.

(18)

VI—Esther Steen. the sixth child and fourth daughter of John Steen and his first wife, Ann Cummins McDole Steen, was born in Darlington, Beaver County, Pennsylvania. September 9. 1811 and died September 9, 1884, aged 73 years She was married to Henry Owrey June 8, 1826, he having been born in 1805, and died February 1, 1890, aged 84 years To them were born the following ten children, the first seven of whom were born in Crawford County, Pennsylvania and the other three at places mentioned

1 Mary Jane Owrey, the eldest child, a daughter of Henry and Esther Steen Owrey, was born October 20 1828 She was married January 28, 1851 to Samuel Long To them were born nine children all born in Lawrence County Pennsylvania Residence, Sewickley, Pennsylvania

  I—Mary E Long, the eldest child of Samuel and Mary J Owrey Long, was born September 18, 1851 She was married, March 12, 1868, to David Fye he having been born in Mercer County, Pennsylvania, March 13, 1843. To them were born the following nine children, all born in Lawrence County Pennsylvania

   1 Reuben Frank Fye was born September 6. 1868. and died (having been killed) August 17. 1895 aged 27 years He was married to Jennie Brown November 8, 1894

   2. Samuel T Fye was born April 9. 1870 He was married to Emma Sigler, January 17, 1892

   3. Mary J. Fye was born May 8. 1872

   4. Sarah A Fye was born July 31. 1874 She was married to William McDanel, November 2 1892

   5 Willis Henry Fye was born July 10, 1877

   6 John S Fye was born February 29 1880

   7 Maud M Fye was born April 2, 1884

   8. Alice S Fye was born October 18, 1887

   9 Elmer Fye was born July 2, 1889

2 Adam Owrey the second child and eldest son of Henry and Esther Steen Owrey was born March 15. 1831 He was married July 3, 1855, to Clara Gibson Residence Ironton, Ohio

3 Anna Eliza Owrey the third child and second daughter of

Henry and Esther Steen Owrey, was born June 9, 1834, and died in infancy.

4 Matthew Steen Owrey, the fourth child and second son of Henry and Esther Steen Owrey, was born March 6, 1837, and died in infancy.

5 Margaret Maria Owrey, the fifth child and third daughter of Henry and Esther Steen Owrey, was born April 15, 1838 She was married October 10, 1860, to William H Clark Residence, West Williamsfield, Ohio

6 Joseph Ball Owrey, the sixth child and third son of Henry and Esther Steen Owrey, was born January 20, 1841. He enlisted in the army, September 10, 1861, in Company A, Seventy-sixth Pennsylvania Infantry, and was killed at Fort Wagner, South Carolina, July 23 1863, in the 23d year of his age

7 Matilda Ann Owrey, the seventh child and fourth daughter of Henry and Esther Steen Owrey was born March 30, 1845 She was married August 1, 1868, to William T Shurlock, he having been born in Beaver County, Pennsylvania, November 28, 1831 Residence, Wampum, Pennsylvania To them eight children were born, all born in Lawrence County, Pennsylvania

    I—Elizabeth Shurlock was born March 18, 1869 She was married December 5, 1889, to Robert McAnlis Residence, Wampum, Pennsylvania

    II—Sara Lillian Shurlock was born July 30, 1871

    III—Margaret McAnlis Shurlock was born August 8, 1874. She was married November 17, 1898, to Charles W Cross Residence near Moravia, Pennsylvania

    IV—Anna Catheryne Shurlock was born August 4 1877

    V—William Samuel Shurlock was born September 10, 1880

    VI—Thomas Shurlock was born January 9, 1883 and died in infancy

    VII—Charles Parkhurst Shurlock was born July 1, 1884

    VIII—Ethel Claire Shurlock was born May 28, 1890

8 John Cummins Owrey, the eighth child and fourth son of Henry and Esther Steen Owrey, was born in Bridgewater, Pennsylvania, May 18, 1848 Residence, Baltimore, Maryland

9 Charles Henry Owrey, the ninth child and fifth son of
Henry and Esther Steen Owrey, was born in New Castle,
Pennsylvania, February 28, 1851. He was married Novem-
ber 10, 1874, to Margaret Robinson, she having been born
July 25, 1852   Residence, New Castle, Pennsylvania   To
them were born eight children, as follows, all born in New
Castle, Pennsylvania

   I —Joseph Edward Owrey was born May 7, 1876

   II —William Oscar Owrey was born November 14 1877

   III —Andrew G Owrey was born April 16, 1880.

   IV —Mabel Claire Owrey was born May 7, 1884

   V —Richard Owrey was born April 20, 1886

   VI —Sarah J Owrey was born March 13, 1888

   VII —Rhoda Belle Owrey was born December 3. 1889

   VIII —Fannie M Owrey was born December 19, 1891

10 William Oscar Owrey, the tenth child and sixth son of
Henry and Esther Steen Owrey. was born at New Castle,
Pennsylvania, May 24, 1853   He was married to Nellie
Messhemer   Residence, Weston, Ohio

VII.—Eliza Steen, the seventh child and fifth daughter of John
Steen and his first wife, Ann Cummins McDole Steen, was
born in Petersburgh, Mahoning County, Ohio, July 16, 1816
She was married May 15, 1834, to James C Mitchell, a merchant and shoemaker, he having been born near Greenville,
Pennsylvania. October 14, 1813, and was drowned at sea
between Cuba and New York   To them were born the following four children

1 William Mitchell was born February 28, 1835, and died
December 29, 1867, leaving no posterity

2 John Steen Mitchell was born November 29, 1836   He was
married July 3, 1860, to Margaret Luse, a daughter of David
and Ellen Luse, of Kennard, Mercer County, Pennsylvania,
she having been born March 25, 1834   Residence, Hartstown, Crawford County, Pennsylvania   To John S and
Margaret L. Mitchell were born the following three children

   I —Sarah M Mitchell was born March 28, 1861. She was
married August 24, 1882. to Myron M Miller, of Hartstown, Pennsylvania. he having been born February 22.

1859   Residence, Hartstown, Pennsylvania   To Myron
M and Sarah M Miller were born the following three
children

.1   Rollin Steen Miller was born June 23, 1883, and died
    April 9, 1887, in the 4th year of his age

2   Samuel Marcus Miller was born April 8, 1889

3   James Milo Miller was born November 3 1893

II —Ellen M Mitchell, the second daughter of John S and
Margaret L Mitchell, was born June 27, 1862   She was
married December 2, 1886, to Harry P. McElroy, of Sum-
merville, Jefferson County, Pennsylvania, he having been
born August 21, 1856   Residence, 153 Herron Avenue,
Pittsburgh, Pennsylvania   To Harry P and Ellen M.
McElroy were born the following four children.

1   Marguerite Pritner McElroy was born December 24,
    1888

2   Marjorie Sarah McElroy was born July 26, 1890

3   Myron Mitchell McElroy was born November 17 1898,
    and died November 3, 1899, aged almost one year

4   Harry Kenneth McElroy was born November 19 1898
    and died January 4, 1899, aged less than two months
    The two last-named were twins

III —James C Mitchell the third child and only son of John
S and Margaret L Mitchell, was born August 23, 1864
He was married May 8 1887, to Lottie Barbour, of Ken-
nard, Mercer County, Pennsylvania, she having been born
April 28, 1864   Residence, Atlantic, Crawford County.
Pennsylvania   To James C and Lottie Barbour Mitchell
were born the following six children   .

1   John Thurman Mitchell was born February 11, 1888

2   Myron Malcolm Mitchell was born February 11, 1890

3   Alice Marie Mitchell was born April 14, 1891, and died
    August 9, 1893, aged 2 years, 3 months and 26 days

4   William Max Mitchell was born August 23, 1893

5   James Milton Mitchell, a twin brother of the preceding,
    was born August 23, 1893, and died September 4, 1896,
    aged 3 years and 12 days.

6   Donna Crystal Mitchell was born January 13, 1897

3 Sarah Mitchell, the third child and eldest daughter of James
C and Eliza Steen Mitchell, was born October 31, 1838, and
died September 29, 1874, aged 35 years, 10 months and 29
days.

4 Annie Mitchell, the fourth and youngest child of James C.
and Eliza Steen Mitchell, was born December 11, 1839, and
died October 14 1840, aged 10 months and 3 days

Eliza Steen Mitchell, the seventh child and fifth daughter of
John and Ann Cummins McDole Steen, was married a second
time, July 29, 1842, to Joseph Ball — a farmer,— of Adamsville, Pennsylvania, he having been born June 29 1815, and
died in Garden Valley, California, in May, 1891 in the 76th
year of his age   Mrs Eliza Steen Mitchell Ball died in Canton, Lewis County, Missouri, March 31, 1886, aged 69 years,
3 months and 16 days   To Joseph and Eliza Steen Mitchell
Ball were born five children, as follows

5 George W Ball, the eldest child of his father, but the fifth
child of his mother, Eliza Steen Mitchell Ball, was born June
30, 1843, and died June 21, 1898, aged 54 years, 11 months
and 21 days He was married, September 13, 1866, to
Morilla J DuMars, of Kennard, Pennsylvania. She having
been born March 13, 1846, and still resides at Kennard,
Mercer County, Pennsylvania   To George W and Morilla
J Ball was born one child, as follows

I —Nannie Belle Ball was born July 15, 1876

6 Morrow B L Ball, the second son of Joseph, but the sixth
child of Eliza Steen Mitchell Ball, was born February 26,
1845, and died July 2, 1865, aged 20 years, 4 months and 6
days

7 Joseph W Ball, the third son of Joseph Ball, being the seventh child of his wife, Eliza Steen Mitchell Ball, was born
in Hancock County, Illinois, near Nauvoo November 9,
1847   He was married by the Rev Thomas Musgrove, of
the Baptist Church, at the home of his wife's parents, in
Walnut Grove, Clarke County, Missouri, June 4, 1871, to
Annie E Childers, a daughter of R L and Mary Childers,
she having been born July 2, 1853   Residence Oklahoma,
Oklahoma County, Oklahoma Territory   Rev Joseph W
Ball writes as follows, giving additional information concerning the family.

OKLAHOMA CITY, March 3, 1900

My parents removed from Hancock County, Illinois to Fort
Madison, Iowa, where we resided for several years From this
place father made his first trip to California, in 1851, leaving his
three boys, George Morrow and myself, with mother He was
gone three years and six months, when he returned home and
remained three years and three months The family then
removed to Macon City, Missouri, from which place father went
to Pike's Peak remaining two years and six months During this
time the Civil War broke out, and mother removed with the
family to Adams County, Illinois, where we all remained until
father returned to us, in 1861 We continued at this place until
the spring of 1863, when father and mother thought best to return
to California again, which we did We started April 28, 1863,
going overland We had to use horses and wagons, and father
had selected the very best that could be had We drove to
Keokuk, Iowa, the roads being muddy, we shipped to Eddyville,
and then drove over to Omaha, where we organized into a train
numbering twenty-six wagons Father was appointed Captain
of the train and we traveled up the North Platte River for nine
hundred miles We had many adventures too numerous to
mention but there was one incident which I will relate. At
Horse Shoe Bend, on the Platte River, we were attacked by the
Sioux Indians, who succeeded in capturing our horses leaving
only one horse in the entire train Fortunately for father, he
was traveling with a train of ox teams, and had extra yokes
and bows so that we were able to get started again, and finally
reached Uncle Wells Phillips, who lived four miles from the
summit, where we stopped for a while and rested up We then
went on to Sacramento, California, where we remained two years,
and returned to the States by way of the Isthmus of Panama,
thence to New York, and from there to Mercer County Pennsylvania, where Brother John S Mitchell and family lived, and near
the place where father and mother were brought up and married
From that place father and mother brother Dan and sister Mary
went West to Illinois leaving brother George and myself in
Mercer County Pennsylvania, where George was married Soon
after his marriage I also went West, to where father and mother
were Not long afterwards I went over into Lewis County, Missouri, where I remained for some time, forming quite a number
of new acquaintances, among whom I was enabled to select a
most worthy and lovable wife, and a new era was begun in my
life In 1887, at the age of forty years, I was licensed to preach
in the M E Church (South), in Knox County Missouri In the
fall of 1893 I was transferred to the Indians Mission Conference,
having a justifiable cause, I withdrew from this Conference and
joined the Congregational Church I am now a licensed minister
in the Southeast Association of the Congregational Church, and
have three appointments I am living on my farm eight miles
west of Oklahoma City, in what is called the wheat belt, and
the wheat is looking well at this writing We have had fourteen
children, thirteen of whom are still living — eight boys and five
girls, twelve were born in Missouri and the two last in Oklahoma
Territory We have two children married, but no grandchildren

    I am yours,   JOSEPH W BALL

The following are the living children of Joseph W and Annie E Ball

I—Morrow B Ball was born March 16, 1872

II—Robert Leonard Ball was born July 10, 1873   He was married in Montana to Miss Jessie Foy

III—Myra N Ball was born April 27, 1875

IV—Joseph Harvey Ball was born May 24, 1877.

V—Arthur Lewis Ball was born March 3, 1880

VI—Katie M Ball was born May 15, 1881   She was married to George McMurry, of Missouri

VII—Nora B Ball was born ——— 18, 1882

VIII—Samuel F Ball was born January 4, 1886

IX—Annie S Ball was born December 16, 1888

X—Decoy Ball was born June 5 1890

XI—Nellie F Ball was born March 22, 1892

XII—Freddie B Ball was born February 9, 1894

XIII—Mary Ruth Ball was born July 1, 1896

8 Daniel Renehart Ball, the fourth son of Joseph Ball, but the eighth child of his wife, Eliza Steen Mitchell Ball, was born June 29, 1854   He was married October 10, 1881, to Melvina J Job, she having been born July 10, 1863   Residence, Canton, Lewis County, Missouri.

9 Mary Belle Ball, the fifth child and only daughter of Joseph Ball, but the ninth child of his wife, Eliza Steen Mitchell Ball, was born June 10, 1857   She was married March 12, 1883, to Alletta C Johnson, of Canton, Lewis County, Missouri, he having been born September 16, 1858   To Alletta C and Mary Belle Ball Johnson was born one son, as follows

I—Joseph Hamilton Johnson was born October 1, 1884 Residence, Canton, Lewis County, Missouri

VIII—Hugh Barnes Steen, the eighth child and third son of John Steen, the eldest child by his second wife, Catherine Barnes Steen, was born in Westmoreland County, Pennsylvania, January 13, 1819, and died in New Castle. Pennsylvania April 13, 1887   He was married near Enon, Lawrence County, Pennsylvania, March 24, 1843, to Ann Johnston, she having been born in County Fermaugh, Ireland September 25, 1819, and died in New Castle, Pennsylvania, May 23, 1897, in the 78th year of her age   They were both earnest Christians.

members of the United Presbyterian Church, and brought up their family in the fear of the Lord. Their bodies now rest in Greenwood cemetery, New Castle, Pennsylvania. Ann Johnston came with her parents to this country in 1825 and located first near Darlington, Beaver County, Pennsylvania, and later near Enon, Pennsylvania, where her young womanhood was spent. The family came to New Castle, Pennsylvania, about 1854, where they afterwards resided. To Hugh Barnes and Ann Johnston Steen were born the following eight children:

1 William Johnston Steen, the eldest son of Capt. Hugh B and Ann J Steen, was born in Bridgewater, Beaver County, Pennsylvania April 27, 1844. He enlisted in the army June 27, 1863, and was discharged August 26 1863. He was married at Tarr Farm, Pennsylvania, September 7 1871 to Lucy Ann Parker, who died in Olean, New York, January 9, 1880. He was married a second time in Leadville, Colorado, in 1884, to Mrs Franklin De Tour. Residence, Cripple Creek, Colorado. To William J Steen and his first wife were born two children as follows.

  I—Edgar Parker Steen, the eldest son of William J and Lucy A Steen, was born at Tarr Farm, Pennsylvania, June 14, 1872.

  II—William Lewis Steen the second son of William J and Lucy A Steen was born at Tarr Farm, Pennsylvania, April 21, 1874.

2 Mara Louisa Steen, the second child and eldest daughter of Capt Hugh B and Ann Johnston Steen, was born in Butler County, Pennsylvania, September 16, 1846. She was married in New Castle, Pennsylvania, December 28 1869, to Richard Addison Parks, who died January 24 1889. They have no children. Residence, New Castle, Pennsylvania.

3 Anna Catherine Steen, the third child and second daughter of Capt Hugh B and Ann Johnston Steen was born in Butler County, Pennsylvania January 13 1849. She removed with her parents to New Castle, Pennsylvania, about 1854, where her permanent home has been ever since. Being a faithful and very successful teacher, she has spent much of her time teaching in other localities. She is a devout Christian, and a very useful member of society. Her mother lived for forty-three years in the same house in New

Castle, Pennsylvania, No 118 South Jefferson Street, which
is still the residence of herself and youngest brother

4 John Walker Steen, the fourth child and second son of
Capt Hugh B and Ann Johnston Steen, was born in Butler
County, Pennsylvania, July 15, 1851   He was married in
Olean, New York July 15, 1880, to Ida May Parker   They
have had no children   John W Steen died in Leadville,
Colorado, November 19, 1880, in the 29th year of his age

5 Elizabeth Eudora Steen the fifth child and third daughter of
Capt Hugh B and Ann Johnston Steen, was born in Butler
County, Pennsylvania, November 15, 1853 and died in New
Castle, Pennsylvania, December 25, 1856, in the fourth year
of her age.

6 Robert Lewis Steen, the sixth child and third son of Capt
Hugh B and Ann Johnston Steen, was born in New Castle,
Pennsylvania, November 11, 1856   R Lewis Steen still
resides in New Castle, Pennsylvania

7 Hugh Craig Steen the seventh child and fourth son of Capt
Hugh B and Ann Johnston Steen, was born in New Castle,
Pennsylvania January 1, 1859   He was married in Buffalo,
New York April 20, 1887, to Sara Myers   Residence. New
Castle, Pennsylvania   To them were born the following four
children

   I —Alice Catherine Steen, the eldest daughter of H Craig
and Sara Myers Steen, was born in New Castle, Pennsylvania, February 26, 1888, and died July 31, 1888

   II —Mary Ethel Steen, the second daughter of H Craig and
Sara Myers Steen, was born in New Castle, Pennsylvania,
October 9, 1889, and died July 9, 1890

   III —Helen Marguerite Steen, the third daughter of H
Craig and Sara Myers Steen, was born in New Castle,
Pennsylvania, June 21, 1891, and died July 27, 1891

   IV —Etta May Steen, the fourth daughter of H Craig and
Sara Myers Steen, was born in Buffalo, New York, June
28, 1892, and died in New Castle, Pennsylvania, March 29,
1899 in the seventh year of her age

8 Andrew Jackson Steen, the eighth child, the fifth and youngest son of Capt Hugh Barnes and Ann Johnston Steen, was
born in New Castle, Pennsylvania July 28, 1863   He was
married in Youngstown, Ohio, July 28, 1886, to Ida May

Roland, who died in New Castle, Pennsylvania, November 25, 1887 Residence, No 118 South Jefferson Street, New Castle, Pennsylvania. To them was born the following child·

I —Richard Andrew Steen, son of Andrew J and Ida May Steen, was born in New Castle Pennsylvania, November 18, 1887

IX —Samuel Steen the ninth child and fourth son of John Steen, the second by his second wife, Catherine Barnes Steen, was born in New Athens, Ohio, October 6, 1821, and died in infancy

X —Robert Lewis Steen, the tenth child and fifth son of John Steen, the third by his second wife Catherine Barnes Steen, was born in New Athens, Harrison County, Ohio June 10, 1823 He was married in Ravenna, Portage County, Ohio, February 29, 1849, to Mary Jane Bunting, she having been born in Hookstown Beaver County, Pennsylvania, and died in Ravenna, Ohio, March 22, 1867 To them were born eight children Robert L Steen was married a second time, in Darlington Beaver County, Pennsylvania, July 4 1871, to Nancy Bartlett Barr, who died in Osage, Kansas May 14, 1874 To them was born one child Robert L Steen was married a third time in Lawrence, Kansas, in 1877 or 1878 to Mrs Elizabeth D McQuiston There were no children to this marriage Robert L Steen died at his home, in Lawrence, Kansas October 13, 1899, aged 76 years, 4 months and 3 days The interment took place at Topeka Kansas, on Monday, October 16, 1899 For years he had been a great sufferer, confined to the house and to his bed for the last four months His affliction was cancer of the face, which at last reached his brain He was not entirely rational for the last two weeks of his life but he had said he was ready and waiting for God to take him home Death was to him a happy release Family residence, Lawrence, Kansas

1 Myra Louisa Steen the eldest daughter of Robert L. and Mary J. Steen, was born in Beaver County, Pennsylvania, October 22, 1849 She was married in New Galilee, Beaver County, Pennsylvania, October 20, 1870, to John Samuel Porter, he having been born in Allegheny County, Pennsylvania, October 11, 1848 They are both members of the Sixth United Presbyterian Church of Pittsburgh Resi-

dence, 327 Hailman Street Pittsburgh, Pennsylvania **To** them were born the following five children

I —Charles Robert Porter was born May 29 1872

II —George Porter was born August 18, 1875

III —John Francis Porter was born June 26, 1878

IV —Vernon Harry Porter was born November 4, 1880

V —Edward Milligan Porter was born November 26, 1885.

2 Robert Alexander Steen, the second child and eldest son of Robert L and Mary J Steen, was born in Bridgewater, Beaver County, Pennsylvania, May 7, 1852 He was married in Council Grove, Kansas, February 27, 1877, to Clara Alice Dillon, she having been born in Darlington, Beaver County, Pennsylvania July 20, 1856 Robert A Steen was County Commissioner of Otero County, Colorado Residence, La Junta, Colorado To them were born the following children

I —Sarah Armstrong Steen, the eldest child of Robert A. and Clara A Steen, was born in Trinidad, Colorado, April 15 1881

II —Walter Strieby Steen, the second child of Robert A and Clara A Steen, was born in Council Grove, Kansas, February 12 1884.

3 Lucy Althea Steen, the third child and second daughter of Robert L and Mary J Steen, was born in Lawrence County, Pennsylvania, January 14, 1853 She was married in Topeka Kansas, March 6, 1873, to Alpheus Hodges, he having been born in Cambridgeboro, Pennsylvania May 4, 1845 Residence, Lakewood, Chautauqua County New York To them were born the following six children

I —Arthur P Hodges was born in Osage City Kansas, November 16 1874

II —Laura M Hodges was born in Scranton, Osage County, Kansas July 14, 1876

III —Ralph A Hodges was born in Topeka Kansas June 8 1878

IV —Alice G Hodges was born in Topeka Kansas April 21, 1880, and died in Scranton, Kansas, August 4, 1880

V —John P Hodges was born in Watts Flats Chautauqua County, New York, March 12, 1882

VI.—Myra L. Hodges was born in Watts Flats, New York, January 3. 1885, and died at the same place January 20, 1886.

4 Charles Henry Oman Steen. the fourth child and second son of Robert L and Mary Jane Steen, was born in Wells County, Indiana, October 8, 1854 He was married in Darlington, Beaver County, Pennsylvania, October 23 1877, to Mary Alice Hanna, she having been born in Darlington, Pennsylvania, August 8, 1854 Residence, Champaign, Illinois. To them were born two children, as follows

I—William Charles Steen was born in Newton Kansas, July 29, 1878

II—Henry Socorro Steen was born in Socorio, New Mexico, September 29 1880

5 Lewis Morgan Steen, the fifth child and third son of Robert L and Mary J Steen, was born in Huntington. Indiana, June 30, 1857 He was married in Scranton. Kansas, March 15, 1877, to Ida May Baxter, she having been born in Osage County, Kansas, January 23, 1861 Residence, La Junta, Colorado To them were born the following four children

I—Hattie Myra Steen was born in Scranton, Kansas September 29, 1878

II.—Lena Alice Steen was born in Scranton, Kansas March 29, 1881

III—John Engle Steen was born in Engle, New Mexico, April 2, 1884

IV—Theo Mamie Steen was born in Scranton Kansas, September 13, 1886

6 John Norton Steen, the sixth child and fourth son of Robert L and Mary J Steen was born in Hannibal Missouri June 27, 1859 He has been an engineer of the Santa Fe Railroad ever since 1879 He was married in Topeka Kansas, December 25 1884, to Cordelia Pasley, a daughter of William Thomas and Mary Adaline Pasley, she having been born in Jackson County, Missouri December 10 1866 Residence, Edmond, Oklahoma Territory. To them was born one son, as follows·

I—Charles John Steen was born in Engle, New Mexico, January 12, 1886

7 Vernon Elliott Steen, the seventh child and fifth son of
Robert L and Mary J Steen, was born in Hannibal, Missouri, May 3, 1861   He was married in Kansas City, Missouri, September 17, 1885, to Minta Elizabeth Powell, she
having been born in Sparta, Indiana, September 16, 1867
They have no children   Residence, Kansas City, Missouri.

8 Hattie Hill Steen, the eighth child and third daughter of
Robert Lewis and Mary Jane Bunting Steen, was born in
Ravenna, Portage County, Ohio, December 30, 1862, and
died in Council Grove, Kansas, December 27, 1874, in the
12th year of her age

9 George Barr Steen, the ninth child and sixth son of Robert
Lewis Steen, the only child by his second wife, Nancy Bartlett Barr Steen, was born in Topeka, Kansas, September 9,
1872 — a clerk   Residence, Topeka, Kansas

XI —Maria Steen, the eleventh child of John Steen, the fourth
child and eldest daughter by his second wife, Catherine Barnes
Steen, was born in Cadiz, Harrison County, Ohio January 3,
1826, and died suddenly of paralysis at Industry, Pennsylvania,
January 8, 1894, aged 68 years and 5 days   She was married
by the Rev A Bowers in Bridgewater, Beaver County, Pennsylvania, October 29, 1846, to Eli McNees, who died April 16,
1891.   To them was born one child, as follows

1 Everette H McNees, the only child of Eli and Maria Steen
McNees, was born February 11, 1865

XII —Mara Louisa Steen, the twelfth child and seventh daughter
of John Steen, the second by his second wife, Catherine Barnes
Steen, was born in Beaver County, Pennsylvania, February
26, 1829, and died in 1846, unmarried, aged 17 years

CHAPTER IV

Joseph Steen, the fourth child and third son of Matthew and
Jane Taylor Steen, was born in Cannonsburgh, Washington
County, Pennsylvania, March 1, 1781, his parents having removed
from Philadelphia, or Eastern Pennsylvania to that place in 1780
He was married in Washington County, Pennsylvania, about

1804, to Elizabeth Steen (a cousin or second cousin, called "Betsy"), and soon afterwards removed to Cadiz, Harrison County, Ohio, where all their children were born The family afterwards returned to Pennsylvania, where Joseph Steen and his wife spent the remainder of their lives   To Joseph and Elizabeth Steen were born the following five children

I —Jane Steen, the eldest child, a daughter of Joseph and Elizabeth Steen, was born in Cadiz, Ohio, about 1805   She was never married, but lived a useful life, and died at the age of 80 years.

II —James Steen, the second child and eldest son of Joseph and Elizabeth Steen, was born in Cadiz Ohio, about 1808   He was married to Elizabeth Chatley (called ' Betsy''), near Darlington, Beaver County, Pennsylvania, probably about 1830 and died a few years later   To James and Elizabeth Chatley Steen were born two children, as follows

  1 Frank Steen was born probably about 1832

  2 Joseph Steen was probably born about 1834

III —John Steen, the third child and second son of Joseph and Elizabeth Steen was born in Cadiz, Ohio, about 1810   He was married in New Castle, Pennsylvania, probably about 1834, to Eliza Campbell, and both of them died in Pennsylvania   To them were born two children, as follows·

  1 Maria Steen

  2 Eliza J Steen

IV.—Matthew Steen, the fourth child and third son of Joseph and Elizabeth Steen, was born in Cadiz, Ohio, probably about 1812   He was married in Beaver County, Pennsylvania, to Anna Parks, probably about 1835, and both of them died in Pennsylvania   To Matthew and Anna Parks Steen were born the following four children·

  1 Taylor Steen

  2 Samuel Steen

  3 Sarah Ann Steen

  4 Daniel L Steen

V —Eliza Steen the fifth child and second daughter of Joseph and Elizabeth Steen, was born in Cadiz, Harrison County Ohio, April 15, 1815 and died in New Castle, Pennsylvania.

December 2 1892, aged 77 years, 7 months and 17 days   She was married near Darlington, Pennsylvania, about 1840, to David Crawford, he having been born in Beaver County, Pennsylvania March 31 1802, and died in 1878 aged 76 years   To them were born the following six children

1 John Crawford, the eldest son of David and Eliza Steen Crawford, was born in New Castle Pennsylvania, January 17, 1842   He was married in October, 1867 to Sophia Branch, and brought up a family of children

2 James Crawford, the second child of David and Eliza Steen Crawford, a twin brother of the preceding, was born in New Castle, Pennsylvania, January 17, 1842 and died in infancy

3 Eliza J Crawford the third child and eldest daughter of David and Eliza Steen Crawford, was born in New Castle, Pennsylvania, January 22, 1846   She was married December 17, 1868 to Samuel McClintock Dickson, he having been born in Harrisville, Butler County, Pennsylvania, March 9, 1839   They lived in New Castle, Pennsylvania To them were born two children, as follows

I—Alice J Dickson, the eldest daughter of Samuel M and Eliza J Dickson, was born in New Castle, Pennsylvania, March 3 1873   She was married in New Castle, Pennsylvania, July 5, 1893, to Elmer C Snyder, he having been born in Kremis, Butler County, Pennsylvania, March 19 1871   Both are devout members of the Lutheran Church   Residence, New Castle Pennsylvania   To them were born the following children

   1 Ralph Dickson Snyder was born in New Castle, Pennsylvania March 3, 1894

   2 Silvia Elizabeth Snyder was born in New Castle, Pennsylvania, February 4, 1896.

II—Jessie Crawford Dickson, the second daughter of Samuel M and Eliza J Crawford Dickson, was born in New Castle, Pennsylvania October 11, 1876   She was married December 8, 1896, to Norman R Miller   Residence, New Castle, Pennsylvania

4 Margaret Crawford the fourth child and second daughter of David and Eliza Steen Crawford, was born in New Castle, Pennsylvania in 1847, and died in her youth

5 David Crawford, the fifth child and third son of David and
   Eliza Steen Crawford, was born in New Castle, Pennsylvania in 1848   He was married and brought up a family
6 Joseph Crawford, the sixth child and fourth son of David
   and Eliza Steen Crawford, was born in New Castle, Pennsylvania, in 1852   He was married and brought up a family

CHAPTER V

Margaret Steen, the fifth child and second daughter of Matthew and Jane Taylor Steen, was born in Cannonsburgh, Washington County, Pennsylvania, October 4 1782, and died in
Beaver County, Pennsylvania, December 3 1844, in the 63d year
of her age   Her father was born in the north of Ireland, and her
parents resided in Philadelphia until 1780 when they removed to
Washington County, Pennsylvania, near Cannonsburgh   Margaret Steen removed with her parents to Beaver County Pennsylvania in 1804, when she was a young woman, and they located
on what was then known as the Platt farm, near the present site
of Beaver Falls, Pennsylvania which at that time was almost a
wilderness   The next season after their arrival in Beaver
County Miss Margaret Steen met a young man who had recently
arrived from Mt Holly New Jersey, his native place, a carpenter and cabinet-maker, who had come to the West to seek his
fortune   His name was Daniel Reeves, and a strong mutual
attachment sprang up between them resulting a few years later
in their marriage   The Reeves family are of Welsh extraction,
and Joseph Reeves resided in Mount Holly New Jersey, where
his body lies buried in the Episcopal cemetery there   Among
his children was a son, also named Joseph Reeves who was born
in Mt Holly New Jersey July 5, 1758, and who afterwards
married Elizabeth Toy, and brought up a family of children
His eldest son Daniel Reeves came to Beaver County, Pennsylvania in 1805 when twenty-two years of age and remained
until death   Margaret Steen was married in 1808 on the Platt
farm near Beaver Falls, Pennsylvania to Daniel Reeves an
excellent and devout Christian man, he having been born in Mt
(19)

Holly, New Jersey, in 1783, and died November 30, 1837, in the 54th year of his age, being drowned in the Beaver River   To them were born the following eight children

I —Eliza Reeves, the eldest daughter of Daniel and Margaret Steen Reeves, was born near Beaver Falls, Pennsylvania, March 9, 1809, and died March 14 1892, aged 83 years and 5 days   She was married in Beaver County, Pennsylvania, January 1, 1828, to Samuel Corbus   To them were born the following seven children·

1. Mary Jane Corbus
2 Thankful Corbus
3 John Corbus
4 Margaret Corbus
5 Daniel Corbus
6. Jesse Corbus
7 Elizabeth Corbus

II —Mary Jane Reeves, the second daughter of Daniel and Margaret Steen Reeves, was born near Beaver Falls Beaver County, Pennsylvania, May 20, 1811, and died April 25, 1884, in the 73d year of her age   She was married in Beaver County, Pennsylvania, October 7, 1834, to David Whitla   To them were born the following nine children

1. William H· Whitla
2 Joseph Whitla
3 Elizabeth Whitla
4 Amanda Whitla
5 Esther Whitla
6 Margaret Ann Whitla.
7 Henry Whitla
8 John Whitla
9 Henry Reeves Whitla

III —Valariah Reeves, the third daughter of Daniel and Margaret Steen Reeves was born near Beaver Falls. Beaver County, Pennsylvania March 27. 1814. and died February 18 1867, in the 53d year of her age   She was married near Beaver Falls, Pennsylvania. October 8. 1834, to William Carter   To them were born the following five children

JOHN REEVES.

1 Charles Carter
2 Adelaide Carter.
3 Margaret Carter
4. Elizabeth Carter.
5 John Carter

IV —Joseph Reeves, the fourth child and eldest son of Daniel and Margaret Steen Reeves, was born near Beaver Falls, Pennsylvania, February 16, 1818, and died July 2, 1876, aged 58 years, 4 months and 16 days He was married July 4, 1843, to Sarah McGahey To them were born the following five children:

1 Mary Jane Reeves
2 Elizabeth Reeves
3 Margaret Reeves.
4 John B Reeves
5 James J. Reeves

V —Esther Reeves, the fifth child and fourth daughter of Daniel and Margaret Steen Reeves, was born near Beaver Falls, Pennsylvania, September 29, 1820, and died ——— She was married July 8, 1841, to Henry Hipple To them were born the following four children

1 James Hipple
2 William Hipple
3 Margaret Hipple
4 Thankful Hipple

VI —Matthew Reeves, the sixth child and second son of Daniel and Margaret Steen Reeves, was born near Beaver Falls, Pennsylvania, February 14 1823, and died March 31, 1823

VII —John Reeves, the seventh child and third son of Daniel and Margaret Steen Reeves, was born near Beaver Falls, Pennsylvania, February 9, 1825 He is a banker and prominent business man, a member and trustee of the Presbyterian Church He was married March 25, 1847, to Cynthia Murphy To them were born ten children Residence, Beaver Falls, Pennsylvania

1. Daniel F Reeves, the eldest son of John and Cynthia M Reeves, was born in Beaver Falls, Pennsylvania, May 6, 1848, and died March 7, 1876, in the 28th year of his age He

was married April 3, 1866, to Mary E Smith   To them was born one child, a daughter, as follows.

I.—Addie G. Reeves, daughter of Daniel F and Mary E Reeves, was born January 11, 1867 She was married February 5, 1885, to Mark Wisener, Jr To them were born two children, as follows

   1 Hazel Wisener was born May 16, 1886

   2 Harry Wisener was born August 22, 1888.

2 Mary A Reeves, the second child and eldest daughter of John and Cynthia M Reeves, was born in Beaver Falls, Pennsylvania, November 22 1849 She was married April 16, 1874, to J F Merriman   To them were born the following four children

   I Susan Merriman was born July 7, 1876, and died December 14, 1877, aged 1 year. 5 months and 7 days

   II —Jessie H Merriman was born January 1, 1881

   III.—Harry N. Merriman was born December 5, 1884

   IV —Ethel Navada Merriman was born November 25, 1891.

3 Ada E Reeves, the third child and second daughter of John and Cynthia M Reeves, was born in Beaver Falls, Pennsylvania, May 17, 1852 She was married October 12 1871, to H W. Nair. To them were born two children, as follows·

   I —Harry W Nair was born May 11, 1872 and died October 13, 1877, aged 5 years. 5 months and 2 days.

   II —Frank M Nair was born December 13, 1877.

4 William H Reeves, the fourth child and second son of John and Cynthia M Reeves, was born in Beaver Falls, Pennsylvania, July 19, 1854, and died June 3, 1860, in the 6th year of his age

5. John Charles Fremont Reeves, the fifth child and third son of John and Cynthia M Reeves, was born in Beaver Falls, Pennsylvania, October 20 1856, and died June 16, 1860, in the 4th year of his age

6 Hannah Reeves, the sixth child and third daughter of John and Cynthia M Reeves, was born in Beaver Falls, Pennsylvania, December 20. 1858 She was married October 2, 1877, to James M. May To them were born the following six children

I—Charles R May was born April 3, 1879

II—John W May was born October 9, 1880

III—James M May, Jr., was born October 14, 1883

IV—Grace May was born November 15, 1885

V—Arthur L May was born April 10, 1887

VI—Marjorie May was born December 24, 1898

7 Jessie Benton Reeves, the seventh child and fourth daughter of John and Cynthia M Reeves, was born in Beaver Falls, Pennsylvania, August 13, 1861 She was married September 16, 1887, to W J. Asdale

8 John Toy Reeves, the eighth child and fourth son of John and Cynthia M Reeves, was born in Beaver Falls, Pennsylvania, November 11, 1863 He was married October 17, 1887, to Lulu N Knight

9 Grace Reeves, the ninth child and fifth daughter of John and Cynthia Murphy Reeves, was born in Beaver Falls, Pennsylvania, September 11, 1866 She was married January 27, 1885, to George W. Coates To them were born the following three children·

I—George W Coates, Jr , was born February 21, 1886

II—Eugene Coates was born February 20, 1887, and died February 24 1887

III—Thomas R Coates was born June 10, 1891

10. Jacob Henrici Reeves, the tenth child and fifth son of John and Cynthia Murphy Reeves, was born in Beaver Falls, Pennsylvania, June 16, 1869, and died December 18, 1876, in the eighth year of his age

VII—Henry Taylor Reeves, the eighth child of Daniel and Margaret Steen Reeves, was born near Beaver Falls, Beaver County, Pennsylvania, October 14, 1827, and died in Jacksonville, Florida, whither he had gone in search of health, November 16, 1889, in the 63d year of his age He was a prominent and successful business man in Beaver Falls, Pennsylvania, for many years, a devout Christian, a member of the Methodist Protestant Church, an influential and useful citizen He was married October 27, 1857, to Sarah Jane Haines The family residence is at Beaver Falls, Pennsylvania The following are their five children

1 Harry W Reeves, the eldest son of Henry Taylor and Sarah
J Haines Reeves, was born in Beaver Falls, Pennsylvania,
April 21, 1860

2 Martha Jane Reeves, the second child and only daughter of
Henry T and Sarah J Reeves, was born in Beaver Falls,
Pennsylvania, April 27, 1862

3 Walter Reeves, the third child and second son of Henry
T and Sarah J Reeves, was born in Beaver Falls, Pennsylvania, March 8, 1864, and died February 24, 1885, in the 21st
year of his age

4 Romulus L B Reeves, the fourth child and third son of
Henry T. and Sarah J Reeves, was born in Beaver Falls,
Pennsylvania, January 1, 1866

5 Albert Reeves, the fifth and youngest son of Henry Taylor
and Sarah Jane Haines Reeves, was born in Beaver Falls,
Pennsylvania, June 21, 1868, and died July 30, 1877, in the
20th year of his age

BOOK FIVE.

DESCENDANTS OF JAMES STEEN.

James Steen was born in Ireland about 1730, was married to Rachel Moore, about 1751, and lived near a place called "The Vow," in County Antrim, Ireland, about eight Irish miles from Coleraine, and near the River Bann. They brought up a family of several children, most of whom emigrated to America.

James Steen was born in the north of Ireland, about 1730, and was married about 1751 to Rachel Moore, of Moore's Lodge, and lived near a place called "The Vow," eight Irish miles from Coleraine, near the bank of the River Bann, in County Antrim, Province of Ulster, Ireland, where he brought up his family. James Steen was a man of sterling integrity of character, was true to his principles, and faithful in his adherence to the doctrines and practices of his ancestors. A grandson, who was named for him, sends the following message to the writer of this record: "Preach Christ and him crucified to the Bethel people under your charge, never forgetting Christ's crown and covenant, your beautiful ancestral family pride. They bowed to no being but their God, and never turned the back to the foe — at Derry, Aughrim, the Boyne, or in defense of William's Liberating Army under Derry's Walls. I suppose you want to make a

family tree, and I must say so, you need not be ashamed of it
Geneva, Calvin, the French reformer — then we fall back on
Scotland, then Ulster in A D 1707." To James and Rachel
Moore Steen were born several children, near "The Vow."

CHAPTER I

Richard Steen, the eldest son of James and Rachel Moore
Steen, was born on the old "Green Hill" farm, near "The Vow."
about 1753 He was married to Flora Shields, who died in early
life Richard Steen was at first a farmer, was afterwards
in the employ of a Mr Bristow, a merchant in the East India
Company He died a widower, in Belfast, about 1828, aged
about 75 years To Richard and Flora Shields Steen were born,
in Ireland, the following seven children

I —Robert Steen was born in County Antrim Ireland He was
married there and brought up a family He was eminent in
his day as a teacher, and lived at Ballyghan, near Coleraine.
James Steen Martin of Philadelphia, was a pupil of his in
English and Algebra in 1836-7

II —Ellen Steen, the second child and eldest daughter of Richard
and Flora Shields Steen, was born in County Antrim, Ireland
She was married and brought up a family

III —Samuel Steen the third child and second son of Richard
and Flora Shields Steen, was born near "The Vow," in
County Antrim, Ireland, and was a successful farmer. He
was married and brought up a family in that locality

IV —John Steen, the fourth child and third son of Richard and
Flora Shields Steen, was born near 'The Vow," in County
Antrim, Ireland — a skillful mechanic He was married and
brought up a family

V —Martha J Steen, the fifth child and youngest daughter of
Richard and Flora Shields Steen, was born near "The Vow"
She was never married

VI —Richard Steen, the sixth child and fourth son of Richard and Flora Shields Steen, was born near "The Vow," in County Antrim, Ireland

VII —Joseph Johnson Steen, the seventh and youngest child of Richard and Flora Shields Steen, was born December 22 1811, upon the same farm as his father, and his grandfather, as well as all his brothers and sisters   He was for many years a merchant tailor in Glasgow, Scotland, and for forty years an elder n the Presbyterian Church   He removed to Iowa U S A, in 1875, and afterwards lived with his son, James E Steen, in Winnipeg, Manitoba, Canada   He was married in Donagh Cloney, County Down, Ireland, July 8, 1832, to Sarah McHartney, she having been born in Liverpool, England, November 5, 1812, and died at the residence of her son, in Winnipeg, Manitoba, Canada, February 5, 1895, aged 82 years and 3 months   To them were born fourteen children only five of whom lived to maturity, as follows

1 Robert Steen was born in 1835, and died at Gibraltar, in May, 1857, in the 22d year of his age, from the effects of the Crimean campaign, in which he served in the Seventy-ninth Cameron Highlanders

2 Agnes Steen a daughter of Joseph J and Sarah McHartney Steen, was born in Glasgow, Scotland, in 1839   She was married to David Grant, and resides with her husband on a farm near Winnipeg, Manitoba, Canada

3 Mary Steen, a daughter of Joseph J and Sarah McHartney Steen, was born in 1842, and died in Glasgow, Scotland, in 1858, aged 16 years

4 James Elder Steen, a son of Joseph J and Sarah McHartney Steen, was born in Glasgow, Scotland, January 13 1845 He went to sea when fourteen years of age and started around Cape Horn   On the first trip the vessel was lost on the Chilian coast   He got ashore and enlisted in the Revolutionary Army of General Galho, whose forces a month later were crushed and scattered   He escaped on a small schooner to Valparaiso, went aboard a British warship called "The Ganges," and joined the naval service for three years   In 1862, with his honorable discharge in his pocket, he arrived home in Glasgow   He afterwards attended the Glasgow University and went into business   In 1874 he

came to New York and from 1877 to 1879 he edited a news-paper in Iowa, then went to Chicago and was employed in a grain commission house   In the autumn of 1881 he located in Winnipeg Manitoba, Canada, where he still continues in prosperous business as the editor and proprietor of "The Commercial,' a large weekly newspaper   James E. Steen was married in Winnipeg, Manitoba, March 14, 1892, to Annie C Rogerson   To them was born a son

I —Charles Joseph Steen, son of James E and Annie C. Steen, was born in Winnipeg, Manitoba, December 13, 1894

5 Eliza May Steen, a daughter of Joseph J and Sarah McHart-ney Steen, was born in Glasgow, Scotland, in 1852, and died in Traer, Tama County, Iowa, November 6, 1880, aged 28 years

CHAPTER II

John Steen, the second son of James and Rachel Moore Steen, was born near "The Vow," in County Antrim, Ireland, in 1755, and died of typhoid fever in Ireland in 1818, in the 63d year of his age   He was married in 1781 to Katherine Cartney, she having been born in 1749, and died November 9, 1829, aged 80 years   John Steen brought up his family in Ireland at Reshai-ken, four miles from "The Vow "   The following are his children, and although some of them may not be recorded here   the seed of the righteous shall never perish"

I —Robert Steen, son of John and Katherine Cartney Steen was born at Reshaiken, four miles from "The Vow,' in County Antrim, Ireland, June 13, 1787, and died in Philadelphia, Penn-sylvania, February 22, 1866 in the 79th year of his age   He removed to America in 1816, and located in Philadelphia, Penn-sylvania, and was employed by Robert Fleming in the grocery and produce trade.   He afterwards established himself in that business, and continued in it for nearly forty years   He retired

from the firm of "Steen, Garratt & Co" about 1857   Robert
Steen was married in Philadelphia, January 19 1836, to Mrs
Margaret R McAdam, the widow of James McAdam, and
whose maiden name was Margaret Ray Service she having
been born in Larne, County Antrim, Ireland, in 1807   She
survived her husband four years, and died in Philadelphia
Pennsylvania, October 28, 1870, aged 63 years   To them were
born the following seven children all born in Philadelphia

1 Mary Service Steen, the eldest child of Robert and Margaret
   R Steen, was born in 1837, and died in February 1893, aged
   56 years   She was married in Philadelphia Pennsylvania,
   July 25, 1861, to the Rev J Addison Henry, D D   a son of
   the Rev Symmes Cleves Henry, D D , he having been born
   in Cranbury, New Jersey, October 28, 1835   He was graduated from the College of New Jersey, in 1857 , studied theology in Princeton, New Jersey   and was ordained and
   installed pastor of Princeton Presbyterian Church, in Philadelphia in 1860 which relation he still retains   Residence,
   3818 Powelton Avenue, Philadelphia, Pennsylvania   To the
   Rev J Addison and Mary S Henry were born the following children

   I —Margaret Steen Henry
   II —Katherine Henry, deceased

2 John Gill Steen, the second child and eldest son of Robert
   and Margaret R Steen was born in 1840   He held a position in the Union Trust Company No 611 Chestnut Street
   Philadelphia, for some years   He was married in Philadelphia, Pennsylvania June 20 1878, to A Lizzie Fulton, who
   died in early life   To them one child was born

   I —Margaret S Steen   Residence, No 401 North Thirty-
      third Street Philadelphia Pennsylvania

3 William Service Steen, the third child and second son of
   Robert and Margaret R Steen, was born August 7 1841
   He was graduated from the University of Pennsylvania in
   1861, and from Princeton Theological Seminary in 1866
   where he afterwards pursued post-graduate studies   He was
   licensed to preach the Gospel by the Old School Presbytery
   of Philadelphia, Central, October 1, 1866, and engaged in
   Home Missionary work in Bradford County Pennsylvania,
   for several years   He was ordained to the full work of the

ministry by the Presbytery of Lackawanna in Wysox Pennsylvania June 7 1881, where he remained three years   The
Rev William S Steen has devoted much of his time to
teaching, in which he has been very successful in Cranbury,
New Jersey Washington. Pennsylvania and Wayne Pennsylvania. He was married near Canonsburgh. Washington County Pennsylvania June 19 1879, to Ellen Ewing
Hallock she having been born near that place. about 1859
Residence. Philadelphia Pennsylvania. To the Rev William S and Ellen E Steen were born two children as follows.

I —Robert Service Steen was born in Wysox Pennsylvania
    May 5, 1880

II.—John Ewing Steen was born in Wysox. Pennsylvania,
    November 2 1881

4 Robert Steen. the fourth child and third son of Robert
and Margaret R Steen was born in 1843 and died in 1844,
when about ten months old

5 Robert James Service Steen. the fifth child and fourth son
of Robert and Margaret R. Steen. was born in 1844 and still
resides in Philadelphia — a traveling salesman.   He was
married in Philadelphia Pennsylvania in May 1870 to
Jessie Davis who died August 7 1871

6 George Johnston Steen. the sixth child and fifth son of
Robert and Margaret R Steen. was born in 1846 and died
in 1847 when about seventeen months old.

7 Katherine Service Steen. the seventh child and second
daughter of Robert and Margaret R Steen was born in
1848. Residence 3818 Powelton Avenue Philadelphia
Pennsylvania

I.—Ellen Steen. the second child and eldest daughter of John
and Katherine Cartney Steen was born near The Vow in
County Antrim. Ireland in 1790 and died April 10 1870
aged 80 years. She was married at the same place in 1812 to
William Martin of The Vow he having been born in
County Antrim Ireland in 1779 and died there January 30.
1865 aged 86 years   They brought up their family in Ireland and never came to the United States but with one exception all their children removed to America and permanently
located The following are the names of their children con-

cerning whom a correspondent wrote: There were no cowards among them in 1861'

1. Alexander Martin was born in 1812, near 'The Vow, in County Antrim, Ireland, and died in Burlington New Jersey in 1888 He was twice married, first to Susan Goldey, and the second time to Mary Lippincott. No children

2 Robert S. Martin inherited the old homestead at "The Vow" in Ireland He was married to Mary Ritchie, and had four children, as follows:

I—James S Martin

II—Margaret S Martin, who married a Mr. Fletcher She died in 1890

III—Ellen S Martin

IV—Annie Martin.

3 William Martin, who was married to Rosalie Halsey, and has two living children, as follows Residence in Kent County, Delaware

I—Robert H Martin

II—Margaret J Martin

4 John M Martin was named for his grandfather John Steen, and died unmarried in November 1897

5 James Steen Martin was born in County Antrim, Ireland January 12, 1820 Like the rest of the family he is a lineal descendant of the Moores — the Moores of Moore Lodge near Coleraine on the County Antrim side of the River Bann In 1840 he removed from Finvoy Parish, County Antrim, Ireland to America and has since resided in Philadelphia, Pennsylvania. For many years he has been a successful business man engaged in the wholesale and retail trade in groceries and provisions at 133 South Front Street He was a brave soldier under the command of General Meade, of the Union troops Senior Captain of the emergency men who pressed General Lee's left flank on the third day's fight at Gettysburg Pennsylvania Here, with others loyal and true he determined to conquer or to die in the struggle He is a life member of the Academy of Natural Sciences of Philadelphia, was President of the Robert Burns Association and delivered the annual address January 25, 1882, has been Director of the Academy of Fine

Arts, and is considered a good judge and a lover of the
beautiful To him ancient history has been a source of great
pleasure He is a devout and earnest Christian, and has
been an influential and very useful citizen His son, R
Steen Martin has been associated with him in business
James Steen Martin was married in Philadelphia, Pennsylvania May 25, 1848 to Eliza Simpson, a daughter of Hood
and Jean Burns Simpson, she having been born in Philadelphia, Pennsylvania, January 19, 1826 To them were
born the following eight children

I —Thomas Hood Martin was born in Philadelphia, Pennsylvania, March 16, 1849, and died March 6, 1865, aged
nearly 16 years

II —Robert Steen Martin was born March 12, 1851 — a
prosperous business man He was married in Philadelphia, Pennsylvania, June 26, 1879 to Kate T Elder, who
died July 12 1883 He was married a second time in
Clinton, New Jersey, to Kate Van Syckle, a daughter of
Joseph and Cyrena Van Syckle, of Clinton New, Jersey,
she having been born August 11 1860 To them were
born the following children

   1 Cyrena Van Syckle Martin was born September 16,
1890

   2 Joseph Van Syckle Martin was born July 6, 1895

   3 Robert Steen Martin, Jr, was born March 17, 1898

III —Jean Burns Martin was born September 6, 1853. Residence, Philadelphia, Pennsylvania

IV —Ellen Steen Martin was born in Philadelphia, Pennsylvania February 2, 1856, and died January 31, 1861, aged
almost five years

V —Eliza Simpson Martin was born in Philadelphia Pennsylvania July 8, 1858, and died June 29 1861, aged nearly
three years

VI —James Renwick Martin was born in Philadelphia, Pennsylvania, February 21 1861

VII —Margaret Steer Martin was born in Philadelphia,
Pennsylvania, July 3 1863

VIII —Grace Simpson Martin was born in Philadelphia,
Pennsylvania, July 3, 1867

6 Anna Jane Martin a daughter of William and Ellen Steen
   Martin, was born near "The Vow," in County Antrim, Ireland January 12, 1822 She was married in Philadelphia,
   Pennsylvania, in 1845, to Alexander Kerr, who died some
   years afterwards leaving her a widow Residence 2002 Race
   Street, Philadelphia Pennsylvania To them were born four
   children, as follows

   I—Ellen Steen Kerr, the eldest child of Alexander and
      Anna J Martin Kerr, was born in Philadelphia, Pennsyl-
      vania, January 14, 1847 and died March 16, 1887, aged
      40 years, 2 months and 2 days She was married January
      16, 1869, to the Rev Archibald McCullagh D D , a Pres-
      byterian clergyman, who is now (1900) pastor of Plymouth
      Congregational Church, at Worcester, Mass To them
      were born the following six children

      1 Alexander Kerr McCullagh was born November 7,
         1871, and was married in March, 1894, to Cornelia E.
         Platt To them was born one child, as follows

         a Helen McCullagh was born in 1898, and died in
            infancy She was the great-great-granddaughter of
            Ellen Steen Martin

      2 Archibald McCullagh Jr was born September 9, 1873
      3 Samuel Kerr McCullagh was born February 21 1875
      4 Martin Kerr McCullagh was born April 12, 1878
      5 Anna Kerr McCullagh was born June 3 1880
      6 Ellen Kerr McCullagh was born June 5, 1884

   II—Samuel Kerr the second child and eldest son of Alex-
      ander and Anna J Martin Kerr, was born December 4,
      1849, and died September 1, 1850

   III—Samuel Thomas Kerr the third child and second son
      of Alexander and Anna J Martin Kerr, was born Decem-
      ber 31, 1852 He was married in Philadelphia Pennsyl-
      vania March 28, 1882, to Caroline M. Damon, she having
      been born November 25, 1860 They are the parents of
      the following four children

      1 Ellen Constance Kerr was born August 30 1883
      2 Carlotta Thetonia Da Costa Bandeira Kerr was born
         November 25 1884
      3 Anna J Kerr was born January 12 1886

   (20)

4. Alexander Kerr, Jr , was born July 1, 1890

IV.—Alexander Martin Kerr, the fourth child and third son
of Alexander and Anna J Martin Kerr, was born May 27,
1856, and died November 25, 1876, in the 21st year of his
age

7 A daughter of William and Ellen Steen Martin was born in
County Antrim, Ireland, probably about 1824 or 1825. She
died in infancy, and her body was interred in the cemetery at
"The Vow "

8 Martha Martin, the eighth and youngest child of William
and Ellen Steen Martin, was born in County Antrim Ireland,
probably about 1828, and died in childhood at "The Vow,"
and was buried there   The dust of these little children lies
in the old family lot of the Steens and the Martins, com-
mingled with that of parents and grandparents, there to rest
in the grave near the banks of the River Bann until the
resurrection day

III —Rachel Moore Steen, the third child and second daughter of
John and Katherine Cartney Steen, was born at "The Vow,"
in Ireland, about 1793   She was married in Philadelphia, by
the Rev Dr Wylie, about 1815, to the Rev Jonathan Gill, an
Ulster man of the Solemn League and Covenant type, connected with either the Associate or Associate Reformed Church
in America   They removed to the West on horseback, crossing over the Allegheny Mountains, and located in Allegheny
County, Pennsylvania. thirteen miles east of Pittsburgh, near
where Brinton Station on the Pennsylvania Railroad is now
located   There, at Tinkle Creek, Mr Gill faithfully preached
Christ to the people, and there their bodies now rest in the
grave   Mr Gill died April 26, 1846   Mrs Rachel M Steen
Gill survived her husband for many years, and died in Allegheny City, Pennsylvania about 1874, in the 91st year of her
age   She used to tell with true ancestral pride how her great-
great-grandfather Steen was imprisoned in the "Bass Rock"
for his religious faith (a place of historic fame as the prison
house of the Covenanters in the cruel reign of Charles II), and
how he was married on the day of his release to an excellent
Christian woman, as consecrated and devout as himself   To
the Rev Jonathan and Rachel M Steen Gill were born the
following children, all born in Allegheny County, Pennsylvania

1 Jane Gill, who was born about 1821, was married to Wilham M Stewart, a coal merchant, who died May 27, 1885. She died January 23, 1888 They were the parents of four children, as follows·

I —Matthew Stewart, who died when a child.

II —Amanda Stewart, who died when she was fifteen years old

III —Margaret Steen Stewart, and

IV —Martha Neil Stewart, who now reside at 936 North Avenue, West Allegheny, Pennsylvania

2 Amanda Gill, the second daughter of Jonathan and Rachel M Steen Gill, was born about 1823, and was married to Rev Albert Johnson, and in 1845 they went as missionaries to India They were both killed in the Indian mutiny, in June, 1857 They had no children

3 Elvira Gill, the third daughter, was born about 1826, and was married to James Logan, and to them were born two children, as follows

I —Albert Logan, who married Susan Murphy He is a manufacturer of bedding and mattresses. They live on Fifth Avenue, Pittsburgh, Pennsylvania, East End

II —Jane Logan was married to John V Shoemaker, M D They have no children Residence, 1519 Walnut Street, Philadelphia, Pennsylvania

4 Amelia Gill was married to the Rev Samuel George, and died in Chambersburgh, Pennsylvania They went to Siam as missionaries, and after ten years of service they returned to Chambersburgh, Pennsylvania, where Mr George preached, and where he still resides They had no children

5 Sarah E Gill, the fifth daughter of Rev. Jonathan and Rachel M Steen Gill, was born in Allegheny County, Pennsylvania, July 15, 1833 She was married March 8, 1860, to John K Caldwell, who is engaged in the brick business They have had three children as follows Residence Chicago, Illinois

I —Nellie Moore Caldwell was born in Washington County, Iowa, June 24, 1862 She was married February 6, 1884, to William Sidney Purington, of Massachusetts Residence, Galesburgh Illinois They have three children, as follows

       1 William Caldwell Purington

       2 Helen Purington

       3 D Stewart Purington

6 Katherine Gill, the sixth daughter of Rev Jonathan and Rachel M Steen Gill, died when she was a young lady

7 Wylie Gill, the seventh child and eldest son of Rev. Jonathan and Rachel M Steen Gill, was a lawyer, and died   He was married to Ann Blair, and had two children, as follows:

    I —Harry Gill, who is a lawyer of Philadelphia   He was married to a Miss Sharpless, of Philadelphia, and has two children

    II —Ellen Moore Gill, who was married to a Mr Moore, and is now living in California

8 John Gill, the youngest son of Jonathan and Rachel M. Steen Gill, was married and had quite a family   He is dead   In the Memorial of the Fattehghur Mission and her martyred missionaries is an account of Mr and Mrs Johnson.   The only surviving child of Mrs Gill is Mrs J K Caldwell, of Chicago   She is now with her daughter, Mrs Purington, of Galesburgh, Illinois

IV — ———— Steen, a daughter of John and Katherine Cartney Steen, was born near The Vow," in County Antrim, Province of Ulster, Ireland, about 1797   She was married to a Mi Young, and removed to the United States of America, where they brought up a family and lived and died

V —John Steen, the fifth child and second son of John and Katherine Cartney Steen, was born near "The Vow," about eight Irish miles from the city of Coleraine, Ireland, about the year 1800   He was a well-to-do farmer.   He was married about 1825 to Lettie Campbell, who died about a year later   In 1827 he removed to America and located in Philadelphia, Pennsylvania, where he died, in 1831

VII —Annie Steen, the seventh child and fifth daughter of John and Katherine Cartney Steen, was born near "The Vow," in County Antrim, Ireland, about the year 1808   She had a sister a little older than herself, whose name does not appear in the foregoing list   Annie Steen removed to America and was married in Philadelphia, Pennsylvania, in 1832, to John Taylor. She brought up her family in Philadelphia, where she lived and died

---

CHAPTER III

Martha Steen, a daughter of James and Rachel Moore Steen, was born on the old "Green Hill" farm, near "The Vow," eight Irish miles from Coleraine, Ireland, about 1781   She was married to David Johnson, a man of kind and generous heart, and a faithful Christian — a good Covenanter   Martha Steen Johnson is reported by one who knew her well in 1827, as a ' grand, good woman "   To David and Martha Steen Johnson was born one child, as follows :

I —Joseph Johnson, son of David and Martha Steen Johnson, and a grandson of James and Rachel M Steen, was born near "The Vow," in County Antrim, Ireland, about 1807   He was married there, and died in early life, leaving one child

: A daughter

BOOK SIX.

DESCENDANTS OF GEORGE STEEN

George Steen was born in Ireland, December 16, 1758, and died on his farm in Tippecanoe County, Indiana, December 16, 1836   He came to America about 1775 with his two brothers, James and John, and located in Lancaster County, Pennsylvania   In 1833 he removed to the then far West, and settled in Tippecanoe County, Indiana   He was married in Lancaster County, Pennsylvania, about 1792, to Anne Gualt, she having been born July 26, 1776, and died May 21, 1857.

George Steen was born in Ireland, December 16, 1758, and died in Tippecanoe County, Indiana, December 16, 1836, aged 78 years   He emigrated to the United States of America about 1775, with his two brothers, James and John, and located in Lancaster County, Pennsylvania, where he continued to reside until May, 1833, when he sold his farm and other possessions and removed with his family to Tippecanoe County, Indiana where he purchased a farm in Sheffield Township, upon which he continued to reside until his death   When George Steen removed from Pennsylvania to Indiana he located near two of his sons, who had previously settled there   George Steen was a prosperous farmer, and a man of sterling worth — a faithful member of

(310)

the Presbyterian Church, in which faith all his children had been brought up   He was married in Lancaster County, Pennsylvania, about 1792, to Anne Gualt, she having been born July 26, 1776, and died May 21, 1857, in the 81st year of her age   To them were born six children

CHAPTER I

Letitia H Steen the eldest child, and a daughter of George and Anne Gualt Steen, was born in Lancaster County, Pennsylvania, August 5, 1793, and died at the home of her son, Amos C Henderson, in Frankfort, Indiana, December 14 1875 in the 83d year of her age   She was married in the city of Lancaster, Pennsylvania, by the Rev. William Author, March 14, 1817, to Amos Henderson, and removed with her husband and father's family to Tippecanoe County, Indiana, in May, 1833, where they continued to reside, until Mr Henderson's death, which took place February 2, 1871   After the death of her husband, Mrs Letitia Steen Henderson made her home with her son, Amos C. Henderson, in Frankfort, Indiana   To Amos and Letitia Steen Henderson were born eight children, as follows.

I —Ann Eliza Henderson, the eldest child of Amos and Letitia H Steen Henderson, was born in Lancaster County Pennsylvania, January 21, 1818, and died December 22 1818 aged 11 months

II —Rachel Henderson, the second daughter of Amos and Letitia H Steen Henderson, was born in Lancaster County, Pennsylvania, April 8, 1819, and died in Dayton, Tippecanoe County, Indiana, April 3, 1883, in the 64th year of her age   She was married first to John G McCain, June 1, 1836, he having been born in Abbeville District, South Carolina, April 1, 1809, and died in Indiana, July 24, 1844, in the 36th year of his age   To them were born four children   Rachel Henderson McCain was married a second time, November 1, 1849, to Benjamin C McCoy, he having been born in Waldo County Maine, March 23, 1818 — a prosperous farmer   Residence, Dayton,

Indiana   The following are the children of these two mar
riages

1 Joseph Van Buren McCain was born August 17. 1837

2. Mary Letitia McCain was born July 9, 1839

3 Benjamin Franklin McCain was born in July, 1841

4 Louisa McCain was born in July, 1843

5 Margaret Jane McCoy, the fifth child of Rachel Henderson,
   and the eldest child by her second husband, was born in
   Howard County, Indiana, September 27 1850, and died
   ——————

6 Anna Laura McCoy was born in Howard County, Indiana,
   September 3, 1852   She was married to a Mr Lamson
   Residence, Rensselaer, Indiana

7 Amos H. McCoy was born in Howard County, Indiana,
   June 29, 1854   Residence, Goodland, Indiana

8 Florence A McCoy was born in Howard County, Indiana
   March 3, 1857   Residence, Mulberry, Indiana

9 John C McCoy was born in Howard County, Indiana,
   March 3, 1859, and died ————————

III —John Franklin Henderson the third child and eldest son
of Amos and Letitia H Steen Henderson, was born in Lancaster County, Pennsylvania, November 23, 1820 and died in
Kokomo, Indiana, July 8, 1888, in the 68th year of his age.
He was a practicing physician in Indiana for many years   He
was married, July 20, 1842, to Cynthia Ann Whitson, she having been born in Clinton County, Ohio, June 5, 1822, and now
resides in Kokomo, Indiana   To them were born seven children, as follows

1 Mary Eliza Henderson, the eldest child of Dr John F and
   Cynthia A Henderson was born March 6, 1843 and died
   June 9, 1844

2 Generous Leander Henderson, the second child and eldest
   son of Dr John F and Cynthia A Henderson, was born
   October 4. 1844   Residence, Kansas City, Missouri

3 John Oscar Henderson, the third child and second son of
   Dr John F and Cynthia A Henderson, was born September 1, 1847   He was Auditor of the State of Indiana   Residence, Indianapolis, Indiana

4 Howard Eugene Henderson, the fourth child and third son of Dr. John F and Cynthia A Henderson, was born December 22, 1849 Residence, Kokomo Indiana

5 Ernest Benton Henderson, the fifth child and fourth son of Dr John F and Cynthia A Henderson, was born November 29, 1853, and died March 12 1854

6 Ernest Lacey Henderson the sixth child and fifth son of Dr John F and Cynthia A Henderson, was born September 3, 1857 Residence, Kansas City, Missouri

7. William Franklin Henderson, the seventh and youngest child of Dr John F and Cynthia A Henderson, was born February 11, 1860 Residence Indianapolis, Indiana

IV —George Hamilton Henderson the fourth child and second son of Amos and Letitia Steen Henderson, was born February 1, 1823, and died, unmarried April 11, 1848 in the 26th year of his age

V —Ann Eliza Henderson, the fifth child and third daughter of Amos and Letitia Steen Henderson, was born in Lancaster County, Pennsylvania, December 12 1824, and died in the State of Iowa, March, 25, 1849, in the 25th year of her age She was married to a Mr McClure and had removed to Iowa

VI —Amos Clemson Henderson, the sixth child and third son of Amos and Letitia Steen Henderson was born at Chambersburgh Pennsylvania August 11, 1827 — a prosperous farmer He was married in Clinton County Indiana, December 1 1850, to Ann Eliza Glick a daughter of Samuel and Sophia Glick, she having been born November 15, 1832 Residence Frankfort Indiana To them were born seven children, as follows

1 Melissa Jane Henderson, the eldest child of Amos C and Ann Eliza Henderson, was born in Clinton County, Indiana, July 21, 1852 She was married, August 6, 1872 to Isaac Michael Residence, Avery Station Indiana

2 Aldora Ann Henderson the second daughter of Amos C and Ann Eliza Henderson, was born in Clinton County, Indiana, October 17, 1854 She was married, December 29, 1875 to William Kyger Residence, Frankfort Indiana

3 Ashbel Willard Henderson, the third child and only son of Amos C and Ann Eliza Henderson, was born in Clinton County Indiana October 5, 1857 He was married Febru-

ary 26, 1885, to Maud Cowden   Residence, Anderson, Indiana

4 Anna Helen Henderson, the fourth child and third daughter of Amos C and Ann Eliza Henderson, was born in Clinton County, Indiana, April 8, 1860, and died June 5, 1869 in the 10th year of her age

5 Ida Josephine Henderson, the fifth child and fourth daughter of Amos C and Ann Eliza Henderson, was born in Clinton County, Indiana April 12, 1863   Residence Frankfort, Indiana.

6 Letitia Linda Henderson, the sixth child and fifth daughter of Amos C and Ann Eliza Henderson, was born in Clinton County, Indiana, January 14, 1866   She was married December 25, 1886, to George Braden   Residence, Frankfort, Indiana.

7 Margaret Luella Henderson, the seventh child and sixth daughter of Amos C and Ann Eliza Henderson, was born in Clinton County, Indiana, September 28, 1867.   Residence, Frankfort, Indiana

VII —Joseph Oscar Henderson, the seventh child and fourth son of Amos and Letitia Steen Henderson, was born in Pennsylvania, August 30, 1829, and died March 12, 1873, in the 44th year of his age   He was married September 24, 1850, to Sarah Ann Parks, who still resides in Kokomo Indiana   To them were born seven children, as follows

1 Luzane Lillie Henderson, the eldest daughter of Joseph Oscar and Sarah Ann Henderson, was born December 20, 1851   She was married June 11, 1877, to George W Stidger he having been born in Meigs County, Ohio, in 1844   Residence, Kokomo Indiana

2 George Hamilton Henderson, the second child and eldest son of Joseph Oscar and Sarah Ann Henderson was born October 12, 1853, and died March 19, 1883 in the 30th year of his age

3 Dorinda Britton Henderson, the third child and second daughter of Joseph Oscar and Sarah Ann Henderson, was born February 15, 1856

4 Adolphus Henderson, the fourth child and second son of Joseph Oscar and Sarah Ann Henderson was born August 9 1859, and died May 4, 1860

5 Electa Henderson, the fifth child and third daughter of Joseph Oscar and Sarah Ann Henderson, was born December 27, 1862, and died February 22, 1870, in the 8th year of her age

6 Charles A Henderson, the sixth child and third son of Joseph Oscar and Sarah Ann Henderson, was born May 7, 1868 Residence, Kokomo, Indiana

7 Otto Henderson, the seventh child and fourth son of Joseph Oscar and Sarah Ann Henderson, was born February 28, 1872, and died February 24, 1873

VII—Margaret Jane Henderson, the eighth child and fourth daughter of Amos and Letitia Steen Henderson, was born in Pennsylvania, March 3 1832, and brought to Indiana by her parents, when she was only one year old She was married to Joseph Garris — a farmer — he having been born in Pennsylvania, and died in Indiana She was married a second time June 4 1868, to Henry B Peters — a farmer — he having been born in Tippecanoe County, Indiana, September 25 1836, and now resides at Mulberry, Indiana Mrs Margaret Jane Peters died at Mulberry, Indiana, June 3, 1879 in the 48th year of her age To them were born two children, as follows

1 Iva Peters, the eldest child, a daughter of Henry B and Margaret Jane Peters, was born December 6 1869, and died in June, 1870

2 Charles H Peters, the second child, a son of Henry B and Margaret Jane Peters was born in Tippecanoe County Indiana, July 10, 1871 Residence Monitor, Tippecanoe County Indiana

CHAPTER II

George Hamilton Steen the second child and eldest son of George and Ann Gualt Steen was born in Salisbury Township, Lancaster County, Pennsylvania, November 3, 1797, and died in Sheffield Township, Tippecanoe County Indiana, April 14 1859 in the 62d year of his age, in the full hope of a blessed

immortality He received his middle name of Hamilton from
his father's mother, whose maiden name was Hamilton He was
a man of sterling Christian character, and highly respected by all
who knew him In 1827 he was chosen and commissioned by the
Governor of Pennsylvania as Captain in the State Militia, the
following being a copy of his commission

PENNSYLVANIA, ss

In the name and by the authority of the Commonwealth of Pennsylvania, I, Andrew Shultz, Governor of the said Commonwealth, to
George H Steen, of the County of Lancaster, Greeting

Know that you, the said George H Steen, being appointed and
returned, are hereby commissioned Captain of the Tenth Company,
Second Battalion, Fifty-first Regiment of the Militia of the Commonwealth of Pennsylvania in the First Brigade of the Fourth Division,
composed of the Militia of the County of Lancaster To have and to
hold this commission, exercising all the powers and discharging all
the duties thereunto lawfully belonging and attached, until the third
day of August one thousand eight hundred and twenty-eight, if you
shall so long behave yourself well and perform the duties required
by law

In testimony whereof I have set my hand and caused the less seal
of the State to be affixed to these presents at Harrisburgh, dated agree-
ably to law, the first day of May, in the year of our Lord one thousand
eight hundred and twenty-seven, and of the Commonwealth the fifty-
first

By the Governor.   J D BANARD,
                        Secretary of the Commonwealth

In the autumn of 1830 Capt George H Steen removed from
Pennsylvania to Indiana, and entered lands in Sheffield Township, Tippecanoe County, where he continued to reside, a prosperous farmer and an honored citizen, until his death On his
removal from Pennsylvania the following testimonial was presented to him

We whose names are hereby subscribed do certify that for many
years we have been personally acquainted with George Hamilton Steen,
an unmarried man, a native of Salisbury Township, Lancaster County,
and State of Pennsylvania, and that, to the best of our knowledge, he
has always borne the character of an honest, sober and industrious man.
August, 1830

WILLIAM ROBINSON	JAMES QUINN
ANDREW BAILEY	JAMES HARRISON
HUGH M McCLINTICK	JOHN LEWIS
JOHN STEEN	GEORGE ZELL
JOHN McCAMERT	WILLIAM EMERY
DAVID JENKINS	ZOGOMORA MILLER
WILLIAM WITMAN	WILLIAM SMITH
J MILLER	GEORGE EMERY
GEORGE IRWIN JAMES	HUGH R MORTON
HUGH ROBINSON	

It was not long after the arrival of Capt George H Steen

in Indiana until his abilities were recognized and his integrity being well known, he soon became a prominent, useful, and influential citizen He was commissioned by the Governor of Indiana First Lieutenant of Cavalry in the Sixty-second Regiment of the State Militia, July 1, 1833 The following is a copy of his commission

NOAH NOBLE,

Governor of the State of Indiana and Commander-in-Chief of the Militia thereof, to all who may see these presents, Greeting

Whereas. It has been certified to me by the proper authority that George H Steen has been duly elected to the office of First Lieutenant of Cavalry in the Sixty-second Regiment of the Militia of the State

Therefore know ye, That in the name and by the authority of the said State, I do hereby commission him, the said George H Steen, First Lieutenant of Cavalry in the said Regiment, to serve from the date hereof, during his good behavior, or until he shall arrive at the age of sixty years

Done at Indianapolis the first day of July, one thousand eight hundred and thirty-three, the eighteenth year of the State, and of the independence of the United States the fifty-seventh

In testimony whereof I have hereunto placed my signature and caused to be affixed the seal of the State, the day and year aforesaid

By the Governor N. Noble

WM SHLEK, Secretary of State

George Hamilton Steen resided in Tippecanoe County, Indiana, from his arrival in 1830, until his death, a period of about twenty-eight years and six months He was married by the Rev James Carnahan at Dayton Indiana, February 26. 1835, to Mary Whitson, a daughter of John and Cynthia Whitson she having been born in Preble County, Ohio May 21, 1813 She was a granddaughter of Solomon and Phoebe Whitson, who were born and married in South Carolina Since the death of her husband Mrs Mary Whitson Steen has resided with her daughter, in Lafayette, Indiana To them were born the following five children:

I —John Whitson Steen the eldest son of George Hamilton and Mary Whitson Steen, was born on the farm, three miles southeast of Dayton in Sheffield Township, Tippecanoe County Indiana, February 7, 1840 He was brought up on the farm, where he lived and labored until 1864 when he removed to Dayton, Indiana and learned the carpenter trade which he followed there In 1875 he removed to Litchfield, Montgomery County Illinois, and in 1886 to Goldman Arkansas County,

Arkansas, where he still resides — a carpenter   He was married in Dayton, Indiana, September 22, 1864, to Drusilla Hadrick, the second daughter of John and Nancy Hadrick, she having been born February 4, 1839, and died in Dayton, Indiana, December 4, 1879, aged 40 years and 10 months   To them were born five children   John Whitson Steen was married a second time, in Louisiana, Missouri, by the Rev A D Pierce a Presbyterian clergyman, May 26, 1881, to Mrs Cynthia McAllen, widow of William McAllen, and a daughter of John and Mary Wandel, she having been born in Hancock County, Indiana, April 9, 1850   To them was born one child   The following are the children of John Whitson Steen

1   Lilly L Steen, the eldest child by his first wife, Drusilla Hadrick Steen, was born in Dayton, Indiana, October 4, 1865, and died October 20, 1865

2   Jessie Letitia Steen, the second daughter of John W and Drusilla H. Steen, was born in Dayton, Indiana February 8, 1867   She was married September 16, 1884, to Charles A Hyer, of Washington C H , Ohio, who died in Columbus, Ohio, February 16, 1891   After the death of her husband, and for seven years previous to her own death, Mrs Hyer worked in the watch factory of Elgin, Illinois   Mrs Jessie L Steen Hyer died in Rensselaer, Indiana, June 3, 1898, aged 31 years, 3 months and 25 days   The following are her children.

I —Frederica Steen Hyer, the eldest daughter of Charles A. and Jessie L Steen Hyer, was born June 18 1885

II —Mattie Leah Hyer, the second daughter of Charles A and Jessie L Steen Hyer, was born May 18, 1887

3   Frank Whitson Steen, the third child and eldest son of John W and Drusilla H Steen, was born in Dayton, Indiana, February 8, 1868, and died June 1 1868

4   Ethel Belle Steen, the fourth child and third daughter of John W and Drusilla H Steen, was born in Dayton, Indiana, June 21, 1870, and died August 3, 1870

5   Edward Hamilton Steen, the fifth child and second son of John W and Drusilla H Steen, was born in Dayton Indiana, August 31 1872 and died September 18 1882 in the 11th year of his age

6 Mary Steen, the sixth child and fourth daughter of John W
Steen, the eldest by his second wife, Cynthia Wandel McAllen
Steen, was born in Goldman, Arkansas, January 7, 1891

II —Harriet Steen, the second child and eldest daughter of
George H and Mary Whitson Steen, was born on her father's
farm, three miles southeast of Dayton, Indiana August 25,
1843. She was married to a Mr Barnhart   Residence,
Lafayette, Indiana

III —Eliza Steen, the third child and second daughter of John
H and Mary Whitson Steen, was born on the home farm of
her father, near Dayton, Indiana, May 31, 1848 She was
married in Lafayette, Indiana December 31, 1864, to Daniel
Harvey Kenyon, a son of Aaron Stratton and Sidney Gualt
Kenyon, he having been born at Waldo, Marion County, Ohio,
August 6, 1842 — a farmer by occupation   Residence Waldo,
Ohio To them were born the following fourteen children.

1 Martha Jane Kenyon, the eldest child of Daniel H and
Eliza Steen Kenyon, was born at Waldo, Ohio, September 8,
1866

2 Jessie Margreeth Kenyon, the second daughter of Daniel H.
and Eliza Steen Kenyon was born at Waldo Ohio, January
18, 1868 and died July 4, 1868

3 George Aaron Kenyon, the third child and eldest son of
Daniel H and Eliza Steen Kenyon was born at Waldo Ohio
August 28, 1869

4 Joseph Hamilton Kenyon, the fourth child and second son
of Daniel H and Eliza Steen Kenyon was born at Waldo,
Ohio, September 15, 1871

5 John David Kenyon, the fifth child and third son of Daniel
H and Eliza Steen Kenyon was born at Waldo, Ohio,
August 5 1873, and died August 17, 1873

6 Mary Ellen Kenyon, the sixth child and third daughter of
Daniel H and Eliza Steen Kenyon, was born at Waldo Ohio,
January 18, 1875

7. Cidna Eliza Kenyon the seventh child and fourth daughter
of Daniel H and Eliza Steen Kenyon, was born at Waldo,
Ohio September 13, 1876

8. Charles Monroe Kenyon, the eighth child and fourth son of
Daniel H and Eliza Steen Kenyon, was born at Waldo Ohio,
February 2, 1878

9 Daniel Harvey Kenyon Jr the ninth child and fifth son of
Daniel Harvey and Eliza Steen Kenyon, was born at Waldo,
Ohio, January 15, 1881

10 Clara Kenyon, the tenth child and fifth daughter of Daniel
H and Eliza Steen Kenyon, was born at Waldo Ohio February 17, 1883 and died April 28, 1886

11 Frederick Antom Kenyon the eleventh child and sixth
son of Daniel H and Eliza Steen Kenyon was born in Delaware Delaware County Ohio February 7 1884

12. James Lee Kenyon, the twelfth child and seventh son of
Daniel H and Eliza Steen Kenyon was born at Waldo,
Ohio, September 1, 1885

13 Frank Steen Kenyon, the thirteenth child and eighth son
of Daniel H and Eliza Steen Kenyon, was born at Waldo,
Ohio, June 22, 1888

14 Stella Hope Kenyon the fourteenth child and sixth daughter of Daniel H and Eliza Steen Kenyon was born at
Waldo, Ohio, May 24, 1891

IV—George Hamilton Steen, Jr, the fourth child and second
son of George Hamilton and Mary Whitson Steen, was born
on the old home farm near Dayton, Tippecanoe County
Indiana, February 29, 1852 where he grew up to manhood
He is a traveling salesman for a wholesale drug house in St
Louis, Missouri He was married at Litchfield Illinois, Sep-
tember 5, 1877 to Ida A Lawrence, the eldest daughter of
Major Joseph and Agnes Lawrence, she having been born in
Litchfield, Illinois, November 26, 1857 To them were born
two children Residence St Louis Missouri

1 Georgia A Steen the eldest daughter of George H and
I Agnes Lawrence Steen, was born in Litchfield, Illinois
June 7 1878

2 Mary Vesta Steen, the second daughter of George H and
Ida Agnes Lawrence Steen, was born in Morrisonville Illinois October 19, 1880

V—Joseph Walker Steen, the fifth child and third son of George
Hamilton and Mary Whitson Steen was born on the farm
near Dayton, Indiana, July 29, 1857 He received his middle
name after Walker Steen, a nephew of his grandfather George
Steen, who left Ireland and went to Scotland, where he married
a Scotch lady He afterwards came to America and became

quite prosperous, and very much respected by all who knew him   Joseph Walker Steen delights in travel and in literature He is unmarried, and seems quite contented with that situation in life   He has followed the occupation of druggist and jeweler, but in 1898 he sold his drug and jewelry store and other property in Rossville, Illinois to spend two years or more in foreign travel in South America Europe, etc   He hopes to see enough of the world by the close of the year 1900 to be ready to return home and go into business again

---

CHAPTER III.

Agnes Walker Steen, also called "Nancy   the third child an 1 second daughter of George and Anne Gualt Steen, was born in Lancaster County, Pennsylvania, in 1801 and died in Tippecanoe County, Indiana, February 27 1845, aged about 44 years In 1833 with her husband, her children, and her father's family, she removed from Pennsylvania to what was then the far West, and located in Tippecanoe County, Indiana, where she spent the remainder of her life   She was married in Pennsylvania by the Rev A. J Ballet, April 28 1825, to Hugh Morton McClintick he having been born April 28, 1804   To them were born ten children, as follows

I —Ann L McClintick, the eldest child of Hugh Morton and Agnes Walker Steen McClintick was born in Pennsylvania, February 1 1826, and died in Tippecanoe County, Indiana, March 31, 1848, in the 23d year of her age

II —James McClintick, the second child and eldest son of Hugh Morton and Agnes Walker Steen McClintick, was born in Pennsylvania March 27, 1827   Residence, Muscoda, Grant County Wisconsin

III —George Steen McClintick the third child and second son of Hugh Morton and Agnes Walker Steen McClintick, was born in Pennsylvania, March 25 1829   Residence Rich Valley Miami County, Indiana

(21)

IV—Jane S McClintick, the fourth child and second daughter
of Hugh Morton and Agnes Walker Steen McClintick, was
born in Pennsylvania, May 15, 1831 She was married to a
Mr Robinson Residence, Cedar Rapids, Boone County,
Nebraska

V—Hugh M. McClintick, the fifth child and third son of Hugh
Morton and Agnes Walker Steen McClintick, was born in
Pennsylvania, October 20, 1832, and died March 13, 1833

VI—Hugh Morton McClintick, Jr, the sixth child and fourth
son of Hugh Morton and Agnes Walker Steen McClintick,
was born in Tippecanoe County, Indiana, February 20, 1834.
He was married, first, October 23, 1856, to Nancy J Robinson,
she having been born October 13, 1834, and died September 2,
1872, in the 38th year of her age To them were born five
children Hugh Morton McClintick was married a second
time, December 1, 1874 to Laura Winkle To them were born
two children Residence, Cedar Rapids, Nebraska

1 George W McClintick, the eldest child of Hugh Morton
and Nancy J McClintick, was born September 24, 1857

2 Sarah L. McClintick, the second child and eldest daughter
of Hugh M and Nancy J Robinson McClintick, was born
March 18, 1859, and died September 16, 1883, in the 25th
year of her age

3 James H McClintick, the third child and second son of
Hugh M and Nancy J McClintick, was born August 25,
1861.

4 Linda May McClintick, the fourth child and second daughter of Hugh M and Nancy J McClintick, was born October
4, 1864 and died October 8, 1865

5 Joseph Morton McClintick, the fifth child and third son of
Hugh M and Nancy J Robinson McClintick, was born
October 28 1866

6 Clarence C McClintick, the sixth child of Hugh Morton
McClintick and the first child by his second wife Laura
Winkle McClintick, was born September 9, 1875, and died
February 20, 1876.

7 Alvin Everett McClintick, the seventh child of Hugh Morton McClintick, and the second child by his second wife,
Laura Winkle McClintick, was born November 3, 1878, and
died January 10, 1881, in the 3d year of his age.

VII —Joseph Hamilton McClintick, the seventh child and fifth son of Hugh Morton and Agnes Walker Steen McClintick, was born in Tippecanoe County, Indiana September 3, 1836 Residence, Portland, Oregon

VIII —Agnes Walker McClintick, the eighth child and third daughter of Hugh Morton and Agnes Walker Steen McClintick, was born in Tippecanoe County, Indiana, May 16, 1838, and died August 22, 1848, in the 11th year of her age

IX —Rachel Marian McClintick, the ninth child and fourth daughter of Hugh Morton and Agnes Walker Steen McClintick, was born in Tippecanoe County, Indiana September 16, 1840 She was married to a Mr Robinson Residence, Cedar Rapids, Nebraska

X —Amzi Wright McClintick, the tenth child and sixth son of Hugh Morton and Agnes Walker Steen McClintick was born in Tippecanoe County Indiana, September 22, 1842 Residence, Grey Eagle, Minnesota

---

CHAPTER IV

Joseph Steen, the fourth child and second son of George and Anne Gualt Steen, was born in Lancaster County Pennsylvania April 21, 1803 He was an intelligent, industrious, and prosperous farmer In the fall of 1830, in company with his brother, George Hamilton Steen, he removed from Pennsylvania to Indiana and entered land in Sheffield Township Tippecanoe County, and settled down and began to open up a farm He was a man of strict integrity, and highly respected by all who knew him While engaged in improving his farm and preparing it for a future home, he was taken sick, and died not long afterwards in Tippecanoe County, Indiana March 10 1833 in the 30th year of his age

CHAPTER V

    John Steen the fiitl child and third son of George and Anne Gualt Steen was born in Lehigh County, Pennsylvania July 29 1808, and died in Clinton County, Indiana, September 12, 1881, in the 74th year of his age He was a farmer by occupation He was mairied in Carlisle, Pennsylvania, April 14, 1833, to Jane D Wright, a daughter of Robeit and Nancy Wright, she having been born in Carlisle, Pennsylvania March 1, 1807 and died in Clinton County, Indiana August 7, 1859, in the 53d year of her age They removed from Pennsylvania with George Steen, his family and other friends, to the then far West, in Tippecanoe County, Indiana, in May, 1833, the next month after their marriage and not long afterwards located in the adjoining county of Clinton, in which they made their permanent home To them were born six children, as follows

I —Robert Wright Steen, the eldest child, a son of John and Jane D Wright Steen a grandson of the George Steen who came from Ireland to America, was born in Tippecanoe County, Indiana January 25, 1835 — a prosperous farmer He was married, January 27, 1858, to Lucinda Nally Residence, Battle Ground, Indiana To them were born the following children.

  1 George Edward Steen was boin at Battle Ground, Indiana He was married, August 14, 1895, to Anna Belle Chenowith Residence, Battle Ground, Indiana To them were born the following:

    I —Olive Lalena Steen was boin at Battle Ground Indiana, September 12, 1896

    II —Esther Evaleen Steen was born at Battle Ground, Indiana January 9, 1890

  2 Mary Elizabeth Steen was born at Battle Ground, Indiana

II —Nancy Holmes Steen the second child and eldest daughter of John and Jane D Wright Steen, was born in Clinton County, Indiana, November 12 1837 She was mairied at the same place October 21, 1852, to John C Allen — a farmer — he having been boin in Ohio, January 2, 1827, and died in Clinton County, Indiana November 27, 1889, in the 63d year of his age Mrs Nancy H Steen Allen still resides near Mulberry, Clinton County, Indiana To them were born nine children, as follows:

1 Henry Albert Allen the eldest son of John C and Nancy H Steen Allen was born in Clinton County, Indiana, January 21, 1854 He is a farmer by occupation He was married, February 3, 1879, to Lillian Carr, she having been born February 13, 1858. Residence, Brookston, White County, Indiana To them were born the following four children

    I —Helen A Allen, the eldest child of Henry Albert and Lillian Carr Allen was born August 26, 1881

    II —Jay C Allen, the second child and eldest son of Henry A and Lillian C Allen, was born July 10 1883

    III —Nancy V Allen, the third child and second daughter of Henry A and Lillian C Allen, was born November 12, 1885

    IV —Albert H Allen, the fourth child and second son of Henry A and Lillian C Allen, was born March 16, 1888

2 Lydia Jane Allen, the second child and eldest daughter of John C and Nancy H Steen Allen, was born in Clinton County, Indiana, November 4, 1855 She was married, January 11, 1888, to John A Cook — a druggist — he having been born October 14, 1852 Residence, Goodland, Indiana To them was born one son, as follows

    I —Raymond Cook a son of John A and Lydia Jane Allen Cook, was born January 13, 1889

3 Harriet Louisa Allen, the third child and second daughter of John C and Nancy H Steen Allen was born in Clinton County, Indiana, September 6, 1857 and died November 8, 1861, in the 5th year of her age

4 Jemima Adaline Allen the fourth child and third daughter of John C and Nancy H Steen Allen, was born in Clinton County, Indiana February 26, 1859 She was married, October 21, 1885, to Dr Dennis M. Kelley, he having been born March 12, 1855 Residence Brookston Indiana

5 George Gordon Allen, the fifth child and second son of John C and Nancy H Steen Allen was born in Clinton County, Indiana, February 19, 1861 — a farmer He was married, December 21, 1888, to Adda Finch, she having been born

September 28, 1865 Residence, near Otterbein, Benton County, Indiana To them one child was born

I —Geneva Allen, daughter of George B and Adda Finch Allen, was born December 22, 1890

6 Elizabeth Ann Allen, the sixth child and fourth daughter of John C and Nancy H Steen Allen, was born in Clinton County, Indiana, August 16, 1862 She was married in Markle, Huntington County, Indiana, June 17, 1885, to the Rev Milton E Nethercut, a minister of the Methodist Episcopal Church, he having been born March 9, 1861. To them one child was born

I —Emory E Nethercut, a son of Rev. M E and Elizabeth A Allen Nethercut, was born April 21, 1886

7 John Edward Allen, the seventh child and third son of John C and Nancy H Steen Allen, was born in Clinton County, Indiana, October 24, 1863 — a druggist. Residence, Mulberry, Indiana

8 Mary Olive Allen, the eighth child and fifth daughter of John C and Nancy H. Steen Allen, was born in Clinton County, Indiana, September 22 1865 She was married, September 5, 1888, to Bert G Small, a son of Rev Gilbert Small, he having been born March 16, 1867 — editor of "The Journal." Residence, Logansport, Indiana To them one child was born

I —Donald Small, a son of Bert G and Mary Olive Allen Small, was born April 21, 1890

9 Robert Wright Allen, the ninth child and fourth son of John C and Nancy H Steen Allen, was born in Clinton County, Indiana, December 14, 1870 — a druggist Residence, Mulberry, Clinton County, Indiana

III.—George Boyd Steen, the third child and second son of John and Jane D Wright Steen, and a grandson of George and Anne Gualt Steen, was born in Tippecanoe County, Indiana, December 22, 1839 — a farmer by occupation He was married in Danville, Illinois, February 25 1863, to Damaris Bush, a daughter of William and Jane Bush she having been born in Dayton, Indiana, April 6 1843 Residence, Ionia, Jewell County, Kansas To them were born eleven children, as follows

1 Orville Bush Steen, the eldest son of George Boyd and
   Damaris Bush Steen, was born in Tippecanoe County, Indiana, January 3, 1865, and died August 19, 1865

2 George Edgar Steen, the second son of George B and
   Damaris B Steen, was born in Tippecanoe County, Indiana,
   March 25, 1866 — clerk of the court, Mankato, Kansas

3 Ralph Lester Steen, the third son of George B. and Damaris
   B Steen, was born in Daviess County, Missouri, March 17,
   1869 — a teacher, Mankato, Kansas

4 Robert Lee Steen, the fourth son of George B. and Damaris
   B Steen, was born in Daviess County, Missouri, March 12
   1871 — a teacher, Jewell City, Kansas

5 Agnes Mary Steen, the fifth child and eldest daughter of
   George B and Damaris B Steen, was born in Jewell County,
   Kansas, October 3, 1873   Residence, Ionia, Kansas

6 Orris Dwight Steen, the sixth child and fifth son of George
   B and Damaris B Steen, was born in Jewell County, Kansas, September 6, 1875   Residence, Ionia, Kansas

7 Morton Colfax Steen, the seventh child and sixth son of
   George B and Damaris B Steen was born in Jewell County,
   Kansas, November 16, 1877   Residence, Ionia, Kansas

8 Maud Lillie Steen, the eighth child and second daughter of
   George B and Damaris B Steen, was born in Jewell County,
   Kansas, December 17, 1879   Residence, Ionia, Kansas

9 Chester Lynn Steen, the ninth child and seventh son of
   George B and Damaris B Steen, was born in Jewell County,
   Kansas, January 28, 1882

10 Clement Earle Steen, the tenth child and eighth son of
    George B and Damaris B Steen, was born in Jewell County,
    Kansas, June 25, 1884   Residence, Ionia, Kansas

11 Leona M Steen, the eleventh child and third daughter of
    George B and Damaris B Steen, was born in Jewell County,
    Kansas, October 27, 1886   Residence, Ionia Kansas

IV —Harriet Eliza Steen, the fourth child and second daughter
of John and Jane D Wright Steen, and a granddaughter of
George and Anne Gualt Steen, was born in Clinton County,
Indiana, March 15, 1842, and died September 30, 1866, in the
25th year of her age   She was married in Tippecanoe County,
Indiana, March 29 1860, to Anthony Noble, he having been

born in Butler County Ohio September 12 1831 and resides near Fithian, Vermilion County, Illinois To them were born three children as follows

1 Huldah Jane Noble the eldest daughter of Anthony and Harriet Eliza Steen Noble, was born May 6, 1861 Residence, Fithian, Illinois

2 Rosa R Noble, the second daughter of Anthony and Harriet Eliza Steen Noble, was born November 15, 1862 Residence Fithian, Illinois

3 Mary Agnes Noble, the third daughter of Anthony and Harriet Eliza Steen Noble, was born April 28, 1864 Residence, Fithian, Illinois

V—Sarah Ann Steen, the fifth child and third daughter of John and Jane D Wright Steen, and a granddaughter of George and Ann Gualt Steen, was born in Clinton County Indiana, January 16, 1846. She was married by the Rev R M Martin, in Danville Vermilion County, Illinois, September 26, 1867, to William Harvey Dearth he having been born in Warren County Ohio November 30 1843 Residence Fithian, Illinois They are the parents of one child, as follows

1 John William Dearth, son of William Harvey and Sarah Ann Steen Dearth was born near Fithian Illinois June 18, 1871 Residence, Fithian, Vermilion County, Illinois

VI—Mary Elizabeth Steen, the sixth child and fourth daughter of John and Jane D Wright Steen and a granddaughter of George and Annie Gualt Steen, was born in Clinton County, Indiana February 12 1848 She was married in Vermilion County, Illinois, January 18, 1866, to Perry T Martin he having been born in Georgetown, Vermilion County Illinois February 16 1843 Residence 346 East Madison Street Danville, Illinois To them were born two children, as follows·

1 Edward Perry Martin the eldest son of Perry T and Mary Elizabeth Steen Martin, was born August 6, 1870 Residence Danville, Illinois

2 Lawson Ellsworth Martin, the second son of Perry T and Mary Elizabeth Steen Martin, was born April 7, 1873 Residence, Danville, Illinois

CHAPTER VI.

Jane Steen, the sixth and youngest child of George and Anne Gualt Steen was born in Lancaster County, Pennsylvania, March 26, 1811, and died in Tippecanoe County, Indiana, October 8, 1836, in the 26th year of her age. She removed with her parents from Pennsylvania to Tippecanoe County Indiana, in May 1833. She was married in Tippecanoe County, Indiana about 1835, to John Adam Peters, by whom she had one child, as follows:

I.—Jane Peters, a daughter of John Adam and Jane Steen Peters, was born in Tippecanoe County, Indiana September 29, 1836. She was married in Clinton County, Indiana February 25, 1857, to William Foresman, he having been born in Circleville, Ohio, September 8 1830. Residence Foresman, Newton County, Indiana. To them were born five children, as follows:

1. Charles A Foresman the eldest son of William and Jane Peters Foresman, was born in Dayton, Tippecanoe County, Indiana, May 29 1859. He is editor of "The Lewiston Teller." He was married in Crawfordsville, Indiana, August 5 1891. Residence, Lewiston, Idaho

2. Robert Bruce Foresman the second son of William and Jane Peters Foresman, was born in Dayton, Indiana, November 10, 1862. He was married in Kentland Indiana, March 20, 1890. To them one child was born. Residence, Kentland, Indiana

3. William Foresman, the third son of William and Jane Peters Foresman, was born in Harristown, Macon County Illinois, September 7, 1864 — a teacher and printer by occupation. Residence, Lewiston, Idaho

4. Marcus F Foresman, the fourth son of William and Jane Peters Foresman was born in Harristown Illinois, November 17, 1867. He was married in Foresman, Indiana, October 16 1890. He is by occupation a teacher and practical printer. Residence, Lewiston, Idaho

5. Harvey Foresman, the fifth son of William and Jane Peters Foresman, was born in Harristown, Illinois, December 3, 1871. Residence, Foresman, Newton County Indiana

BOOK SEVEN.

DESCENDANTS OF FREDERICK STEEN.

Frederick Steen was born in Lancaster County, Pennsylvania, in 1755 He was married about 1785 to Katherine Rector, and removed to Harrison County Kentucky near Cynthiana where all his four children were born and brought up He died in Knox County, Kentucky, killed by a stroke of lightning, about 1815 After his death the family removed to Missouri.

Frederick Steen was born in Lancaster County, Pennsylvania, in 1755 and died in Knox County, Kentucky, about 1815, killed by a stroke of lightning, when about sixty years of age He was married about 1785 to Katherine Rector, whose parents came from Holland, and consequently belonged to the Pennsylvania Dutch stock she having been born in Pennsylvania about 1759 and died in Gasconade County, Missouri, in 1863 in the 104th year of her age One of the brothers of Katherine Rector Steen became Surveyor General of the State of Missouri in an early day, and is supposed to be the father or grandfather of ex-Governor Rector, of Arkansas Frederick Steen was a man of large frame, quite stout, and weighed considerably more than two hundred pounds Not long after his marriage he removed from Pennsylvania, and located upon a farm near Cynthiana, in Harrison County, Kentucky, where all his four children were

(330)

born and brought up.   He was a successful and practical farmer.
All his children were industrious and prosperous.   Several years
after the death of Frederick Steen his wife and children emigrated
to the State of Missouri, where a numerous posterity still
remains   To Frederick and Katherine Rector Steen were born
the following children· Elizabeth, William, John, and Frances
Steen

CHAPTER I

Elizabeth Steen the eldest child, a daughter of Frederick and
Katherine Rector Steen, was born on her father's farm, near
Cynthiana Harrison County, Kentucky, in 1791   She was mar-
ried to William R Bohan, and in the year 1833 removed to the
State of Missouri with her husband, who located on lands in
Pettis County near the site of the present city of Sedalia, where
many of their descendants still remain   They were the parents
of five children, as follows

I —James Bohan
II —John Bohan
III —William Bohan
   1 Walter S Bohan
IV —Frances Bohan, who was married to a Mr Watson
V —Sarah Bohan, who was married to a Mr Ray

CHAPTER II

William Steen, the second child and eldest son of Frederick
and Katherine Rector Steen, was born upon his father's farm
near Cynthiana, Harrison County, Kentucky October 14, 1795,
and died in Douglas Prairie, Missouri, July 25, 1869, in the 74th

year of his age   In 1832 he removed from Kentucky to Gasconade County, Missouri, and located on what is now known
as Douglas Prairie, where at the time of his death, he owned a
large and valuable estate of five hundred acres of land   He was
married in Roane County, Tennessee, September 14, 1818, to
Elizabeth Rector, (a daughter of Richard Rector who was born
October 7, 1784, and Frances Smith Rector, who was born September 1, 1789), she having been born in Roane County Tennessee, July 19, 1804, and died on Douglas Prairie, Gasconade
County, Missouri, June 29, 1856 in the 52d year of her age. To
them were born three children, as follows

I —Susan Steen, the eldest child, a daughter of William and
   Elizabeth Rector Steen, was born in Roane County Tennessee,
   January 14, 1822, and died October 10, 1865, in the 44th year
   of her age   She was married May 15, 1853, to James Finley
   They had no children

II —Mary Steen, the second daughter of William and Elizabeth
   Rector Steen, was born in Roane County, Tennessee, November 12, 1824   She was married at the home of her parents, on
   Douglas Prairie, in Gasconade County, Missouri, September
   15, 1844, to John Walters, he having been born in South Carolina, September 10, 1817   Residence, Steen's Prairie, Missouri   To them were born two children, as follows

   1 Sarah Elizabeth Walters, the eldest daughter of John and
      and Mary Steen Walters, was born in Maries County, Mis-
      souri, February 19, 1848   She was married at the same
      place, October 3 1867, to Mons Randolph Matthews, he
      having been born in Gasconade County Missouri, March 16,
      1846   Residence, Steen's Prairie, Maries County Missour'
      To them were born three children, as follows

      I —Sarah Margretta Matthews, the eldest child, a daughter
         of Mons Randolph and Sarah Elizabeth Matthews was
         born in Gasconade County, Missouri, July 31, 1869   She
         was married at the same place, January 3, 1889, to Jacob
         Willoughby, he having been born in Maries County, Mis-
         souri, July 2, 1869

      II —Mary Elizabeth Matthews, the second daughter of M
         R and Sarah Elizabeth Walters Matthews, was born at
         Gasconade County, Missouri, April 11, 1872, and died
         August 20, 1875 in the fourth year of her age

III—Honora Florence Matthews, the third daughter of Mons Randolph and Sarah Elizabeth Walter Matthews, was born in Gasconade County, Missouri, November 20, 1877

2 Margietta Walter the second daughter of John and Mary Steen Walter, was born in Maries County, Missouri, December 9, 1850 She was married at the same place November 15, 1871, to John Henry Arrendall, he having been born in Maries County, Missouri, December 23, 1848 They have no children Residence, Steen's Prairie, Missouri

III—Sarah Ann Steen, the third daughter of William and Elizabeth Rector Steen, was born in Roane County, Tennessee, December 22 1826 She was married in Gasconade County, Missouri, May 30, 1848, to Robert Milne, who was a Christian minister and died March 17, 1865, in the 39th year of her age Her husband, Rev Robert Milne, was born in Ohio June 2, 1823, and died August 8, 1890, in the 67th year of his age To them were born the following children

1 Mary E Milne the eldest child, a daughter of Robert and Sarah Ann Steen Milne, was born March 25, 1849 She was married December 11, 1864 to George R Sullivan She was married a second time April 11 1871, to Joseph Beesley, who died May 5, 1898 To the first marriage was born one child, and to the second marriage five children The following are the children of Mary E Milne Sullivan-Beesley

I—George W Sullivan a son of George R and Mary E Milne Sullivan was born September 13, 1865 and died February 1 1888 in the 23d year of his age

II—Charles E Beesley the second son of Mary E Milne, the first child by her second husband, Joseph Beesley, was born March 16, 1872

III—Nancy V J Beesley, daughter of Joseph and Mary E Milne Beesley, was born September 4 1874, and was married September 16 1893, to William T Pennington

IV—Mary E Beesley, daughter of Joseph and Mary E Milne Beesley was born June 4 1878

I—Martha C Beesley, daughter of Joseph and Mary E Milne Beesley was born January 5, 1882

VI—Isaac H Beesley, a son of Joseph and Mary F. Milne Beesley, was born September 6, 1885. Residence, Topaz, Douglas County, Missouri

2 Nancy Malinda Milne the second child, a daughter of Robert and Sarah Ann Steen Milne, was born in Gasconade County, Missouri, November 28, 1852, and was brought up in her father s family in Missouri and Kansas. She was married in Ozark County, Missouri, December 9, 1880, to Francis Marion Herndon, he having been born in Ozark County, Missouri, October 22, 1855. Residence, Silverton, Douglas County, Missouri. To them were born two children, as follows

I—Otis Alvin Herndon, the eldest son of Francis M and Nancy M Herndon, was born in Douglas County, Missouri, January 6, 1882

II—Elmer Benona Herndon, the second son of Francis M. and Nancy M Herndon, was born in Douglas County, Missouri, October 8 1884

3 Melissa Caroline Milne, the third child, a daughter of Robert and Sarah Ann Steen Milne, was born in Gasconade County, Missouri, November 25, 1854, and died at Alva, Missouri, November 2, 1887, in the 33d year of her age. She was married to Thomas A Kay, by whom she had two children. Family residence, Alva, Missouri

I—Dewey Hershel Kay

II—Carrie Ethel Kay

4 William Harvey Milne, the fourth child and eldest son of Robert and Sarah Ann Steen Milne, was born in Gasconade County, Missouri, March 23, 1856. He was married to Mary Cox, and removed to Table Rock, Nebraska, where they still reside. The following are their children

I—Frank Clark Milne

II—William Albert Milne

III—Robert Ohe Milne

IV—Benjamin Alvin Milne

5 Louisa Gabriela Milne, the fifth child and fourth daughter of Robert and Sarah Ann Steen Milne, was born in Gasconade County, Missouri, August 6, 1859. She was married near Polo, Missouri, October 7, 1875, to Thomas Benton

Moore, he having been born June 30, 1850 Residence, Polo, Caldwell County, Missouri To them were born the following six children:

I.—Mary Ellen Moore, the eldest daughter of Thomas B and Louisa G Milne Moore, was born September 30, 1876 She was married January 8, 1892, to Charles C Barr, he having been born September 13 1867

II—Nancy Pearl Moore, the second daughter of Thomas B and Louisa G. Moore, was born March 12, 1878

III—Carrie Virginia Moore, the third daughter of Thomas B and Louisa G Moore, was born November 30, 1879, and died January 8, 1883

IV—Sarah Helena Moore, the fourth daughter of Thomas B and Louisa G Moore, was born March 3, 1882

V.—Walter Benton Moore the fifth child and only son of Thomas B and Louisa G Moore, was born November 30, 1883, and died March 3, 1884

VI—Myrtle Moore the sixth child and fifth daughter of Thomas B and Louisa G Moore, was born September 8, 1890, and died December 19, 1890

6 Sarah Ella Milne, called "Ella," the sixth child and fifth daughter of Robert and Sarah Ann Steen Milne was born in Mt Vernon, Lawrence County, Missouri, March 23, 1861 This was at the beginning of the Civil War Money was scarce and hard to get, and the little girl was called "Hard Times" until peace was declared when her parents decided to call her Sarah Ella Milne When fourteen years of age she taught two terms of private school, and afterwards the public school for several years She has written quite a number of short poems She was married July 15, 1879 to Robert Bruce Martin, a son of Andrew and Margaret Martin, he having been born in Douglas County, Missouri, December 10, 1844 — a farmer — and died in 1896, aged 52 years To this marriage was born one child, as follows

I—Ira Martin, a son of Robert B and S Ella Milne Martin, was born in Lawrence County, Missouri, January 20, 1881 Residence, Salem, Oregon

Sarah Ella Milne Martin was married a second time, in Salem, Oregon June 1, 1898, to Charles Leonidas Watt, a son of Joseph and Sarah E. Watt, he having been born January 18, 1852   Residence, Salem, Oregon

7. James Robert Milne, the seventh child and second son of Robert and Sarah Ann Steen Milne, was born near Spring Hill, Kansas, February 18 1863   He was married in Gasconade County Missouri, March 28 1888, to Mary S Hutchins, she having been born October 13 1867   Residence, near Polo, Caldwell County, Missouri   To them was born one child, as follows·

   I —Katherine Belle Milne, daughter of James R and Mary S Milne, was born near Polo, Missouri, August 12, 1890

8 Susan Emily Milne, the eighth and youngest child, the sixth daughter of Robert and Sarah Ann Steen Milne, was born near Spring Hill, Kansas, March 10, 1865.   She was married near Ava Douglas County, Missouri August 1, 1883, to Jesse Oliver Casto, he having been born near Kingston, Caldwell County, Missouri, February 20, 1862 — a farmer. Residence, Harmony, Lewis County, Washington   To them were born the following children·

   I —Hattie May Casto, the eldest daughter of Jesse O and S Emma Milne Casto, was born in Caldwell Missouri, June 14, 1884, and died June 16, 1887, aged three years

   II —Ethel Lavina Casto, the second daughter of Jesse O and S Emma Milne Casto, was born in Caldwell County, Missouri, August 17 1886

   III —Olive Priscilla Casto, the third daughter of Jesse O. and S Emma Milne Casto was born in Caldwell County, Missouri, May 31, 1893

IV —William Francis Marion Steen, the fourth child and eldest son of William and Elizabeth Rector Steen, was born in Roane County, Tennessee, February 14, 1828.   He was taken by his parents to Missouri, in 1834, when a little boy, only six years old   His father's family settled permanently on a farm in Douglas Prairie, in Gasconade County, eighty-five miles west of St Louis   When a young man he went to Marion County Iowa, and in 1850 crossed the plains to California. He worked in the mines in Placerville, Georgetown, Downieville, and on the Yuba River   In 1852 he went to the Southern diggings at Sonora and the following year purchased a farm in Calaveras County, ten miles from Jacksonville, California, where he remained one year   In 1854 he sold his farm and went to Sydney, Australia   In 1856 he went to the Nelson District, in New Zealand and the following year returned to Sydney   In 1858 he went to Rocky River, in 1859 to Clarence River, in 1860 to the Lamon Flats, and was there at the time of the Chinese riot   In 1861 he went to Sydney again thence to the Lachlan River diggings in New South Wales   He left there in 1862 and went to New England, Clarence River, and the Loam diggings   In 1864 he went to Queensland and 'anded at Rockhampton from whence he proceeded to the Peak Down diggings   In 1865 he went prospecting and discovered gold at the Star River, and afterwards at Cape River In 1867 he went to Gilbert River, and in 1870 to Ravenswood In 1875 he went to Clammany, three hundred miles west of Ravenswood and only remained three months, then returned to Ravenswood, Queensland, Australia, where he has ever since resided His occupation has been that of a gold miner and trader in stocks — sometimes with plenty of money and sometimes with none   In May, 1886, he returned to America on a visit to friends and relatives. William Francis Marion Steen was married in Ravenswood, Queensland, Australia December 12, 1871, to Ann Shaw Gane she having been born in London, England, August 8, 1839   To them were born six children, all born in Ravenswood Queensland Australia, and brought up in the Church of England

1 Elizabeth Ann Steen, the eldest daughter of William F. M and Ann Shaw Gane Steen, was born September 5, 1872

2 Sarah Amelia Steen, the second daughter of William F M and Ann Shaw Gane Steen, was born August 14, 1874.

3 Eliza Jane Steen, the third daughter of William F M and Ann Shaw Gane Steen, was born July 19, 1876

4 Francis Robert Steen, the fourth child and eldest son of William F M and Ann Shaw Gane Steen, was born September 27, 1878

5 Benjamin Steen, the fifth child and second son of William F M and Ann Shaw Gane Steen, was born February 23 1880

6 Rebecca Steen, the sixth child and fourth daughter of William F M and Ann Shaw Gane Steen, was born May 8 1883   Residence, Ravenswood, Queensland, Australia
   (22)

V —Americus Vespucius Steen, the fifth child and second son
of William and Elizabeth Rector Steen, was born in Roane
County, Tennessee, February 12, 1830 He was brought by
his parents to Missouri when a little child, and grew to manhood on his father s farm, on Douglas Prairie, in Gasconade
County In 1850 he crossed the plains to California, and died
from dysentery, near Placerville, soon after reaching the State,
in the 21st year of his age

VI —Richard Rector Steen, the sixth child and third son of
William and Elizabeth Rector Steen, was born in Roane
County, Tennessee, September 6, 1831 and brought by his par-
ents to Douglas Prairie, in Gasconade County, Missouri, in
1834, when only three years old Here he grew up on his
father s farm, an industrious, intelligent, and successful man
He has always followed the occupation of a farmer. He was
married in Maries County, Missouri, December 11, 1873, to
Sarah Elizabeth Lovelace, a daughter of Thomas Jonas and
Mary Susan Lovelace, she having been born in Franklin
County, Missouri, April 4, 1854 They have no children.
Residence, near Springfield, Greene County, Missouri

VII —John C Steen, the seventh child and fourth son of William and Elizabeth Rector Steen, was born in Roane County,
Tennessee, February 6, 1833 and brought by his parents the
next year to Douglas Prairie Gasconade County, Missouri.
Here he grew up to manhood an intelligent industrious, and
successful farmer He was married, October 22, 1868, to
Laura Arundell Residence, Oak Hill, Missouri

VIII —Jasper Newton Steen, the eighth child and fifth son of
William and Elizabeth Rector Steen, was born on Douglas
Prairie, in Gasconade County, Missouri, March 1, 1835 Here
he grew to manhood and worked on his father's farm Residence, Red Bird, Gasconade County, Missouri

IX —Frederick Carlisle Steen, the ninth child and sixth son of
William and Elizabeth Rector Steen, was born on Douglas
Prairie, in Gasconade County, Missouri, February 15, 1831,
and brought up on his father's farm He is a successful farmer
He was married in Owensville, Gasconade County, Missouri,
February 22, 1859, to Martha Jane Thompson, a daughter of
William and Deliah Thompson, she having been born in
Franklin County, Missouri, February 22, 1838 To them were
born four children Residence, St James, Missouri

R. RECTOR STEEN.

1 Wilson Newton Steen, the eldest son of Frederick C and
Martha Jane Thompson Steen, was born in Gasconade
County, Missouri, January 26, 1862   He is by occupation
a cooper   Residence, St James, Missouri

2 Laura Alice Steen, the second child and only daughter of
Frederick C. and Martha Jane Thompson Steen, was born in
Gasconade County, Missouri, October 4, 1866   She is by
occupation a teacher   Residence, St James, Missouri

3 Early Steen, the third child and second son of Frederick C
and Martha Jane Thompson Steen was born in Mt Vernon
Lawrence County Missouri December 7, 1873, and died in
St. James, Missouri, November 7, 1874 aged 11 months.

4 Ernest Steen the fourth child and third son of Frederick
C and Martha Jane Thompson Steen was born in St James,
Missouri, December 25, 1875   Residence, St James Mis-
souri

X—George Washington Lafayette Steen, the tenth child and
seventh son of William and Elizabeth Rector Steen, was born
on Douglas Prairie, in Gasconade County Missouri July 4
1841, and brought up on his father's farm   He is by occupation a farmer   He was married in 1862 to Louisa Boiler   To
them was born one child   Residence, Deepwater Henry
County, Missouri

XI—Elizabeth Parthenia Steen, the eleventh child and fourth
daughter of William and Elizabeth Rector Steen was born
on Douglas Prairie in Gasconade County, Missouri October
29, 1845, and brought up on her father's farm   She was married at that place, June 5 1864, to John Gatz, he having been
born in Hassiah, Germany April 7 1841   They have no children.   Residence on Douglas Prairie, Missouri

---

CHAPTER III

John Steen, the third child and second son of Frederick and
Katherine Rector Steen, was born upon his father's farm, near
Cynthiana, Harrison County Kentucky February 4 1805   He

was an industrious, energetic and successful farmer   In 1832,
when he was about 27 years of age, he removed from Kentucky
to Missouri and located upon a farm   He secured a large tract
of land on what is now known as "Steen's Prairie," in Maries
County, Missouri, which prairie was named after him.   Here he
continued to reside until his death, February 14 1847, aged 42
years   He was married, July 28, 1838, to Mary A J Mitchell,
who died in Hopkins County, Texas, May 22, 1870   To them
were born a family of five children, as follows

I —Elizabeth Jane Steen, the eldest daughter of John and Mary
    A J Steen, was born at Steen s Prairie Maries County, Mis-
    souri, August 4, 1839 and died September 7, 1847, aged 8
    years 1 month and 3 days

II —Martha Ann Steen, the second daughter of John and Mary
    A J Steen was born at Steen s Prairie, Maries County, Mis-
    souri, March 13 1841, and died April 18, 1855, aged 14 years,
    1 month and 5 days

III —Enoch M Steen the third child and eldest son of John
    and Mary A J Steen, was born at Steen s Prairie, in Maries
    County, Missouri, January 18 1843, and died in Hopkins
    County, Texas, January 26 1871 aged 28 years and 8 days
    He was married in Hopkins County, Texas, in 1868, to Jeanie
    Wells, who died in Hopkins County Texas, in 1871   To them
    were born two daughters, both of whom were married and were
    still living at last accounts

IV —William Marvin Steen, the fourth child and second son of
    John and Mary A J Steen, was born at Steen s Prairie, in
    Maries County Missouri, February 20, 1845, and died Decem-
    ber 21, 1845 aged 9 months and 22 days.

V —John Logan Steen, the fifth child and third son of John and
    Mary A J Steen, was born a few days after his father's death
    at Steen s Prairie, Maries County, Missouri, February 25 1847
    — a prosperous farmer   He was married in Denton County,
    Texas February 25, 1872 to Elizabeth Matilda Reynolds
    Residence, Graham Young County, Texas   To them were
    born the following eight children

    1 Zirrel J Steen the eldest child of John L and Elizabeth M
    Steen, was born in Denton County Texas December 27,
    1872

2 Walter P Steen, the second child of John L and Elizabeth
   M Steen, was born in Denton County, Texas, April 28
   1875

3 Wilham H Steen, the third child of John L and Elizabeth
   M Steen was born in Archer County, Texas, August 12,
   1878

4 Myrtle Steen the fourth child of John L and Elizabeth M
   Steen, was born in Archer County, Texas, March 31, 1881

5 Oliver G Steen, the fifth child of John L and Elizabeth M.
   Steen, was born in Archer County, Texas, July 18, 1883

6 Pearl Steen, the sixth child of John L and Elizabeth M
   Steen, was born in Archer County, Texas, November 4,
   1888

7 Ruby Steen, the seventh child of John L and Elizabeth M
   Steen, was born in Archer County, Texas, July 17, 1891

8 Alberta Jewell Steen, the eighth child of John L and Elizabeth M Steen, was born in Archer County Texas, December
   13, 1894

CHAPTER IV.

Frances Steen, the fourth child and second daughter of
Frederick and Katherine Rector Steen, was born on her father's
farm, near Cynthiana, Harrison County, Kentucky, May 8, 1806,
where she grew up to womanhood She was married in 1823, to
Francis R Douglas — a farmer — he having been born October
16, 1799 Mr. Douglas early emigrated to what was then the
far West He was the first settler permanently located on what
is now known as "Douglas Prairie," in Gasconade County, Missouri, which prairie took its name from him Here he continued
to reside for many years brought up his family, and owned a
large and valuable landed estate The following are their
children

I —Frederick J Douglas, the eldest son of Francis R and Frances Steen Douglas, was born February 10, 1824   He was married in St Louis, Missouri, in 1849, to Ann Denny, and died in St Louis, Missouri, February 17, 1875, aged 51 years and 7 days

II —Mary Ann Douglas, the second child and eldest daughter of Francis R. and Frances Steen Douglas, was born April 24, 1826   She was married to S G Trower, and died in early life

III —Enoch S Douglas, the third child and second son of Francis R and Frances Steen Douglas, was born October 23, 1831   He was married to Elizabeth Moore

IV —Lorinda V Douglas, the fourth child and second daughter of Francis R and Frances Steen Douglas, was born September 29, 1833   She was married to F Crabtree   Residence, No 1523 Cherry Street, Kansas City, Missouri

V —William M Douglas, the fifth child and third son of Francis R and Frances Steen Douglas was born July 5, 1835   He was married to Sarah Litton   Residence, Kansas City, Missouri

VI —Malinda E Douglas, the sixth child and third daughter of Francis R and Frances Steen Douglas, was born April 11, 1838   She was married to F Spence, and died ————

VII —Amanda M Douglas, the seventh child and fourth daughter of Francis R and Frances Steen Douglas, was born on Douglas Prairie, in Gasconade County Missouri, September 22 1841   She was married at the same place, July 28, 1858, to Dr George W Wyatt, a successful practicing physician, he having been born in Waterloo, Illinois, August 8, 1834   To them were born two children   Residence, Ash Grove, Missouri

   1 Milliard Clay Wyatt, the eldest son of Dr George W and Amanda M Douglas Wyatt, was born in Gasconade County, Missouri, September 12 1861   He was married, December 17, 1883, to Genevieve Reynolds, she having been born in St Louis Missouri, August 8, 1862   To them the following child was born

      I —Ethel Lynn Wyatt, a daughter of Milliard Clay and Genevieve Reynolds Wyatt, was born July 2, 1885

2 Marion Grant Wyatt, the second son of Dr George W and Amanda S Douglas Wyatt, was born in St Louis County, Missouri, February 16, 1864. He is the editor of the "Ash Grove American.' Residence, Ash Grove, Greene County, Missouri.

VIII —George W Douglas, the fourth son, the eighth and youngest child of Francis R and Frances Steen Douglas, was born on Douglas Prairie, in Gasconade County, Missouri, March 11, 1850 He was married to Mary Austin, by whom he brought up a family of children.

CHAPTER V

The record of Enoch Steen and his descendants is inserted here, although the writer is at a loss to know just where it ought to be placed.

Enoch Steen, a son of William Steen was born on his father's farm, near Harrodsburgh, Kentucky, February 22, 1800, and died in Kansas City, Missouri, January 22, 1880, in the 80th year of his age Enoch Steen served as a soldier and officer in the United States Army for a period of about forty-eight years, i e, from 1832 until his death, in 1880 When the Civil War broke out he was Colonel, commanding the fort at Walla Walla, Washington Territory There is a mountain in Idaho called "Steen's Mountain " named after him in consequence of a severe battle he fought at that place with the Snake Indians, in 1858 or 1859 He was retired from active service in the United States Army, about 1868, as Lieutenant Colonel of the Second United States Cavalry Col Enoch Steen was married three times and had children by his first and second wife, but none by his third He was married first in St. Louis, Missouri, in 1824, to Mrs

Mary Rector McPherson Her maiden name was Mary Rector.
To them were born three children He was married a second
time in 1849, to Mrs Mary Selkirk Walsh, whose maiden name
was Mary Selkirk by whom he had two children His second
wife died in 1862 He was married a third time, March 4, 1869,
to Mrs Amelia McGee Evans, who was born in Shelby County,
Kentucky, June 17, 1813, and who died in 1898, in Kansas City,
Missouri The following are the names of the children by Col
Enoch Steen, so far as they were known to the writer

I —Constance Steen, the eldest child of Col Enoch Steen and
his first wife was born about 1825 She was married to Commander Reed of the United States Navy, who was killed in
an action on the Mississippi River during the Civil War, and
his wife died a few years later

II —Laura Steen the second daughter of Col Enoch Steen and
his first wife, Mary Rector McPherson Steen, was born in
1826 She was married to Dr Marson, a surgeon in the
Southern Army Afterward she was married to Colonel
Tucker of the United States Army In 1893 she was living
quietly at her home on Olive Street, St Louis, Missouri

III —Alexander Early Steen was the only son of Colonel Enoch
Steen At the beginning of the Civil War he was a Captain in
the United States Army stationed at Ringgold Barracks,
Texas He resigned his commission and gave his services and
his life to the South He was very soon placed in command
of a brigade in the Confederate Army, and served with great
bravery and distinction throughout the war and was killed in
one of the last battles at Prairie Grove, Arkansas He was
married to a planter's daughter in the South and to them were
born a son and a daughter

IV —Arabella Steen, called 'Belle,' a daughter of Col Enoch
Steen by his second wife, Mary Selkirk Walsh Steen was born
in 1854 She was married in 1872 to John Waterman who
died about 1885 Arabella Steen Waterman died in Kansas
City, Missouri, in 1888 aged 34 years She was the mother of
one child

  1 Birdie Steen Waterman, a daughter of John and Arabella
  Steen Waterman was born in Kansas City Missouri in 1873,
  and now resides with her grandmother

V.—Catherine Steen, called "Kate," a daughter of Col Enoch Steen by his second wife, Mary Selkirk Walsh Steen, was born in 1856 She was married in Kansas City, Missouri, to Stephen Koth, in 1873 To them were born four children Residence, Kansas City, Missouri

BOOK EIGHT.

DESCENDANTS OF MOSES STEEN.

Moses Steen was born in Culmore, near Londonderry, Ireland, in 1718. He was married to a Miss Nelson, and brought up his family there. He died December 19, 1795, aged 77 years. His ancestors were originally refugees from persecution. They came from Scotland into Ireland as early as the reign of James I., probably about 1620, and settled on the banks of the Foyle.

Moses Steen was born at Culmore, Ireland, near Londonderry, in 1718, and died at the same place, December 19, 1795, aged 77 years. The old homestead at Culmore is a delightful place, overlooking Loch Foyle, and a fine prospect out to the sea. All the vessels that enter the harbor pass near by, and the view from beneath the shady trees is picturesque and interesting. The house stands upon a gentle slope above the water, and the ruins of the old church, where the family used to worship, is in full view. The cemetery near by marks the final resting-place of Moses Steen, his wife, several of their children, and many of their descendants. The ancestors of Moses Steen were originally refugees from Romish persecution in Holland. Leaving everything behind them except their religion, they first came into Scotland, where they remained for some time. They afterwards crossed over into Ireland as early as the reign of James I., prob-

(348)

ably about 1620, or perhaps a few years later They settled at
Culmore, on the banks of the Foyle, about four miles below Londonderry In the course of time they were scattered abroad,
and families of Steens sprang up in many different localities
They were a noble band of earnest Presbyterian Christians, who
had been called to suffer for their religious principles, but determined to maintain their freedom of conscience and liberty of
worship at all hazards. Moses Steen was married near Londonderry, about 1750, to a Miss Nelson, she having been born in
1721, and died August 12, 1784 They lived at Culmore, where
they brought up a family of children They often conversed with
the men who defended Londonderry from the 18th of December
until the close of the awful siege Moses Steen used to tell his
children and his grandchildren how that during the terrible siege
of 1688 his own father and grandfather were driven under the
walls of Derry by Rouen, the French General, in order that their
privations and cries might compel the besieged to surrender
The cruel plan however, failed It enabled the weak and help-
less in the city to get out, and the able-bodied to go in and carry
on the defense until William, the Prince of Orange, succeeded
in breaking through the blockade, and by his conquering army
and shiploads of provisions brought relief to the starving Protestants To Moses Steen and his wife, formerly a Miss Nelson,
were born three children, as follows Thomas, Alexander, and
Mary Steen

There is also a William Steen so closely related to this family that the record of himself and his descendants is inserted as
Chapter IV of this Book

CHAPTER I

Thomas Steen, the eldest son of Moses Steen and his wife,
formerly a Miss Nelson, was born at the old homestead, at Culmore, near Londonderry Ireland, in 1759, and died December 31,
1845, aged 86 years Thomas Steen was a prosperous business
man, a most enterprising merchant of Londonderry, and had a
vessel at sea He was a devout and earnest Christian a faithful

and enthusiastic member of the Presbyterian Church bringing up his family in the fear of the Lord. He was married, about 1788, to Rebecca Bonner, she having been born in 1763, and died December 17, 1846, aged 83 years. Her body was laid away to rest beside that of her husband, in the Culmore ceme- tery. To them were born nine children, as follows

I.—Isabella Steen, the eldest child, a daughter of Thomas and Rebecca Bonner Steen, was born in Londonderry, Ireland, in 1789, and died December 31, 1869, aged 80 years. She was married, about 1812, to John McCalley, and brought up a family of eight children, whose mortal remains now lie side by side in the Culmore cemetery. Their names are as follows:

1   Richard McCalley
2   William McCalley
3   John McCalley
4   Jane McCalley.
5   Isabella McCalley
6   Maria McCalley
7   Caroline McCalley
8   Annie McCalley

II.—William Steen, the second child and eldest son of Thomas and Rebecca Bonner Steen, was born in Londonderry, Ireland, in 1793, and died March 27, 1838. He was never married, was a devout Christian, and a prosperous merchant of Londonderry. His body was laid away to rest in the Culmore cemetery

III.—Alexander Steen, M D , the third child and second son of Thomas and Rebecca Bonner Steen, was born in London- derry, Ireland, in 1794, and died there September 14, 1870, aged 76 years. He was educated as a physician, and attained a high standing. He was court physician at St Petersburgh, Russia, during the latter part of the reign of Nicholas I , who died in St Petersburgh, March 2, 1855. He was a physician in the Refuge Hospital, St Petersburgh, Russia, but returned to Ireland, in his old age, and died there. His body rests in the Culmore cemetery. Dr Alexander Steen was twice mar- ried, first to a Miss Hill, by whom he had two children. After her death he was married a second time to a Miss Griffith, by

whom he also had two children The following are the names
of his children in the order of their birth:

1 William Steen
2 Emma Steen
3 Eliza Steen
4 Alexander Steen

IV —Moses Steen the fourth child and third son of Thomas and
Rebecca Bonner Steen, was born in Londonderry, Ireland,
about 1796, and died in Limavady, County Londonderry, Ireland, in 1856, aged about 60 years He was a merchant of
Limavady, doing a large business in the shoe trade He was
an earnest Christian, and brought up his children as such He
was married, about 1818, to Mary Simpson, who died in 1850,
by whom he had seven children, as follows:

1 Thomas Steen, the eldest son of Moses and Mary Simpson
Steen, was born in Limavady, Ireland, about 1820
2 Alexander Steen, the second son of Moses and Mary Simpson Steen, was born in Limavady, Ireland, about 1822
3 William Steen, the third son of Moses and Mary Simpson
Steen, was born in Limavady, Ireland, about 1824.
4 Lucinda Steen, the fourth child and eldest daughter of
Moses and Mary Simpson Steen, was born in Limavady,
Ireland, about 1825
5 Rebecca Steen, the fifth child and second daughter of Moses
and Mary Simpson Steen, was born in Limavady, Ireland,
about 1826
6 Amelia Winton Steen the sixth child and third daughter of
Moses and Mary Simpson Steen, was born in Limavady,
Ireland, about 1828
7. George Steen, the seventh child, the fourth and youngest
son of Moses and Mary Simpson Steen, was born in Limavady, Ireland in 1820 He was educated in the University
of Glasgow, Scotland, and ordained a minister of the Presbyterian Church in 1854, and installed pastor of the congregation in Keady, Ireland On this occasion the Rev John
Hall, D D, late of New York City, preached the installa-
tion sermon Rev George Steen still continues pastor of
this church in Keady, which position he has now (1900) held
for forty-six years He was married, in 1864, to Janet Lysle

Ross, she having been born in 1843. Residence, Keady, County Armagh, Ireland. To them were born six children, as follows·

I—James Ross Steen, M D , the eldest son of Rev. George and Janet L Ross Steen, was born in Limavady. Ireland, in 1867   He is now a physician in London, England

II—George Bonner Steen, the second son of Rev George and Janet L Ross Steen, was born in Keady, Ireland, in 1869 — a banker   Residence, Carrickmacross, Ireland

III—Ernest Lysle Steen, the third son of Rev George and Janet L. Ross Steen, was born in Keady, Ireland, in 1870 — a banker — Carrickmacross, Ireland

IV—Ilicia Lysle Steen, the fourth child of Rev George and Janet L Ross Steen, was born in Keady Ireland in 1872 She lives with her brother, Dr Steen, in London, England

V.—Olive Georgia Steen the fifth child and second daughter of Rev George and Janet L Ross Steen, was born in Keady, Ireland, in 1875   She was married to Henry Hobart Dorman, M D , in Keady, Ireland — a physician Residence, Keady, Ireland

   1 Olive Steen Dorman, a daughter of Dr Henry H and Olive G Steen Dorman, was born in Keady, Ireland, November, 1895

VI—Wilfred Alexander Steen, the sixth child, the fourth and youngest son of Rev George and Janet Lysle Ross Steen, was born in Keady, Ireland, in 1879 — a medical student, London, England.

V —Archibald Steen. the fifth child and fourth son of Thomas Bonner Steen, was born in Londonderry, Ireland, about 1798 He was an energetic and successful business man, was never married   He sailed on the ocean, and was never afterwards heard from·, was probably drowned at sea

VI —Thomas Steen, the sixth child and fifth son of Thomas and Rebecca Bonner Steen, was born in Londonderry, Ireland, in the year 1800   He was a prosperous merchant of Londonderry, a devout Christian, was never married, and died December 24, 1856, aged 56 years   His body rests in the old cemetery at Culmore, Ireland

VII —Elizabeth Steen, the seventh child and second daughter of Thomas and Rebecca Bonner Steen, was born in Londonderry, Ireland, about the year 1803 She was married to James Walker, by whom she had one child, as follows
1 Thomas Walker

VIII —Rebecca Steen, the eighth child and third daughter of Thomas and Rebecca Bonner Steen, was born in Londonderry, Ireland, about the year 1805, and died unmarried

IX —George Steen, the ninth child, the fifth and youngest son of Thomas and Rebecca Bonner Steen, was born in Londonderry, Ireland, April 11, 1807, and died at his residence in Limavady, County Londonderry, Ireland, in 1897, in the 91st year of his age He was married, December 24, 1833, to Margaret Thompson, of Bally Garnet, who died at White Hill Limavady, Ireland, November 29, 1891, after a happy married life of nearly fifty-eight years George Steen was ordained a Presbyterian clergyman, and installed pastor of a Presbyterian Church, near Limavady, Ireland, March 10, 1833, which he continued to serve for twelve years, until the organization of the Second Presbyterian Church in Limavady, when he was called to the pastorate of that church, and installed over it March 31, 1845 This relation he continued to hold until his death, a period of about 52 years and 6 months His active ministry in the vicinity of Limavady was a faithful, able and devoted service of more than sixty-four years In many respects he was a remarkable man — strong physically, mentally and religiously The writer visited his home in 1896, and found him in the 90th year of his age, still actively engaged in preaching the Gospel regularly once each Sabbath, with a warm heart and a mind of clear and quick perception, deeply interested in all the religious, literary and civil affairs of the day At that advanced age he was a good conversationalist and as host acted with the energy, grace, and dignity of an alderman of fifty years To the Rev George and Margaret Thomson Steen were born the following five children

1 Alexander Nelson Steen, the eldest son of Rev George and Margaret Thompson Steen was born in Limavady, County, Londonderry, Ireland, about 1836 He is a grain dealer in Liverpool Residence, No 40 Beaumont Street, Liverpool, England

(23)

2 William Steen, the second son of Rev George and Margaret Thompson Steen was born in Limavady, County Londonderry, Ireland, May 12, 1839   He is a manager of the Northern Bank   He was married at Naveny, Ballybofey, County Donegal, Ireland, to Mary Craig Holmes, she having been born at that place December 11 1855   They have no children   Residence, Newtown Stewart, County Tyrone, Ireland

3 Thomas Scott Steen, the third son of Rev George and Margaret Thompson Steen, was born in Limavady, County Londonderry, Ireland, in 1841   He is a prominent business man of Londonderry, a wholesale and retail colonial merchant, shipping goods to Australia and New Zealand Thomas S Steen is a devout and earnest Christian, a faithful member and ruling elder of the First Presbyterian Church of Londonderry, and was a Commissioner to the General Assembly in 1896   He is a man of large influence and has been chosen by the government a Justice of the Peace for the County of Londonderry   He was married first, to a lady who died not long afterwards   He was married a second time, to Mary Hunter, of Londonderry   Residence, Victoria Park, Warren Hill, Londonderry, Ireland   To them were born three children

    I — ——— Steen, the eldest daughter of Thomas S and Mary Hunter Steen, was born in Londonderry, Ireland and died ————

    II —Alice M T Steen, the second daughter of Thomas S and Mary Hunter Steen, was born in Londonderry, Ireland, April 28, 1884

    III —Mary Steen, the third daughter of Thomas S and Mary Hunter Steen, was born in Londonderry, Ireland, and died

4 Henrietta Cook Steen, the fourth child and only daughter of Rev George and Margaret Thompson Steen, was born in Limavady, County Londonderry, Ireland, about 1845   She was married to a Mr Strahan, who died early in life   Mrs Henrietta C Strahan resides in Coleraine Ireland with her three children, as follows

    I —Ettie Strahan

    II —George Strahan

Rev. George Steen, M.A.
(Born 1807; Died 1897.)

III —Jack Strahan.

5 Joseph Thompson Steen, the fifth child and youngest son of Rev George and Margaret Thompson Steen, was born at White Hill, Limavady, Ireland, February 19, 1849 He is by trade a colonial merchant He was married in Limavady, Ireland, July 11, 1878, to Maud Mary Moody, she having been born there in June, 1859 To them was born one child Residence, 27 Stanthorpe Road, Stratham, London, England, S W

  I —Ethel Margaret Thompson Steen, daughter of Joseph Thompson and Maud Mary Moody Steen, was born in London, England, April 7, 1879 Residence, London, England

CHAPTER II

Alexander Steen, the second son of Moses Steen and his wife (formerly a Miss Nelson), was born at Fountain Hill, Londonderry, Ireland about 1752 He was a sea captain, commander of a merchant ship called 'The Happy Return,' which sailed between Londonderry and New York He was also a partner with his brother in the mercantile business Alexander Steen died of a fever, in New York City He was married, and had three sons and one daughter, as follows. Robert, John, Alexander, and Mary

I—Robert Steen a son of Alexander Steen and a grandson of Moses Steen and his wife (formerly a Miss Nelson), was probably born in Londonderry Ireland, about 1750

II—John Steen, a son of Alexander Steen (who was a sea captain and commander of the merchant vessel "The Happy Return," sailing between New York and Londonderry), and a grandson of Moses Steen and his wife (formerly a Miss Nelson), was probably born in Londonderry Ireland about 1752 where he grew up to manhood He was married, about 1774, to Martha Cresswell, and brought up a family in Ireland

  1 Robert Steen, a son of John and Martha Cresswell Steen, was born at Fountain Hill, Londonderry, Ireland, Novem-

ber 22, 1775 where he spent his early life   He was married
in the Cathedral at Londonderry, July 12, 1803, to Mary
Ann Floyd and brought up his family at Culmore, Ireland
To them were born the following ten children

I —George Steen, the eldest son of Robert and Mary Ann
Floyd Steen, was born in Culmore, County, Donegal, Ireland, about 1804, where he lived and died

II —Martha Steen the second child and eldest daughter of
Robert and Mary Ann Floyd Steen, was born in Culmore,
Ireland about 1806, in which locality she spent her life

III —John Floyd Steen, the third child and second son of
Robert and Mary Ann Floyd Steen was born in Culmore,
County Donegal, Ireland, January 15, 1808   In 1831 he
removed to New York City, New York, where he con
tinued to reside until his death, in 1873 at the age of 65
years   He was married in New York City, in February,
1844, to Nancy Hamilton   To them were born three
children as follows

1 John Floyd Steen the eldest child and only son of John
Floyd and Nancy Hamilton Steen was born in New
York City January 6 1845 where he grew up to man-
hood and received his education   He was ordained a
deacon in the Protestant Episcopal Church, in Trinity
Church New York City, June 7, 1867, by the Rt Rev
Horatio Potter D D , Bishop of New York   He was
ordained to the priesthood, February 2, 1869 by the Rt
Rev John Johns D D Bishop of Virginia, with Rev
Stephen H Tyng, D D , and Rev Edward Anthon
assisting presbyters   From June, 1867, until February
1 1870 he was rector of St Paul's Church, White
Haven, Pennsylvania, and assistant minister in the
Church of the Holy Trinity, New York   He was
installed rector of Memorial Chapel in New York City,
February 1, 1870 which position he still retains   The
Rev John Floyd Steen was married in Kidder Town-
ship Carbon County Pennsylvania, September 15, 1868,
to Martha Porter   They have no children   Residence,
261 West Forty-second Street New York City New
York

REV. JOHN FLOYD STEEN.

2 Mary Elizabeth Leslie Steen, the second child and eldest daughter of John Floyd and Nancy Hamilton Steen, was born in New York City, New York, February 23, 1847, and died September 29, 1883, in the 37th year of her age. She was married in New York City, September 26, 1867, to Andrew Strangford, of Northampton Massachusetts, he having been born in Londonderry, Ireland, in February, 1842. His residence is No 121 Centre Street, Chicopee, Massachusetts. To them were born three children, all born in Easthampton, Massachusetts

a Samuel Floyd Strangford, the eldest child of Andrew and Mary Elizabeth Leslie Steen Strangford, was born March 19, 1869 — a printer by trade. He was married in Springfield Massachusetts, November 24, 1892, to Helen Louise Williams. Residence, Revere, Suffolk County, Massachusetts

b. Alice Hamilton Strangford the second child and only daughter of Andrew and Mary Elizabeth Leslie Steen Strangford, was born October 29, 1870. She was married in East Hampton, Massachusetts, October 15 1894, to Frank Ernest Smith. Residence, Pueblo Colorado

c William Edward Strangford, the third and youngest child, the second son of Andrew and Mary Elizabeth Leslie Steen Strangford was born October 1, 1872 He was married in Brooklyn, New York, November 26, 1896, to Lulu Frary, of Southampton, Massachusetts. Residence, Easthampton, Massachusetts. To them was born one child, as follows

aa. Raymond Lewis Strangford was born in Easthampton, Massachusetts March 28, 1898

3 Martha Frances Steen, the third and youngest child, the second daughter of John Floyd and Nancy Hamilton Steen, was born in New York City, New York, December 27, 1860, where she was brought up. She was married in New York City, February 15, 1881, to Henry Oscar Beebe, he having been born in Westfield, Massachusetts, August 6, 1855. Mr Beebe is of the firm of "Beebe & Van Schaik," at No 32 Broad Street, New

York City New York   Residence, New York City, New York   To them were born two children, as follows

    a Annie Elizabeth Beebe, the eldest child of Henry Oscar and Martha Frances Steen Beebe, was born June 23, 1882

    b. Floyd Steen Beebe the second child of Henry Oscar and Martha Frances Steen Beebe, was born August 18, 1888, and died July 6, 1889

IV—Mary Anne Steen the fourth child and second daughter of Robert and Mary Ann Floyd Steen, was born in Culmore, Ireland, about 1810.

V—Robert Steen, the fifth child and third son of Robert and Mary Ann Floyd Steen was born in Culmore, Ireland, about 1812

VI—Alexander Steen the sixth child and fourth son of Robert and Mary Ann Floyd Steen, was born in Culmore, Ireland about 1814

VII—Sarah Jane Steen the seventh child and third daughter of Robert and Mary Ann Floyd Steen was born in Culmore Ireland about 1816

VIII—Mary Steen the eighth child and fourth daughter of Robert and Mary Ann Floyd Steen, was born in Culmore, Ireland, about 1818

IX—Margaret Steen, the ninth child and fifth daughter of Robert and Mary Ann Floyd Steen was born in Culmore, Ireland about 1820

X—William Steen, the tenth child and fifth son of Robert and Mary Ann Floyd Steen was born in Culmore, County Donegal, Ireland about four miles down the River Foyle, below Londonderry, about 1822, and died unmarried

III—Alexander Steen who was the third son of Alexander Steen who was the second son of Moses Steen and his wife (formerly a Miss Nelson) was born, probably, in Londonderry, Ireland about 1755

IV—Mary Steen the fourth child and only daughter of Alexander Steen the sea captain, who commanded the ship "The Happy Return," sailing between Londonderry and New York, and a granddaughter of the Moses Steen who married a Miss

Nelson, was probably born in Londonderry, Ireland, about 1758 or 1759

CHAPTER III

Mary Steen, the only daughter of Moses Steen and his wife (formerly a Miss Nelson) and whose father was in the siege of Derry in 1688 was born in Londonderry. No record

---

CHAPTER IV

DESCENDANTS OF WILLIAM STEEN

This William Steen was not a descendant of Moses Steen as would be supposed by the name appearing at this place. He was the only son of a William Steen who had a first cousin by the name of Thomas Steen that lived in Londonderry. It is probable that he was a descendant of a brother of the Moses Steen who married a Miss Nelson, and whose record we have not obtained. Thus the father of William Steen was a full cousin to Thomas Steen the son of Moses Steen whose father and grandfather were in the siege of Derry. At any rate, they were closely related families.

I.—William Steen, a son of William Steen and possibly a grandnephew of Moses Steen, was born at Culmore County Donegal near Londonderry Ireland, in 1774. He was married in 1795, to Rebecca Weyhe she having been born in Linmore, Ireland, in 1774. After marriage they continued to live in Culmore, County Donegal until 1822 when they removed with their whole family to America, and located on a farm on the Credit River (a stream which flows into Lake Ontario) situated in Toronto Township, in the County of Peel, Ontario, Canada about four miles from the present village of Streets-

ville, and about twenty miles from the city of Toronto   Here
n this new country they opened up a farm, and by industry
and economy became prosperous   The whole family were
sturdy Presbyterians, as their fathers were, having been
brought up and educated in that faith for generations.   They
have exerted a great influence in molding the character of the
people in that whole region, which influence a numerous posterity still perpetuates   A large proportion of the Steen family relationship living near Streetsville are prosperous farmers,
and a healthy race   Nearly all of them are members of the
Presbyterian Church, and worship together in the congregation
of the Presbyterian Church in Streetsville, Ontario, and form a
large portion of that congregation   It was the writer's great
privilege to visit this locality, associate with these friends, and
worship in this church, in the autumn of 1896   To William and
Rebecca Weylie Steen were born eleven children as follows:

1 Mary Steen, the eldest child, a daughter of William and
Rebecca Weylie Steen, was born in Culmore, Ireland, about
1798   She was married at the home of her parents, on the
Credit River, near Streetsville, Ontario, in 1823, to John
Brown, who came to America in the same ship from County
Donegal, Ireland   They resided in York County, Ontario.
To John and Mary Steen Brown were born thirteen children.
The last place they lived was at Cleveland, Ohio, U. S A.
Among their children were four whose names are unknown
to the writer, but the names of the following nine of their
children are given

I —Rebecca Brown
II —Nathaniel Brown
III —Mary Ann Brown
IV —Jane Brown
V —Nancy Brown
VI —John Brown
VII —Isabella Brown.
VIII —Sarah Brown
IX —Rachel Brown

They live somewhere in the United States of America

2 Nathaniel Steen, the second child and eldest son of William
and Rebecca Weylie Steen, was born in Culmore, Ireland,

about 1800, and died near Streetsville, Ontario, Canada, in 1867 — a prosperous farmer He was married near Streetsville, Ontario, in 1829, to Isabella McKenzie, she having been born near Belfast, Ireland, in 1801, and died near Streetsville, in February, 1894, aged 93 years To them were born the following children

I—Rebecca Steen, the eldest daughter of Nathaniel and Isabella McKenzie Steen, was born near Streetsville, Ontario, June 1, 1838 She was married, March 16, 1859, to Mark Stevenson, he having been born April 9, 1826 To them were born the following children.

  1 William John Stevenson was born August 27, 1860

  2 Nathaniel James Stevenson was born October 13, 1861

  3 Thomas Wright Stevenson was born June 8, 1864

  4 Isabella Jane Stevenson was born November 29, 1866

  5 Mary Hannah Stevenson was born September 24, 1868

  6 Rebecca Elma Stevenson was born December 16, 1871

  7 Mark Usher Stevenson was born September 24, 1874

II—William Steen, the second child and eldest son of Nathaniel and Isabella McKenzie Steen, was born near Streetsville, Ontario, November 13, 1839 He was an invalid, unable to walk, but a very intelligent man He died July 31, 1888, aged 48 years, 8 months and 18 days

III—Nathaniel Steen, the third child and second son of Nathaniel and Isabella McKenzie Steen, was born near Streetsville, Ontario, March 23, 1841 — an influential citizen a successful farmer, and an elder of the Presbyterian Church His farm joins that of each of his sisters' husbands now living, so that they all dwell together, near each other, in the most pleasant associations Nathaniel Steen was married near Streetsville, Ontario, September 24, 1866, to Margery Jane Cummins, she having been born June 5, 1840 Residence, near Streetsville, Ontario To them were born the following children:

  1 Isabella Margaret Steen, the eldest child of Nathaniel and Margery Jane Cummins Steen, was born near Streetsville, Ontario, February 26, 1868, and died February 24, 1874

2 William Ephraim Wellington Steen, the second child
and only son of Nathaniel and Margery Jane Cummins
Steen, was born near Streetsville, Ontario, February 26,
1869 — a prosperous farmer, a fine singer, and leader
of the choir   He was married near Streetsville, Ontario,
December 31, 1895, to Mary Simpson, she having been
born August 23, 1872   Residence, Streetsville, Ontario

3 Elizabeth Mary Amanda Steen, the third child and
second daughter of Nathaniel and Margery Jane Cummins Steen, was born near Streetsville, Ontario, September 15, 1871   She was married at the home of her
parents, June 28, 1899, to Anson. Harvey Forster, of
Toronto, he having been born October 23, 1868   Residence, Toronto, Ontario, Canada

4 Julia Edith Elmina Steen, the fourth and youngest
child of Nathaniel and Margery Jane Cummins Steen,
was born near Streetsville, Ontario, December 3, 1874.
Residence, near Streetsville, Ontario

IV — Mary Hannah Steen, the fourth child and second
daughter of Nathaniel and Isabella McKenzie Steen, was
born near Streetsville Ontario, January 24 1844   She
was married at the same place   October 29, 1862, to
Thomas McCracken — a prosperous farmer — he having
been born November 6, 1834   Residence, near Streetsville, Ontario   To them were born the following children all born on the home farm, near Streetsville

1 Isabella McCracken was born October 8 1864

2 Jane McCracken was born September 18, 1866

3 Lisetta Victoria McCracken was born February 12,
1869

4 Nathaniel Steen McCracken was born July 1, 1870

5 Thomas Cayne McCracken was born August 2, 1871,
and died ————

6 William James Breckinridge McCracken was born
August 8, 1872 and died ————

7 Augusta Rebecca McCracken was born August 3 1874

8 Mary Elvira McCracken was born November 30, 1875.

9 Ephraim Weyhe McCracken was born July 25, 1877

NATHANIEL STEEN.

10 William Jacob Kennedy McCracken was born August 17, 1880

11 Thomas Mark Evert McCracken was born January 19, 1882

12 Hannah Alice Mary McCracken was born December 18, 1884

V—Ephraim Steen, the fifth child and third son of Nathaniel and Isabella McKenzie Steen, was born near Streetsville, Ontario, April 27, 1847 — a successful farmer Some years before his death he suffered the loss of his right arm and after the amputation his system never regained its former vigor He died near Streetsville, Ontario in June 1893 in the 47th year of his age He was married near Streetsville, June 23, 1871, to Mary Ritchey she having been born July 21 1848 Family residence the old homestead, near Streetsville Ontario To them were born the following children, all born at the old Steen family homestead, on the Credit River near Streetsville Ontario

1 Nathaniel Ritchey Steen the eldest son of Ephraim and Mary Ritchey Steen was born June 9 1872, and died ————.

2 Samuel Dilman Steen, the second son of Ephraim and Mary Ritchey Steen, was born December 29, 1873

3 Nathaniel Robb Steen, the third son of Ephraim and Mary Ritchey Steen, was born August 29 1875

4 Thomas Weylie Steen the fourth son of Ephraim and Mary Ritchey Steen was born September 24 1877

5 Isabella Jane Steen, called "Belle, the fifth child and only daughter of Ephraim and Mary Ritchey Steen, was born July 15 1879, at the old family home on the Credit River, where her great-grandfather, William Steen first settled in America She was married at the same place, June 2', 1890, to James Ritchey Residence, Detroit, Michigan

6 William Stevenson Steen, the sixth child and fifth son of Ephraim and Mary Ritchey Steen, was born June 4, 1883

(24)

7 Ephraim James Randolph Steen, the seventh child and sixth son of Ephraim and Mary Ritchey Steen was born April 9, 1886

8 Francis Benard Steen, the eighth child and seventh son of Ephraim and Mary Ritchey Steen, was born June 9, 1888

3 Ephraim Steen, the third child and second son of William and Rebecca Weyhe Steen, of Culmore Ireland, and a descendant of Moses Steen and his wife (formerly a Miss Nelson), was born in Culmore, Ireland, about 1803   In 1822 he removed with his parents to America, and located on the Credit River in Toronto Township, County of Peel, Ontario, Canada   He was an industrious energetic, and successful farmer   He was married near Streetsville Ontario, in 1830, to Jane Douglas she having been born in Ballenlong Perthshire Scotland   They spent their lives in Toronto Township, County of Peel near Streetsville, where many of their descendants still remain   To them were born seven children, as follows

1 —Rebecca Steen, the eldest child, a daughter of Ephraim and Jane Douglas Steen, was born in Toronto Township, County of Peel Ontario October 22, 1831   She was married in the same locality, December 30, 1851, to John Weyhe, he having been born April 23, 1821   Residence, Glanford Ontario Canada   To them were born nine children, as follows, all born near Glanford, Ontario, Canada

1 Jane Weyhe was born August 10, 1853

2 John Weyhe was born September 11, 1854

3 Isaac Weyhe was born November 22, 1855

4 Mary Ann Weyhe was born December 3, 1857

6 Rebecca Weyhe was born February 23, 1859

6 William Weyhe was born September 5, 1860

7 Agnes Weyhe was born February 12, 1862 and died

8 Frances Weyhe was born April 9 1864 and died

9 Sarah Weyhe was born September 2 1868

II—William Steen, the second child and eldest son of Ephraim and Jane Douglas Steen, was born in Toronto, Township, County of Peel about four miles from Streetsville, Ontario July 4 1833 — a farmer and afterwards a business man. He was married near Streetsville, October 22, 1860 to Ann Matilda Miller, she having been born August 15, 1840. Residence, in Streetsville Ontario. To them were born ten children, as follows

1 Ephraim Erie Steen, the eldest son of William and Ann Matilda Steen was born near Streetsville Ontario April 19 1862. Residence Brandon Manitoba, Canada

2 John Crombie Steen, the second child and a twin brother of the preceding was born near Streetsville Ontario, April 19, 1862, and died February 14, 1895, aged 32 years 9 months and 25 days

3 Mary Jane Steen, the third child and eldest daughter of William and Ann Matilda Miller Steen, was born near Streetsville Ontario February 28, 1864, and died April 5, 1864, aged 1 month and 16 days

4 Margaret Anna Matilda Steen, the fourth child and second daughter of William and Ann Matilda Miller Steen, was born near Streetsville Ontario, November 20 1865. She was married in Streetsville Ontario, May 22, 1894, to William Couse he having been born February 22 1860. Residence, Streetsville Ontario. To them was born one child

a William Harold Couse was born May 31, 1895

5 William Waldie Steen, the fifth child and third son of William and Ann Matilda Miller Steen, was born near Streetsville, Ontario, April 19, 1868, and died October 22, 1870 aged 24 years, 6 months and 3 days

6 Robert Irwin Steen, the sixth child and fourth son of William and Ann Matilda Miller Steen, was born near Streetsville, Ontario, July 6, 1870

7 Sarah Agnes Steen the seventh child and third daughter of William and Ann Matilda Miller Steen, was born near Streetsville Ontario, July 29, 1872. She was married in Streetsville, Ontario, August 3 1898 to William

Benjamin Wiedenhamer, he having been born December 24, 1869   Residence, Streetsville, Ontario   To them was born one child

    a Frederick Carl Wiedenhamer was born September 5, 1899

8 Charles Breckinridge Steen, the eighth child and fifth son of William and Ann Matilda Miller Steen, was born near Streetsville, Ontario, October 8, 1874

9 Catherine Rebecca Steen, the ninth child and fourth daughter of William and Ann Matilda Miller Steen, was born near Streetsville, Ontario, February 24, 1877

10 William James Goodesham Steen, the tenth child and sixth son of William and Ann Matilda Miller Steen, was born near Streetsville, Ontario, February 18, 1880. Residence, Streetsville, Ontario, Canada

III —Robert Steen, the third child and second son of Ephraim and Jane Douglas Steen, was born in Toronto Township, County of Peel, about four miles from Streetsville, Ontario April 5 1835 — a successful farmer   He was married February 12, 1862 to Margaret Graham, she having been born August 4, 1839   Residence, near Streetsville, Ontario   To them were born eight children, as follows all born near Streetsville Ontario   ,

1 Jane Steen, the eldest child of Robert and Margaret Graham Steen was born December 29, 1862   She was married December 27, 1890, to Seth Harket Pattulo, he having been born November 12, 1849   To them was born one child, as follows·

    a James Granam Pattulo was born January 1, 1892

2 Mary Ann Steen, the second daughter of Robert and Margaret Graham Steen, was born July 19, 1864   She was married April 13 1887 to Andrew George Orr, he having been born November 1 1864   To them was born one child, as follows.

    a Margaret Edna Orr was born March 8, 1890

3 Albert Edward Steen, the third child and eldest son of Robert and Margaret Graham Steen was born July 19, 1864 (a twin brother to Mary Ann Steen Orr)   He was married, December 29, 1890, to Isabella Ford, she hav-

ing been born March 6 1861 To them two children were born, as follows

a Francis Wilfred Steen, the eldest child of Albert Edward and Isabella Ford Steen, was born November 3, 1891

b Myrtle Jessie Steen the second child of Albert Edward and Isabella Ford Steen, was born March 7 1893

4 Elizabeth Margaret Steen, the fourth child and third daughter of Robert and Margaret Graham Steen, was born August 29 1866 She was married, September 16, 1891, to Albert Charles Bigger, he having been born July, 1868 To them was born one child, as follows:

a Eva Mildred Bigger was born October 10 1892

5 Clara Jennette Steen, the fifth child and fourth daughter of Robert and Margaret Graham Steen, was born July 24, 1870

6 Eveline Steen the sixth child and fifth daughter of Robert and Margaret Graham Steen, was born December 23, 1874 She was married near Streetsville, Ontario, July 1 1897 to Robert Buck

7 Josephine Rebecca Steen the seventh child and sixth daughter of Robert and Margaret Graham Steen was born July 3, 1878

8 Douglas Steen, the eighth child and youngest son of Robert and Margaret Graham Steen, was born November 15, 1882 Residence, near Streetsville, Ontario

II'—Janet Steen, the fourth child and second daughter of Ephraim and Jane Douglas Steen, was born in Toronto Township, County of Peel about four miles from Streetsville, Ontario, December 13, 1836 She was married, May 13, 1874, to Trueman Dixon Hall They never had any children Their post-office address is Orangeville, Ontario, Canada

V'—Jane Steen, the fifth child and third daughter of Ephraim and Jane Douglas Steen, was born in Toronto Township, County of Peel about four miles from Streetsville, Ontario, March 19, 1840. She was married February 17, 1859, to James Waldie, he having been born in January,

1832. and died —————— The family residence is in
Streetsville, Ontario, Canada To them were born eight
children, as follows

1 Isabella Jane Waldie, the eldest child of James and
Jane Steen Waldie, was born in Streetsville, Ontario,
December 9 1859

2 Janetta Waldie, the second daughter of James and Jane
Steen Waldie, was born in Streetsville. Ontario, June 16,
1862, and died ——————

3 Rebecca Ann Waldie the third daughter of James and
Jane Steen Waldie, was born in Streetsville, Ontario,
November 5, 1865

4 James Waldie, the fourth child and eldest son of James
and Jane Steen Waldie, was born March 29, 1867 and
died ——— —

5 Wilhelmina Waldie, the fifth child and fourth daughter
of James and Jane Steen Waldie was born September 4,
1868, and died ——————

6 John Robert Waldie the sixth child and second son of
James and Jane Steen Waldie, was born October 9,
1869 and died ——————

7 Ephraim Douglas Waidie the seventh child and third
son of James and Jane Steen Waldie, was born October
11, 1871 and died ——— —

8 Sarah Matilda Margaret Waldie, the eighth child and
fifth daughter of James and Jane Steen Waldie was
born January 6 1873, and died ——————

V I —Ephraim Steen, the sixth child and third son of Ephraim and Jane Douglas Steen was born in Toronto Township County of Peel, about four miles from Streetsville,
Ontario, March 15 1842 — a prosperous farmer He
was married, January 15, 1867 to Elizabeth Evans, she
having been born February 27 1843 Their post-office
address is Streetsville Ontario, Canada To them were
born seven children, as follows

1 Charlotte Jane Victoria Steen, the eldest child of
Ephraim and Elizabeth Evans Steen was born near
Streetsville, Ontario May 24, 1871, and died January 25,
1891

2 Waldie Hunter Douglas Steen, the second child and
   eldest son of Ephraim and Elizabeth Evans Steen was
   born near Streetsville Ontario, June 8, 1873 He was
   married, December 23, 1897, to Lavina Matthews she
   having been born November 25 1873 To them was
   born one child

   a Victoria Hattie Irene Steen was born September 29
      1898

3 Ethel May Susarnah Steen, the third child and second
   daughter of Ephraim and Elizabeth Evans Steen was
   born near Streetsville, Ontario May 1 1875

4 Evans Star Steen the fourth child and second son of
   Ephraim and Elizabeth Evans Steen, was born near
   Streetsville Ontario, September 5 1877 He was married July 1, 1898 to Frances Elizabeth Williams, she
   having been born June 23 1878

5 Ephraim Breckinridge Campbell Steen the fifth child
   and third son of Ephraim and Elizabeth Evans Steen
   was born near Streetsville, Ontario, October 16 1879

6 Mabel Ruth Steen the sixth child and third daughter
   of Ephraim and Elizabeth Evans Steen was born near
   Streetsville, Ontario, August 4 1881

7 Robert Joseph Herbert Steen the seventh child and
   youngest son of Ephraim and Elizabeth Evans Steen
   was born near Streetsville Ontario October 1 1883

VII —Nathaniel Steen the seventh child and fourth son of
   Ephraim and Jane Douglas Steen, was born in Toronto
   Township, County of Peel about four miles from Streetsville, Ontario November 25 1845 — a prosperous farmer.
   He was married May 23, 1871, to Sarah Ann Danby she
   having been born April 27, 1847 Their post-office
   address is Meadowvale, Ontario Canada To them were
   born five children, as follows

   1 James Danby Steen, the eldest child of Nathaniel and
      Sarah Ann Danby Steen was born near Meadowvale,
      Ontario, September 21 1873

   2 Ephraim Dufferin Steen the second son of Nathaniel
      and Sarah Ann Danby Steen was born near Meadow-
      vale Ontario July 6, 1876

3 Matilda Jane Steen the third child and only daughter
of Nathaniel and Sarah Ann Danby Steen was born
near Meadowvale, Ontario July 24, 1883

4 Ernest Stanley Steen, the fourth child and third son of
Nathaniel and Sarah Ann Danby Steen, was born near
Meadowvale, Ontario, August 20, 1887

5 Wilfred Nathaniel Steen, the fifth child and fourth son
of Nathaniel and Sarah Ann Danby Steen, was born
near Meadowvale Ontario, February 1, 1893

4 Nancy Steen, the fourth child and second daughter of William and Rebecca Weylie Steen, of Culmore, County Donegal, Ireland and a descendant of Moses Steen and his wife
(formerly a Miss Nelson) was born in Culmore, Ireland,
about the year 1805 In 1822 she removed with her parents
and the whole family to America, and located with them on
the Credit River, in Toronto Township in the County of
Peel, about four miles from the present village of Streetsville, Ontario, Canada   She was married in the same place
in 1826, to James Kennedy, he having been born in Schenec-
tady, New York and came to Canada from the State of Connecticut, U S A   They lived in Toronto Township York
County, Ontario   To James and Nancy Steen Kennedy
were born the following ten children

I —Nancy Kennedy was born March 8, 1828

II —Rebecca Kennedy was born March 30, 1829

III —James Kennedy was born October 17 1830

IV —Jane Kennedy was born April 27, 1832

V —John Kennedy was born December 15, 1834

VI —Simon Kennedy was born November 12 1836

VII —Samuel Kennedy was born August 25 1838

VIII —William Henry Kennedy was born July 30, 1840

IX —Isabella Kennedy was born April 28, 1842

X —Mary Ann Kennedy was born May 28 1843

5 Jane Steen the fifth child and third daughter of William
and Rebecca Weylie Steen, was born in Culmore, County
Donegal Ireland, about 1808, and removed with her father's
family to America in 1822 She was married at the home
of her parents, on the Credit River, about four miles from

Streetsville, Ontario, in 1829, to Jacob McCracken, he having been born near Londonderry, Ireland. They lived in Toronto Township, York County, Ontario. To Jacob and Jane Steen McCracken were born the following six children:

I—Rebecca McCracken was born November 5 1832.

II—Thomas McCracken was born November 6, 1834

III—William McCracken was born August 9, 1836

IV—Jacob McCracken was born February 25, 1840

V—James McCracken was born September 23, 1841

VI—Jane McCracken was born July 9 1843

6 Rebecca Steen, the sixth child and fourth daughter of William and Rebecca Weyhe Steen was born in Culmore, Ireland, about 1810, and was brought by her parents to their new home in Canada in 1822. She was married at the home of her parents on the Credit River, about four miles from Streetsville Ontario, in 1831, to Hugh Henan, he having been born in County Down, Ireland. They lived in Toronto Township, County of York, Ontario, Canada. To Hugh and Rebecca Steen Henan were born the following five children.

I—Jane Henan was born April 13, 1833

II—William Henan was born October 2, 1834

III—Robert Henan was born February 16 1835

II—Sarah Henan was born May 14, 1838

I—Hugh Henan was born September 27, 1840

7 Ann Steen, the seventh child and fifth daughter of William and Rebecca Weyhe Steen was born in Culmore, County Donegal, Ireland, about 1812, and was brought to America by her parents, in 1822. She was married in Toronto Township, County of Peel, about four miles from Streetsville, Ontario, in 1831 to Archibald McKinney, he having been born near Belfast Ireland. They resided in the County of York, Ontario, Canada. To them were born the following eight children

I—Hannah McKinney

II—Archibald McKinney

III—Rebecca McKinney

II—Sarah McKinney

V —James McKinney
VI —Jeremiah McKinney
VII —Daniel McKinney
VIII —Matilda McKinney

8 William Steen, the eighth child and third son of William
and Rebecca Weyhe Steen was born in Culmore, County
Donegal, Ireland, four miles from Londonderry, about
1814 and was brought to Canada by his parents in 1822
when he was a little boy   He grew up to manhood on his
father's farm, on the Credit River in Toronto Township
County of Peel, four miles from Streetsville, Ontario   He
removed in early life to the State of New York, and ever
afterwards made his home at Buffalo, New York   He was
married in Buffalo, New York, in 1835, to Mary Mills   To
them were born nine children, as follows

I —Nathaniel Steen, the eldest son of William and Mary
Mills Steen, was born in Buffalo, New York, October 28,
1837, and died at his home in Milwaukee Wisconsin,
December 21, 1895 in the 59th year of his age   He was
an intelligent and industrious man — a carpenter and
builder by occupation   He was married in Milwaukee
Wisconsin, July 25 1865, to Susan Sceets   To them were
born six children, as follows   The family residence is No
220 Hanover Street Milwaukee, Wisconsin

  1 Helen Nathalie Steen the eldest daughter of Nathaniel
     and Susan Sceets Steen, was born in St Joseph, Mis-
     souri, in 1867   Residence, Milwaukee, Wisconsin

  2 Susan Elizabeth Steen the second daughter of Nathan
     iel and Susan Sceets Steen, was born in St Joseph, Mis-
     souri, in 1870   Residence, Milwaukee, Wisconsin

  3 May Rebecca Steen, the third daughter of Nathaniel
     and Susan Sceets Steen, was born in St Joseph Mis-
     souri, in 1872   Residence Milwaukee Wisconsin

  4 William Irving Steen, the fourth child and eldest son of
     Nathaniel and Susan Steen, was born in St
     Joseph, Missouri, in 1874, and grew up in his father's
     family   About 1896 he removed to the West, seeking
     a milder climate than that of Wisconsin

  5 Ada Marguerite Steen, the fifth child and fourth daugh-

ter of Nathaniel and Susan Sceets Steen, was born in St
Joseph, Missouri, in 1876. Residence, Milwaukee Wisconsin

o Everett Hale Steen the sixth child and youngest son of
Nathaniel and Susan Sceets Steen, was born in St.
Joseph Missouri, March 21 1883, and died in Milwau-
kee, Wisconsin March 19, 1892, aged 9 years

II—Robert Steen the second son of William and Mary
Mills Steen, was born in Buffalo New York, about 1839
He removed to the West, and some years ago was Sheriff
of Mojave County, Arizona

III—Nancy Steen, the third child and eldest daughter of
William and Mary Mills Steen was born in Buffalo, New
York, about 1841

IV—William Steen, the fourth child and third son of William and Mary Mills Steen, was born in Buffalo, New
York, about 1843

V Ephraim Steen, the fifth child and fourth son of William
and Mary Mills Steen was born in Buffalo New York,
about 1845

VI—John Steen the sixth child and fifth son of William
and Mary Mills Steen, was born in Buffalo, New York,
about 1848

VII—Moses Steen, the seventh child and sixth son of William and Mary Mills Steen, was born in Buffalo, New
York about 1851 He was married and removed to
Mineral Park Arizona where himself, wife and child
— the whole family — were killed in the autumn or winter
of 1883 They were crushed to death, or smothered by
the caving in of his home, caused by a snowslide coming
down against it from the mountain

VIII—Sarah Steen the eighth child and second daughter of
William and Mary Mills Steen, was born in Buffalo New
York about 1853

IX—Thomas Steen the ninth and youngest child of William
and Mary Mills Steen, was born in Buffalo, New York,
about 1855

9 Isabella Steen, the ninth child and sixth daughter of William and Rebecca Weyhe Steen was born in Culmore

County Donegal, Ireland, in 1813, and brought to Canada by her parents in 1822, when she was just a little girl She was married at the old Steen homestead, on the Credit River, four miles from Streetsville, Ontario, in 1834 to John Leslie, he having been born in the Highlands of Scotland   They resided on a farm, near Streetsville, Ontario, and brought up a family of children   Mr Leslie died a number of years ago, and Isabella Steen Leslie died at her home, January 13, 1897, aged about 84 years   Her funeral, in the Presbyterian Church was largely attended from all parts of the county, and deep regret was felt that her death closed the doors of one of the oldest homes in Peel, which for more than half a century was gladly opened to all who cared to enter, but especially to friends   That home of which she was ever the presiding genius was one of well-known hospitality through out the sixty-two years of her life therein, for she left the same house as a corpse into which she entered as a bride, three score and two years before   Her most estimable sister, Mrs Sarah Irwin, of Toronto is now the only survivor of that large early pioneer family   The body of Mrs Leslie was lovingly laid away to rest in the Streetsville cemetery   To John and Isabella Steen Leslie were born the following nine children all born near Streetsville, Ontario

I —William Leslie was born May 27 1836

II —Esther E Leslie was born December 23, 1837

III —Rebecca Leslie was born March 11, 1840

IV —John Leslie was born December 9, 1841

V —James Leslie was born August 10 1843

VI —George Leslie was born January 8, 1846

VII —Nathaniel Leslie was born March 16, 1848

VIII —Robert U Leslie was born February 22, 1850

IX —Mary Jane Leslie was born January 21, 1852

10 Matilda Steen the tenth child and seventh daughter of William and Rebecca Weyhe Steen, was born in Culmore, County Donegal, Ireland, in 1816, and was brought to Canada by her parents when she was a little child   She grew up to womanhood on the old Steen homestead, on the Credit River, about four miles from Streetsville, Ontario   Here she was married, in 1836 to Francis Motheral, from the

SARAH STEEN IRWIN.

State of Pennsylvania, he having been born November 16, 1805 They located in Streetsville, Ontario To Francis and Matilda Steer Motheral were born the following nine children

I —Rebecca Motheral was born July 19 1837

I —John Motheral was born October 26 1838

III —William Motheral was born January 13, 1840

IV —Margaret Motheral was born October 14, 1841

V —Ephraim Motheral was born September 5, 1843

VI —James Motheral was born August 27, 1846

VII —David Motheral was born ————

VIII —Francis Motheral was born ————

IX —George Motheral was born ————

11 Sarah Steen, the eleventh child and eighth daughter of William and Rebecca Weyhe Steen, was born in Culmore, County Donegal, Ireland in 1819, and was brought by her parents, with the whole family, to Canada, in 1822, when she was very young She was brought up on her father's farm, on the Credit River in Toronto Township, County of Peel, about four miles from Streetsville Ontario Here she was married, in 1839, to John Irwin he having been born near Sligo, Ireland, in 1807, and died in 1871, aged 64 years Mrs Sarah Steen Irwin now (1900) resides with her eldest daughter and family Residence, No 227 Huron Street, Toronto, Canada To John and Sarah Steen Irwin were born ten children as follows all born in Toronto Township, County of Peel Ontario, Canada

I —Margaret Irwin the eldest child of John and Sarah Steen Irwin was born August 12, 1840 She was married, May 21 1861 to the Rev Anson Green Forster, a Presbyterian clergyman, who died in 1871 Family residence, Toronto, Canada. To Anson Green and Margaret Irwin Forster were born the following four children.

1 George Spurgeon Forster was born May 2, 1862

2 Albert Irwin Forster was born March 12, 1864

3 John Cowper Forster was born July 15, 1866

4 Anson Harvey Forster was born October 23, 1868 He was married near Streetsville Ontario June 28 1899 to

Elizabeth Mary Amanda Steen, a daughter of Nathaniel and Margery J Steen, she having been born near Streetsville, Ontario, September 15, 1871   Residence, Toronto, Ontario Canada

II —George Irwin, the second child and eldest son of John and Sarah Steen Irwin, was born March 1, 1842, and died in 1844

III —Rebecca Irwin, the third child and second daughter of John and Sarah Steen Irwin, was born July 27, 1844   She was married, September 21, 1866, to John James Price, of Peel County Ontario, where they still reside   To John James and Rebecca Irwin Price were born the following seven children

  1 William John Henry Price was born July 1, 1867

  2 Rebecca Adaline Price was born November 9, 1869

  3 Frances Margaret Anne Price was born December 27, 1870

  4 Sarah Lottie Florence Price was born June 9, 1872

  5 Ella Jane Price was born February 1, 1876

  6 James Alfred Price was born August 19, 1879

  7 Elizabeth Alice Price was born July 1, 1881

IV —William F Irwin, the fourth child and second son of John and Sarah Steen Irwin, was born June 7, 1846   He was married November 17, 1875, to Eva Johnston of Peel County, Ontario   Residence, Brandon, Manitoba, Canada   To William F and Eva Johnston Irwin were born the following six children.

  1 Marsden Frank Irwin was born September 24 1876

  2 Sadie Maud Margaret Irwin was born March 31, 1878

  3 Wilhelmina Evangeline Irwin was born March 28, 1879

  4 Frederick John Irwin was born February 28 1881

  5 Alice Lavina Irwin was born January 28 1883

  6 William McBride Irwin was born November 10, 1885.

V —Sarah Jane Irwin, the fifth child and third daughter of John and Sarah Steen Irwin, was born December 8, 1848   She was married June 27 1871, to John Woods, of Peel County, Ontario, where they still reside   To John and

Sarah Jane Irwin Woods were born the following nine children

1 Laura Irwin Woods was born November 27 1872

2 Marion Gregg Woods was born December 1, 1874

3 Irwin John Crombie Woods was born September 25, 1876

4 Edward Blacke Woods was born July 22, 1878

5 James Garfield Woods was born April 4, 1880

6 George Brown Woods was born November 17, 1882

7 Wilfred Gordon Woods was born March 27. 1885

8 Sarah Victoria Woods was born July 10, 1887

9 Margaret Elizabeth Stephenia Woods was born January 23, 1890

11—Matilda Irwin, the sixth child and fourth daughter of John and Sarah Steen Irwin, was born October 25, 1850 She was married, March 27, 1872, to Asa Hall, of Churchville, Peel County, Ontario They afterwards removed to the United States, locating first in Illinois, and finally settling on a fruit farm near Azuza, California A delightful silver wedding anniversary at their home was held March 27, 1897, in honor of the twenty-five years of their happy married life Among the interesting things on that occasion, Mrs J J Morgan read "She Liked Him Rale Weel," and Mr E O Gale, of Chicago, read the following original poem

TO MR AND MRS ASA HALL ON THEIR SILVER WEDDING

How these occasions conjure up those days we all remember,
When Love's bright June ruled all the year, with roses hid
   December,
When we first wooed these wives of ours and felt so much
   elated
In looking forward to the time when to them we'd be mated
How bright to us appeared those days, no matter what the
   weather.
Yet brighter far the evenings were in bringing us together,
And oft in thought we walk those lanes with arms entwined
   serenely,
And gaze again on that dear girl who walked with us so
   queenly.
Those blissful hours do we recall, so filled with holy pleasure,
We would not blot their memory out for any earthly treasure

If love can give to hearts in youth so much of pure enjoyment,
Can it be wise for married folks to find it no employment?
If we conceived ecstatic bliss when we our troth had plighted,
Should we not happier be to-day for all these years united?
Our lives are shaped by little things, by chafings or caressings,
Who keeps in age the love of youth, holds fast the highest blessings
And when at length the hour came so happy, yet momentous,
We took her hand whose heart we claimed the Lord had kindly sent us,
We felt a knightly chivalry, to us e'en now appealing,
As we to cherish, love, protect, with sacred vows were sealing

We needed not those vows to bind, though friends had given weeping,
We felt the bride, through God, would find true bliss when in our keeping
As we those idols of their homes with us away were taking,
We saw we filled those homes with sighs, left hearts there almost breaking,
Yet we had such abiding faith in the roseate hues before us,
We knew our love eclipsing theirs, for her who did adore us
Tis true we could not sound that love, but sure it was abiding,
And in our souls we pledged for life its strength to her confiding

And knowing that our friends as guest have always welcomed Cupid,—
And who does not, as years roll by, grow more supremely stupid?—
We with our hearts congratulate to find them still pursuing
Those little courtesies of life we all paid in our wooing;
But apt in time to quite ignore, and much thereby is missing,
For who would think of praising wives or startle them by kissing!
Yet being boarder now and then, should I catch "Ase and Tilly"
Forgetting they had married been, were still remaining silly
Do you suppose I'd neighbors tell, as fun at Hall in making?
Not much, lest it like measles prove, which are so awful taking.
Keep on, my friends, in future years, as in these five-and-twenty,
And may the Father, who is Love, crown you with love and plenty

To Asa and Matilda Irwin Hall were born the following three children

1 Sarah Gertrude Hall was born at Woodstock, Ontario, October 11, 1875 and died at River Forest, Illinois, June 13, 1883, in the 8th year of her age

2 Irwin Russell Hall was born at Woodstock, Ontario, August 17, 1878 — insurance clerk for W A Alexander & Co, "The Rookery," Chicago, Illinois

3 Almon Asa Hall was born at Woodstock, Ontario,

February 17, 1881. Troop L, Fourth United States Calvary, at Manila, Philippine Islands Residence, Azuza, California

VII —Mary Alice Irwin, the seventh child and fifth daughter of John and Sarah Steen Irwin, was born December 6, 1852 M Alice Irwin was married November 3, 1875, to George W. Johnston, of Peel County, Ontario Residence, Toronto, Canada To George W and M Alice Irwin Johnston were born the following three children

1 Irwin McKenzie Johnston was born February 19, 1879

2 Alice Gerelda Johnston was born December 11, 1882

3 Sarah Rebecca Edna Johnston was born December 28, 1886

VIII —John Irwin, the eighth child and third son of John and Sarah Steen Irwin, was born May 23, 1854 He was married December 27, 1883, to Matilda McClelland, of Peel County, Ontario, where they still reside To John and Matilda McClelland Irwin were born the following four children

1 John George Murray Irwin was born November 5, 1884

2 Robert James Glassford Irwin was born February 27, 1888

3 Oswald Yale Irwin was born October 3 1892

4 Arthur Beaty Irwin was born October 3 1892 The last-named were twins

IX —George Irwin, the ninth child and fourth son of John and Sarah Steen Irwin, was born August 4, 1856 He was married, May 16, 1888, to Mary Olive Adamson, of Peel County, Ontario, where they still reside To George and Mary Olive Adamson Irwin were born the following two children

1 Olive Stilwell Irwin was born September 26, 1895

2. George Arthur Adamson Irwin was born December 21 1898

X —Robert Ure Irwin, the tenth child and the fifth and youngest son of John and Sarah Steen Irwin, was born August 30, 1859 He was married, November 20 1882, to

Jane Ritchey, of Peel County, Ontario York County,
Ontario, was subdivided about 1845 to form York and
Peel Counties Robert Irwin and family reside at
Orangeville, Ontario, Canada To Robert Ure and Jen-
nie Ritchey Irwin were born the following five children

1 Edith Gertrude Irwin was born September 21, 1883

2 Samuel John Ure Irwin was born November 10, 1886

3. Wilfred Leslie Irwin was born June 26, 1892

4. Gladys Maxwell Irwin was born June 21, 1897

5. Robert Goldie Irwin was born November 21, 1898

BOOK NINE.

DESCENDANTS OF JOHN STEEN, OF BALLENEY

John Steen was born in Ireland in 1759, and died in May, 1852, aged 93 years His grandfather was one of the persecuted Scotch that came into Ireland He was married in 1778 to Nancy Schoals who was also born in 1759, and died December 17, 1847 aged 88 years They brought up a family of six children all born on the townland of Balleney, near Coleraine, Ireland

John Steen, of Balleney, County Londonderry, was the grandson of one of the persecuted Scotchmen who came over into Ireland with three brothers at the same time He was born in 1759, and died in May, 1852, aged 93 years, and his body was laid away to rest in Downhill cemetery, near Castlerock He was married, in 1778, to Nancy Schoals, she having been born in 1759, and died December 17, 1847, aged 88 years Her body rests by the side of her husband John Steen came to Balleney from Largentea, about four miles southeast of Limavady about the year 1784, and bought the townland of Balleney nearly two hundred acres, upon which he continued to reside during the remainder of his life. He was a prosperous farmer He lived to see the fifth generation from himself coming through his eldest son James, his grandson John, and his great-grandson James,

(389)

whose little daughter he lived to see and dandle upon his knee
To John Steen, of Balleney, and his wife, Nancy Schoals Steen,
the following six children were born   James, Thomas, Conolly,
Philip, John, and Isaiah Steen

CHAPTER I.

James Steen, the eldest son of John and Nancy Schoals
Steen, was born on the townland of Balleney, near Coleraine,
Ireland, in 1779 or 1780   He was married, about 1806, to Mary
Kerr, by whom he had two children   He was married a second
time to a Miss Clark, by whom he brought up a family of chil-
dren   He was also married a third time to a lady whose name is
not known to the writer of this record, by whom he brought up a
family.   The old family home of the Steens of the townland of
Balleney is situated near the sea, in the northern portion of the
County of Londonderry, nearly between Castlerock and Port
Stewart   To James Steen and his first wife, Mary Kerr Steen,
were born the following children

I —Nancy Steen, a daughter of James and Mary Kerr Steen, was
   born in Balleney, Ireland, in 1807

II —John Steen, a son of James and Mary Keir Steen (a twin
   brother of the preceding), was born in Balleney, Ireland in
   1807, and died in May, 1833, aged 26 years   He was married
   about 1828, to Mary Ann Smith, by whom he had three children, as follows

   1 James Steen, the eldest child and only son of John and Mary
      Ann Steen, was born about 1830   He was married, about
      1850, to Jane Baxter, of Coleraine, by whom he had at least
      one daughter, whom its great-great-grandfather lived to see
      and dandle upon his knee
      I — ——— Steen, a daughter of James and Jane Baxter
         Steen, removed with their family to America, where this
         James Steen died, leaving descendants in this country
   2 Mary Ann Steen, the second child and eldest daughter of
      John and Mary Ann Steen, and a sister of the James Steen

who married Jane Baxter, was born about 1832 She removed to America with her brother and his family

3 Isabella Steen, the third child and second daughter of John and Mary Ann Steen, was born about 1833 She removed to America with her brother James and his family, and her sister

James Steen, the eldest son of John and Nancy Schoals Steen, of Balleney, brought up a family by his second wife, a Miss Clark, of which the writer has no record By his third wife also he brought up a family of children, whose record the writer could not ascertain Two of his grandchildren by his third wife were living a few years ago in Poway Valley, San Diego County, California Miss Matilda Moore, then living with her brother, Alexander Moore, could probably give full information in regard to his family by his third marriage This James Steen came to America with his family very early in the nineteenth century, and has left a very numerous posterity

CHAPTER II

Thomas Steen the second son of John and Nancy Schoals Steen, was born on the old homestead, in the townland of Balleney, County Londonderry, Ireland, in 1782 or 1783 He was married probably about 1808 to "Ginney Boreland," by whom he had three children, as follows

I.—Nancy Ann Steen the eldest daughter of Thomas and Ginney Boreland Steen, was born in Ireland about 1810 She removed with her brother and sister to the United States of America

II —Samuel Steen, the second child and only son of Thomas and Ginney Boreland Steen, was born in Ireland about 1812. He removed to the United States of America and located in Cincinnati, Ohio, where he died, unmarried

III —Martha Steen, the third and youngest child of Thomas and Ginney Boreland Steen, was born in Ireland about 1814 She removed to the United States of America with her brother and sister

CHAPTER III

Conolly Steen, the third son of John and Nancy Schoals Steen was born at the old home of his father, in the townland of Balleney, County Londonderry, Ireland in 1790, and died May 30, 1867 aged 77 years He was buried near the grave of his father in Downhill cemetery, near Castlerock He was a successful farmer He was married, in 1832, to Rachel Caskey, she having been born in 1809, and died October 29, 1893, aged 84 years To them were born eight children, as follows

I --Nancy Steen, called Nannie, the eldest child of Conolly and Rachel Caskey Steen, was born in the townland of Balleney, County Londonderry, Ireland, October 30, 1833 She often heard her grandfather say that his grandfather was one of the persecuted Scotch that came over into Ireland for religious freedom, and that he was one of three brothers who came over at the same time Nancy Steen is unmarried Residence, Strabane, County Tyrone, Ireland

II —John Steen the second child and eldest son of Conolly and Rachel Caskey Steen, was born in Balleney, March 24, 1835 He was married, July 9, 1873, to Margaret Pollock They have no children Residence, Mt Sandel, Coleraine, County Londonderry, Ireland

III —Robert Steen, the third child and second son of Conolly and Rachel Caskey Steen was born in Balleney December 29, 1836 — a practical farmer Residence, Lake View House, Drum, County Monaghan, Ireland

IV —James Steen, the fourth child and third son of Conolly and Rachel Caskey Steen, was born in Balleney, May 27 1839 He was ordained a Presbyterian clergyman in the Presbyterian

Church of Drum, County Monaghan, Ireland, May 29, 1866
He was installed pastor of Castleban County Mayo, May 11,
1880, and installed pastor of the Presbyterian Church in Wexford, Ireland, May 29, 1888, where he still continues He was
married, July 14, 1875, to Margaret Whyte Robertson, eldest
daughter of William Robertson a manufacturer of Dunfern-
line, Scotland Residence, Bay View Manse Wexford Ireland To them were born three children, as follows

1 William Robertson Steen, the eldest son of Rev James and
Maggie W Steen, was born in Drum, County Monaghan,
Ireland, April 22 1877 Residence, Wexford, Ireland

2 May Robertson Steen, the second child and only daughter of
Rev James and Maggie W Steen, was born in Drum
County Monaghan Ireland, July 6, 1878, and died September
26, 1886, in the 9th year of her age

3 James Conolly Steen the third child and second son of Rev
James and Maggie W Steen, was born in Castleban, County
Mayo, Ireland, March 18, 1882 Residence, Wexford Ire-
land

V—Eliza Jane Steen the fifth child and second daughter of
Conolly and Rachel Caskey Steen, was born in Balleney, Sep-
tember 22, 1841 She was married November 7, 1872, to
William Glenn—a farmer Residence Drumslade, County
Londonderry, Ireland To them were born five children as
follows

1 Mary Eliza Glenn, the eldest child of William and Eliza
Jane Steen Glenn, was born March 22, 1875

2 Rachel Glenn the second daughter of William and Eliza
Jane Steen Glenn, was born December 6 1876

3 William Hugh Glenn, the third child and only son of William and Eliza Jane Steen Glenn, was born January 28, 1880

4 Margaret Glenn, called " Maggie " the fourth child and third
daughter of William and Eliza Jane Steen Glenn, was born
March 15 1881

5 Annie Ida Glenn the fifth and youngest child of William
and Eliza Jane Steen Glenn, was born December 15 1886
Residence, Drumslade, County Londonderry, Ireland

VI —Margaret Steen, called Maggie, the sixth child and third daughter of Conolly and Rachel Caskey Steen, was born in Balleney, February 22, 1844   She was married, June 14, 1864, to John McMillan, a merchant of Londonderry, he having been born February 22, 1842, and died August 17, 1875, in the 34th year of his age   To them were born six children, as follows:

1   Elizabeth McMillan, the eldest child of John and Margaret Steen McMillan, was born in Londonderry, Ireland, April 10, 1865

2   Annie McMillan, the second daughter of John and Margaret Steen McMillan, was born in Londonderry, Ireland, October 6, 1867   She was married, July 23, 1889, to Rev C C M Dickey, B A , of Draperstown, County Derry, Ireland   To them were born the following

I —Robert Steen Dickey was born June 19, 1890

II —Alfred Charles Dickey was born September 25, 1893.

III —Norah Dickey was born December 24, 1894

3   John Steen McMillan, the third child and eldest son of John and Margaret Steen McMillan, was born in Londonderry, Ireland, October 21, 1868

4   Margaret McMillan, called ' Maggie ' the fourth child and third daughter of John and Margaret Steen McMillan, was born in Londonderry, Ireland, May 1, 1870

5   Robert McMillan, the fifth child and second son of John and Margaret Steen McMillan, was born in Londonderry, Ireland December 3, 1871, and died February 16, 1882, in the 11th year of his age.

6   James Steen McMillan the sixth and youngest child of John and Margaret Steen McMillan, was born in Londonderry, Ireland, July 22, 1873

VII —Rachel Steen, the seventh child and fourth daughter of Conolly and Rachel Caskey Steen, was born in Balleney, December 2, 1847   She was married, April 9 1878, to James R Gallagher, a merchant of Coleraine   Residence Coleraine, Ireland   To them were born four children, as follows:

1   Joseph Gallagher, the eldest child of James R and Rachel Steen Gallagher, was born in Coleraine, Ireland January 16, 1879, and died March 14, 1893, in the 15th year of his age

2 James Gallagher, the second son of James R and Rachel Steen Gallagher, was born in Coleraine, Ireland, March 6, 1880

3 Robert Gallagher, the third son of James R and Rachel Steen Gallagher, was born in Coleraine, Ireland, September 11, 1881

4 Kathleen Gallagher, the fourth child and only daughter of James R and Rachel Steen Gallagher, was born in Coleraine, Ireland, June 2, 1883

VIII —Mary Steen, the eighth and youngest child, the fifth daughter of Conolly and Rachel Caskey Steen, was born in Balleney, County Londonderry, Ireland, June 1 1852 She is unmarried. Residence, Lake View, County Monaghan, Ireland

CHAPTER IV

Philip Steen, the fourth son of John and Nancy Schoals Steen, was born at Balleney, in 1791, and died October 27, 1858, aged 67 years — a successful and prosperous farmer He was married in 1823 to Mary Wray, she having been born in 1801, and died November 17, 1890, aged 89 years. To them were born seven children, as follows

I —Mary Jane Steen, the eldest child, a daughter of Philip and Mary Wray Steen, was born at Balleney, October 28, 1824 She was married, in 1843, to John Dunne, of Dartries Cottage, Articlave, Castlerock, Ireland, and who died about 1870 To them were born five children, as follows

1 Jane Dunne, the eldest child, a daughter of John and Mary Jane Steen Dunne, was born at Dartries Cottage, about 1844

2 Mary Ann Dunne, the second daughter of John and Mary Jane Steen Dunne, was born at Dartries Cottage about 1846 She was married to Thomas MacAfee, who was a permanent Land Commissioner

3 Thomas Steen Dunne the third child and eldest son of John and Mary Jane Steen Dunne, was born at Dartries Cottage, Articlave, about 1848 He was also an Irish Land Commissioner, well known in the northern counties, and a Liberal Unionist His friendship was true and steadfast and those who knew him best, loved him most He was warmly attached to the Presbyterian Church, and rarely absent from its services when able to attend He died at his residence, Dartries Cottage, Articlave, Saturday, February 16 1896, aged about 48 years

4 William Dunne, the fourth child and second son of John and Mary Jane Steen Dunne, was born at Dartries Cottage Articlave, about 1850 When a young man he emigrated to the United States of America, and died ————

5 Isabella Steen Dunne, the fifth and youngest child of John and Mary Jane Steen Dunne, was born at Articlave, near Castlerock, Ireland, about 1853 or 1854

II —John Steen, the second child and eldest son of Philip and Mary Wray Steen, was born in the old home of his grandfather, John Steen, of Balleney, September 16 1827 He formerly lived at Doey, Port Stewart, on the Sea, but now resides at Dunboe House Articlave, near Castlerock County Londonderry, Ireland, in a fine old Episcopal residence which he purchased at the time of the disestablishment of that Church in Ireland He holds a commission as Justice of the Peace for County Londonderry, Ireland He visited the United States of America in 1893 attending the World's Exposition in Chicago He was ordained an elder in the Presbyterian Church at Port Stewart, September 20, 1853, and installed elder in the First Dunboe Presbyterian Church in May, 1896, and wields a wide religious influence He was married, December 20, 1853, to Nancy Kerr To them were born two children, as follows

1 Marion Steen, the eldest child, a daughter of John and Nancy Kerr Steen, was born at Doey, Port Stewart October 12, 1854 She was married at the same place on her 28th birthday, October 12, 1882, to William Hutton, of Donaghadee, Ireland, where she resided nearly fifteen years She died at Ballygraney House, Donaghadee, County Down Ireland, July 21, 1897, in the 43d year of her age, and her

JOHN STEEN, J. P.

body was lovingly laid away to rest in the Dunboe cemetery, July 23, 1897 To them one child was born, as follows

I—John Steen Hutton, a son of William and Marion Steen Hutton, was born in Donaghadee, County Down, Ireland, August 28, 1883

2 John Kerr Steen, the second child and only son of John and Nancy Kerr Steen, was born at Doey, Port Stewart, January 18, 1858, and died while a student in medicine in Edinburgh University, January 27, 1877, aged 19 years His body was tenderly laid away to rest in the Dunboe cemetery He was a young man of bright promise and noble character, was a brilliant student, progressing rapidly, when his life work was ended He had taken the "Joseph Black Medal" in practical chemistry, and also a certificate in surgery and physiology in the University of Glasgow

III—James Steen the third child and second son of Philip and Mary Wray Steen, was born at Balleney, February 12 1829 — a prosperous farmer He was married, May 30, 1867, to Mary Dunne Residence, Inchna, Ballymoney, County Antrim, Ireland To them were born nine children, as follows

1 Mary Wray Steen, the eldest child, a daughter of James and Mary Dunne Steen, was born at Inchna, September 27 1868

2 William Steen, the second child and eldest son of James and Mary Dunne Steen, was born June 12, 1870

3 Annie Steen, the third child and second daughter of James and Mary Dunne Steen, was born November 9, 1871

4 Jane Steen, the fourth child and third daughter of James and Mary Dunne Steen, was born May 16, 1873

5 Isabella Steen, the fifth child and fourth daughter of James and Mary Dunne Steen, was born August 8, 1875

6 Elizabeth Steen, the sixth child and fifth daughter of James and Mary Dunne Steen was born August 25, 1877, and died May 14 1880

7 James Philip Steen, the seventh child and second son of James and Mary Dunne Steen, was born January 31, 1879, and died April 26 1880

8 Sarah Margaret Steen the eighth child and sixth daughter of James and Mary Dunne Steen, was born August 30, 1881

9 Agnes Hamil Steen, the ninth child and seventh daughter of James and Mary Dunne Steen, was born November 21, 1882

I\ —Thomas Steen, the fourth child and third son of Philip and Mary Wray Steen, was born at the old homestead, in Balleney January 13, 1831 He was drowned while bathing in the River Bann, August 9, 1851 in the 21st year of his age

V —Robert Steen, the fifth child and fourth son of Philip and Mary Wray Steen, was born in the old homestead, at Balleney, January 10, 1833, where he still resides — a successful farmer He was married, July 9, 1868, to Sarah Lynd, a sister of the Rev Dr Lynd, of May Street Presbyterian Church Belfast, Ireland   Residence Balleney House, near Coleraine, Ireland, P L G. To them were born seven children, as follows

1 John Wilson Steen, the eldest child, a son of Robert and Sarah Lynd Steen, was born at Balleney July 2, 1869

2 Mary Steen, the second child and eldest daughter of Robert and Sarah Lynd Steen, was born at Balleney, December 25, 1870

3 Anna Belle Steen, the third child and second daughter of Robert and Sarah Lynd Steen, was born at Balleney, August 27, 1872

4 Robert Steen, the fourth child and second son of Robert and Sarah Lynd Steen, was born at Balleney, November 23, 1875 Studied medicine in Belfast, Ireland

5 Hugh Barkhe Steen, a twin brother of the preceding, was born at Balleney, November 23, 1875. Studied medicine in Belfast, Ireland

6 Thomas Steen, the sixth child and fourth son of Robert and Sarah Lynd Steen, was born at Balleney July 2, 1878

7 Alexander Steen, the seventh child and fifth son of Robert and Sarah Lynd Steen, was born at Balleney, August 5, 1882

VI —Isabella Steen, the sixth child and second daughter of
+ Philip and Mary Wray Steen was born at the homestead, at Balleney, April 15, 1838 She was married, February 26 1863, to George Hanson, of Bally Lintagh, who died October 25, 1867 To them one child was born, as follows

1 Janet Rankin Hanson was born June 3, 1866.

Isabella Steen Hanson was married a second time, October 25, 1870, to Dr Alexander Kennedy, who died October 25, 1885 To them were born the following children

2 Mary Caroline Kennedy was born June 12, 1873

3 Alexander Frederick Kennedy was born August 25 1875 Family residence, Kana Vista Adelaide Park, Belfast, Ireland

VII —Cochran Steen, the seventh child and fifth son of Philip and Mary Wray Steen, was born at Balleney, May 23, 1840 He was married to Lucy Hunter, of Londonderry To them were born three children He is a stock broker, with residence on Royal Avenue Belfast Ireland

1 William Hunter Steen, the eldest son of Cochran and Lucy Hunter Steen was born October 19, 1874.

2 James Hunter Steen, the second son of Cochran and Lucy Hunter Steen, was born July 8, 1876

3 Cochran John Campbell Steen, the third son of Cochran and Lucy Hunter Steen, was born May 11, 1878

CHAPTER V

John Steen, the fifth son of John and Nancy Schoals Steen of Balleney, was born at the old homestead, in the townland of Balleney, in County Londonderry, Ireland, about 1793 or 1794 He was a prosperous farmer of Malin Head, in the Parish of Dunboe near Coleraine Ireland He lived to be an old man of about 80 years of age, and died about 1873 or 1874 He was married first, probably about 1818, to Ann Kerr, by whom he had three children He was married a second time in 1825, to Nancy Robinson, by whom he had two children He brought up his family in the Presbyterian Church in Ireland, of which they all became full members He was the father of the following five children

I—James Steen the eldest son of John and Ann Kerr Steen, of Malin Head, Parish of Dunboe, was born at Malin Head in 1819, and died, February 9, 1875, aged 56 years. He was a farmer living at Castlebotheny, Parish of Killowen, Coleraine, Ireland. He was married, about 1842, to Mary Finley, she having been born in 1822, and died March 5, 1896, aged 72 years. To them were born ten children, as follows

1 John Steen, the eldest child, a son of James and Mary Finley Steen, was born in Castlebotheney, Parish of Killowen, Coleraine, March 20, 1843. He was educated at Crannagh Hill National School, Coleraine Academy, and Queen's College, Belfast. He entered college in 1860, and was graduated in 1863, receiving the degree of B A. In the autumn of the same year he entered the Presbyterian Assembly's Theological College, where he pursued his theological studies. He was ordained a Presbyterian clergyman, May 26, 1868, by the Presbytery of Monaghan, and placed over the Presbyterian congregation of Smithborough, County Monaghan, Ireland. On October 27, 1880, he was installed pastor of Glenelly Presbyterian Church by the Presbytery of Strabane, where he still remains, a faithful and devoted minister of the Gospel. The Rev John Steen was married in Cormeallagh August 14, 1889, to Eliza Huey Derwock. To them three children have been born, as follows

 I—James Steen, the eldest child, a son of the Rev John and Eliza H. Steen, was born May 16, 1890

 II—Mary Steen, the second child, a daughter of the Rev John and Eliza H Steen, was born February 9, 1892

 III—John Steen, the third child and second son of the Rev John and Eliza H Steen, was born June 17, 1894. Residence, Plumbridge, County Tyrone, Ireland

2 Ann Steen, the second child and eldest daughter of James and Mary Finley Steen, was born at Malin Head, Parish of Killowen, Coleraine, about 1845

3 Robert Steen, the third child and second son of James and Mary Finley Steen, was born at Malin Head, Parish of Killowen, Coleraine, about 1847

4 Thomas Steen, the fourth child and third son of James and Mary Finley Steen, was born about 1849

5 James Steen the fifth child and fourth son of James and Mary Finley Steen, was born about 1851

6 Eliza Steen, the sixth child and second daughter of James and Mary Finley Steen, was born about 1853

7 Mary Steen, the seventh child and third daughter of James and Mary Finley Steen was born about 1855

8 Matthew Steen, the eighth child and fifth son of James and Mary Finley Steen, was born about 1857

9 Nancy Steen, the ninth child and fourth daughter of James and Mary Finley Steen was born about 1859

10 Jane Steen, the youngest child and daughter of James and Mary Finley Steen, was born at Castlebotheny, Parish of Killowen, Coleraine, about 1861

II —Thomas Steen, the second son of John and Ann Kerr Steen, was born at Malin Head, in the Parish of Dunboe, near Coleraine Ireland, in 1823, and died in New Orleans, Louisiana, September 25, 1856, aged about 33 years He was brought up in the Presbyterian Church in Ireland and removed to America in 1843 when only about 20 years of age, and located permanently in New Orleans, Louisiana. He was married in New Orleans Louisiana by the Rev. Charles W Whitall, April 29 1852, to Mary Trelford, a daughter of William and Sarah Wilson Trelford (who had emigrated from Belfast, Ireland, first to Mexico and then to New Orleans, in 1836,) she having been born in Castle Dawson, Ireland February 14 1826, and died in New Orleans Louisiana, September 26, 1879, in the 54th year of her age, having survived her husband twenty-three years To them were born two children, as follows

1 Thomas Jackson Steen, the eldest son of Thomas and Mary Trelford Steen, was born in New Orleans, Louisiana, January 8, 1854 He is by occupation a 'contracting slater' He was married in New Orleans, Louisiana February 4 1880, to Emma Jane Medd a daughter of James Medd of Indiana, and Jane Brady Medd formerly from Ireland she having been born in New Orleans, Louisiana, March 1, 1858 Residence 109 Gasquet Street, New Orleans Louisiana To them were born the following five children, all born in New Orleans, Louisiana

I —Mary Steen, the eldest child, a daughter of Thomas J and Emma J Medd Steen, was born December 19, 1880

II —Veronica Steen, the second daughter of Thomas J and Emma J Medd Steen, was born November 12, 1882

III —Thomas Steen, the third child and eldest son of Thomas J and Emma J Medd Steen, was born July 6, 1884

IV —Ethel Steen, the fourth child and third daughter of Thomas J and Emma J Medd Steen, was born March 4, 1889

V —Alexander Trelford Steen, the fifth and youngest child of Thomas J and Emma J Medd Steen, was born March 30, 1891

2 Clark Steen, the second and youngest child of Thomas and Mary Trelford Steen, was born in New Orleans, Louisiana, October 7, 1855, where he was educated, grew to manhood and permanently settled in business He was for many years bookkeeper in the City Treasury Office in New Orleans, and is prominent in business matters He was married by the Rev Father Thomas O Neil, a Roman Catholic priest, in New Orleans, Louisiana, January 24 1882, to Mary Leah Brune, a daughter of Henry Brune, of France, and Theressa Tilliere Brune, of Belgium, she having been born in New Orleans, Louisiana, January 24, 1861 Residence, New Orleans, Louisiana To them were born seven children as follows, all born in New Orleans, Louisiana

I —Mary Leah Steen, the eldest daughter of Clark and Mary Leah Brune Steen, was born November 9 1882

II —Theressa Tilliere Steen, the second daughter of Clark and Mary Leah Brune Steen, was born August 10, 1884, and died August 8, 1888

III —Clara Clark Steen, the third daughter of Clark and Mary Leah Brune Steen, was born January 12, 1886

IV —Clark Eugene Steen, the fourth child and eldest son of Clark and Mary Leah Brune Steen, was born May 9 1887

V —Thomas Harry Steen the fifth child and second son of Clark and Mary Leah Brune Steen was born November 25, 1888, and died May 22 1889

I I—Alfred Alexander Steen, the sixth child and third son of Clark and Mary Leah Brune Steen was born April 14, 1890

I II—William James Steen, the seventh child and fourth son of Clark and Mary Leah Brune Steen, was born September 10, 1897.

III—Mary Steen, the third child, a daughter of John and Ann Kerr Steen, was born at Malin Head, Parish of Dunboe, near Coleraine, Ireland, about 1824 She was married to Robert Burns

IV—Martha Steen, the fourth child and second daughter of John Steen, and the first child by his second wife, Nancy Robinson Steen was born at Balleney, in 1827

V—Isabella Steen, the fifth child and third daughter of John Steen, and the second daughter by his second wife, Nancy Robinson Steen, was born at Balleney in 1829

CHAPTER VI

Isaiah Steen, the sixth son and youngest child of John and Nancy Schoals Steen, of Balleney, and who were born in 1759, was born at the old homestead, in the townland of Balleney near Coleraine, Ireland, in 1798, and died in Belfast Ireland, greatly beloved and honored, August 3, 1871, aged 73 years He was educated in the College at Belfast, and ordained a minister of the Presbyterian Church about 1824 He was installed pastor of the church at Bally Copeland, near Donaghadee in County Down, Ireland, where he remained nine years, when he was chosen head master of the Mathematical Department of the Royal Academical Institution in Belfast, a position he held for thirty-seven years, being a most painstaking and conscientious teacher He was married, about 1825, to Isabella Carmichael, a daughter of John Carmichael, she having been born in 1802, and died August 13, 1841, aged 39 years He was married a second time, December 21, 1855, to Dorothy Smith Peile, a daughter of William Peile, of Workington, England, she having been born in 1815, and died March 30, 1889, aged 74 years To the Rev Prof Isaiah Steen and his first wife were born eight children, and to his second wife one son

I —John Carmichael Steen, the eldest son of Rev Isaiah and Isabella Carmichael Steen, was born in Donaghadee, County Down, Ireland, February 5. 1826 He was educated in Belfast, and went to Scotland, where, by examination, he secured the position of master of Madias Academy Cupar Fife where he remained five years In 1851 he went to Edinburgh as teacher in Park Place Institution, a high-class school for the education of young ladies In 1857 he purchased the good will of the establishment, and became proprietor, and head master which position he held until the time of his death, in 1886, aged 60 years He was thus a prominent and successful teacher for about forty years He was married to Elizabeth Jane Barnett, the eldest daughter of James Barnett a merchant of Belfast For several years Mrs Steen has been Secretary of the Ladies' Foreign Missionary Society of the Presbyterian Church in Ireland Family residence, 30 College Gardens, Belfast, Ireland To them were born nine children

r. Elizabeth Wallace Steen, the eldest child of John Carmichael and Elizabeth Jane Barnett Steen, was born in Edinburgh, Scotland, in January, 1861 She was married, September 11, 1894, to William Durham McBride, a merchant of Belfast Residence, 12 University Square, Belfast, Ireland

2 Helen Steen, the second daughter of John C and Elizabeth J Barnett Steen, was born in Edinburgh, Scotland, in June, 1862 and died in December, 1862

3 Edith Carmichael Steen, the third daughter of John C and Elizabeth J Barnett Steen, was born in Edinburgh Scotland, in October, 1863 Edith C. Steen worked for several years in a Soldiers' Home in Ireland, but is now in a Soldiers' Home at Rewal-Pinde, in India

4 Annie Livingstone Steen, the fourth daughter of John C and Elizabeth J Barnett Steen, was born in Edinburgh Scotland, in December, 1864 A missionary nurse in Nagpore, India

5 Alice Eustace Steen, the fifth daughter of John C and Elizabeth J Barnett Steen, was born in Edinburgh, Scotland, in September, 1867 Residence, Belfast, Ireland

6 Eveline Edgar Steen, the sixth daughter of John C and Elizabeth J Barnett Steen, was born in Edinburgh, Scotland, in March 1869, and died in February, 1870

7 James Barnett Steen, the seventh child and eldest son of John C and Elizabeth J Barnett Steen, was born in Edinburgh, Scotland, in December, 1870. J Barnett Steen was married in September, 1900, and is engaged in active business Residence, Belfast, Ireland

8 Mary Harvey Steen, the eighth child and seventh daughter of John C and Elizabeth J Barnett Steen, was born in Edinburgh, Scotland, in December, 1873 A missionary nurse in India since 1898

9 John Edgar Steen, the ninth and youngest child, and the second son of Prof John C and Elizabeth J Barnett Steen, was born in Edinburgh, Scotland, in February, 1876 Residence Belfast, Ireland

II —Thomas Steen, the second son of Rev Isaiah and Isabella Carmichael Steen, was born in Donaghadee, Ireland, December 22, 1827, and died April 1, 1874, in the 47th year of his age He was married to Eleanor Dinnen, a daughter of Mr Dinnen, of Cabin Hill, Belfast Thomas Steen lived for some years in Dublin, Ireland, and was connected with the National Board of Education He was afterwards appointed Inspector of Factories in England Mrs Eleanor Dinnen Steen now resides in Cabin Hill, Belfast, Ireland

III —Robert Steen, Ph D , the third son of Rev Isaiah and Isabella Carmichael Steen, was born in Donaghadee, County Down, Ireland, May 9 1830, and died in Belfast, November 3, 1893, in the 64th year of his age He was educated in the Royal Academical Institution, and in Belfast College He also studied in London, and spent four years on the Continent in Hamburgh and Himelin, where he thoroughly learned the German language He spent one year in the College at Geneva, two years at the University of Bonn, and took his degree of Ph D at the University of Leipsic. He studied theology three years, took first prize in Hebrew, and prizes in other subjects He did not enter the ministry, but was chosen elder

in Fitzroy Avenue Presbyterian Church, Belfast, and Superintendent of the City Mission   He was elected head master of
the Classical Department of the Royal Academical Institution
in Belfast, and entered upon his work there on May 1 1856,
which position he held for thirty-five years   Dr Robert Steen
was a gentleman of very amiable qualities, a great favorite
with his pupils who, for more than a quarter of a century, were
educated in the institution   He was, if possible, held in still
higher esteem by the vast number of young gentlemen who
passed through the boarding school connected with his department, and thus had a closer acquaintance with him and better
opportunities for knowing him in the private relationship of
life   The following article is copied from "The Northern
Whig," a Belfast newspaper, published the day after his death·

Death, ever busy in our midst, has removed yet another man
who has played the part of wide usefulness in the community   The
announcement in our columns of the passing away of Dr Robert
Steen will awake no mere perfunctory expressions of regret   So
long and so closely connected with the Royal Academical Institution,
apart from his extended social relations   he had come in contact
with large numbers of those who afterwards came to occupy prominent positions in the learned professions and in the business world
Of these it is not too much to say that those who first knew him as a
teacher came to value him as a friend, his friendship thus linking
the associations of a pleasant school life with those of an after
career   This was the inevitable result of the fine personal qualities
of the man   Ever mindful of the educational interests of those
intrusted to him   never careless in matters of discipline, those
interests were all the better served, and discipline all the more
readily maintained, through the kindliness of heart, the cheery
manners and unfailing geniality which were characteristic of him
It was a matter of sincere regret to all who had been under his
care, and to his many friends, when failing health rendered it
advisable that he should relinquish the position he had occupied so
long, though they would have been well contented that he should
for any other reason enter upon a period of merited leisure   The
cordial attachment felt toward him was clearly shown at the time
of his retirement, and will be more strongly marked in the sorrow
manifested in his decease

Dr Robert Steen was married, June 30 1858, to Annie Carmichael, a daughter of David Carmichael, a merchant of Belfast, she having been born October 11, 1834   To them were
born eleven children   Family residence, 5 Dunclin Malone
Road, Belfast, Ireland

1. Annie Isabel Steen, the eldest child of Dr Robert and
   Annie Carmichael Steen, was born in Belfast, Ireland, Octo-

PROF. ROBERT STEEN, PH.D.

ber 31, 1859, and died at the residence of her brother, at Owetor Ferry, England, August 13, 1890, in the 31st year of her age.

2 Marion Louisa Steen, the second daughter of Dr Robert and Annie Carmichael Steen, was born in Belfast, Ireland, July 30, 1861 Residence, Belfast, Ireland

3 William Carmichael Steen, M D , the third child and eldest son of Dr Robert and Annie Carmichael Steen, was born in Belfast, Ireland, March 6, 1863 He was educated in Queen's College, Belfast, and in London Medical College. He located first at Owetor Ferry, England, where he had a good practice and remained several years After the death of his father he removed to Belfast, so as to be near his mother Dr William C Steen was married by the Rev J Joseph, at St Andrew's Street Church, Cambridge, England, February 17, 1900, to Margaret Lilley, youngest daughter of the late William Eaden Lilley, of Thorpe House Cambridge Residence, Thomasville, Lisburn Road Belfast, Ireland

4 David Miller Steen the fourth child and second son of Dr Robert and Annie Carmichael Steen, was born in Belfast, Ireland, December 26 1864 He is now in the civil service, acting judge in Tangalle, Ceylon He was married, July 9, 1895, to Elsie Orr, a daughter of T Carmichael Orr, of Glasgow, Scotland Residence, Tangalle, Ceylon.

5 Elizabeth Barnett Steen, the fifth child and third daughter of Dr Robert and Annie Carmichael Steen, was born in Belfast, Ireland, January 21, 1867 She was married, October 19, 1893, to Robert E Workman, a merchant of Belfast, and a son of John Workman, J P Residence Eglantine Avenue, Belfast, Ireland To them was born

I—Arthur Coates Workman, a son of Robert E and Elizabeth Barnett Steen Workman, was born in Belfast, Ireland, July 18, 1895

6 Ida Frances Steen, the sixth child and fourth daughter of Dr Robert and Annie Carmichael Steen, was born in Belfast, Ireland, September 28, 1868, and died February 26, 1870

7 Robert Hunter Steen, M D , the seventh child and third son of Dr Robert and Annie Carmichael Steen, was born in Belfast, Ireland, May 29, 1870 He was graduated from London University and is now household physician at St Mary's Hospital Residence, London, England

8 Edward Steen, the eighth child and fourth son of Dr Robert and Annie Carmichael Steen, was born in Belfast, Ireland, April 1, 1872 — a builder and contractor Residence, 5 Dunelin, Malone Road, Belfast, Ireland.

9 Harold Steen, the ninth child and fifth son of Dr Robert and Annie Carmichael Steen, was born in Belfast, Ireland, December 1, 1873 and died March 16, 1875

10 John Howard Steen, the tenth child and sixth son of Dr Robert and Annie Carmichael Steen, was born in Belfast, Ireland, October 28, 1877 and died June 17, 1879

11 Thomas Arnold Steen, the eleventh child and seventh son of Dr Robert and Annie Carmichael Steen, was born in Belfast, Ireland, July 30, 1879 — a student Residence, 5 Dunelin, Malone Road, Belfast, Ireland

IV —Agnes Steen, the fourth child and eldest daughter of Rev Isaiah and Isabella Carmichael Steen, was born in Donaghadee, County Down, Ireland June 13, 1832 the day on which her father was chosen head master of the Royal Academical Institution in Belfast She was married in Belfast, Ireland, October 30, 1855, to Walter Burns, a son of the Rev William Hamilton Burns, D D , (who was for twenty years minister at Dun, Forfarshire, and forty years minister at Kelayth Sterlingshire, Scotland,) he having been born at Kelayth, Sterlingshire, Scotland August 16, 1824 He was for ten years joint proprietor of ' The Fife Herald ' and is now a music publisher and composer in Belfast He was the author of the words and music of "The Prince and Princess of Wales Anthem," in 1885, the "Vienna Jubilee Anthem," in 1887, and forty-five hymn tunes, etc Walter Burns' father had a brother William Chalmers Burns, who was a Chinese missionary, and also another brother, the Rev Islam Burns, D D , who was a professor of theology in Glasgow, Scotland To them were born five children

1 Elizabeth Isabella Burns, the eldest daughter of Walter and

Agnes Steen Burns, was born in Cupar Fife, Scotland August 11, 1856

2 William Hamilton Burns the second child and eldest son of Walter and Agnes Steen Burns was born in Newry, Ireland, March 12, 1859 — a music dealer and piano tuner

3. Walker Chalmers Burns, the third child and second son of Walter and Agnes Steen Burns was born in Newry, Ireland, July 26, 1861, and died in October 1861

4 Charlotte Alexandrina Chalmers Burns, the fourth child and second daughter of Walter and Agnes Steen Burns, was born in Newry Ireland April 7 1865   Residence Belfast, Ireland

5 Agnes Louisa Burns, the fifth and youngest child the third daughter of Walter and Agnes Steen Burns was born in Newry, Ireland July 17, 1871   She is a fine singer, a soprano vocalist   At the Royal Academy of Music, where she received her musical education she received five silver and bronze medals for solo singing, sight reading, and harmony besides honor certificates for piano playing, teaching etc   She also obtained the medal from the Society of Arts, in August, 1895   Residence, Belfast, Ireland

V—James Steen the fifth child and fourth son of Rev Isaiah and Isabella Carmichael Steen, was born in Belfast, Ireland, November 17, 1834 and died, unmarried, March 30 1868, in the 34th year of his age.

VI—Hunter Steen, the sixth child and fifth son of Rev Isaiah and Isabella Carmichael Steen was born in Belfast, Ireland, December 23 1836 — a manufacturer in Belfast Ireland   He was married, June 1 1869, to Mary Jane Clarke, a daughter of Mr Clarke of Parkville Belfast   To them were born three children   Residence 3 Dunelm Malone Road Belfast Ireland

1 Carrie Louisa Steen, the eldest child of Hunter and Mary Jane Clarke Steen, was born in Belfast Ireland October 10 1870.

2 Hunter Carmichael Steen the second child and eldest son of Hunter and Mary Jane Clarke Steen, was born in Belfast, Ireland, August 10, 1872   He is now Lieutenant of the Bombay Lancers   Residence, Neemuck Bombay India

3 James Clarke Steen, the third child and second son of Hunter and Mary Jane Clarke Steen, was born in Belfast, Ireland, December 21, 1873 Residence. 3 Dunelin, Malone Road, Belfast. Ireland.

VII —Margaret Steen, the seventh child and second daughter of Rev Isaiah and Isabella Carmichael Steen, was born in Belfast, Ireland. April 11 1839 She was married, June 24 1863, to David Martin, a wholesale trader and seed merchant of Newry Ireland, he having been born in Rathfriline, Ireland, September 15 1837 Residence, Littleton, Newry, Ireland To them were born nine children

1. William Wallace Martin, the eldest child of David and Margaret Steen Martin, was born in Newry, Ireland, August 6, 1864

2 Henry Carmichael Martin, the second son of David and Margaret Steen Martin, was born in Newry Ireland, September 18, 1865

3 Isabella Steen Martin, the third child and eldest daughter of David and Margaret Steen Martin, was born in Newry, Ireland, March 15, 1867

4 Elizabeth Wallace Martin, the fourth child and second daughter of David and Margaret Steen Martin, was born in Newry Ireland. October 20, 1868, and died in June, 1869

5 Kathleen Edgar Martin, the fifth child and third daughter of David and Margaret Steen Martin, was born in Newry, Ireland, March 24 1871

6 David Herbert Martin, the sixth child and third son of David and Margaret Steen Martin, was born in Newry Ireland. May 17 1874

7 Margaret May Martin, the seventh child and fourth daughter of David and Margaret Steen Martin, was born in Newry, Ireland, March 23, 1877

8 Annie Beatrice Martin, the eighth child and fifth daughter of David and Margaret Steen Martin, was born in Newry, Ireland, January 24, 1881

9 Norman Hudson Martin, the ninth child and fourth son of David and Margaret Steen Martin, was born in Newry Ireland, October 10, 1884 Residence, Littleton, Newry Ireland

VIII.—William Steen, the eighth child and sixth son of Rev Prof Isaiah and Isabella Carmichael Steen, was born in Belfast, Ireland. August 9, 1841, and died September 27, 1841

IX —William Peile Steen the ninth child and seventh son of the Rev Prof Isaiah Steen, the first and only child by his second wife, Dorothy Smith Peile Steen, was born in Belfast, Ireland, February 27, 1857   He was educated in Queens College, Belfast, where he received the degrees of B A and M A He also studied in London University, and took the degree of M A there   He was for a time head master of Sullivan School, Hollyroad, County Down, Ireland, and afterwards head master of the Lisburn School   He now holds an educational appointment in Burlington House, Cambridge. England. He was married, July 30 1894 to Ethel Louisa Needham, a daughter of Mr Needham, of Yountbridge, Wells, England   Res-dence, Queen Anne s Terrace, Cambridge, England

BOOK TEN.

DESCENDANTS OF MATTHEW STEEN

Matthew Steen was the youngest son of James Steen, of County Tyrone, Ireland He was born in Tyrone, Ireland, in 1771, and died in Noble County, Ohio, February 11 1868, in the 97th year of his age. He came to America in 1793 and located first in Westmoreland County, Pennsylvania, and afterwards settled permanently in Noble County, Ohio He was married in Adams County, Pennsylvania, February 1, 1800, to Margaret Campbell, and brought up a family of seven children

Matthew Steen was the son of James Steen who lived in County Tyrone, Ireland, where he was married about 1756, and brought up a family of six children, whose names were as follows John Steen Elizabeth Steen Jane Steen, Mary Steen, Martha Steen, and Matthew Steen, the latter being the only one of the family known to his descendants to have removed to America, and whose record is known to the writer Matthew Steen was born in the City of Tyrone, County Tyrone, Ireland, in 1771, removed to America in 1793, when about 22 years of age, and located first in Westmoreland County, Pennsylvania He was married in Adams County, Pennsylvania, February 1, 1800, to Margaret Campbell, she having been born in Adams County, Pennsylvania, in 1774, and died in Noble County, Ohio, October 19, 1858 aged about 74 years For several years after his marriage Matthew Steen and family resided in Adams County, Pennsylvania, then removed to Washington County, Pennsylvania, and finally settled in Noble County, Ohio, where he died, February 11, 1868, in the 97th year of his age Matthew Steen was a man of sterling character, a member of the United Presbyterian Church, and a ruling elder for many years In this church all his children were brought up and continued in full membership until its final abandonment in the community in which they lived, when they united with the Presbyterian Church, with which the family have been connected ever since To them were born seven children

I.—William Ferguson Steen, the eldest child, and a son of Matthew and Margaret Campbell Steen, was born in Adams County, Pennsylvania November 5, 1800, and died in Sharon, Noble County, Ohio, April 23, 1885, in the 85th year of his age He was married in Jefferson County, Ohio, November 5, 1832, to Elizabeth Francis, whose parents came from Ireland, and who died in Cadiz, Harrison County, Ohio, about January 1, 1834 To them one child was born William Ferguson Steen was married a second time, in Jefferson County, Ohio, to Martha Francis, a cousin of his first wife, and whose parents also came from Ireland, she having been born March 17, 1808 To them were born two children, one son, and one daughter

  1 James Francis Steen, a son of William Ferguson Steen and his first wife, Elizabeth Francis Steen, was born in Cadiz, Harrison County, Ohio, December 5, 1833 He was married in Morgan County, Ohio, by the Rev George M Hisey, February 1, 1861, to Abigail Minta Walls, she having been born in Morgan County, Ohio, November 8, 1840 James F Steen is by occupation a merchant Residence, Caldwell, Noble County Ohio To them were born five children

    1—Loren C Steen, the eldest child of James F and Abigail M Steen, was born in Sharon, Noble County, Ohio, January 1, 1863. He was married in Caldwell, Ohio, April 12, 1888, to Lulu Belle Dilley, she having been born in Cald-

(27)

well, Ohio   Loren C Steen is a merchant of Zanesville
Residence, Zanesville, Ohio   To them were born two
children

    1 Leone Lillian Steen, the elder child, a daughter of
      Loren C. and Lulu Belle Steen, was born January 5,
      1889

    2 Paul Herbert Steen, the second child, a son of Loren
      C and Lulu Belle Steen, was born December 10, 1890

II —Albina Frances Steen, the second child and only daughter of James F. and Abigail M Steen, was born in Sharon,
Ohio, May 4, 1865. and died January 19, 1867, in the
second year of her age

III —Malcom Steen, the third child and second son of
James F and Abigail M. Steen, was born in Sharon, Ohio,
February 28, 1869   Residence, Caldwell, Ohio

IV --Harry Burns Steen, the fourth child and third son of
James F and Abigail M Steen, was born in Sharon, Ohio,
August 4, 1870   Residence, Caldwell, Ohio

V —James Wilbur Steen, the fifth child and fourth son of
James F and Abigail M Steen, was born in Sharon, Ohio,
March 16, 1879   Residence, Caldwell, Noble County,
Ohio

2   Matthew Steen, the second son of William Ferguson Steen,
and the first child by his second wife, Martha Francis Steen,
and thus a half brother to James F Steen was born in Harrison County, Ohio, October 5, 1838   He was married by
the Rev. Ellis Daniels, August 21, 1866, to Elizabeth Jane
Winder, she having been born December 31, 1845   Matthew Steen is a merchant   Residence, Sharon, Noble
County, Ohio

I —John William Steen, the eldest child, a son of Matthew
and Elizabeth Jane Steen, was born in Sharon, Ohio, July
28, 1867

II —Clement Alexander Steen, the second son of Matthew
and Elizabeth Jane Steen, was born in Sharon, Ohio, September 12, 1870

III —Jessie Martha Steen, the third child and only daughter
of Matthew and Elizabeth Jane Steen, was born in Sharon,
Ohio, April 19, 1883.

IV —Frank W Steen, the fourth and youngest child and the third son of Matthew and Elizabeth Jane Steen, was born in Sharon, Ohio, February 22, 1877

3 Margaret Ann Steen the third child and only daughter of William Ferguson Steen, and the second child by his second wife, Martha Francis Steen, was born in Harrison County, Ohio, May 31, 1845 She was married in Sharon, Ohio, by the Rev William Galbreath December 31, 1875 to Simeon Socrates McFarland, he having been born in Warren County Virginia December 16 1851, and died November 15, 1886, in the 35th year of his age Family residence, Sharon, Noble County, Ohio To them were born two children

I Anna Lesta McFarland the elder child, a daughter of Simeon S and Margaret Ann Steen McFarland was born in Sharon, Ohio, September 12 1876

II —John William McFarland, the second child a son of Simeon S and Margaret Ann Steen McFarland, was born in Sharon, Ohio, April 30, 1879

II —Sarah Steen, the second child and eldest daughter of Matthew and Margaret Campbell Steen, was born in Adams County, Pennsylvania, September 3, 1803, and died September 23 1874, aged 71 years She was married in Harrison County, Ohio, November 28, 1828, to James Porter, he having been born near Taylorstown, Washington County, Pennsylvania, May 30, 1805, and died March 20, 1842 in the 37th year of his age To them were born two children one son and one daughter

1 James Porter, the elder child of James and Sarah Steen Porter was born in Cadiz, Ohio, October 3, 1829 He was married to Catherine Lyons, November 18, 1856 she having been born in Sharon Ohio June 17 1830 Residence, Keiths Noble County, Ohio To them were born seven children

I —George Irwin Porter the eldest child, a son of James and Catherine Lyons Porter, was born September 5, 1857.

II —Margaret Leonora Porter, the second child and eldest daughter of James and Catherine Lyons Porter, was born July 30, 1859

III —Sarah Adelaide Porter, the third child and second
daughter of James and Catherine Lyons Porter, was born
August 30, 1861

IV —James Augustus Porter, the fourth child and second
son of James and Catherine Lyons Porter, was born January 24, 1864.

V —Angelia Porter, the fifth child and third daughter of
James and Catherine Lyons Porter, was born December
19, 1865.

VI —Arabella May Porter, the sixth child and fourth daughter of James and Catherine Lyons Porter, was born February 26, 1868, and died October 13, 1869

VII.—Emma Hannah Porter, the seventh and youngest
child, the fifth daughter of James and Catherine Lyons
Porter, was born August 26, 1870

2 Sarah Campbell Porter, the second child, a daughter of
James and Sarah Steen Porter, was born in Cadiz, Harrison
County, Ohio, September 13, 1837 She was married in
Sharon, Ohio, by the Rev. Randall Ross, pastor of the Uni-
ted Presbyterian Church, April 20, 1854, to Charles Eckels
Srack — a house carpenter — he having been born in Bel-
mont County, Ohio, July 27, 1825 They continued to live
in Ohio until 1877, when they removed to Brookville, Saline
County, Kansas   Residence, Brookville, Kansas   To them
were born seven children

I —James Porter Srack, the eldest child, a son of Charles
E. and Sarah C Porter Srack, was born in Sharon Ohio,
August 14, 1855   He was married, September 30, 1873
to Nancy Ann Tilton   Residence, Brookville, Kansas.
To them were born three children, as follows

  1 Bertha Srack, the eldest child of James P and Nancy
  Ann Srack, was born February 16, 1876

  2 Lorah Srack, the second daughter of James P and
  Nancy Ann Srack, was born February 17, 1879

  3 Charles Drennan Srack, the third child and only son
  of James P and Nancy Ann Srack, was born August
  22, 1887

II —Adam Drennan Srack, the second son of Charles E
and Sarah C Porter Srack, was born in Sharon, Ohio,

February 10, 1858, and died in Sharon, Ohio, January 5, 1862, in the 4th year of his age

III—Willey Charles Srack, the third son of Charles E. and Sarah C. Porter Srack, was born in Sharon, Ohio, June 5, 1860. Residence, Brookville, Kansas

IV—Mary Frances Adelaide Srack, the fourth child and the elder daughter of Charles E. and Sarah C. Porter Srack, was born in Sharon, Ohio, December 14, 1862 Residence, Brookville, Kansas

V—John Elmer Srack, the fifth child and fourth son of Charles E. and Sarah C. Porter Srack, was born in Sharon, Ohio, July 26, 1865. Residence, Brookville, Kansas

VI—Laura Belle Srack, the sixth child and second daughter of Charles E. and Sarah C. Porter Srack, was born in Sharon, Ohio, June 15, 1870, and died in Noble County, Ohio, May 27, 1876, in the 6th year of her age

VII—McLaren Srack, the seventh and youngest child of Charles Eckels and Sarah Campbell Porter Srack, was born in Sharon, Ohio, July 8, 1873 Residence Brookville, Kansas

III—Elizabeth Steen, the third child of Matthew and Margaret Campbell Steen, was born in Adams County, Pennsylvania, September 17, 1804, and died in Keiths, Noble County, Ohio, February 10, 1892, in the 38th year of her age She was an amiable, devout and very useful Christian woman, a member of the Presbyterian Church, quietly exerting a wide religious influence She was never married

IV—James Campbell Steen, the fourth child and second son of Matthew and Margaret Campbell Steen, was born in Washington County, Pennsylvania, June 12, 1808, and died in Oceola, Crawford County, Ohio, June 20, 1885. aged 77 years He was married in Columbiana County, Ohio, in 1830, to Mary McCloskey, she having been born in Columbiana County, Ohio, April 1, 1806 In 1893 she was still living in Oceola, Crawford County, Ohio, in a ripe old age, but in excellent health To them one child was born

1 John Clark Steen, a son of James Campbell and Mary McCloskey Steen, was born in Columbiana County, Ohio, May 5, 1831. He was formerly a tailor by occupation, but is

now a farmer   He was married in Oceola, Ohio, November 18 1852, to Rachel Carlisle, she having been born in Columbiana County, Ohio, September 16 183—   Family residence, Oceola, Crawford County, Ohio   To them were born two children

I —Harietta Jane Steen, the elder daughter of John Clark and Rachel Carlisle Steen, was born in Oceola, Ohio, June 28, 1853   Residence, Oceola, Ohio

II —Frank Laverne Steen, the second child of John Clark and Rachel Carlisle Steen, was born in Oceola, Ohio, March 2, 1866   Residence, Oceola, Ohio

V —Jane Steen the fifth child and third daughter of Matthew and Margaret Campbell Steen, was born in Washington County, Pennsylvania, June 11, 1811   She was married in Harrison County, Ohio in September, 1847, to Joseph Sharp, and died July 3, 1849 in the 39th year of her age   To them one child was born

1 Jane Sharp, the only child of Joseph and Jane Steen Sharp, was born in Harrison County, Ohio, June 29, 1849, and died ————

VI —Margaret Steen, the sixth child and fourth daughter of Matthew and Margaret Campbell Steen, was born in Washington County, Pennsylvania, March 17, 1813, and died October 2, 1863 in the 51st year of her age   She was married in Morgan County, Ohio, August 17. 1848, to Nathan Jones Ramsey, he having been born in Chester County, Pennsylvania, December 27, 1825   To them were born two children

1 David Steen Ramsey, the elder child of Nathan Jones and Margaret Steen Ramsey, was born in Harrison County, Ohio, May 29, 1849   He was married, February 28, 1871, to Hannah Francis, she having been born November 10, 1846   Residence Haga, Noble County, Ohio   To them were three children born

I —Walter Francis Ramsey, the eldest son of David Steen and Hannah Francis Ramsey, was born in Noble County, Ohio, March 17, 1872

II —Nathan Augustus Ramsey, the second son of David Steen and Hannah Francis Ramsey, was born in Noble County, Ohio. June 22, 1875

III—Loren Steen Ramsey, the third and youngest son of David Steen and Hannah Francis Ramsey, was born in Noble County, Ohio, December 1, 1877

2 Mary Ann Ramsey, the second child of Nathan Jones and Margaret Steen Ramsey, was born in Harrison County, Ohio, October 1, 1851, and died May 20, 1853, in the second year of her age

VII—Mary Steen, the seventh and youngest child, the fifth daughter of Matthew and Margaret Campbell Steen, was born in Harrison County, Ohio, May 6, 1822. She was brought up by her parents in the United Presbyterian Church, of which she was for many years a member After its disorganization in the community in which she lived, she united with the Presbyterian Church She was a woman of devout Christian character and extensive usefulness, was never married, and lived to a good old age She died, about 1896, in the sure and certain hope of a blessed immortality Her residence had been at Keiths, Noble County Ohio

BOOK ELEVEN.

DESCENDANTS OF JAMES STEEN.

James Steen was born in the North of Ireland, early removed to America, and located in what is now Chester County, Pennsylvania He was for many years an elder of the Doe Run Presbyterian Church He was married to Nancy Jordan, and brought up a family of ten children

James Steen was born in the North of Ireland, early removed to America, and located in what is now Chester County, Pennsylvania, where he spent a long and useful life He was a farmer, and at the time of his death an elder in the Doe Run Presbyterian Church He was married to Nancy Jordan, and brought up a family of ten children, who were all trained in "the nurture and admonition of the Lord "

I—Margaret Steen was the eldest child of James and Nancy Jordan Steen She was born in Newlin Township, Chester County, Pennsylvania (No genealogical record has been received for this work)

II—John Steen, the second child of James and Nancy Jordan Steen, was born in Newlin Township, Chester County, Pennsylvania (No genealogical record received)

(424)

III—Stuart Steen, the third child of James and Nancy Jordan Steen, was born in Newlin Township, Chester County, Pennsylvania (No genealogical record received)

IV—Isaiah Steen, the fourth child of James and Nancy Jordan Steen, was born in Newlin Township, Chester County, Pennsylvania   He was married to Amelia ———— They probably removed in early life to Washington County, in Western Pennsylvania, where they spent their lives and brought up a family of several children   Two of their sons graduated from Washington College, and occupied useful stations in life Among their children were probably the following:

1 James T Steen, a son of Isaiah and Amelia Steen, was born in Washington, Washington County, Pennsylvania   He was graduated from Washington College in 1811   He was a law student in Newark, Delaware, and Baltimore, Maryland   He was a teacher by profession, and taught in York, Pennsylvania, Abington, six years, and Govanstown fourteen years   He was married, May 7, 1833, to Sarah E. McComas   He died of paralysis in Baltimore, Maryland, April 13, 1855   James T and Sarah E Steen were probably the parents of some of the Steens who lived in Baltimore and vicinity

2 George Washington Steen, a son of Isaiah and Amelia Steen, was probably born in Washington, Pennsylvania   He was married to Ann Eliza House Booth, and they lived and died in Baltimore, Maryland   To them were born four children

   1—George Washington Steen, the eldest son of George W. and Ann Eliza H Steen, was born in Baltimore, Maryland, in 1838   He was married by the Rev Dr Crau, pastor of the First Lutheran Church of Baltimore, to Mary F Hickman, she having been born in Baltimore, Maryland, November 17, 1838   George W Steen resided in Washington, D C, for several years, and was a clerk in the Surgeon General's office   He died July 13, 1880, aged 42 years, leaving a wife and family of five children. Residence, 2006 Biddle Street, Baltimore, Maryland

      1 George Washington Steen, the eldest son of George W. and Mary F Steen, was born in Washington, D C, February 10 1868 — a canmaker   He was married, in Baltimore, Maryland, June 15, 1892, to Rosa Roberts

Keithley she having been born November 27, 1865 Residence, Baltimore, Maryland   To them was born:

a Myrtle Esther Steen, a daughter of George W and Rosa R K Steen, was born March 23, 1893, and died August 28, 1893

2 Ann Eliza Steen, the second child and only daughter of George W and Mary F Steen, was born October 13, 1871   Residence, Baltimore, Maryland

3 Hiram Grant Steen, the third child and second son of George W and Mary F Steen, was born January 15, 1873 — a canmaker   Residence, Baltimore, Maryland

4 Samuel House Steen, the fourth child and third son of George W. and Mary F Steen, was born March 21, 1875

5 Lawrence Hickman Steen, the fifth child and fourth son of George W and Mary F Steen, was born April 22, 1877   Residence, Baltimore, Maryland

II —James Steen, the second son of George W and Ann Eliza Booth Steen, was born in Baltimore, Maryland, about 1840   He removed to the West

III —Samuel Isaiah Steen, the third son of George W and Ann Eliza Booth Steen, was born in Baltimore, Maryland, about 1842, and died ————

IV —Susan Steen, the fourth child and only daughter of George W and Ann Eliza Booth Steen, was born in Baltimore, Maryland, about 1845, and died ————

3 Isaiah Steen, a son of Isaiah and Amelia Steen, was born in Washington, Pennsylvania, in 1812, and was graduated from Washington College in 1833 — a lawyer by profession   He studied law at Washington, Pennsylvania, and Wellsburgh, Virginia, from 1833 to 1835. He practiced law in Wheeling, West Virginia, from 1836 until 1839, and in Wellsburgh, Virginia, from 1839 until 1863   He was prosecuting attorney of Hancock County, Virginia, from 1844, until 1852   He died from typhoid fever in Cincinnati, Ohio, May 30, 1863   He was married, October 20, 1839, to Theressa M Klein, to whom were born several children   The widow resided near Cincinnati Ohio, in 1883

V —Ann Steen, the fifth child and second daughter of James and Nancy Jordan Steen, was born in Newlin Township, Chester County, Pennsylvania (No genealogical record received)

VI—Hugh Jordan Steen, the sixth child and fourth son of James and Nancy Jordan Steen, was born in Newlin Township, Chester County, Pennsylvania He was married to Susan Burns They spent their lives in the same locality where they exerted an extensive influence for good They were the parents of three children

1 James H Steen was born in Newlin Township, Chester County, Pennsylvania, November 30, 1818 He was a successful farmer, and for many years a ruling elder in Doe Run Presbyterian Church He was married, December 2, 1841, to Elizabeth Strode To them were born seven children, as follows

I —Susannah Chrisman Steen

II —William Strode Steen.

III —Mary Elizabeth Steen

IV —David James Steen

V —Thomas Truman Steen

VI —Emma Belle Steen

VII —Hugh Jordan Steen

2 Jordan Steen, the second son of Hugh Jordan and Susan Burns Steen, was born in Newlin Township, Chester County, Pennsylvania about 1821

3 Hugh Steen, the third son of Hugh Jordan and Susan Burns Steen, was born in Newlin Township, Chester County, Pennsylvania, about 1824

VII —Sarah Steen, the seventh child and third daughter of James and Nancy Jordan Steen was born in Chester County, Pennsylvania (No genealogical record received)

VIII —James Steen, the eighth child and fifth son of James and Nancy Jordan Steen, was born in Newlin Township, Chester County, Pennsylvania He was married about 1813, to Ruth Harlan, and brought up a family of children in Chester County, Pennsylvania The record of one son only is given

1 John Steen, a son of James and Ruth Harlan Steen, and a grandson of James and Nancy Jordan Steen, was born near

Doe Run, Chester County, Pennsylvania, January 5, 1819.
He was married to Ann Steen, a cousin, she having been
born June 8, 1820 To them were born four children

I —Albert Judson Steen, deceased.

II —Anna Steen   Residence, Bryn Mawr, Pennsylvania

III —Margaret Thompson Steen   Residence, Bryn Mawr,
Pennsylvania.

IV —William Ezekiel Steen, a son of John and Ann Steen,
a grandson of James and Ruth Harlan Steen, and a great-
grandson of James and Nancy Jordan Steen, was born in
Philadelphia Pennsylvania, November 27, 1847 He is an
influential citizen and a ruling elder in the Presbyterian
Church at Bryn Mawr, Montgomery County, Pennsylvania   He was married in Philadelphia, Pennsylvania,
October 22, 1875, to Kate Irene Smith To them were
born three children   Residence, Bryn Mawr, Pennsylvania

  1 William Adam Steen, the eldest child of William Ezekiel and Kate Irene Steen, was born November 16, 1876,
  and died February 28, 1878

  2 Katherine Elizabeth Steen, the second child and eldest
  daughter of William Ezekiel and Kate Irene Steen, was
  born June 3, 1880

  3 Dorothy Anne Steen, the third child and second daughter of William Ezekiel and Kate Irene Steen, was born
  October 22, 1890

IX —Katherine Steen, the ninth child and fourth daughter of
James and Nancy Jordan Steen, was born in Newlin Township,
Chester County, Pennsylvania (No genealogical record of
her family has been received)

X —Samuel Steen, the tenth child and sixth son of James and
Nancy Jordan Steen (who early emigrated from Ireland and
settled in Chester County, Pennsylvania), was born in Newlin
Township, Chester County, Pennsylvania (No family record
received)

BOOK TWELVE.

DESCENDANTS OF JAMES STEEN

James Steen was born in the Province of Ulster, Ireland
He was married to Ann Scales, and brought up a family of at
least four children   Many of his descendants are in America

CHAPTER I

John Steen, a son of James and Ann Scales Steen, was born
in Ireland   He was married to Margaret George, and brought
up a family of children   Among them was—

I —David Steen, a son of John and Margaret George Steen, was
born in Ireland   He was married to Eleanor Peoples, and
came to America   They lived in New Jersey, and brought up
a family of children, as follows

  1. James Steen, a son of David and Eleanor Peoples Steen,
was married to Elizabeth Christie, and brought up a family
of five children, as follows:

    I —David Steen, a son of James and Elizabeth Christie
Steen, was married to Kate Hines   To them were born
six children, as follows·

1 Mary Steen

2 David Steen

3 John D Steen

4 Kate Steen

5 Harry Steen

6 William Steen

II —James Steen, the second son of James and Elizabeth Christie Steen, was married to Ann Purcell

III —John Steen, the third son of James and Elizabeth Christie Steen, was married to Rosanna McCrosson To them were born three children, as follows

1 James Steen, a son of John and Rosanna McCrosson Steen was born March 27, 1852 He was graduated from Princeton College, New Jersey, in 1871, and received the degree of A M. in 1873 He was admitted to the bar by the Supreme Court of New Jersey in 1874 In 1883 he was elected a ruling elder of the Shrewsbury Presbyterian Church which office he still holds He was chosen Commissioner to the General Assembly of the Presbyterian Church from the Presbytery of Monmouth in 1885, and again in 1895 He was a member of the Synodical Historical Committee, and delivered the address in the old Tennant Church, in 1895, on Scotch-Irish and Huguenot settlers of Monmouth County, New Jersey He was Mayor of Eatontown, and President of its Board of Education He was a member of the New Jersey Law and Order League, and as an attorney was instrumental in punishing and driving out of business many indecent bookmakers and gamblers in the vicinity He was married, December 1 1875, to Miriam Seabrook Holmes Residence, Eatontown, New Jersey

2 John A Steen, the second son of John and Rosanna McCrosson Steen

3 William Steen, the third son of John and Rosanna McCrosson Steen, deceased

IV —Robert Steen the fourth son of James and Elizabeth Christie Steen, was married to Ellen Sherlock To them were born six children, as follows:

1 Alexander M Steen, the eldest child and only son of
Robert and Ellen Sherlock Steen, was born near Coleraine, Ireland, April 17, 1862, and removed with his
parents to America about 1868   He spent his early life
in Trenton, New Jersey   He was graduated from the
Medical Department of the University of Pennsylvania,
at Philadelphia March 15, 1882, and practiced medicine
for seven years in Trenton, New Jersey   He was married and in December, 1889, removed to Florida, where
he is still engaged in the practice of medicine   Residence, Palatka, Florida

2 Mary Jarvis Steen

3 Ellen D Steen

4 Martha Steen

5 Elizabeth Steen

6 Margaret M Steen

I—Margaret Steen, the fifth child, a daughter of James and
Elizabeth Christie Steen, was married to William Purcell
To them were born two children, as follows

  1 William Purcell

  2 James Purcell

2 John Steen, the second son of David and Eleanor Peoples
Steen, was married to Rosanna George   To them was born

  I—William James Steen, who became a minister of the
  gospel.

3 Ellen Steen, the third child and eldest daughter of David
and Eleanor Peoples Steen, was married and lives with her
family in Trenton, New Jersey

4 Martha Steen, the fourth child and second daughter of
David and Eleanor Peoples Steen, lived in New Jersey

5 Mary Ann Steen the fifth child and third daughter of David
and Eleanor Peoples Steen, was married to Andrew Stewart
To them were born two children, as follows.

  I—David Stewart

  II—William Stewart

6 William Steen the fifth and youngest child, the third son of
David and Eleanor Peoples Steen, lived in Pennsylvania

CHAPTER II

James Steen, the second son of James and Ann Scales Steen, was born in Ballybay, County Monaghan, in the Province of Ulster, Ireland   He was married there to Jane Small a Scotch Covenanter, who was related to the Pedens and Smalls of Edinburgh, Scotland.   They removed to America, about 1793, with their daughter Mary, and a nephew, George A Steen, and lived in Philadelphia, Pennsylvania, many years   They removed to Washington, D C , where they resided several years, and finally settled in Morgantown, Virginia, where they spent the remainder of their lives   James Steen was by trade a carpenter   To them were born six children

I —Mary Steen, the eldest child, a daughter of James and Jane Small Steen, was born in Ireland   She was married in Philadelphia, Pennsylvania, to Robert Brown, who died, leaving three sons, as follows
1 James Brown
2 David Brown
3 John Brown
   After her husband's death, Mary Steen Brown removed with her parents to Morgantown, Virginia   She was afterwards married to William Berkshire — a farmer — of Monongalia County, Virginia, by whom she had one daughter, as follows
4. Jane Berkshire was born in Virginia, and died, unmarried, in Baltimore, Maryland, in 1890

II —Eliza A Steen the second daughter of James and Jane Small Steen, was born in Philadelphia, Pennsylvania, June 17, 1799, and died at her home, in Clarksburg, Virginia, May 10, 1866, in the 67th year of her age   When twelve years of age she united with the Presbyterian Church in Philadelphia, under the ministry of the Rev Dr Potts   In Washington, D C , she was a member of the church of which the Rev John F Clarke was pastor   She removed to Clarksburgh, Virginia in 1824, and for some time taught school, having for one of her pupils the mother of Stonewall Jackson, the celebrated Confederate General   She was one of the original members of the

Clarksburgh Presbyterian Church, having brought her letter from Morgantown, Virginia, for the purpose of uniting in the organization. Eliza A Steen was married ————, to John Davis, who came to Clarksburgh from Woodstock, Shenandoah County, Virginia, he having been born there in 1796, and died in Clarksburgh, Virginia, November 9, 1863, in the 67th year of his age. He was an elder in the Presbyterian Church for more than fifty years. To them were born seven children

1 Sarah E Davis, the eldest child of John and Eliza A Steen Davis, was born in Clarksburgh, Virginia, and died when two years old

2 Mary C Davis, the second daughter of John and Eliza A Steen Davis, was born in Clarksburgh, Virginia and died when two years old

3 Jane S Davis, the third daughter of John and Eliza A Steen Davis, was born in Clarksburgh, Virginia. She was married to A B Thorn, and died two weeks afterwards of scarlet fever, aged 21 years.

4 William O Davis, the fourth child and eldest son of John and Eliza A Steen Davis, was born in Clarksburgh, Virginia, and died when six years old

5 John J Davis, the fifth child and second son of John and Eliza A Steen Davis, was born in Clarksburgh Virginia where he still resides. He is a prominent attorney-at-law, and an elder in the Presbyterian Church. John J Davis was married, August 21, 1862, to Anna Kennedy a daughter of W W Kennedy, of Baltimore, Maryland. To them were born six children

   I —Miriam Davis, the eldest child, a daughter of John J and Anna Kennedy Davis, was born in Clarksburgh Virginia and died in infancy

   II —Catherine Estella Davis, the second daughter of John J and Anna Kennedy Davis was born in Clarksburgh, Virginia, and died when six years old

   III —Lillie Davis, the third daughter of John J and Anna Kennedy Davis was born in Clarksburgh Virginia. She was married to Hon John A Preston the son of a Scotch-Irish Presbyterian minister, and is himself an elder in the Presbyterian Church. Residence Lewisburgh Virginia

(28)

IV —Emma Davis, the fourth daughter of John J and Anna Kennedy Davis, was born in Clarksburgh, Virginia

V —Anna H Davis, the fifth daughter of John J and Anna Kennedy Davis, was born in Clarksburgh, Virginia

VI —John W Davis, the sixth child and only son of John J and Anna Kennedy Davis, was born in Clarksburgh, Virginia   He is an attorney-at-law, associated with his father in practice

6 R C Davis, the sixth child and third son of John and Eliza A Steen Davis, was born in Clarksburgh, Virginia   He is an attorney-at-law   Residence Louisville, Kentucky

7 Anna Davis, the seventh and youngest child of John and Eliza A Steen Davis, was born in Clarksburgh, Virginia   She was married to the Rev Robert H Blackford, a Presbyterian minister   Residence, Hastings, New York

III —Sarah Steen, the third daughter of James and Jane Small Steen, was born in Philadelphia, Pennsylvania, about 1802   She was married to John Hanway   To them was born one son

1 Col W A Hanway   Residence Baltimore Maryland

IV —Jane Steen, the fourth daughter of James and Jane Small Steen, was born in Philadelphia, Pennsylvania, about 1805, and died unmarried

V —Margaret Steen, the fifth daughter of James and Jane Small Steen, was born in Philadelphia, Pennsylvania, about 1807, and died unmarried

VI —John A Steen, the sixth child and only son of James and Jane Small Steen, was born in Philadelphia, Pennsylvania, about 1810   He was married in West Virginia, and removed to Ralls County Missouri, where they afterwards lived and died   He was the father of two children

1 Robert Steen a son of John A Steen and wife was born in Ralls County, Missouri   He was married in Ralls County, Missouri where he brought up a family

2 Matilda Steen a daughter of John A Steen and wife, was born in Ralls County, Missouri, where she was also married and brought up a family

CHAPTER III

———

Rose Steen, the third child and eldest daughter of James and Ann Scales Steen, was born in Ballybay, County Monaghan, Ireland. She removed to America about 1793. She was married near Philadelphia, Pennsylvania, to a Mr Ritchie and continued to live and died there. They had no children.

——— ———

CHAPTER IV

———

Edward Steen the third son, the fourth child of James and Ann Scales Steen, was born in Ballybay, County Monaghan, Ireland, where he lived and died. He was married in Ireland, and brought up a family. One of his sons came to America.

I—George A Steen a son of Edward Steen and his wife, was born in Ballybay, County Monaghan Ireland. He removed to America with his uncle, James Steen, about 1793. He became a Colonel in the United States Army, and died about 1865

BOOK THIRTEEN.

DESCENDANTS OF ROBERT M STEEN

Robert M. Steen was born in Londonderry, Ireland, November 16, 1810, and died at his home, near Sturges, Missouri, January 12, 1894, in the 84th year of his age He was brought to America by his father when a small child He went to sea when only about eight years of age. and spent his early life there He was married in Indiana, in 1836, to Jane Culbertson, and removed to Missouri, where he brought up a family of nine children

---

Robert Mae Steen was the son of a John Steen who was born and brought up in the North of Ireland, and removed with his family to America when his children were very young. and located in Kittanning, Armstrong County, Pennsylvania. where he continued to reside John Steen had one son at least, in addition to Robert M Steen, whose name was also John Steen He, too, resided in Kittanning, Pennsylvania, where it is supposed he brought up his family

Robert Mae Steen was born in Londonderry. Ireland, November 16, 1810, and died at his home. near Sturges Missouri January 12, 1894, in the 84th year of his age When just a small boy, about the year 1818, he ran away from home, and went to sea, where he spent his early life He never returned to his father's family in Pennsylvania, and had but little knowledge of them Robert M. Steen was married in Gibson County, Indiana, in 1836, to Jane Culbertson, a daughter of Andrew Culbertson, she having been born in Gibson County, Indiana, January 17, 1821 The Culbertsons were originally Scotch Covenanters, who took refuge in the North of Ireland from the persecutions of Claverhouse and others From Ireland they emigrated to America and settled in Pennsylvania They are now widely scattered, and live in many States This family is Scotch-Irish on both sides, and well connected In 1839 Robert M Steen and his wife removed to the West and located upon a farm in Rich Hill Township, Livingston County, Missouri, where they continued to reside, and where they brought up a family of nine children Mrs Jane Culbertson Steen was still living on this farm in 1900 The post-office address is Sturges, Missouri

I —John Andrew Steen, the eldest child, a son of Robert M. and Jane Culbertson Steen, was born in Rich Hill Township, Livingston County, Missouri June 18, 1840 He was named after both of his grandparents — John Steen and Andrew Culbertson In 1860, when he was twenty years of age, he removed to Texas, and the next year enlisted in the Confederate Army He served under General Bragg during the Civil War 1861 to 1865 He was badly wounded in battle at Richmond, Kentucky, and left on the field as dead, but afterwards he was picked up and carried to the hospital, where he was carefully treated by Dr D M Barkley, and finally recovered He was for many years a prominent attorney-at-law, and County Judge of Concho County Texas, until his death, October 5, 1899 He was widely known and an influential citizen Judge John A Steen was married in Denton County, Texas January 18, 1871, to Rebecca Frances Manning, she having been born in Springfield, Missouri, March 4, 1847 They were the parents of six children Family residence, Paint Rock Concho County, Texas

  1 Lewis Manning Steen, the eldest child, a son of Judge John A and Rebecca F. Steen, was born in Denton County, Texas, March 2, 1873

  2 Mary Jane Steen, called "Mamie," the second child and only daughter of Judge John A and Rebecca F Steen, was born in Denton County, Texas, April 19, 1874 She was married to a Mr Thornton about 1898 Residence, Paint Rock, Texas

3 Robert Lee Steen, the third child and second son of Judge
John A and Rebecca F Steen, was born in Denton County,
Texas, March 8, 1879

4 Benjamin Franklin Steen, the fourth child and third son of
Judge John A and Rebecca F Steen, was born in Tarrant
County Texas, January 8, 1881

5 Peter Smith Steen, the fifth child and fourth son of Judge
John A and Rebecca F Steen, was born in Tarrant County,
Texas, December 15 1883

6 Guy Eldon Steen, the sixth and youngest child, the fifth son
of Judge John A and Rebecca F Steen, was born in Paint
Rock, Concho County, Texas, May 31, 1887

II —Mary Ann Steen, the second child and eldest daughter of
Robert M and Jane Culbertson Steen, was born at the old
homestead, near Sturges, Livingston County, Missouri, July
2, 1842, where she still resides with her mother and brother

III —James Knox Polk Steen, the third child and second son
of Robert M and Jane Culbertson Steen, was born near Sturges, Livingston County, Missouri August 1, 1846 He is a
successful farmer, and well-known Baptist clergyman He is
unmarried and resides at the old homestead with his mother
and sister Residence, near Sturges, Missouri

IV —Robert Taylor Steen the fourth child and third son of
Robert M and Jane Culbertson Steen, was born near Sturges,
Livingston County, Missouri May 13, 1849 He is a farmer
by occupation, and has resided in Missouri, California, Indian
Territory, and Texas He was married in Cottonwood, Cal-
lahan County, Texas, August 5, 1877, to Rebecca Nancy Hay-
worth, she having been born in Birdville, Tarrant County,
Texas, December 15, 1855 To them have been born eight
children The family residence is near London, Kimble
County, Texas.

1 Sarah Frances Steen, the eldest child, a daughter of Robert
T and Rebecca N Steen, was born in Stephens County
Texas, November 25, 1878

2 Alice Jane Steen, the second daughter of Robert T and
Rebecca N Steen, was born in Stephens County, Texas,
April 4, 1880

3 Solomon Lee Steen, the third child and eldest son of Robert

REV. JAMES K. P. STEEN.

T and Rebecca N Steen, was born in Stephens County, Texas, May 27, 1881

4. John Henry Steen, the fourth child and second son of Robert T. and Rebecca N Steen, was born in Menard County, Texas, February 4, 1883

5 Keziah Mary Steen, the fifth child and third daughter of Robert T and Rebecca N Steen, was born in Menard County, Texas, September 23 1884

6 Martin Robert Steen the sixth child and third son of Robert T and Rebecca N Steen, was born in Menard County, Texas, August 7, 1886

7 Laura Nancy Steen, the seventh child and fourth daughter of Robert T. and Rebecca N. Steen, was born in Menard County, Texas, July 11, 1890

8 Paul Napoleon Steen, the eighth child and fourth son of Robert Taylor and Rebecca Nancy Steen, was born in Menard County, Texas, August 17, 1894

V —Letitia Frances Steen, the fifth child and second daughter of Robert M and Jane Culbertson Steen, was born near Sturges, Livingston County, Missouri November 9 1852 She was married in September, 1877 to Jacob M Crowe, he having been born in Illinois January 16, 1857 To them were born seven children Residence Chula, Livingston County, Missouri

1 Benjamin Dillon Crowe, the eldest child, a son of Jacob M and Letitia Frances Steen Crowe, was born September 20, 1878

2 James K Crowe, the second son of Jacob M and Letitia Frances Steen Crowe, was born September 2, 1879

3 Mary Jane Crowe the third child and eldest daughter of Jacob M and Letitia Frances Steen Crowe, was born December 5 1881

4 Sarah Cleavis Crowe, the fourth child and second daughter of Jacob M and Letitia Frances Steen Crowe, was born October 23, 1884

5 George Clarence Crowe the fifth child and third son of Jacob M and Letitia Frances Steen Crowe was born July 1, 1887

6 Spurgeon Crowe, the sixth child and fourth son of Jacob M and Letitia Frances Steen Crowe, was born June 26, 1890

7 Nancy Crowe, the seventh child and third daughter of Jacob M and Letitia Frances Steen Crowe, was born July 5 1893

VI—Sarah Jane Steen, the sixth child and third daughter of Robert M and Jane Culbertson Steen, was born near Sturges, Missouri, February 27, 1855 and died August 14, 1871, in the 17th year of her age

VII—William Alexander Steen the seventh child and fourth son of Robert M and Jane Culbertson Steen, was born near Sturges, Missouri April 20 1857, and died September 7, 1876, in the 20th year of his age.

VIII—George Washington Steen the eighth child and fifth son of Robert M and Jane Culbertson Steen, was born near Sturges, Missouri, May 22 1859 He is a farmer by occupation. He was married in Livingston County Missouri March 14, 1886, to Elizabeth Uhlmacher, she having been born in Hartford, Wisconsin July 7, 1861 To them were born three children Family residence, near Sturges, Missouri

  1 Fay Steen, the eldest child, a son of George W and Elizabeth U Steen, was born April 9, 1887

  2 Robert Nicholas Steen, the second son of George W and Elizabeth U Steen, was born March 21, 1889

  3 Neva Steen, the third child and only daughter of George Washington and Elizabeth Uhlmacher Steen, was born May 29, 1892

IX—Francis Marion Steen, the ninth and youngest child, the sixth son of Robert M and Jane Culbertson Steen, was born near Sturges Livingston County, Missouri, August 22, 1862 He is by occupation a farmer He was married in Chillicothe, Livingston County, Missouri, November 21, 1888, to Mary Elizabeth Anderson, she having been born in Livingston County, Missouri, September 6, 1868 To them have been born four children Family residence, near Chillicothe, Missouri

  1 Allen M Steen, the eldest child, a son of Francis M and Mary E Steen, was born near Chillicothe, Missouri, November 2, 1889

  2 Alta May Steen, the second child and only daughter of Francis M and Mary E Steen, was born near Chillicothe, Missouri, February 27 1891

3 James Earl Steen, the third child and second son of Francis M and Mary E Steen, was born near Chillicothe, Missouri, July 7, 1893

4 Lucian LeRoy Steen, the fourth child and third son of Francis Marion and Mary Elizabeth Steen was born near Chillicothe, Missouri, April 1 1895

BOOK FOURTEEN.

DESCENDANTS OF JAMES STEEN

James Steen was born in Antrim, County Antrim, Ireland, in 1714, where he spent a long and useful life He was married to a Miss Hoilinger, and brought up a large family He was thrown from his buggy by a runaway horse in 1796, from the effects of which he died, in the 82d year of his age

---

James Steen was born in Antrim, County Antrim, Ireland, in the Province of Ulster, in 1714, and there spent a long and useful life He had a brother who lived in the same locality whose name was Alexander Steen, an influential citizen See Book Fifteen

James Steen was married to a Miss Hollinger, and brought up a family of several children. He was thrown from a buggy by a runaway horse, from the effects of which he died, in 1796, in the 82d year of his age This branch of the Steen family came into Ireland with Oliver Cromwell, the Scotts, and Livingstons, non-Conformist Scotch ministers, who left Scotland in the days of persecution and settled first in Killinsky, in County Down, and afterwards located at Antrim in the county of the same name They were staunch Presbyterians, and descended from a Scotch Presbyterian minister, and continued to have representatives of the family in the ministry To James Steen and his wife were

(444)

born several children, one of whom was named Silas Steen, whose record is given below

---

CHAPTER I.

Silas Steen, a son of James and —— Hollinger Steen was born in Antrim, in the County of Antrim, and Province of Ulster, Ireland, in 1757, where he continued to reside until his death, in 1827, aged about 70 years. He was married to Agnes Scott about 1778, and brought up a family of five children.

I —Jane Steen, the eldest child, a daughter of Silas and Agnes Scott Steen, was born in Antrim, County Antrim, Ireland, in 1779. She was married to James McNealy, and brought up a family of ten children, as follows:

1 James McNealy

2. John McNealy.

3 Silas McNealy

4 George McNealy

5 Joseph McNealy

6 —— McNealy.

7 Nancy McNealy

8 Jane McNealy

9 Margaret McNealy

10 Anne McNealy, who married a Mr Bashford, by whom she had at least two children, as follows

I —Charles Bashford, who lived in Scotland and died there

II —John Bashford, who married Rebecca Hughes. To them were born five children, as follows

1 Margaret Bashford, who married a Mr Cooper, who died. She is now a widow, residing in New York State

2 Fannie Bashford, who married a Mr Stokes who died. She is now a widow, residing in Belfast, Ireland

3 Jane Bashford, who married a Mr Morton. To them

were born at least three children, as follows, all of whom are now dead:

    a James Morton

    b William Morton

    c Joseph Morton

    4 Rebecca Bashford, who is now a teacher in New York State

    5 Agnes Bashford, who now lives in Belfast Ireland

II —James Steen, the second child and eldest son of Silas and Agnes Scott Steen, was born in Antrim, Ireland, in 1781 He removed to America about 1810, to join an uncle by the name of Scott, who was then an Adjutant General in the British Army at Montreal Canada On the vessel in which he crossed the ocean was a family by the name of Campbell with whom he became intimately acquainted, and afterwards married a daughter of this family Her name was Sarah Campbell called "Sallie " After the death of his uncle he removed to Vicksburgh, Mississippi, and thence to Natchez, Mississippi, or vice versa We have no record of his children

III —Elizabeth Steen, the third child and second daughter of Silas and Agnes Scott Steen, was born in Antrim Ireland, in 1784 She was married to Job Foster, and died in 1840, aged about 56 years To Job and Elizabeth Steen Foster were born six children, as follows

    1 Anne Foster, who married a Mr Magee

    2 Robert Foster

    3 Sophia Foster

    4 Jane Eliza Foster

    5 Margaret Foster

    6 Joseph Foster

After the death of their mother, the younger children removed to England with their father

IV —Margaret Steen, the fourth child and third daughter of Silas and Agnes Scott Steen, was born in Antrim, County Antrim, Ireland, February 23, 1788 She was married by the Rev Mr Montgomery, of Antrim, Ireland, in June, 1816, to John Steen, a son of William and Mary Gill Steen, and a grandson of Alexander and Jane Stewart Steen Hence Margaret Steen and her husband were both descended by different lines from

the same great-grandfather Steen, and were second cousins
They continued to reside in Antrim, Ireland as long as they
lived Margaret Steen died December 9 1863, aged 75 years,
9 months and 18 days   John Steen was born in Antrim, Ireland, in February, 1787 and lived to a good old age   He was
a noted singer in his day, having been trained in voice culture
in England in his early years   He was precentor in a large
church in Antrim for more than forty years   He had many
tempting offers to go to other places, and sing in other churches
of different denominations, but nothing could tempt him away.
A writer, in speaking of him, says 'I only voice the senti-
ment of others when I say that I never heard such volume and
sweetness of voice combined   To John and Margaret Steen
were born nine children, and all brought up in the fear of the
Lord

1 Margaret Steen, the eldest child a daughter of John and
   Margaret Steen, was born in Antrim, Ireland, June 9, 1818,
   and died in Belfast, Ireland, February 5, 1853 She was
   never married

2 Anne Steen, the second daughter of John and Margaret
   Steen, was born in Antrim, County Antrim, and Province of
   Ulster, Ireland, January 20, 1820   She removed to America
   in 1857, resided for a time in San Francisco, and finally
   made her home with her sister at 767 Alice Street, Oakland,
   California   She died May 25, 1893, aged 73 years 4 months
   and 5 days   She was an amiable, devout, and useful Christian woman

3 Dorothea Steen, the third daughter of John and Margaret
   Steen, was born in Antrim, Ireland, December 21, 1821 and
   died in Belfast Ireland October 19, 1852, aged 30 years, 10
   months and 2 days

4 Eliza Steen, the fourth daughter of John and Margaret
   Steen, was born in Antrim County Antrim, in the Province
   of Ulster Ireland, June 22 1824, and died in Oakland, California, on Sabbath, December 10, 1899 in the full hope of a
   glorious resurrection   The funeral took place the following
   Wednesday and her body was tenderly laid away to rest
   in the cemetery. She was married by the Rev Mr Early
   in Antrim Ireland, August 24 1843 to John Johnson and
   the same year removed to America   They were devout
   Christians and useful citizens   Family residence 767 Alice

Street Oakland. California. They are the parents of the following four children:

I —John Steen Johnson, the eldest child. a son of John and Eliza Steen Johnson, was born in San Francisco, California, April 17, 1852 He was married, April 15, 1879, to Annie Neff Vanderslice. To them were born five children, as follows

  1 Milton Francis Johnson the eldest child and only son of John Steen and Annie Neff Johnson, was born June 27 1881

  2 Alice Jane Johnson, the second child and eldest daughter of John S and Annie N Johnson, was born October 15, 1883

  3 Elva May Johnson, the third child and second daughter of John S and Annie N. Johnson, was born May 28, 1885

  4 Gertrude Sherman Johnson, the fourth child and third daughter of John S and Annie N Johnson, was born July 31, 1887 and died March 8 1889, in the second year of her age

  5 Alma Vanderslice Johnson, the fifth child and fourth daughter of John S and Annie N Johnson, was born January 17, 1889

II —Thomas Alexander Johnson, the second son of John and Eliza Steen Johnson, was born in San Francisco, California. May 17, 1859, and died November 7 1859

III —Annie Margaret Johnson, the third child and eldest daughter of John and Eliza Steen Johnson, was born in San Francisco, California, July 23, 1862

IV —Alice Mary Johnson, the fourth child and second daughter of John and Eliza Steen Johnson, was born in Oakland California, September 19, 1864 She was married, June 5, 1890, to George B M Gray To them were born three children, as follows

  1 Harold Granville Gray was born May 5, 1894

  2 Everett Johnson Gray was born December 29 1895

  3 Gerald Harry Gray was born in Oakland. California May 26, 1899

5. Fannie Steen, the fifth daughter of John and Margaret Steen, was born in Antrim, Ireland, in September, 1825, and died the same month

6. Fannie Steen (or Frances), the second child of the same name (the former having died when but a few days old), and the sixth daughter of John and Margaret Steen, was born in Antrim, Ireland, August 23, 1826 She removed to America and was married in San Francisco, California, September 10, 1856, to Reuel Robinson, from Mt Vernon Maine To them were born three children Residence, South Seattle, Washington

   I.—Clara Eleanor Robinson, the eldest child, a daughter of Reuel and Frances (Fannie) Steen Robinson, was born June 29, 1859 She was married, May 22, 1884, to F. A. Detering Residence, South Seattle, Washington. To them were born the following children

     1 Clara Eleanor Detering was born in Seattle, Washington, May 8, 1886

     2 Reuel Frederick Detering was born in Seattle, Washington, April 10, 1892, and died June 16, 1892

   II.—Walter Steen Robinson, the second child and only son of Reuel and Frances Steen Robinson, was born June 20, 1861, and died June 10, 1862

   III—Frances Matilda Robinson, the third child and second daughter of Reuel and Frances Steen Robinson, was born April 9 1866 Residence, South Seattle, Washington

7 Matilda Steen, the seventh daughter of John and Margaret Steen, was born in Antrim, Ireland, June 13, 1830 She removed to America and was married in San Francisco California, by the Rev. William A Scott, D D , October 16, 1857, to Thomas Henderson. She died in Oakland, California, April 10, 1875 aged 44 years, 9 months and 28 days The family residence is at 767 Alice Street, Oakland, California To Thomas and Matilda Steen Henderson were born four children, as follows

   I—John Henry Henderson, the eldest son of Thomas and Matilda Steen Henderson, was born September 21, 1858 Residence, Oakland, California

   II—William Steen Henderson, the second son of Thomas

(29)

and Matilda Steen Henderson was born February 11, 1860, and died in February, 1866, aged 6 years

III —George Logan Henderson, the third son of Thomas and Matilda Steen Henderson, was born March 6, 1863. He was married, July 18, 1889, to Bessie Bostwick Graves Residence, Oakland, California To them were born five children, as follows

1. Herman Bryant Henderson, the eldest child of George L and Bessie B Henderson, was born August 31, 1890.

2. George Logan Henderson, the second child of George L and Bessie B Henderson, was born October 14, 1891.

3. Donald Williams Henderson, the third child of George L and Bessie B Henderson, was born March 17, 1894

4. Muriel Henderson, the fourth child of George L and Bessie B Henderson, was born October 31, 1895

5 Dorothy Steen Henderson, the fifth child of George L. and Bessie B Henderson, was born April 12, 1899

IV —Fannie Matilda Henderson, the fourth child and only daughter of Thomas and Matilda Steen Henderson was born March 24, 1866. She was married, March 29, 1900, to William Edgar Beck Residence, Oakland, California

8. William John Steen, the eighth child and only son of John and Margaret Steen, was born in Antrim, Ireland, February 1, 1832. He removed to America in 1848, and spent the remainder of his life in California He died, unmarried, at Calistoga Springs, California, June 13, 1860, aged 27 years, 8 months and 12 days

9 Eleanor Steen, the ninth child and eighth daughter of John and Margaret Steen, was born in Antrim, Ireland July 19, 1835, and died in Belfast, Ireland, December 11, 1897, aged 62 years, 4 months and 22 days She was married, June 12, 1865, to John Williamson, who died some years ago They resided in Belfast, Ireland, and never had any children

V —Ann Steen, the fifth child and fourth daughter of Silas and Agnes Scott Steen, was born in Antrim, Ireland, about 1790 She was married, about 1814, to William Johnston, and they lived in Belfast, Ireland To them were born seven children.

1 Jane Johnston, the eldest child, a daughter of William and Ann Steen Johnston, was born in Belfast, Ireland, about 1815. She was married to a Mr Stewart

2 Ann Johnston, the second daughter of William and Ann
Steen Johnston, was born in Belfast, Ireland, April 21, 1817,
and died November 8, 1889, in the 73d year of her age She
was married, October 1, 1841, to Robert Gilmore, he having
been born June 8, 1819, and died in July, 1896, aged 77 years.
They were the parents of nine children

   I —Susan Gilmore, the eldest child, a daughter of Robert
and Ann Johnston Gilmore, was born September 19, 1842
She was married, April 2, 1862, to John Frew. Residence,
Downpatrick, Ireland

   II —May Gilmore, the second daughter of Robert and Ann
Johnston Gilmore, was born February 27, 1844 She was
married, May 29, 1894, to John Iles, he having been born
July 8 1844, and died in 1900 in the 56th year of his age
Family residence, Blackpool, England

   III —Margaret Ann Gilmore, the third daughter of Robert
and Ann Johnston Gilmore, was born December 9, 1845
She was married, December 29, 1868, to William Cuddy
Residence, Ligoniel, County Down, Ireland

   IV —Joseph Gilmore, the fourth child and only son of Robert and Ann Johnston Gilmore, was born March 17, 1848,
and was married, in 1873, to Mary Elizabeth Barlow

   V —Eliza Gilmore, the fifth child and fourth daughter of
Robert and Ann Johnston Gilmore, was born May 26,
1850 She was married to Edward Bradshaw, he having
been born April 10, 1850 Residence, Blackpool England

   VI —Fannie Steen Gilmore, the sixth child and fifth daughter of Robert and Ann Johnston Gilmore, was born June
29, 1852. She was married to James Lingard, he having
been born May 26, 1848 Residence, Blackpool, England

   VII —Barbara Reba Gilmore was born July 30, 1857

   VIII —Leah Gilmore was born June 28, 1859

   IX —Louise Matilda Gilmore was born December 16, 1861.

3 Eliza Johnston, the third daughter of William and Ann
Steen Johnston, was born in Belfast, Ireland, in 1822 She
was married to a Mr James Rodgers, in 1842, and died in
June, 1858, aged 36 years. James Rodgers was born in

Dungannon, Ireland, was by occupation a mill manager, and died in Belfast, March 27, 1881   To James and Eliza Johnston Rodgers were born the following children

I—Mary Ann Rodgers was born in 1843

II.—William Rodgers was born in 1844

III—Johnston Rodgers was born in 1846, and died in 1889, aged 43 years

IV—James Rodgers was born in 1849, and married abroad

V—Robert Henry Rodgers was born in 1852, and died in 1868, aged 16 years

VI—John Rodgers was born in 1854, and died in 1887, aged 33 years.

VII—Elizabeth Rodgers was born in 1857

4 Margaret Johnston, the fourth daughter of William and Ann Steen Johnston, was born about 1823

5 William Johnston, the fifth child and elder son of William and Ann Steen Johnston, was born about 1825

6 John Johnston, the sixth child and second son of William and Ann Steen Johnston, was born about 1828

7 Susan Johnston, the seventh and youngest child, and the fifth daughter of William and Ann Steen Johnston, was born about 1830.

BOOK FIFTEEN.

DESCENDANTS OF ALEXANDER STEEN.

Alexander Steen was born in Antrim, County Antrim, and Province of Ulster, Ireland, in 1716, and spent his life there. He was married to Jane Stewart, and brought up a family of seven children, whose descendants are now very widely scattered. He was killed by a gunshot on the day of the battle of Antrim as he sat under an arbor in his own private garden, in June, 1798, in the 82d year of his age.

Alexander Steen was born in the city of Antrim, County of Antrim, and Province of Ulster, Ireland, in 1716, where he spent a long and useful life. He had a brother, James Steen, who lived in the same locality, and left a numerous but now very widely scattered posterity. Both James and Alexander Steen were staunch Presbyterian Christians, and their children were all brought up in that faith. For the descendants of James Steen in part see Book Fourteen.

Alexander Steen was married to Jane Stewart, and brought up a family of seven children. He died from the effects of a gunshot wound, which he received as he was quietly sitting under an arbor in his own private garden, on the day of the battle of

(453)

Antrim, in June, 1798, in company with his youngest son   He was eighty-two years old when he died.   It was never known whether the shot that caused his death was intentional or merely accidental   Alexander Steen had nothing whatever to do with the political troubles of the times, but his friends felt it to be unsafe to investigate the matter, lest they should share a similar fate   Alexander Steen was an influential and useful citizen, and spent his whole life in Antrim, Ireland   To himself and wife were born the following seven children   William, Frances, John, Jane, James, ————, and Mary Steen.

CHAPTER I.

William Steen, the eldest child, a son of Alexander and Jane Stewart Steen, was born in the city and County of Antrim, Ireland, in 1762, and died in 1825 aged 64 years   He was married, first, to Mary Gill, by whom he had six children   He was married a second time to Martha Johnson by whom he had three children, making nine in all   Hence he has left a numerous posterity now widely scattered throughout Europe, Australia and America

I —Mary Steen, the eldest child, a daughter of William and Mary Gill Steen, was born in the City and County of Antrim, Ireland, in 1784, and died in 1854, aged 70 years   She was married, about 1808, to James Magee, by whom she had the following nine children

1 William Magee, the eldest child, a son of James and Mary Steen Magee, was born about 1809, and died in 1849, during the epidemic in Belfast, aged about 40 years

2 James Magee, the second son of James and Mary Steen Magee, was born about 1811, and died in Antrim, Ireland, in 1881, aged about 70 years

3 John Magee, the third son of James and Mary Steen Magee, was born in Antrim Ireland, about 1813, and removed from the place in early life

4 Martha Magee, the fourth child and eldest daughter of James and Mary Steen Magee, was born about 1815 She was married to Thomas Johnson, but is now a widow Residence, Belfast, Ireland

5 Alexander Magee, the fifth child and fourth son of James and Mary Steen Magee, was born about 1817, and died in Belfast, Ireland, during the epidemic plague in 1849, aged about 31 years

6 Thomas Magee, the sixth child and fifth son of James and Mary Steen Magee, was born about 1819, and left Antrim many years ago

7 Mary Magee, the seventh child and second daughter of James and Mary Steen Magee, was born about 1821, and in early life removed from Antrim with her brothers, John and Thomas Magee

8 Jane Magee, the eighth child and third daughter of James and Mary Steen Magee, was born in 1822, and died of lung disease in 1846 aged 24 years

9 Margaret Magee, the ninth and youngest child, the fourth daughter of James and Mary Steen Magee, was born in Antrim, Ireland, in 1824, and died of lung disease in 1846, aged 22 years

II —John Steen, the second child and eldest son of William and Mary Gill Steen (a grandson of Alexander and Jane Stewart Steen), was born in Antrim, Ireland, in February, 1787 He was married in Antrim by the Rev Mr Montgomery, of that place, in June, 1816, to Margaret Steen (a daughter of Silas and Agnes Scott Steen, and a granddaughter of James and ——— Hollinger Steen), she having been born in Antrim, Ireland, February 23, 1788, and died December 9, 1863, aged 75 years, 9 months and 18 days John Steen and Margaret Steen, his wife, were second cousins both having descended by different lines from the same great-grandfather Steen, who was the son of a Scotch Presbyterian minister They spent a long, happy and useful life in Antrim, where they were universally respected John Steen was quite a noted singer in those days, having in early life received a thorough training in voice culture in England He was the precentor of a large church in Antrim for more than forty years He had many tempting offers to go and sing in other places, and in churches of different denominations, but nothing could entice him away

A voice of such richness, sweetness and volume combined, as he possessed, is very seldom found To John and Margaret Steen were born the following nine children, all brought up in the fear of the Lord·

1 Margaret Steen, the eldest child of John and Margaret Steen, was born in Antrim, Ireland, June 9, 1818, and died in Belfast, Ireland, February 5, 1853, aged 44 years, 4 months and 4 days She was never married

2 Anne Steen, the second daughter of John and Margaret Steen, was born in Antrim, Ireland, January 20, 1820. She removed to America in 1857, and made her home with her sister, at 767 Alice Street, Oakland, California, where she died May 25, 1893, aged 73 years, 4 months and 5 days. She was never married, and was an amiable, devout and useful Christian woman, a member of the Methodist Episcopal Church at the time of her death.

3 Dorothea Steen, the third daughter of John and Margaret Steen, was born in Antrim, Ireland, December 21, 1821, and died in Belfast, Ireland, October 19, 1852, aged 30 years, 10 months and 2 days. She was never married.

4 Eliza Steen, the fourth daughter of John and Margaret Steen, was born in Antrim Ireland, June 22, 1824, and died at the family residence, in Oakland, California, on the holy Sabbath, December 10, 1899, in the sure and certain hope of a glorious immortality. Her funeral took place on Wednesday, December 13, and her body was tenderly laid away to rest until the resurrection morning. She was married in Antrim, Ireland, by the Rev Mr Early, of that place, August 24, 1843, to John Johnson The same year of their marriage they removed to California, in the United States of America For some time they resided in San Francisco, and afterwards located at 767 Alice Street, Oakland, California, where the family still resides They are all faithful and devout Christians, active members of the Methodist Episcopal Church To John and Eliza Steen Johnson were born the following four children.

I—John Steen Johnson, the eldest son of John and Eliza Steen Johnson, was born in San Francisco, California, April 17, 1852 He was married, April 15, 1879, to Annie Neff Vandersliee Residence, Oakland, California To them were born five children, as follows·

1 Milton Francis Johnson was born June 27, 1881.

2 Alice Jane Johnson was born October 15, 1883

3 Elva May Johnson was born May 28, 1885

4. Gertrude Sherman Johnson was born July 31, 1887, and died March 8, 1889

5 Alma Vanderslice Johnson was born January 17, 1889.

II —Thomas Alexander Johnson, the second son of John and Eliza Steen Johnson, was born in San Francisco, California, May 17, 1859, and died November 7, 1859, aged 5 months and 21 days

III —Annie Margaret Johnson, the third child and eldest daughter of John and Eliza Steen Johnson, was born in San Francisco, California, July 23, 1862 — a teacher. Residence, Oakland, California.

IV —Alice Mary Johnson, the fourth child, the second and youngest daughter of John and Eliza Steen Johnson, was born in Oakland, California, September 19, 1864 She was married in Oakland, California, June 5, 1890, to George B. M Gray Residence, Oakland, California To them were born the following children.

   1 Harold Granville Gray was born in Oakland, California, May 5, 1894.

   2 Everett Johnson Gray was born in Oakland, California, December 29, 1895.

   3. Gerald Harry Gray was born in Oakland, California. May 26, 1899.

5 Fannie Steen (or Frances), the fifth daughter of John and Margaret Steen, was born and died in Antrim, Ireland, in September, 1825

6 Fannie Steen (or Frances), the second child of the same name (the former having died when only a few days old), and the sixth daughter of John and Margaret Steen, was born in Antrim, Ireland, August 23, 1826 She removed to America in early life, and lived in San Francisco, California, where she was married by the Rev William A Scott, D D, September 10, 1856, to Reuel Robinson, of Mt. Vernon, Maine. Residence, South Seattle, Washington To Reuel and Fannie Steen Robinson were born the following three children·

I —Clara Eleanor Robinson, the eldest child, a daughter of Reuel and Frances (Fannie) Steen Robinson, was born in Seattle Washington, June 29, 1859 She was married, May 22, 1884, to F A Detering Residence, South Seattle, Washington To F A and Clara E Detering were born the following children

   1 Clara Eleanor Detering was born in South Seattle, Washington, May 8, 1886

   2. Reuel Frederick Detering was born in South Seattle, Washington, April 10, 1892, and died June 16, 1892, aged 2 months and 6 days

II —Walter Steen Robinson, the second child and only son of Reuel and Frances (Fannie) Steen Robinson, was born in South Seattle, Washington, June 20, 1861, and died June 10, 1862, aged 1 year, lacking 10 days

III —Frances Matilda Robinson, the third child, and second daughter of Reuel and Frances Steen Robinson, was born in South Seattle, Washington, April 9, 1866. Residence, South Seattle, Washington

7 Matilda Steen, the seventh daughter of John and Margaret Steen, was born in Antrim, Ireland, June 13, 1830 She early removed to America, and resided in San Francisco, California, where she was married by the Rev William A Scott, D D, October 16, 1857, to Thomas Henderson, of Oakland, California She died at their home in Oakland, California, April 10, 1875, aged 44 years, 9 months and 28 days Family residence, Oakland, California To Thomas and Matilda Steen Henderson were born four children, as follows

I —John Henry Henderson, the eldest son of Thomas and Matilda Steen Henderson, was born in Oakland, California, September 21, 1858 Residence, Oakland, California.

II —William Steen Henderson the second son of Thomas and Matilda Steen Henderson, was born in Oakland, California, February 11, 1860, and died in February, 1866, aged 6 years

III —George Logan Henderson, the third son of Thomas and Matilda Steen Henderson, was born in Oakland, California, March 6, 1863 He was married, July 18, 1889 to

Bessie Bostwick Graves. Residence, Oakland, California
To them were born five children, as follows

1 Henry Bryant Henderson was born in Oakland, California, August 31, 1890
2 George Logan Henderson was born October 14, 1891
3 Donald William Henderson was born March 17, 1894.
4 Muriel Henderson was born October 31, 1895.
5 Dorothy Steen Henderson was born April 12, 1899

IV.—Frances Matilda Henderson, the fourth child and only daughter of Thomas and Matilda Steen Henderson, was born in Oakland, California, March 24, 1866 She was married, March 29, 1900, to William Edgar Beck Residence, Oakland, California

8. William John Steen, the eighth child and only son of John and Margaret Steen, was born in Antrim, Ireland, February 1, 1832. He removed to America in 1848, and lived in San Francisco, California, for some time He died, unmarried, at Calistoga Springs, Napa County, California, June 13, 1860, aged 27 years, 8 months and 12 days

9 Eleanor Steen, the ninth child and eighth daughter of John and Margaret Steen, was born in Antrim, Ireland, July 19, 1835, and died in Belfast, Ireland, December 11, 1897, aged 62 years, 4 months and 22 days She was married, June 12, 1865, to John Williamson, who died several years ago They resided in Belfast, Ireland, but never had any children

III —Dorothea Steen, the third child and second daughter of William and Mary Gill Steen, was born in Antrim, Ireland, about 1789 She was married to Robert Adams. In 1823 Robert and Dorothea Steen Adams removed to the United States of America When they had reached this country with their family, and were landing at their destination, Mrs Dorothea Steen Adams, with a little babe in her arms, fell from the gangplank into the sea and was drowned, but the child was rescued To Robert and Dorothea Steen Adams were born the following six children

I —Robert Adams
II —John Adams
III —William Adams
IV —Samuel Adams.

V —Margaret Adams

VI —Eliza Adams, who married a Mr Harris, and resided with her family in Mobile, Alabama

IV —Margaret Steen, the fourth child and third daughter of William and Mary Gill Steen, was born in Antrim. Ireland, about 1792 She was married to Alexander Riddell, about 1818, and died in 1876, aged about 82 years To Alexander and Margaret Steen Riddell were born the following four children

I.—Robert Riddell

II —Sarah Riddell, who married a Mr. Miller

III —George Riddell.

IV —Mary Riddell, who married a Mr Williamson, and lived in Belfast, Ireland She is now a widow

V —Alexander Steen, the fifth child and second son of William and Mary Gill Steen, was born in Antrim, Ireland, about 1794. He was married to Eliza Johnson, a niece of Martha Johnson, who had become his father's second wife. To Alexander and Eliza Johnson Steen were born the following children

1 James Steen, the eldest son of Alexander and Eliza Johnson Steen, was born in Antrim, Ireland, about 1826, and lived and died in that locality.

2 John Steen, the second son of Alexander and Eliza Johnson Steen, was born in Antrim, Ireland, about 1829. He was married and removed to Wolverhampton, England, where he carried on the book and stationery trade, and where he died He was the father of four children, two sons and two daughters, as follows.

I —Alfred Steen, the eldest son of John Steen, and a grandson of Alexander and Eliza Johnson Steen, died at the home of Mrs Martha Steen Blair, his grandfather's sister, and his body was buried in the Antrim cemetery

II —John Dunbar Steen, the second son of John Steen, and a grandson of Alexander and Eliza Johnson Steen, was born in Antrim, Ireland. He was married by the Rev J R Stratton, at Stevens, Kirkstall, England. about 1893, to Maud Crowe, the third daughter of George Francis Crowe, of Kirkstall, Leeds. England John D Steen is engaged in the book and stationery trade at Wolverhampton, England.

III.—Lucy Elizabeth Steen, called "Lily," was born in Antrim, Ireland   Residence, Wolverhampton, England.

IV—Kate Annie Ellen Steen, called "Kittie," a daughter of John Steen, and a sister of John D Steen, was born in Antrim, Ireland, and resides with her brother, at Wolverhampton, England

3 Mary Steen, the third child and eldest daughter of Alexander and Eliza Johnson Steen, was born in Antrim, Ireland, about 1831   After the death of her father she removed with her mother and her two youngest children, to Queensland, Australia

4 William Steen, the fourth child and third son of Alexander and Eliza Johnson Steen was born in Antrim, Ireland, about 1833   After his father's death he removed with his mother and his sisters, Mary and Margaret to Queensland, Australia   He afterwards located in New Zealand

5 Margaret Steen, the fifth child and second daughter of Alexander and Eliza Johnson Steen, was born in Antrim, Ireland, about 1835   After the death of her father she removed with her mother, her brother William, and sister Mary to Queensland, Australia

VI —Thomasina Steen, the sixth child and fourth daughter of William and Mary Gill Steen, was born in Antrim Ireland, about 1796   She was married to a Mr. Young, and died in 1876, aged about 80 years

VII —William Steen, the seventh child and third son of William Steen, but his eldest child by his second wife, Martha Johnson Steen, was born in Antrim, Ireland about 1809 and died in 1874, aged about 65 years

VIII —Anne Steen, the eighth child of William Steen, the second child and eldest daughter by his second wife, Martha Johnson Steen, was born in Antrim, Ireland, about 1813   She was married to a Mr. Shannon, and died in 1887, aged 74 years

IX —Martha Steen, the ninth child and sixth daughter of William Steen, but the third child and second daughter by his second wife, Martha Johnson Steen, was born in Antrim, Ireland, about 1815   She was married to a Mr Blair, and died in 1889, aged about 74 years   She was the mother of the following children·

- 1 Anne Blair was born in Antrim, Ireland   She was married
to a Mr Anderson   She is now a widow, with one daughter
- 2 William Blair was born in Antrim, Ireland   He now carries on his father's business as a cabinet-maker, and superin-
tends a farm left by his uncle William.
- 3 Hester Blair was born in Antrim, Ireland, and now resides
with her brother there

CHAPTER II

Frances Steen, called "Fannie," the second child, the eldest
daughter of Alexander and Jane Stewart Steen, was born in
Antrim, Ireland, about 1765   She was married to Robert Craig,
and brought up a family of four children, as follows

I —Margaret Craig, who married Joseph McLariman, and
brought up a family of children   Their daughter, Ann McLariman, died in 1893, very old   At that time two others of their
children were still living

II —Sarah Craig, the second daughter of Robert and Frances
Steen Craig, who married James Murdock and brought up a
family of children

III —Samuel Craig, the third child and eldest son of Robert and
Frances Steen Craig, was born in 1794   He was married and
brought up a large family of children, who are now widely
scattered   He has one daughter living in Glasgow, Scotland
Samuel Craig died in November, 1890, aged 96 years   He was
quite strong and active until after he was 90 years old

IV —John Craig, the fourth and youngest child of Robert and
Frances Steen Craig, died many years ago

CHAPTER III

John Steen, the third child and second son of Alexander and Jane Stewart Steen, was born in Antrim, Ireland, about 1768 He was married and had two daughters, brought up in England, as follows.

I —Jane Steen, the eldest daughter of John Steen, and a grand-daughter of Alexander and Jane Stewart Steen, was married to a Mr Fogg, but left no children.

II —Fannie Steen, the second daughter of John Steen, died unmarried

CHAPTER IV.

Jane Steen, the fourth child and second daughter of Alexander and Jane Stewart Steen was born in Antrim, Ireland, about 1770 She was married to Robert Alexander, principal of the Male Department of the Lancastrian School in Antrim She was principal of the Girls' Department in the same institution, which position she held until her death, in 1810, when she was about forty years of age To Robert and Jane Steen Alexander were born the following six children

I —John Alexander was born in Antrim, Ireland, about 1792, and afterwards held his father's position as principal of the Lancastrian School He married a Miss Forbes, of Antrim, and removed to England, where he received a lucrative position in the British Excise

II —James Alexander, the second son of Robert and Jane Steen Alexander, was born in Antrim, about 1795 He removed to the United States of America in 1827 or 1828, and probably settled in Baltimore, Maryland

III —Hannah Alexander, the third child and elder daughter of
Robert and Jane Steen Alexander, was born in Antrim, Ireland, about 1797   She was never married, and made her home
with her brother John

IV —Robert Alexander, the fourth child and third son of Robert
and Jane Steen Alexander, was born in Antrim, Ireland, about
the year 1800   He removed to the United States of America
with his brother James, in 1827 or 1828   He located in Baltimore, Maryland, where the two brothers kept a shoe store.
He was married in Baltimore, but died soon afterwards

V —William Alexander, the fifth child and fourth son of Robert
and Jane Steen Alexander, was born in Antrim, Ireland, about
1803   He joined the British Army, and died young

VI —Jane Alexander, the sixth child, the second and younger
daughter of Robert and Jane Steen Alexander, was born in
Antrim, Ireland, about 1805   She was never married, and
always made her home with her eldest brother John

CHAPTER V

James Steen, the fifth child and third son of Alexander and
Jane Stewart Steen, was born in Antrim, Ireland, in 1773, and
died about 1854, in the 81st year of his age   He was married,
and brought up a family of children   He was ordained as a minister of the Gospel rather late in life   He was the assistant pastor,
perhaps for fifteen years, of an Independent Congregation at
Donaghmore, under the Rev Mr Hanson   He was an earnest
Christian, and held in high esteem by those who knew him   The
Rev James Steen was the father of the following four children:

I —Alexander Steen—

II —James Steen—

III —Thomas Steen—

who removed to the United States of America between the
years 1830 and 1832   Alexander Steen and James Steen both
died comparatively young, but Thomas Steen lived to be

advanced in life, and for many years kept "The Planters' Hotel" in New Orleans, Louisiana

IV —John Steen, the fourth and youngest son of the Rev James Steen, was born in Antrim, Ireland, where he continued to reside.

CHAPTER VI.

—— Steen, a son of Alexander and Jane Stewart Steen, was born in Antrim, Ireland, about 1775 He was married, and brought up a family Among his children there was one whose name was James, and he was generally known as "James Steen of Clady " He owned a "Bleaching Green" at Clady, which was only a few miles from Antrim To this James Steen of Clady, who was a grandson of Alexander and Jane Stewart Steen, the following seven children were born

I —John Steen

II —James Steen.

III —Henry Steen

IV —William Steen.

V —Alexander Steen, who succeeded his father in the bleaching business for a time, but afterwards went into the grain trade He spent his whole life on his father's old place at Clady, where he died He was a large man, over six feet high, very handsome, genial, warm-hearted and "every inch a Steen " He was married and had four children, as follows.

  1 Eleanor Steen, who was married to Walter Campbell, of Belfast, Ireland

  2 Elizabeth Steen, who died young

  3 Mary Steen, who died in youth

  4 Margaret Steen

VI —Elizabeth Steen, a daughter of "James Steen of Clady," was married to a Mr Hunter, who at that time kept a wholesale and retail dry goods store

  (30)

VII.—Mary Steen, another daughter of "James Steen of Clady," was married to a Mr Boyd. They had no children.

CHAPTER VII

Mary Steen, the seventh child of Alexander and Jane Stewart Steen, was born in Antrim, County Antrim, Ireland, probably about 1780   She was married to Thomas Wright.   They had no children

---

CHAPTER VIII

Jane Steen, another daughter of Alexander Steen was born in Antrim, Ireland   She was married to John Bruce, by whom she had two children, as follows

I —John Bruce, the eldest son of John and Jane Steen Bruce, was born in Antrim, County of Antrim, Ireland   He was married to a Miss Hanna   To John and —— Hanna Bruce were born three sons and one daughter, who left Antrim before 1820   John Bruce, the eldest son of John and Jane Steen Bruce, was married a second time to Mary Martin by whom he had four children, all born in Antrim, and all of them remarkably handsome

5 Alexander Bruce was born in 1781, and was never married

6 Sarah Bruce was born about 1805   She was married to William Leetch, who was proprietor of the "Antrim Arms Hotel " She died in 1890, aged about 85 years

7 Mary Bruce was born in 1808; was never married   She lived in Antrim, and died in May, 1892, aged 84 years

8. Matilda Bruce was born in 1810, and was never married She died about 1884, aged 74 years.

II.—Fannie Bruce, the second child of John and Jane Steen Bruce. was born in Antrim, Ireland. She was married to Thomas Johnson, who owned a paper mill at Bogshead, near Antrim   To them were born the following five children:

1 Esther Johnson, who was married

2 Jane Johnson, who married a Mr. Brown, and had three daughters, all dead.

3 John Johnson, who married a Miss Charters and died rather young leaving one daughter.

4 James Johnson, who married a Miss Johnson and died early in life.

5 Thomas Johnson, who married Martha Magee, a daughter of James and Mary Steen Magee. He is now dead. but his wife resides in Belfast, Ireland, with a son, Thomas Johnson, and a granddaughter

BOOK SIXTEEN

DESCENDANTS OF DAVID STEEN.

David Steen was born in County Londonderry, Ireland, and twice married. Some of his descendants came to America, and resided in New York, Pennsylvania, and Ohio.

David Steen was born in the County of Londonderry, Ireland, and lived at Terrydromont. His father was probably the James Steen who lived in Ireland, and whose second wife was named McGeorge, so that there were two sets of children. David Steen was married and brought up his family in Ireland, consisting of nine children, some of whom emigrated to the United States of America, but he spent his whole life in Ireland, and died there, it is said, at the age of 103 years.

CHAPTER I

I.—James Steen, the eldest son of David Steen, was born about 1800. Lived and died in Ireland.

II.—Martha Steen, the second child and eldest daughter of David Steen, was born in the County of Londonderry, Ireland, about

1803. She emigrated with her brother to America, and resided first in the State of New York, in Livingston County, and afterwards came with her brother into Pennsylvania   .

III.—Ellen Steen, the third child and second daughter of David Steen, was born in the County of Londonderry, Ireland, about 1805 She emigrated to America with her brother William and two of her sisters

IV.—Margaret Steen, the fourth child and third daughter of David Steen, was born in the County of Londonderry, Ireland, about 1807, and spent her whole life there

V.—Mary Ann Steen, the fifth child and fourth daughter of David Steen, was born in the County of Londonderry, Ireland, about 1809 She emigrated to America with her brother William and her two sisters, Martha and Ellen Steen, and all first lived in Livingston County, New York, and afterwards in Butler County, Pennsylvania

VI.—Jane Steen, the sixth child and fifth daughter of David Steen, was born in the County of Londonderry, Ireland, about 1811, where she lived and died

VII.—Eliza Steen, the seventh child and sixth daughter of David Steen, was born in the County of Londonderry, Ireland, about 1814, and spent her whole life there.

VIII.—William Wilson Steen, the eighth child and second son of David Steen, was born in the County of Londonderry, Ireland, in March, 1816, and died at Conoquenessing, Butler County, Pennsylvania, May 26, 1886, in the 71st year of his age In his early life William W Steen removed from Ireland and came into the United States of America, bringing with him three of his sisters, Martha, Ellen, and Mary Ann, and located first in Livingston County, New York They afterwards removed to Conoquenessing, Butler County, Pennsylvania, where they all continued until death William W Steen was married in York Center, Livingston County, New York, June 23, 1840, to Jane Conley, she having been born in the County of Londonderry, Ireland, April 26, 1822 To them were born the following twelve children·

  1 David C Steen, the eldest son of William W and Jane Conley Steen, was born at York Center, Livingston County, New York, May 6, 1841 In the American Civil War he

enlisted in the army, and was killed in battle at Weldon, Virginia, August 19. 1864, in the 24th year of his age.

2   Daniel Steen, the second son of William W and Jane Conley Steen, was born in Pittsburgh, Allegheny County, Pennsylvania, August 28, 1842, and is by occupation a farmer. He was married at Waterford, Erie County, Pennsylvania, January 7. 1869, to Elizabeth M. King, she having been born at Waterford, Pennsylvania, November 22, 1858.   Residence, Waterford, Erie County, Pennsylvania   To them were born the following five children, all born near Waterford, Pennsylvania.

I.—William King Steen, the eldest child of Daniel and Elizabeth M Steen, was born May 1, 1871.   Residence, Waterford, Pennsylvania

II —Inez Jane Steen, the second child and eldest daughter of Daniel and Elizabeth M. Steen, was born November 28, 1872, and died April 27, 1879, aged 6 years, 4 months and 29 days.

III —James McConnell Steen, the third child and second son of Daniel and Elizabeth M Steen, was born February 5, 1874, and died May 4, 1879, aged 5 years, 2 months and 29 days

IV.—Iona Laverne Steen, the fourth child and second daughter of Daniel and Elizabeth M Steen, was born May 8. 1876   Residence, Waterford, Pennsylvania.

V —Reid Wilson Steen, the fifth and youngest child, and the third son of Daniel and Elizabeth M Steen, was born December 8, 1878.   Residence, Waterford, Pennsylvania.

3. Ellen Elizabeth Steen, the third child and eldest daughter of William W and Jane Conley Steen, was born at Conoquenessing, Butler County, Pennsylvania, October 14, 1844. She was married at the same place, June 30, 1870, to Hiram Graham.   To them were born the following ten children.

I —Jennie Theressa Graham, the eldest child of Hiram and Ellen E. Steen Graham, was born May 1, 1871

II.—Lizzie Idonia Graham, the second daughter of Hiram and Ellen E Steen Graham, was born October 11, 1872.

III —William Alexander Graham, the third child and eldest son of Hiram and Ellen E Steen Graham. was born June 18, 1874

IV —Laura Fantasia Graham, the fourth child and third daughter of Hiram and Ellen E. Steen Graham, was born March 16, 1876

V.—Hiram McKee Graham, the fifth child and second son of Hiram and Ellen E. Steen Graham, was born October 18, 1878

VI —Harriet Vestina Graham, the sixth child and fourth daughter of Hiram and Ellen E Steen Graham, was born June 17, 1880

VII —Margaret Ellen Graham, the seventh child and fifth daughter of Hiram and Ellen E Steen Graham, was born May 9, 1882

VIII —Raney Graham, the eighth child and third son of Hiram and Ellen E. Steen Graham, was born November 8, 1884, and died June 8, 1886, aged 1 year and 7 months.

IX —Sidney Bertha Graham, the ninth child and sixth daughter of Hiram and Ellen E Steen Graham, was born December 6, 1887

X —John Steen Graham, the tenth child and fourth son of Hiram and Ellen E Steen Graham, was born June 24, 1890

4. Nancy Steen, the fourth child and second daughter of William W and Jane Conley Steen, was born at Conoquenessing. Butler County, Pennsylvania, December 21, 1846. She was married at the same place, January 22, 1872, to Jacob Cleffer Brandon To them were born the following ten children. Residence, Grove City, Mercer County, Pennsylvania

I —Dora Estella Brandon, the eldest child of Jacob C. and Nancy Steen Brandon, was born December 28, 1872, and died December 24, 1878, aged 5 years, 11 months and 26 days

II.—William John Brandon, the second child and eldest son of Jacob C. and Nancy Steen Brandon, was born March 3, 1874

III.—Jennie Elmina Brandon, the third child and second daughter of Jacob C and Nancy Steen Brandon, was born October 28, 1876.

IV —Cameron Galbreath Brandon, the fourth child and second son of Jacob C. and Nancy Steen Brandon, was born April 27, 1878.

V —Raymond Arthur Brandon, the fifth child and third son of Jacob C and Nancy Steen Brandon, was born July 19, 1881, and died July 18, 1882, aged 1 year, lacking one day.

VI —Tina Lovetta Brandon, the sixth child and third daughter of Jacob C and Nancy Steen Brandon, was born February 25, 1883 and died January 10, 1884, aged 10 months and 15 days

VII —Ethel Claire Brandon, the seventh child and fourth daughter of Jacob C and Nancy Steen Brandon, was born November 6, 1884

VIII —Ora Dight Brandon, the eighth child and fifth daughter of Jacob C and Nancy Steen Brandon, was born October 13, 1886.

IX —Maggie Marie Brandon, the ninth child and sixth daughter of Jacob C and Nancy Steen Brandon, was born August 21, 1888, and died July 22, 1889, aged 11 months and 1 day

X —Loyal Jamison Brandon, the tenth child and fourth son of Jacob C and Nancy Steen Brandon, was born September 16, 1890.

5   Martha Steen, the fifth child and third daughter of William W. and Jane Conley Steen, was born at Conoquenessing, Butler County. Pennsylvania, September 2, 1849   She was married at the same place, October 2, 1877, to John M. Rose. To them were born five children, as follows   Residence, Conoquenessing, Butler County, Pennsylvania

I.—Levi M Rose, the eldest child of John M and Martha Steen Rose, was born December 2, 1878

II —William W Rose, the second son of John M. and Martha Steen Rose, was born May 3, 1880

III —David Irwin Rose, the third son of John M and Martha Steen Rose, was born October 31, 1881

IV —Nora Violetta Rose, the fourth child and only daughter of John M. and Martha Steen Rose. was born November 22, 1884

V.—Samuel Hall Rose, the fifth child and fourth son of John M. and Martha Steen Rose, was born September 30, 1886

6 Mary Steen, the sixth child and fourth daughter of William W and Jane Conley Steen, was born at Conoquenessing, Butler County, Pennsylvania, September 26, 1850, and died February 25, 1857, aged 6 years, 4 months and 29 days.

7 Harriet Steen, the seventh child and fifth daughter of William W and Jane Conley Steen, was born at Conoquenessing, Pennsylvania, January 26, 1854, and died February 23, 1863, aged 9 years and 27 days

8 Mary Jane Steen, the eighth child and sixth daughter of William W and Jane Conley Steen, was born at Conoquenessing, Pennsylvania, May 3, 1856.

9 Sarah A Steen, the ninth child and seventh daughter of William W and Jane Conley Steen, was born at Conoquenessing, Pennsylvania, May 11, 1858, and died February 21, 1863, aged 4 years, 9 months and 10 days

10 William J Steen, the tenth child and third son of William W and Jane Conley Steen, was born in Conoquenessing, Pennsylvania, May 28, 1860, and died February 21, 1863, aged 2 years, 8 months and 24 days

11 James Henderson Steen, the eleventh child and fourth son of William and Jane Conley Steen, was born at Conoquenessing, Pennsylvania, March 8, 1863. He was married October 30, 1888, to Emma Lissa Roder, who died March 26, 1892 To them was born one child, as follows. Residence, Conoquenessing, Pennsylvania

   I—Willa May Steen, the only child of James H and Emma Lissa Steen, was born at Conoquenessing, Pennsylvania, March 11, 1892

12 Samuel R Steen, the twelfth child and fifth son of William Wilson and Jane Conley Steen, was born at Conoquenessing, Butler County, Pennsylvania, April 25, 1865, and died September 5, 1890, aged 25 years, 4 months and 20 days He was married, February 8, 1888, to Milla Nora Graham. To them were born the following two children

   I—Orrie Henderson Steen, the eldest son of Samuel R and Milla Nora Steen, was born February 15, 1889

II —Norman Edmund Steen, the second son of Samuel R. and Milla Nora Steen, was born August 1, 1890, and died August 21, 1890, aged 20 days.

IX —John Steen, the ninth child and third son of David Steen of Terrydromont, County Londonderry, Ireland, was born in County Londonderry, Ireland, about 1818. He was married and brought up a large family in Ireland

---

CHAPTER II.

David Steen, another of the same name, was born in the North of Ireland, and spent the whole of his long life there   He had a brother whose name was John Steen, who emigrated to America and lived near Bucyrus, Ohio — a prosperous farmer. He was married and brought up his family near Bucyrus, Crawford County, Ohio   This John Steen used to visit his nephew, Charles A Steen, after the latter's marriage, at Berlin Heights, Erie County, Ohio   After the death of John Steen, at Bucyrus, Ohio, in 1858, the families neglected to keep up their acquaintance, and no record of the descendants of this John Steen has been received

David Steen was married in Ireland, about 1795, to Mary Elizabeth Armstrong, called "Betsy," and to them were born at least two children, as follows·

I —Charles Armstrong Steen, a son of David and Mary Elizabeth Steen, was born in the city of Armagh, County of Armagh, Ireland, December 25, 1797, and removed to the United States of America about 1831   He died at Berlin Heights, Erie County, Ohio, January 12, 1858, in the 61st year of his age. He was married at Berlin Heights, Erie County, Ohio, in 1842, to Mrs Lorenda Stevens Sexton, a widow, she having been born in Lima, New York, December 26, 1809, and died at Berlin Heights, Erie County, Ohio, February 19, 1889, in the 80th year of her age   To them were born four children, as follows.

ɪ Eliza Jane Steen, the eldest child, a daughter of Charles Armstrong and Lorenda Stevens Sexton Steen, was born at Berlin Heights, Erie County, Ohio, January 31, 1843   She was married at the same place, January 8, 1866, to Benjamin Emmett Deeeley, he having been born in Sandusky, Erie County, Ohio, August 31, 1841   Residence, Sandusky, Ohio.   To them were born four children, as follows:

> *I.*—Mary Josephine Deeley, the eldest child, a daughter of Benjamin E. and Eliza J. Steen Deeley, was born in Sandusky, Ohio, November 9, 1868.

> *II*—Sarah Elizabeth Deeley, the second daughter of Benjamin E and Eliza J. Steen Deeley, was born in Sandusky, Ohio, August 28, 1871.

> *III.*—Stanton Emmett Deeley, the third child and only son of Benjamin E. and Eliza J. Steen Deeley, was born in Sandusky, Ohio, October 19, 1873.

> *IV.*—Annie Laurie Deeley, the fourth child and third daughter of Benjamin Emmett and Eliza Jane Steen Deeley, was born in Sandusky, Ohio, January 27, 1878.

2 David Orlando Steen, the second child and eldest son of Charles A and Lorenda S. S Steen, was born at Berlin Heights, Erie County, Ohio, March 9, 1845. He was married in Ohio. September 10, 1868, to Julia Ann Weinare, she having been born in Ohio August 20, 1846. For five years after their marriage they continued to live in Ohio, but removed to the West in 1873   They have since then lived in Nebraska and Iowa   To them were born six children, as follows. Residence, Oskaloosa, Iowa

> *I*—Herbert Orlando Steen, the eldest son of David O and Julia A. Steen, was born in Erie County, Ohio, July 20, 1870

> *II*—William Henry Steen, the second son of David O. and Julia A Steen, was born in Erie County, Ohio, March 15, 1872.

> *III*—Charles Frederick Steen, the third son of David O and Julia A Steen, was born May 10, 1875

> *IV*—Sarah Lorenda Steen, the fourth child and eldest daughter of David O. and Julia A. Steen, was born September 28, 1878.

V —Robert Alden Steen, the fifth child and fourth son of David O and Julia A Steen, was born July 12, 1887.

VI —Hattie Eleanor Steen, the sixth child and second daughter of David Orlando and Julia Ann Steen, was born September 24, 1889

3 Mary Olmstead Steen, the third child and second daughter of Charles A and Lorenda S. S Steen, was born at Berlin Heights, Erie County, Ohio, May 20, 1849 She was married at the same place, January 25, 1870, to George Fitch Hill, a son of Dr Benjamin Lord and Joanna Greer Hill, he having been born at Birmingham, Erie County, Ohio, May 3, 1847. Residence, Berlin Heights, Ohio To them were born four children, as follows.

I.—Maora Belle Hill, the eldest daughter of George F. and Mary O. Steen Hill, was born at Berlin Heights, Ohio, April 22, 1871

II.—Inez Aletha Hill, the second daughter of George F and Mary O. Steen Hill, was born at Berlin Heights, Ohio, September 5, 1877.

III —Lysle Steen Hill, the third child and eldest son of George F. and Mary O Steen Hill, was born at Berlin Heights, Ohio, March 19, 1881.

IV —Harvey Coit Hill, the fourth child and second son of George Fitch and Mary Olmstead Steen Hill, was born at Berlin Heights, Ohio, June 4, 1885

4. Charles Fabine Steen, the fourth child. the second and youngest son of Charles Armstrong and Lorenda Stevens Sexton Steen, was born at Perkins, Erie County, Ohio, May 17, 1857. He was married, March 3, 1875, to Sarah L Modine, she having been born in Erie County, Ohio, November 13, 1850 To them were born four children, as follows Residence, Sandusky, Ohio.

I —Harry M Steen, the eldest son of Charles F and Sarah L. Steen, was born in Sandusky, Ohio, May 6, 1876, and died March 26, 1884, aged 7 years, 10 months and 20 days

II —Ada L Steen, the second child and eldest daughter of Charles F and Sarah L Steen, was born in Sandusky, Ohio, February 3, 1880

III —Alpha H. Steen, the third child and second daughter of Charles F. and Sarah L. Steen, a twin sister of the above, was born in Sandusky, Ohio, February 3, 1880

IV.—Rollin Egbert Steen, the fourth child and second son of Charles Fabine and Sarah L. Steen, was born in Sandusky, Ohio, April 15, 1895

II —Barbara Steen, a daughter of David and Mary Elizabeth Armstrong Steen, and a sister of Charles Armstrong Steen, was born and brought up in Ireland She was married there, and is said to have died on her wedding day

BOOK SEVENTEEN.

The Coat of Arms of the Steens of Holland is—"A Shield of Gold, with an eight-pointed, red (vermilion) star, surmounted by a rose of the same color."

DESCENDANTS OF JAMES STEEN.

James Steen was born in Malpos, England, May 19, 1761, was married to Elizabeth Wood, in Chester, England, in December, 1785, removed to America in 1795, and located in Brattleboro, Vermont, where he resided with his family for twenty-three years In 1818 he removed to Richland, New York, where he died in 1826

James Steen was born in Malpos, Cheshire County, England, six miles from the city of Chester, May 19. 1761 and died in Richland, New York, February 19, 1826, in the 65th year of his age   He was a land owner in England, and a house builder by trade   Owing to the political troubles in 1793, high taxes, and the press gang going about the country enlisting men for the army and navy, peaceably if they could, but forcibly if they must, he sold his property in England for what he could get and removed to America in 1795. His great-grandfather removed from Holland into the North of England about the year 1700, where he spent the remainder of his life and brought up his family there

James Steen was married in Chester, England, in December, 1785, to Miss Elizabeth Wood, she having been born in that city January 7, 1759, and died in Brattleboro, Vermont, in March

(478)

1813, in the 55th year of her age. On leaving England, a Mr.
Nelson, of London, heartily recommended him to Kish Booth,
Esq., of Boston, Massachusetts, whom he found on the ship
"Galen," on which they made their journey to America. Through
this friend Mr. Steen obtained a letter of introduction to the Rev.
William Wells, D.D., who had then recently been called as the
only pastor in Brattleboro, Vermont, to which place he went
with his wife and family in 1795. Here he continued to live for
twenty-three years — a prosperous and useful citizen. His wife
and all his children having died, except one son and his only
daughter, he removed to Richland, New York, in 1818, which
was then a forest. He took with him to his new home his only
daughter, leaving his only living son upon the old homestead
in Brattleboro, Vermont. At Richland he maintained himself
and daughter by farming and working at his old-time trade as a
house carpenter. After eight years' residence at Richland, New
York, he died, February 19, 1826. His was the first grave ever
made at Richland, and its location is shown by the following
little chart:

The grave of James Steen lies at the front of the others,
nearer to the pond, irregular as to line, and without a headstone
to mark the spot. He was a noble Christian gentleman, who
exerted in his day a wide influence for good. He was a Presbyterian in faith, industrious, studious, intelligent, and highly
esteemed by all who knew him. To James and Elizabeth Wood
Steen were born seven children, only two of whom lived to
maturity.

I.—James Steen, the eldest son of James and Elizabeth Wood
    Steen, was born in Chester, England, in July, 1787, and died
    in September of the same year.

II —James Steen (2nd), the second son of James and Elizabeth Wood Steen, was born in Chester, England, in October, 1788, and died the same year.

III —William Steen, the third son of James and Elizabeth Wood Steen, was born in Chester, England, in 1791, and died in Brattleboro, Vermont, in 1797, when about six years old

IV —James Steen (3rd), the fourth son of James and Elizabeth Wood Steen, was born in Chester, England, in 1794, and died in Brattleboro, Vermont, in 1800, when about six years old

V —Joseph Steen, the fifth son of James and Elizabeth Wood Steen, was born in Brattleboro, Vermont, March 4, 1797, where he lived a long and useful life   He died in peace in the Christian faith, August 7. 1881, in the 85th year of his age, and his body was tenderly laid away to rest in the Brattleboro cemetery   The following extract from "The History of Brattleboro, Vermont," which was published two years before his death, is given to show the character of the man, and the estimation in which he was held by those who knew him best

The familiar form of this gentleman and his present quiet operations in the book and stationery business, continued since 1830, give no idea to the present generation, aside from the business aforesaid, what he has been and done in the period of eighty-two years since his birth in this place   The generation now passing off the stage of life have ever considered him an important acquisition, a tower of strength to any cause his honest convictions led him to advocate And it is fortunate for this community that his power and influence has always been in the right direction   He has been a strong man, physically and mentally, often exercising the attributes in times of adversity advantageously to the condition of others less fortunate than himself   From his aid and counsels the latter have received courage and inspiration to face the ills of life   During his mercantile operations he has published eleven thousand royal octavo Bibles of fifteen hundred pages each,   eleven thousand encyclopedias of religious knowledge of fifteen hundred pages each,   two thousand school Bibles,   one thousand pocket Testaments, besides large numbers of school books   Printing was hard work then, done by hand power, often stimulated by alcohol in the form of whisky, black strap, rum or rye gin   For being a solitary exception in total abstinence from all intoxicating liquors, Mr. Steen was ridiculed by his fellow workmen   but he lived to see many of them fill drunkards' graves   In 1830 he was foremost in the Washingtonian movement. The self-reliant, independent character of the man is apparent from the foregoing, as also it was in every period of his life where decisive action was required   Mr Steen obeyed the Scriptural command, "Prove all things, and hold fast that which is good "   Over sixty years ago he joined the Congregational Church, and has been superintendent of the Sunday-school over twenty-five years, and is yet the oldest member of these institutions   In 1838 he tried Democracy

JOSEPH STEEN.
(Born 1797. and died 1881.)

under Van Buren's administration, and for a short time was editor and proprietor of the "Windham County Democrat," but in 1840 he again voted the Whig ticket, editing a Whig campaign paper, called "The Flail,' which had a circulation of five thousand per week

Mr Steen was the agent here for paying pensions to the soldiers of the Revolution, continuing this duty till the last died   He was assignee in bankruptcy for Windham County in 1844, Justice of the Peace in 1848, and still held the office of Selectman in 1854-55   He was chosen school committee to put in operation the graded school system in 1841—a plan of his own designing. He was severely censured by a wealthy man for his action respecting schools, but neither wealth nor position could ever shut his mouth   He was always ready to sell books, but never his principles

Joseph Steen was married, in 1821, to Eliza Miller of Heath Massachusetts, she having been born in 1800, and died in Brattleboro, Vermont, in October, 1881. To them were born five children

1 William Curtis Steen, the eldest son of Joseph and Eliza Miller Steen, was born in Brattleboro, Vermont December 20, 1824, and died March 3, 1863, in the 39th year of his age He was married, April 27, 1846, to Ruth Louisa Crossett, she having been born January 13, 1825   To them were born five children, as follows

I.—Louisa Annie Steen, the eldest child of William Curtis and Ruth Louisa Steen, was born November 12, 1848 She was married, June 22, 1869, to William Wallace Harvey, he having been born June 6, 1848   Residence, Constantine Michigan   To them were born the following six children, all born in Constantine, Michigan, where they still reside

1 George Crossett Harvey, the eldest son of William W and Louisa Annie Steen Harvey, was born July 28, 1870

2 Helen W Harvey, the second child and eldest daughter of William W and Louisa Annie Steen Harvey, was born December 2, 1872, and died the same day

3 William Steen Harvey, the third child and second son of William W. and Louisa Annie Steen Harvey, was born February 14, 1874.

4 Laura Abbott Harvey, the fourth child and second daughter of William W and Louisa Annie Steen Harvey, was born September 20, 1876

5 Laura Harvey, the fifth child and third daughter of William W. and Louisa Annie Steen Harvey, was born December 14, 1878, and died August 12, 1881, in the third year of her age.

6 Wallace Norman Harvey, the sixth child, the third and youngest son of William Wallace and Louisa Annie Steen Harvey, was born November 30, 1881

II —Joseph Crossett Steen, the second child and eldest son of William Curtis and Ruth Louisa Steen, was born January 2, 1851, and died in Brattleboro, Vermont, September 7, 1882, in the 32d year of his age

III —Emma Eliza Steen, the third child and second daughter of William Curtis and Ruth Louisa Steen, was born March 1, 1854, and died in Baltimore, Maryland, September 10, 1882, in the 29th year of her age She was married, April 23, 1881, to Dr Alfred Wanstall, by whom she had one child, as follows

1 Charles Steen Wanstall was born in Baltimore, Maryland, May 18, 1882, and died January 22, 1884, in the second year of his age

IV —William Payson Steen, the fourth child and second son of William Curtis and Ruth L Steen, was born February 18, 1857 He was married, May 4 1893, to Ruth Debora Little Residence, Phoenix, Arizona

V —Edward Frank Steen, the fifth child and third son of William Curtis and Ruth L Steen, was born at Bennington, Vermont, September 27, 1863, and died the same day

2 Edward Tyler Steen, the second son of Joseph and Eliza Miller Steen, was born in Brattleboro, Vermont, December 5, 1826 He was apprenticed to his trade when he was fourteen years of age, and has followed ever since the occupation of mechanical engineer He has invented a patent quartz mill, hydraulic house-raising machinery, wave power, etc. He is now engaged in the foundry business in San Francisco, California He was married, February 18, 1856, to Mary M Salisbury Residence, San Francisco California They have no children

3 Joseph Franklin Steen, the third son of Joseph and Eliza Miller Steen, was born in Brattleboro, Vermont March 16, 1829 He was married in East Abington Massachusetts,

May 22, 1851, to Laura Jane Flye. He left the old home in Vermont in 1858, and has followed the occupation of clerk, book-seller and is now a farmer He has no children Residence, near Del Rosa, California

4 James Wood Steen, the fourth son of Joseph and Eliza Miller Steen, was born in Brattleboro, Vermont, in 1833, and died in 1834

5 Anna Elizabeth Steen, the fifth child and only daughter of Joseph and Eliza Miller Steen, was born in Brattleboro, Vermont, July 4 1836 She was married at the same place in September, 1875, to Frank Edward Flint, a druggist, of Westfield, Massachusetts Residence, Lynn, Massachusetts The following are their children

    I—Ethel Steen Flint a daughter of Frank Edward and Anna Elizabeth Steen Flint, was born September 2, 1876, and died January 9, 1878, in the second year of her age

    II—Bertha Steen Flint, an adopted daughter of Frank E and Anna E Steen Flint, was born in 1879

VI—Job Steen, the sixth son of James and Elizabeth Wood Steen, was born in Brattleboro, Vermont, in 1800 and died, unmarried, in 1822, aged 22 years

VII—Mary Ann Steen, the seventh child and only daughter of James and Elizabeth Wood Steen, was born in Brattleboro, Vermont, October 27, 1803 and died in Richland, New York, August 11, 1842 in the 39th year of her age She was married at Richland, New York, about 1824 to Jonathan Ferguson, he having been born at Hoosac, New York, February 24, 1802, and died in Richland, New York, March 12, 1857 in the 56th year of his age To them were born the following six children

1 Mary Elizabeth Ferguson the eldest child of Jonathan and Mary Ann Steen Ferguson, was born in Richland, New York, about 1827 (?) She was married at the same place to John Potter, and died August 30, 1854, aged about 27 years (?) They had no children

2 Charlotte Maria Ferguson, the second daughter of Jonathan and Mary Ann Steen Ferguson, was born in Richland, New York, May 4, 1831 She was married in Richland, New York, July 4, 1853, to Hezekiah Henry Mellen he

having been born in Richland, New York September 28, 1820, and died of heart failure in Minneapolis, Minnesota, December 13, 1893, in the 74th year of his age   Mr Mellen was a surveyor by occupation   He served in the War of the Rebellion for two years as Quartermaster for the 147th Regiment of New York Volunteer Infantry, and was afterwards a merchant in Richland, New York   The family residence is now (1900) in Minneapolis, Minnesota   To them were born the following children·

I —Frank H Mellen, the eldest child of Hezekiah H and Charlotte M Mellen was born in Richland, New York, March 2, 1855   He was married at Laconia, New York, to Mary M Hydorn   Residence, 212 West Twenty-seventh Street, Minneapolis, Minnesota   To them were born the following five children

    1. Marguerite Mellen, the eldest child of Frank H and Mary M Mellen, was born November 14, 1887, and died April 13, 1888, aged 5 months

    2 Paul H Mellen, the second child and eldest son of Frank H and Mary M Mellen, was born April 20, 1889, and died November 7, 1889, aged 6 months and 18 days

    3 George H. Mellen, the third child and second son of Frank H and Mary M Mellen, was born July 29, 1891.

    4 Edith A Mellen, the fourth child and second daughter of Frank H and Mary M Mellen, was born August 22, 1893, and died April 2, 1894, aged 7 months and 10 days.

    5 Doris A. Mellen, the fifth child and third son of Frank H and Mary M Mellen, was born in Minneapolis, Minnesota, July 29, 1898

II —Elizabeth Mellen, the second child, a daughter of Hezekiah H and Charlotte M Mellen, was born in Richland, New York, March 8, 1857   She was married to William F Ripsom, of Minneapolis, Minnesota   To them was born one child   Residence, North Minneapolis, Minnesota

    1 Lulu B Ripsom, a daughter of William F and Elizabeth Mellen Ripsom, was born in Minneapolis, Minnesota, March 9, 1887   Residence, North Minneapolis, Minnesota

3 Joseph Steen Ferguson, the third child and eldest son of
Jonathan and Mary Ann Steen Ferguson, was born in Richland, New York, July 7, 1832, and died, unmarried, March 1,
1852, in the 20th year of his age

4 DeWitt C Ferguson, the fourth child and second son of
Jonathan and Mary Ann Steen Ferguson, was born in Richland New York, in 1834, and died in July, 1863, aged 29
years He was married in Richland, New York, August 15,
1860, to Alice Mellen No children

5 Jerome C. Ferguson the fifth child and third son of Jonathan and Mary Ann Steen Ferguson, was born in Richland,
New York, January 22, 1838 He was married at the same
place, to Mary Storm Residence, Richland, New York
To them were born two children, as follows

I.—Steen Ferguson, the elder child, a son of Jerome C and
Mary Storm Ferguson, was born in Richland, New York,
August 25, 1864 He was married at Harrisville, New
York, to Eva Streeter Residence, Harrisville, New York
To them was born one child

1 A daughter Residence, Harrisville, New York

II —Ettie Ferguson, the second child, a daughter of Jerome
C and Mary Storm Ferguson, was born in Richland, New
York, December 5, 1866, and died, unmarried, in Minneapolis, Minnesota, August 14, 1890, in the 24th year of
her age

6 Franklin F Ferguson, the sixth and youngest child and
the fourth son of Jonathan and Mary Ann Steen Ferguson,
was born in Richland, New York, August 14, 1840 He
was married in Richland New York, May 2, 1863, to Addie
Storm Residence, Clermont, Iowa To them were born
the following children.

I —Arthur Ferguson, the elder child, a son of Franklin F
and Addie Storm Ferguson, was born April 20, 1864
Residence, Clermont, Iowa.

II —Carrie M Ferguson, the second child, a daughter of
Franklin F and Addie Storm Ferguson, was born
November 11, 1865 Residence, Clermont, Iowa

BOOK EIGHTEEN.

MISCELLANEOUS STEEN FAMILIES OF SCOTCH-IRISH DESCENT

CHAPTER I

John Steen came from Scotland into Ireland and located upon a farm on Fountain Hill, near Londonderry, where he built a house about 1750, in which he spent the remainder of his life There were other Steens living in the same locality, who did not belong to that family This John Steen was married and had two children — one son and one daughter — whose names were William and Dinah

I —William Steen, the eldest child of John Steen, as above was born at Fountain Hill, near Londonderry Ireland probably about 1773 He held the lands formerly occupied by his father, and carried on a large dyeing and linen weaving trade He was married probably about 1797, to Sarah Long of Clandy County Londonderry, Ireland To them were born five children, as follows

1 John Steen, the eldest child of William and Sarah Long Steen, was born at Fountain Hill, near Londonderry, Ireland, about 1798, where he resided until 1830, when he removed to New York, in the United States of America He afterwards died, unmarried, in New York City

2 James Steen, the second son of William and Sarah Long Steen, was born at Fountain Hill near Londonderry Ireland, in October, 1800, where he was brought up and spent his early life He was given a liberal education, and ordained to the ministry of the Reformed Presbyterian Church in 1839 He continued an active and faithful minister and missionary of that Church until the year 1843, when he united with the Presbyterian Church in Ireland, and was chosen pastor of a church near Newry where he remained until his death He lived under the reign of four British sovereigns, and died in Newry, Ireland, July 17, 1896 in the 96th year of his age He was a minister of the gospel for a period of fifty-seven years, and at the time of his death he was the oldest minister in the Presbyterian Church in Ireland Rev James Steen was married to Sarah Doran, of County Down, Ireland To them were born seven children, three daughters and four sons Two daughters and one son died very young The following four children lived to maturity

I —Edward James Steen, a son of the Rev James and Sarah Doran Steen, died unmarried, in the 24th year of his age

II —Leopold Steen, a son of the Rev James and Sarah Doran Steen was born and brought up in Ireland but removed to Australia He is unmarried Residence, Adelaide, South Australia

III —Frederick Charles Steen, a son of the Rev James and Sarah Doran Steen, was born and brought up in Ireland He is now — 1900 — unmarried Residence Newry Ireland

IV —Clarissa Sarah Steen, a daughter of the Rev James and Sarah Doran Steen, was born and brought up in Ireland She was married in 1883 to Frederick Rigsby, a leather merchant To them were born eight children, three boys and five girls — all living in 1900

3 Margaret Steen, the third child and eldest daughter of William and Sarah Long Steen, was born at Fountain Hill near Londonderry, Ireland, about 1803, where she was brought up She was married to Thomas McElwee of County Londonderry, Ireland by whom she brought up a family of children

4 Dinah Steen, the fourth child and second daughter of William and Sarah Long Steen, was born at Fountain Hill,

near Londonderry, Ireland, about 1805 and was brought up there   She was married to a Mr Floyd, her cousin, by whom she had a large family of children   They emigrated to America

5   Matilda Steen, the fifth child and youngest daughter of William and Sarah Long Steen, was born at Fountain Hill, near Londonderry, Ireland, about 1808, where she was brought up and educated   She was married to a Mr Irwin, of Londonderry   To them were born five children, two sons and three daughters   Residence, Londonderry, Ireland

   I —James Irwin, a son of Matilda Steen Irwin, was born in Londonderry, Ireland   He is married, and now — 1900 — living on the old place at Fountain Hill, near Londonderry, Ireland   He has no children

   II —William John Irwin, a son of Matilda Steen Irwin, was born and brought up at Fountain Hill, near Londonderry, Ireland   He was married and removed to Australia, where he is engaged in the drapery business   He has no children   Residence, Geelong, Victoria, Australia

   III —One daughter of Matilda Steen Irwin was born and brought up at Londonderry, Ireland   She was married to James Lindsay a grocery merchant   They have a large family   Residence, Melbourne, Australia

   IV —*V* —Two other daughters of Matilda Steen Irwin, who were born in Londonderry, Ireland, are now — 1900 — unmarried   Residence, Melbourne Victoria, Australia

---

CHAPTER II

John Steen was born and brought up in Ireland, and was by occupation a farmer.   He was married in Ireland, about 1770, to Elizabeth Carus, and came to America about 1777   They located in Cumberland County, Pennsylvania, where he brought up a family of eight children, four boys and four girls, as follows

I—James Steen, the eldest son of John and Elizabeth Carus Steen, was born in Ireland about 1772 He was brought by his parents to America when about five years of age, and grew up to manhood in Cumberland County, Pennsylvania

II—John Steen, the second son of John and Elizabeth Carus Steen, was born in Ireland in 1775, and brought by his parents to America when a little child only about two years old He lived with his parents and grew up to manhood in Cumberland County, Pennsylvania, and was a carpenter by trade He was married near Carlisle, Pennsylvania, in 1819, to Mary Davidson, she having been born near Carlisle, Cumberland County, Pennsylvania, about the year 1800 After his marriage he continued to live in Pennsylvania for about four years, or until about 1823, when they removed to Wayne County, Ohio, where they afterwards made their home To them were born ten children, eight sons and two daughters, as follows

1 Emily Steen, the eldest child of John and Mary Davidson Steen was born near Carlisle, Pennsylvania, in 1820, and brought by her parents to their new home in Ohio when she was a small child

2 William Steen, the second child and eldest son of John and Mary Davidson Steen, was born near Carlisle, Pennsylvania in 1822, and brought by his parents to their new home in Wayne County, Ohio, about the next year

3 John Steen, the third child and second son of John and Mary Davidson Steen, was born in Wayne County, Ohio, August 8, 1824, where he grew up to manhood He was married to Catherine Chambers she having been born in Crawford County, Ohio, in January, 1827 To them were born nine children, six of whom are still living in 1900 as follows

> I—Elias Steen, a son of John and Catherine Chambers Steen, was born near Bucyrus, Crawford County, Ohio, August 8 1849, and is by occupation a carpenter He was married in Findlay, Ohio, September 3, 1871, to Sarah Ann Bare, she having been born near Bloomdale Wood County Ohio, May 6, 1854 Residence, Vanlue, Ohio To them were born four children

>> 1 John Benjamin Steen, the eldest child of Elias and Sarah Ann Bare Steen, was born May 1, 1872 — a teacher

2 . Charles Millard Steen, the second son of Elias and
Sarah Ann Bare Steen, was born February 23. 1874 — a
teacher

3 James Allen Steen, the third son of Elias and Sarah Ann
Bare Steen, was born January 14, 1879 — a teacher

4 Albert Oscar Steen the fourth and youngest son of
Elias and Sarah Ann Bare Steen, was born January 5,
1883 — a student.

II —Nathaniel Steen, a son of John and Catherine Chambers
Steen, now — 1900 — resides at Vanlue, Ohio

III —D M Steen, a son of John and Catherine Chambers
Steen, now — 1900 — resides in Findlay, Hancock County,
Ohio

IV —Charles E Steen, a son of John and Catherine Chambers Steen, now — 1900 — is a hardware merchant   Residence, Findlay, Ohio

V —E A Steen, a son of John and Catherine Chambers
Steen, now — 1900 — resides in Findlay, Ohio

VI —James M Steen, a son of John and Catherine Chambers
Steen, is now — 1900 — a hardware merchant   Residence, Findlay, Ohio

4 Joseph Steen, the fourth child and third son of John and
Mary Davidson Steen, was born and brought up in
Wayne County, Ohio   He now — 1900 — lives in Crawford
County, Ohio

5 James Steen, the fifth child and fourth son of John and
Mary Davidson Steen, was born in Wayne County, Ohio,
in September, 1828, where he spent his early life   His
present residence, in 1900, is in Crawford County

6 David Steen, the sixth child and fifth son of John and Mary
Davidson Steen, was born in Wayne County, Ohio, in 1830

7 Elizabeth Steen, the seventh child and second daughter of
John and Mary Davidson Steen, was born in Wayne County,
Ohio in October, 1832

8 Samuel Steen the eighth child and sixth son of John and
Mary Davidson Steen, was born in Wayne County, Ohio,
April 17, 1834

9 Nathaniel Steen, the ninth child and seventh son of John
and Mary Davidson Steen, was born in Wayne County,

Ohio, in May, 1836   He resides, in 1900, in Crawford County, Ohio

10 Moses Steen, the tenth child and eighth son of John and Mary Davidson Steen, was born in Wayne County, Ohio, in 1838

III —William Steen, the third son of John and Elizabeth Carus Steen, was probably born, soon after the arrival of his parents from Ireland, in Cumberland County, Pennsylvania, about 1778, where he spent his early life   He was twice married and lived and died at Barkley's Row, in Cumberland County, Pennsylvania   He was the father of at least four children two sons and two daughters, whose names are as follows

  1 William Steen, born in Pennsylvania, and was still living in Illinois in 1898

  2 John Steen, born in Pennsylvania and died at Barkley s Row, September 7, 1807   He was married in Pennsylvania to Mary Steward, who died April 15, 1881   They were the parents of ten children, all born in Cumberland County, Pennsylvania

  I —James Steen, born December 25, 1841, still living

  II —John Steen, still living

  III —Mary Ellen Steen, still living

  IV —Alice Steen, still living

  V —Mariette Steen, born March 12, 1844   She was married to James H Quinn, by whom she had eleven children seven sons and four daughters, of whom two boys and three girls are dead   The names of the living are John, James, William, Charles, Ethel, residing in Denver, Colorado, and Harry, who joined the United States Navy.

  VI —Kate Steen, born about 1853, and died about 1882

  VII —Jane Ann Steen, deceased

  VIII —Emily Steen deceased

  IX —*X* —Two other daughters, who are now dead

  3 Emily Steen, who married a Mr. Ikelman in 1865 and both are now dead

  4 Elizabeth Steen, who married a Mr Peters, of Harrisburgh, Pennsylvania, and died, leaving one child

IV —David Steen the fourth son of John and Elizabeth Carus Steen, was born near Carlisle, Cumberland County, Pennsylvania, probably about 1780, where he was brought up and spent his life

V —Barbara Steen, the fifth child and eldest daughter of John and Elizabeth Carus Steen, was born near Carlisle, in Cumberland County, Pennsylvania, where she spent her life

VI —Elizabeth Steen, a daughter of John and Elizabeth Carus Steen, was born and brought up near Carlisle, Pennsylvania

VII —Emily Steen, a daughter of John and Elizabeth Carus Steen, was born and brought up near Carlisle, Pennsylvania.

VIII —Jane Steen, a daughter of John and Elizabeth Carus Steen, was born and brought up near Carlisle, Pennsylvania.

Three of the above daughters of John and Elizabeth Carus Steen were married to three brothers, whose names were John, James and Joseph Stuart John Stuart was a Judge in the Courts of Cumberland County, Pennsylvania, for many years

CHAPTER III

Arthur Steen was born in the North of Ireland, was married, and lived at Castle Wray, near Londonderry, where he brought up his family At least three of his children came to America, two sons and one daughter The eldest son came about 1830, and the others probably about 1839 They were all members and worshiped in the Protestant Episcopal Church during their lives The following are the names of the children.

I —William Steen, a son of Arthur Steen, was born in Ireland, and emigrated to the United States of America, from Castle Wray, about the year 1830 He was married, and came first to New York, and afterwards lived in Philadelphia for some time. He again removed to the South, and settled in Mobile, Alabama, where he died shortly after the Mexican War After the death of William Steen, his widow and the large family which had been born to them returned to the North, and located in Brooklyn, Long Island, New York Of this family, only three of the children are known to the writer of this record.

1 ———— Steen a daughter of William Steen, was born about ———— She was married to John Cameron, about 1860, an artist in the employ of Currier & Ives publishers of lithographic pictures, ever since he was a boy — over sixty-five years in the service They now — 1900 — reside on a small farm near Jamesport, Long Island, Suffolk County, New York

2 Benjamin S Steen, Major of the Fourteenth New York National Guards, of Brooklyn, of which he is a veteran — and now Inspector of the Custom House — is also a son of this William Steen Residence, 65 Miller Avenue, Brooklyn New York

   I —Catherine A Steen teacher 65 Miller Avenue, Brooklyn, New York

   II —W A Steen, carpenter, 65 Miller Avenue, Brooklyn, New York

3 Edward Steen, probably a son of William Steen, a Sea Captain on the route between New York and Richmond Virginia Residence, 386 Green Avenue, Brooklyn, New York.

   I —Dora H Steen a daughter of Edward Steen — same address

   II —John Steen, 448 Warren Street, Brooklyn. New York

   III —Andrew Steen, 448 Warren Street, Brooklyn, New York

II —Mary Steen, a daughter of Arthur Steen, was born in Ireland, and came to America She died in New York City many years ago

III —John Lamma Steen, a son of Arthur Steen, was born in Castle Wray, near Londonderry Ireland, about 1785, and emigrated to America about 1838 or 1839 He was twice married, his first wife dying early He was married a second time to Fanny Hood, she having been born in Donegal, Ireland, and died in Oakfield, Fond du Lac County Wisconsin, in 1858 To John L Steen were born ten children, as follows, the first child being by his first wife, and all the rest by his second wife, Fanny Hood Steen

1 Jane Steen, the eldest child, was born at Castle Wray, Ireland, probably about 1810, came to America with her father, and was married to James Hayes, of New York City

2 Arthur Hood Steen, the second child and the eldest son of John L and Fanny Hood Steen was born in Ireland, February 6, 1814, and died in Oakfield, Fond du Lac County, Wisconsin, September 13 1882, aged 68 years, 7 months and 7 days   He was married in New York City, January 3, 1841, to Frances Filbey, she having been born in England, and died in Oakfield Wisconsin, August 13, 1851   They lived for some time in Astoria, Long Island, New York, but removed to Oakfield Wisconsin where they spent the remainder of their lives   To them were born five children, as follows

   I —Frances Anne Steen, the eldest child of Arthur H and Frances Filbey Steen, was born March 7, 1844, and died February 18, 1881, in the 37th year of her age

   II —Mary Susanna Steen, the second daughter of Arthur H and Frances Filbey Steen, was born October 11, 1845

   III —Joseph Filbey Steen, the third child and eldest son of Arthur H and Frances Filbey Steen, was born July 17, 1847

   IV —John Allen Steen, the fourth child and second son of Arthur H and Frances Filbey Steen, was born February 1, 1849, and died May 8, 1878, aged 29 years, 3 months and 7 days

   V —Arthur Henry Steen, the fifth and youngest child of Arthur H and Frances Filbey Steen, was born June 16, 1850   He was graduated from Rush Medical College, Chicago, Illinois, February 14, 1874, and is engaged in the successful practice of medicine at Cottage Grove, Minnesota   Dr Arthur H Steen has in his possession the original Masonic jewel which was many years ago presented to Robert Steen, and no doubt this jewel belonged to the parchment now in possession of George H Steen, of Chicago, Illinois   Dr Arthur H Steen was married, April 9, 1887, to Eva Perkins she having been born in Canada February 7 1862   They have no children living   Residence, Cottage Grove Minnesota

3 Elizabeth Steen, the third child, the second by John L and Fanny Hood Steen, was born in Ireland, and emigrated to America with her parents She was married to Thomas Burns, and brought up a family of children. They have one son, Dr. J. W. Burns, who is Secretary of the Fond du Lac County Association Residence, Oakfield, Wisconsin

4 Fanny Steen, the fourth child, the third of John L and Fanny Hood Steen, was born in Ireland, and died

5 Mary Steen, the fifth child, the third daughter of John L and Fanny Hood Steen, was born in Ireland in 1823, and brought to America by her parents She was married by an Episcopal clergyman in New York, in 1844, to John Forsythe, he having been born in 1816 They afterwards removed to Wisconsin where they brought up a family of eight children, five of whom are dead — only three sons remaining. Two sons are away from home, and the other one cultivates their large farm near Waucousta, Wisconsin Mr. and Mrs John Forsythe are now — 1900 — in their old age, residing near Waucousta, Fond du Lac County, Wisconsin

6 John Morris Steen, the sixth child the fifth of John L and Fanny Hood Steen, was born in Ireland, probably about 1825, and died

7 Margaret Steen, the seventh child the sixth of John L and Fanny Hood Steen, was born in Ireland, probably about 1828, and emigrated to America with her parents She was married to a Mr Thompson, and now (1900) resides at Dee River, New York

8 William Steen, the eighth child, the seventh of John L and Fanny Hood Steen, was born in Ireland, probably about 1830 and died J F Steen, of Oakfield, Wis, is probably a son of his

9 Anne Steen, the ninth child, the eighth of John L and Fanny Hood Steen, was born in Ireland, probably about 1832, and died

10 Robert Lyman Steen, the tenth child of John L Steen but the ninth child of John L and Fanny Hood Steen, was born in Castle Wray, near Londonderry, Ireland, May 12, 1834, and died in Walla Walla, Washington, February 19
(32)

1899, in the 65th year of his age He was extensively engaged in the mercantile and railroad business, and resided at different times in New Lisbon, Wisconsin, La Crosse, Wisconsin, and Marion, Iowa He was married in New Lisbon, Wisconsin, March 5, 1859, to Katheryn Callahan, she having been born in Geneva, New York, December 23, 1842, and died in Marion, Iowa, November 11, 1894, in the 52d year of her age To them were born the nine following children·

I—Herbert Lesley Steen, the eldest son of Robert L and Katheryn Callahan Steen, was born at La Crosse, Wisconsin, December 27, 1850 He is connected with the Chicago, Milwaukee and St Paul Railway He was married, at New Lisbon, Wisconsin, April 26, 1883, to Carrie Leight Residence, Delmar Iowa To them were born the following children

  1 Charles Lesley Steen was born in New Lisbon, Wisconsin, October 5, 1884, and died October 19, 1884

  2 Irma Minnie Steen was born in Louisa Iowa January 10, 1886

  3 William Ray Steen was born in Delmar, Iowa, August 7 1891

II—Lillian Beatrice Steen, the second child and eldest daughter of Robert L and Katheryn Callahan Steen, was born in La Crosse, Wisconsin, March 13, 1861, and resides with her brothers in Chicago, Illinois

III—Horace Arthur Steen, the third child and second son of Robert L and Katheryn Callahan Steen, was born at La Crosse, Wisconsin, December 18, 1862 He is connected with the Great Northern Railway Company Residence, Kerkhoven, Swift County Minnesota He was married at Portage City, Wisconsin June 28, 1893, to Emma Frundt, she having been born in Portage City Wisconsin, September 6, 1868 To them were born the following

  1 Harold Horace Steen was born in Cayuga North Dakota, April 12, 1894

  2 Gladys Katheryn Steen was born at Kerkhoven Minnesota, September 21, 1895

  3 Myrtle Dorothy Steen was born at Kerkhoven Minnesota, July 27, 1897

IV—Laura Harmony Steen, the fourth child and second daughter of Robert L and Katheryn Callahan Steen, was born at La Crosse, Wisconsin, October 26, 1866 She resides with her brothers in Chicago, Illinois

V—Minnie May Steen, the fifth child and third daughter of Robert L and Katheryn Callahan Steen, was born at La Crosse, Wisconsin, October 6, 1868 She was married at Marion, Iowa, June 5 1889, to William Elijah Elliott, he having been born at Marion, Iowa, November 28, 1866 He is now — 1900 — the manager of "The Elliott Button Fastener Company," and also Secretary and foreign representative of the National Machine Company Residence, Grand Rapids Michigan To Wm E and Minnie Steen Elliott were born the following

　1 A daughter born at Marion, Iowa, February 25, 1891 and died the same day.

　2 A son born at Grand Rapids, Michigan July 15, 1894, and died July 19, 1894

VI—George Henry Steen, the sixth child and third son of Robert L and Katheryn Callahan Steen, was born at New Lisbon, Wisconsin, August 6, 1870 He is now — 1900 — connected with the Chicago and Northwestern Railway Company His sister writes that he is now in possession of an old parchment which was given by his Grandfather Steen to his father, probably because his name was Robert Steen It may possibly indicate relationship with the Robert Steen of Book One She says "It is a certificate of membership in good standing of Robert Steen in a certain Masonic Lodge, in a certain place dating, if I remember correctly, some time in 1700 I saw the paper a few weeks ago (1899), while in Chicago, and pored over it some time, but failed to make out the place as the writing had become so indistinct" George H Steen resides at 1224 West Adams Street, Chicago Illinois

VII—Eldridge Robert Steen the seventh child and fourth son of Robert L and Katheryn Callahan Steen, was born at New Lisbon, Wisconsin, May 14, 1872 He is connected with the "Singer Sewing Machine Company" Residence, Chicago, Illinois

VIII —IX —Fred Edwin Steen, and Frank Charles Steen, the eighth and ninth children, and the fifth and sixth sons of Robert L. and Katheryn Callahan Steen, were born in New Lisbon, Wisconsin, October 26, 1877 They are now — 1900 — connected with the Bushnell Reaper Works Residence, Chicago, Illinois

CHAPTER IV

William Steen, a silk weaver by occupation, was born in the North of Ireland in 1813 He had at least two brothers and one sister, i e, Archibald Steen, John Steen and Rachel Steen, who removed to Scotland, where they made their home William Steen was married about 1839 to Eliza J McClaine, who was born in the North of Ireland in 1810 They early removed to America and located permanently in New York City To them were born five children

I —Alexander Steen, the eldest child of William and Eliza J Steen, was born in the North of Ireland, October 20, 1840, and was brought by his parents to America He died in New York City, and was buried in Sypes Hill cemetery

II —James Steen, the second son of William and Eliza J Steen, was born in the North of Ireland, May 18, 1843 and was brought by his parents to America He was married in the Presbyterian Church, corner Twenty-eighth Street and Ninth Avenue, New York City, September 7, 1864, to Eliza Cecelia Sheridan, she having been born June 22, 1846 , To them were born six children. Residence, 350 West Forty-second Street, New York, New York

  1 Anna Steen, the eldest child of James and Eliza C Steen, was born in New York City, June 25, 1867

  2 Eliza Cecelia Steen, the second daughter of James and Eliza C Steen, was born in New York City, September 25 1869

  3. Francis William Steen, the third child and eldest son of James and Eliza C Steen, was born in New York City, June 30, 1872

4 Alexander Steen, the fourth child and second son of James and Eliza C. Steen, was born in New York City, December 18, 1874

5. James Steen, the fifth child and third son of James and Eliza C Steen, was born in New York City, November 19, 1876.

6. Florence Rebecca Steen, the sixth child and third daughter of James and Eliza C Steen, was born in New York City November 9, 1885

III —William John Steen, the third son of William and Eliza J Steen, was born in the North of Ireland, October 20, 1844, and brought by his parents to America He died in New York City, and was buried in Sypes Hill cemetery

IV —Martha Steen, the fourth child and elder daughter of William and Eliza J Steen, was born September 12, 1846 She died in New York City, and was buried in Sypes Hill cemetery

V —Janet Steen, the fifth child and second daughter of William and Eliza Jane McClane Steen, was born August 7, 1848. She died in New York City, and was buried in Sypes Hill cemetery.

CHAPTER V.

Thomas Steen was born in County Antrim, Ireland, where he was married, brought up his family, lived and died After his death, in 1849, his wife and children removed to Scotland, where they remained for five years In 1854 they came to New York City, where Mrs. Steen died the same year, and was buried in Greenwood cemetery, Brooklyn, New York To Thomas Steen and his wife were born three children.

I —Robert Steen, the eldest child of Thomas Steen, was born in County Antrim, Ireland, in 1835, and died in New York City, September 6, 1888, in the 53d year of his age His body was laid to rest in Greenwood cemetery, by the side of his mother, and two of his children He was a devout and earnest Presbyterian Christian, and died as he lived, in the hope of a blessed immortality   Robert Steen came to New York with his mother and the family, in 1854, when he was 19 years of age   He was married in New York City, January 30, 1858, to Rose A Brady, a daughter of Thomas and Bridget Denning Brady, she having been born in Killenkare, County Cavan, Ireland, November 1, 1839   Residence, 97 King Street, New York City   To Thomas and Rose A Steen were born four children, two of whom, a son and a daughter, died, and are buried in Greenwood cemetery   The other children are as follows

1   Thomas Steen, a son of Robert and Rose A Steen, was born in New York City, January 16 1862   Residence 97 King Street, New York, New York

2   Robert J. Steen, a son of Robert and Rose A Steen, was born in New York City, March 25, 1867   Residence, 97 King Street, New York, New York

II —Matilda Steen, the second child and eldest daughter of Thomas Steen, was born in County Antrim Ireland about 1838, and came to New York from Scotland in 1854, when she was about 16 years of age   She was married in New York City to a Mr Meloy   She died in Jersey City, New Jersey, in 1875, leaving two children,

1   William L Meloy, and

2   Matilda Meloy, both of whom are now married and have families of their own

III —Nancy Steen, the third child and second daughter of Thomas Steen was born in County Antrim Ireland, about 1840   After her father's death, in 1849, she removed with her mother and family to Scotland, and in 1854 to New York City   She afterwards returned to Scotland, and was married to a Mr. Montgomery.

CHAPTER VI

John Steen was born in Culmore, near Londonderry, Ireland, about 1770, and died in 1840, aged about 70 years   He was married to Ellen Hays, by whom he had four children   After her death he was married a second time to Katherine Boyle, she

having been born about 1791, and died in 1843, aged about 52
years To John Steen and his second wife were born six children.

I.—John Steen, the eldest son of John and Ellen Hays Steen, was
born near Moville, Ireland, about 1809 After his mother's
death he came to America, and lived near Philadelphia, in the
employment of the government, before the Civil War He afterwards went to Alaska on a sailing expedition, and was not
heard from

II —James Steen, the second son of John and Ellen Hays Steen,
was born near Moville, Ireland about 1811, and died in
Wilmington, Delaware, in 1880, aged 69 years. He also came
to America after his mother's death, and located in Wilmington, Delaware. He was married in Wilmington, Delaware,
about 1836, to Mary Cook. To them was born one child, as
follows

    1 John Steen, a son of James and Mary Cook Steen, was born
    in Wilmington, Delaware, about 1846, where he still resides
    He is married and has one child

III —Thomas Steen, the third son of John and Ellen Hays Steen,
was born near Moville, Ireland, about 1814, where he continued
to make his home until his death He was by occupation a
fisherman upon the sea He was married to a Miss Dobbins.
To them were born two children

    1 Isaac Steen

    2 Annie Steen.

IV —Katherine Steen, the fourth child and only daughter of John
and Ellen Hays Steen, was born near Moville, Ireland, about
1818 She removed to America and was married in Hartford,
Connecticut, to William Pierce To them one child was born,
as follows

    1 Katherine Pierce, a daughter of William and Katherine
    Steen Pierce, was born in Hartford, Connecticut She was
    married in 1882 to Ed Reisel. To them were born five
    children. Residence, Hartford, Connecticut

V —Jane Steen, the fifth child and second daughter of John Steen,
the eldest child by his second wife, Katherine Boyle Steen, was
born near Moville, Ireland, about 1824, and died in Newark,
Ohio, in 1870 She removed to the United States of America,
and was married in Newark, Ohio, to John Pierce, who was

killed in the Civil War To them were born two children, as follows

1 Rebecca Pierce
2 Mamie Pierce

After their mother's death these children went to Hartford, Connecticut, to the family of William Pierce

VI —Rosanna Steen, the sixth child and third daughter of John Steen, the second child by his second wife, Katherine Boyle Steen, was born near Moville, Ireland about 1828, and came to America with her sister in 1862 She first lived in Hartford, Connecticut, and afterwards removed to Newark, Ohio, where she was married to William J Conley, baggage master at the railway station To them were born four children Residence, Newark Ohio

VII.—Matilda Steen, the seventh child of John Steen the third by his second wife, Katherine Boyle Steen, was born near Moville, Ireland, and came to America in 1862 She went to Hartford, Connecticut, and lived with her sister for a few years She was married, in 1868 to John Coombs a nurseryman and fruit-grower To them were born three children Residence, Hartford, Connecticut

1 Mamie Coombs
2 Katie Coombs
3 Joseph Coombs

VIII —Margaret Steen, the eighth child of John Steen, and the fourth daughter by his second wife, Katherine Boyle Steen, was born in 1847, near Moville, Ireland, one mile toward London-derry, near the water front overlooking the sea She came with her brothers to America in 1864, landing at New York, and going at once to Hartford, Connecticut She afterwards removed to the home of her eldest half-sister, in Newark, Ohio, where she died in 1866, aged about 19 years

IX —Andrew Steen, the ninth child of John Steen, the fifth child and eldest son of his second wife, Katherine Boyle Steen, was born near Moville, Ireland, in 1849, and came to America in 1864 with his sister Margaret and his brother William He went to Hartford, Connecticut, and resided two years with his half-brother, then joined the United States army and served three years, principally in the Southern States, being honorably

discharged in Texas in 1869   He was employed in a hat and
fur store in Hartford, Connecticut, from 1870 to 1876, and in a
nursery and greenhouse from 1877 to 1879   He was employed
in iron foundries in Galveston, Texas, Chicago Illinois, and
Omaha, Nebraska, from 1880 to 1886, Portland, Oregon, 1886
to 1889, Stockton, California, 1889 to 1895, and Denver, Colorado, since July, 1895

X —Wilham Steen, the tenth and youngest child of John Steen,
the sixth child by his second wife, Katherine Boyle Steen, was
born near Moville, Ireland, in 1851   He came to America in
1864 with his brother and his sister Margaret   He remained
for a while in Hartford, Connecticut, and then went to his half-
brother James, at Wilmington, Delaware, where he continued
to reside.   He worked at dredging for oysters, and owned his
own boat   He died in Wilmington, Delaware, in 1869, aged 18
years

CHAPTER VII

C N Steen was the son of a Robert Steen, and born in Ireland (probably about 1808)   He was married in Ireland to Elizabeth McGarey, about 1833, and brought up his family in Ireland
To them were born five children

I.—Robert Steen, the eldest child of C N and Elizabeth McGarey
Steen, was born in County Monaghan, Ireland, August 11,
1835, and died in Ireland, April 10 1875, in the 40th year of his
age   He was married on Shrove Tuesday, 1863, in County
Monaghan Ireland, to Margaret Kelley, a daughter of William
Kelley, she having been born in Derry Bush, County Mona-
ghan, Ireland, and now resides at 82 Horatio Street New York
City, New York   To them were born eight children

  1 Wilham Steen, the eldest child of Robert and Margaret
    Kelley Steen, was born in Ireland, March 24 1864, and died
    in October, 1867

  2. Katherine Steen, the second child and eldest daughter of
    Robert and Margaret Kelley Steen, was born in Ireland,
    September 28, 1865 and died in July, 1867

3 Elizabeth Steen, the third child and second daughter of Robert and Margaret Kelley Steen, was born in Ireland, February 21, 1867 Residence, 82 Horatio Street, New York City, New York

4 Sarah Steen, the fourth child and third daughter of Robert and Margaret Kelley Steen, was born in Ireland, November 18, 1868 Residence, 82 Horatio Street, New York, New York

5 Robert Steen the fifth child and second son of Robert and Margaret Kelley Steen was born in Ireland about 1870, and died in infancy

6 Robert Steen (2nd), the sixth child and third son of Robert and Margaret Kelley Steen, was born in Ireland about 1871, and died soon afterwards

7 Thomas Steen, the seventh child and fourth son of Robert and Margaret Kelley Steen, was born in Ireland about 1873, and died

8 Infant son, the eighth child of Robert and Margaret Kelley Steen, was born in Ireland about 1875, and died in infancy

II —Richard Steen, the second son of C N and Elizabeth Mc-Garey Steen, was born in County Monaghan, Ireland, probably about 1837 He was married to Bridget McGarey, and died from consumption in 1877, when about 40 years of age To them were born two children

 1 Richard Steen, a son of Richard and Bridget McGarey Steen, was born probably about 1861 Residence, 629 East Twelfth Street, New York, New York

 2 William Steen, a son of Richard and Bridget McGarey Steen was born probably about 1863 Residence, 629 East Twelfth Street, New York, New York

III —William Steen, the third son of C N and Elizabeth Mc-Garey Steen, was born on the Town Land of Cornline, in County Monaghan, Ireland, October 20, 1844 He was by occupation "an enamel worker" He was married in the Church of the Nativity, New York City, April 27 1873, to Hannah McGrath, a full cousin of his brother Robert Steen's wife, a daughter of John and Sarah M McGrath, she having been born at Castleblaney, County Monaghan, Ireland, in 1841 William Steen left his home, No 30 Brown Street, New York City, December 25, 1878 well and happy, to visit his brother, then living on Twelfth Street, between Avenues C and D, and was never afterwards seen or heard from by his family   Search for him was diligently made, and in twelve months the report of his loss was made by the city authorities, which is now upon record   He was the father of three children   His widow, Mrs. Hannah McGrath Steen, now resides at 2385 Hoffman Street, Fordham, New York, New York

1 Sarah Steen, the eldest child of William and Hannah Mc-Grath Steen, was born in New York City, April 24, 1874

2 John Steen, the second child and only son of William and Hannah McGrath Steen, was born in New York City, April 1, 1876

3 Mary Steen, the third child and the younger daughter of William and Hannah McGrath Steen, was born in New York City, May 25, 1879   Family residence, 2385 Hoffman Street, Fordham, New York, New York

IV—John Steen, the fourth son of C N and Elizabeth McGarey Steen, was born in County Monaghan, Ireland   probably about 1846   He resided in New York City, and died early in 1881, aged about 35 years

V—Katherine Steen, the only daughter, the fifth and youngest child of C N and Elizabeth McGarey Steen, was born in County Monaghan, Ireland   probably about 1849

The following persons, not given elsewhere reside in New York City

1 Henry Steen, carpenter, 235 East 102d Street New York, New York

2 Jacob Steen, 205 East 73d Street, New York New York

3 James Steen, cigar dealer, 1845 Amsterdam Avenue, New York, New York

---

Sallie Pate Steen wrote an interesting story, entitled "Burt Colby's Assistant," which was published in "The Youth's Companion," of Boston, Massachusetts, December 24 1891

Rev Frederick J Steen, a son of Christian A and Julia Steen, was born in New York in September, 1867   He was graduated from the University of Toronto receiving the degree of B A. in 1888, and M A in 1890   He studied theology in Wycliffe College, Toronto, and was ordained a deacon in the Protestant Episcopal Church in 1893, and a priest in 1894   He served a church in Berlin for three years, and was then appointed Professor of Ecclesiastical History and Apologetics in Montreal Theological College   In 1897 he became special preacher in Christ's Church, Montreal   Residence, Montreal, Ontario, Canada

William Steen was a son of Thomas and Emily Steen, and lived in Vicksburgh, Mississippi   His wife's name was Amanda, and they had four sons, as follows: 1 William Steen 2 James Steen   3 Cornelius Steen 4 Henry Steen, who was born in Vicksburgh, Mississippi, July 26, 1871, and has been absent from the old home for several years   Residence, Denver, Colorado

Alexander Steen lived in the vicinity of Belfast, Ireland and brought up his family there   He had a son whose name was—
1 —William James Steen, who brought up his family in the same locality   He had a son—
  1 William Steen, who spent the greater portion of his life in Belfast, where the family resided   He has a son still living whose name is—
   1 —William Steen, who is now (1900) in the Northern Bank of Ireland

CHAPTER VIII

William M Steen was born in Dublin, Ireland, and removed to the United States of America about 1780   He was married to Elizabeth Breckinridge, called "Peggy," and located upon a farm in Allegheny County, Pennsylvania. To them were born at least four children

I.—William M Steen, Jr , a son of William M and Elizabeth Breckinridge Steen, was born in Allegheny County, Pennsylvania, in 1790, and brought up on his father's farm He was married in 1815 to Margaret Thompson, a daughter of Alexander and Elizabeth Thompson, who were born in Tipperary, Ireland, about 1765, emigrated to America, and located upon a farm in Crawford County, Pennsylvania, near where the city of Titusville now stands Margaret Thompson was born near Pleasantville, Pennsylvania, July 19, 1795, and in 1896 was still living near that place, in the 102d year of her age A letter from her son to the writer says

"William M Steen once owned a farm of three hundred acres in Butler County, Pennsylvania, which he traded for a tract of five hundred acres, which included the site where Pithole City was afterwards built. After the death of William M Steen his wife traded that tract of land for a farm on Sugar Creek This was before the great oil excitement in Pennsylvania, and the farm at Pithole afterwards brought an enormous sum of money, the celebrated V S oil well being located upon it, which alone produced about three thousand barrels a day "

He says again

"William M and Margaret Thompson Steen were the parents of eighteen children—nine boys and nine girls—all of them except four being still alive (1896) Eight of their sons enlisted in the army during the American Civil War and each faithfully served his country for four years during which time they became very widely scattered They were all in the first battle of Bull Run in 1861, but never met again during the war "

The following are the names of the children of William M and Margaret Thompson Steen (except two whose names are not given, and who probably died in infancy)

1 Joseph Clark Steen, born in 1816
2 Alexander T Steer, born in 1818
3 John N Steeen, born in 1820
4. Jesse F Steen born in 1822
5 Amos Steen, born in 1823
6 Christian Steen, born in 1824
7 George Steen, born in 1826

8 James A. Steen, born in 1827

9 Elizabeth Steen, born in 1829.

10 Margaret Steen, born in 1831

11 Esther Ann Steen, born in 1832

12 Jane Steen, born in 1834

13 Matilda Steen, born in 1838

14 Christina Steen, born in 1840

15 Mary Ann Steen, born in 1842

16 William M Steen, the youngest child of William M and Margaret Thompson Steen, was born on the "Steen farm," near Pleasantville Venango County, Pennsylvania, July 19, 1844 He was married by the Rev J R Lindsay, January 24, 1873, to Esther Beers, she having been born in 1856. To them have been born "twenty children, ' so says the "Oil City Derrick," a newspaper published in the city in which they live   This William M Steen (whose father and grandfather are reported as having the same name) served as a private soldier for two years and a half in the 69th Regiment, New York Volunteers, and one and one-half years in Company E, 57th Regiment of Pennsylvania Volunteers He was wounded in the battles at Antietam, Gettysburgh, the Wilderness, and Yellow Tavern, in front of Petersburgh He is a member of Stowe Post, G A R, of Tidioute, Pennsylvania, and a pensioner   Residence, Oil City, Pennsylvania

II —Robert Steen, a son of William M and Elizabeth Breckinridge Steen, was born in Allegheny County, Pennsylvania, about 1793, and removed to the West in early life

III —Christie Ann Steen, a daughter of William M and Elizabeth Breckinridge Steen, was born near Pittsburgh, in Allegheny County, Pennsylvania, about 1796   She lived in Butler County, Pennsylvania, and owned a farm

IV —Ibbie Steen, a daughter of William M and Elizabeth Breckinridge Steen, was born near Pittsburgh, in Allegheny County, Pennsylvania, about 1799   She also lived in Butler County, Pennsylvania, and owned a large farm there

CHAPTER IX.

OTHER STEENS IN TEXAS

Judge John A Steen, of Paint Rock, Concho County, Texas, writes

"I came into Texas in 1860, and have met several Steens and heard of several more   They figured considerably in the early history of Mississippi, Louisiana and Texas   The old ones are mostly dead, but their descendants are yet to be found   They are all of Scotch-Irish descent   I saw several Steens when in Bragg's army, east of the Mississippi, but do not know their place of residence   Major Steen, an old settler at Beeville Bee County, Texas a prominent and noted character, was, I think, from Louisiana   Judge Max Steen was killed in Old Mexico about 1891 He was a judge in one of the southern counties of Texas   There was a John Steen in Bosque County, Texas, years ago   Also, the family of C C Steen, known as the   Kit Steen family   He also had a brother Abe Steen, and a sister who married a Mr Bennett, living somewhere in the Indian Territory, I think in the Choctaw Nation.   The Steens in Bosque County, Texas, are the children of John Steen and George Steen, who came into the State from Southeast Missouri   I knew George Steen well during the war   John Steen was killed there   I have heard different reports concerning it as that he was mobbed as a spy, and that he was killed by the Indians, but I never did know the truth of the matter   At any rate, I hear that he was a good man, and that his sons were good men   Richard C Steen belongs I think, to a different family than the Steen's Creek Steens of which you wrote   That is, they are not closely connected, but still are of the same stock of the early Steens of that country   They lived near Steenston Lowndes County Mississippi, but over the line in Alabama "

Jefferson William Steen was born and brought up in Madison County Mississippi, and died in Texas in March 1885   He had two brothers, Thomas Steen and David Steen, both are dead, but their families are living either in Madison or in Hinds

County, Mississippi Jefferson William Steen was married and brought up a family of nine children—eight sons and one daughter, all still living in 1899 His eldest son is Charles Steen, whose post-office address is Cobb, Freestone County, Texas, and his seventh child is Richard C Steen, of Mexia, Texas, who has resided there since 1884, selling goods for his brother-in-law, F G Robertson, the merchant

Richard Steen, a part of whose family settled in Texas, was born in North Carolina, but lived, brought up his family, and died in Missouri He was married to Juda McCarrell, and had a family of eight children, four sons and four daughters, as follows

I —James Steen

II —George Steen, who came into Texas in early life

III —John Brannon Steen, who came into Texas and was killed there

IV —William Steen; the only one of the children of Richard and Juda Steen, now living (1899) Residence. Marshfield, Missouri

V —Elvira Steen

VI —Margaret Steen

VII —Rebecca Steen

VIII —Maria Steen

John Brannon Steen, the third child of Richard and Juda McCarrell Steen, as given in the above list, was born in Stoddard County, Missouri, October 17, 1837, and early removed into Texas He was married, December 11, 1858, to Parmelia T Roper, and brought up a family of children in Texas, three of whom are still living in 1900, as follows.

1 J R Steen, whose residence is near Towle P O , Bosque County, Texas.

2 Josie Steen Craig, who resides at Sherman, Grayson County, Texas

3 George J Steen, who was born in Texas October 17, 1865, and was married November 13, 1884, to Nellie Wood, she having been born in Texas February 15, 1867 They reside on a farm near Towle P O , Bosque County, Texas To them were born the following children

I —Newton Steen was born December 22, 1885 and died
    November 14, 1886

II —Ada Steen was born June 2, 1887, and died November
    10, 1889

III —Wessie Steen was born August 30, 1889

IV —Jennie Steen was born May 26. 1891

V —Bertie Steen was born July 14, 1893

VI —Susie Steen was born August 3, 1895

VII —Beulah Steen was born March 7, 1897.

BOOK NINETEEN.

MISCELLANEOUS STEEN FAMILIES FROM SCANDINAVIA (Norway, Sweden, Denmark, Etc.)

The Coat of Arms of this branch is the "Head, Neck and Breast of the Phoenix Bird in Gold '

CHAPTER I ·

Rasmus Jansen Steen, the son of a government ship builder, was born in Svendborg Island of Fuenen, probably about 1786 He was married about 1815 to Helena Keppelgard, to whom were born several children, who, like their father and their grandfather, were fond of a seafaring life

I —Richard Christian Steen, the eldest son of Rasmus Jansen and Helena Keppelgard Steen, was born in North Germany, probably about 1817

II —Maria Madeline Steen, the second child and eldest daughter of Rasmus Jansen and Helena Keppelgard Steen, was born in North Germany, probably about 1820

III —Asmus Frederick Steen, the third child and second son of Rasmus Jansen and Helena Keppelgard Steen, was born in Cappeln, North Germany, April 2, 1822 He came to America in 1838, when only about sixteen years of age He worked at ship building in Chicago, Muskegon, St Louis and New Orleans He afterwards went to sea as a ship carpenter, and visited nearly every seaboard nation, then returned to America and located in New York City He afterwards purchased a home in Haddam, Connecticut, where he still resides He was married, April 29, 1849, to Elizabeth May Allbar, to whom three children were born as follows

1 Alphonso Charles Steen, the eldest child of Asmus Frederick and Elizabeth May Allbar Steen, was born in London, England, January 16, 1854 He was married at 334 East Ninth Street, New York City, January 6, 1876 to Katherine Amelia Marsh, she having been born in Newark, New Jersey, June 7, 1854 Residence, 1019 East 136th Street, New York City. To them were born six children

> *I* —Sarah Elizabeth Steen, the eldest child of Alphonso C and Katherine Amelia Steen, was born in New York City, April 6 1877.

> *II.*—Edward Charles Steen, the second child and eldest son of Alphonso C and Katherine Amelia Steen, was born in Haddam, Middlesex County, Connecticut, October 11, 1879.

> *III* —Lillian Victoria Steen, the third child and second daughter of Alphonso C and Katherine Amelia Steen, was born in New York City, December 3 1882

> *IV* —William Haddon Steen, the fourth child and second son of Alphonso C and Katherine Amelia Steen, was born in New York City, January 3, 1884

> *V* —Joseph Alphonso Steen, the fifth child and third son of Alphonso C and Katherine Amelia Steen, was born in New York City, October 13, 1887

> *VI* —Martha Freeman Steen, the sixth child and third daughter of Alphonso Charles and Katherine Amelia Steen, was born in New York City, November 7, 1889

2 Joe Leon Spurgeon Steen, the second son of Asmus Frederick and Elizabeth May Allbar Steen, was born February 2, 1858 He is a good mechanic, but when tired of life on shore would rather go to sea and work at half the wages, visiting different counties and peoples Residence, Haddam, Connecticut

3 Asmus Haddon Steen, the third son of Asmus Frederick and Elizabeth May Allbar Steen, was born in Haddam, Connecticut, February 12, 1860 Residence, Jersey City, New Jersey

IV —Charles August Steen, the fourth child and third son of Rasmus Jansen and Helena Keppelgard Steen, was born in North Germany about 1824.

V —William Steen, the fifth child and fourth son of Rasmus Jansen and Helena Keppelgard Steen, was born in North Germany about 1827 He went out in a ship which was lost at sea, and was never heard from afterwards

VI —Johannes Steen, the sixth child and youngest son of Rasmus Jansen and Helena Keppelgard Steen, was born in North Germany about 1829 He also took to the sea, and after sailing the Spanish main for several years, went to California at the time of the gold excitement there From thence he went to Oregon, and afterwards to New York City, from whence, in 1856, he sailed for Europe as chief officer of one of the largest vessels then afloat, and with the intention of visiting his aged mother But one morning on the voyage, as he stood beside his commander, he was washed overboard by a heavy sea sweeping across the vessel

---

CHAPTER II

Carl Ludwig Steen was born in Magdeburg, Prussia, in 1785, and emigrated to Norway about 1805 He was married in Norway to a Miss Kirsten, to whom were born four children, as follows:

I —William Steen, the eldest son of Carl Ludwig Steen and his wife, formerly a Miss Kirsten, was born in Norway, probably about 1815 He was drowned

II —Carl Ludwig Steen, the second son of Carl Ludwig and his ' wife, formerly a Miss Kirsten, was born in Norway, probably about 1818, where he was brought up He was married, December 4 1844, to Ragnhild Leverine, and had two children, as follows·

  1 Dorothea Leverine Steen, the first child of Carl Ludwig and Ragnhild Leverine Steen, was born in Norway about 1845

2 Ludwig Adolph Steen, the second child, a son of Carl Ludwig and Ragnhild Leverine Steen, was born in Norway, probably about 1848 He has traveled quite extensively, and finally made his home in America For several years he was a member of the New York ' Society for the Prevention of Cruelty to Children." He was married in New York City, September 8, 1888, to Emma Christian Residence, Passaic, New Jersey To them was born one child, as follows:

I —Karin Ragnhild Steen, a daughter of Ludwig Adolph and Emma Christian Steen, was born in New York City, about 1890.

III.—Bertha Steen, a daughter of the Carl Ludwig Steen that was born in Prussia in 1785, and removed to Norway about 1805, was born in Norway, probably about 1820, where she continued to reside

IV —Johann Christian Steen, the fourth child and third son of the Carl Ludwig Steen that was born in Prussia in 1785 and emigrated to Norway about 1805, was born in Norway, probably about 1822, where he was brought up He was married in Norway in 1846, and is the father of two children, as follows

1 Bernhardina Steen

2 Camilla Steen

CHAPTER III.

Heinrich Steen was born in Germany, where he was married and brought up a large family of children One of his sons was married to Christina Mans and had seven children

I —Johann Steen, a son of Heinrich Steen, was born in Germany, probably about 1788, where he was brought up and continued to live He was married in Germany, probably about 1813, to Christina Mans to whom seven children were born, as follows

1 August Steen, the eldest son of Johann and Christina Mans Steen, was born about 1814

2 Adolph Steen, the second son of Johann and Christina Mans Steen, was born about 1816

3 Flora Steen, the third child and eldest daughter of Johann and Christina Mans Steen, was born about 1818

4 Louisa Steen, the fourth child and second daughter of Johann and Christina Mans Steen, was born about 1820

5 Johanna Steen, the fifth child and third daughter of Johann and Christina Mans Steen, was born about 1822

6 Rosa Steen, the sixth child and fourth daughter of Johann and Christina Mans Steen, was born about 1825

7 Ferdinand Johann Frederick Steen, the seventh child and third son of Johann and Christina Mans Steen, was born in Germany, October 7, 1827, where he was brought up. He was married in Germany, May 7, 1856, to Margretta Kleingown. To them were born seven children, as follows

I —Johannes Steen, the eldest child of Ferdinand J F. and Margretta Kleingown Steen, was born in Germany, November 20, 1857

II —Carl Heinrich Steen, the second son of Ferdinand J F. and Margretta Kleingown Steen, was born in Germany, August 15, 1860, on the Island of Femern, an island of Prussia, in the Province of Schleswig-Holstein, separated from Holstein by the Femern Sound, and from the Danish Island of Laaland by the Femern Belt He is by occupation a cabinet maker, and has resided in Germany, Iowa, and California He was married in Davenport, Iowa, June 25, 1887, to Emma Gertrude Reick, she also having been born on the Island of Femern They have no children Residence, 826 Union Street, San Francisco, California

III —Caroline Steen, the third child and eldest daughter of Ferdinand J F and Margretta Kleingown Steen, was born October 4, 1862

IV —Clara Steen, the fourth child and second daughter of Ferdinand J F and Margretta Kleingown Steen, was born October 27, 1864

V —Bernhard Steen, the fifth child and third son of Ferdinand J. F. and Margretta Kleingown Steen, was born November 27, 1866

VI —Kathinka Steen, the sixth child and third daughter of Ferdinand J F and Margretta Kleingown Steen, was born November 4, 1868

VII —Christiana Steen, the seventh and youngest child, the fourth daughter of Ferdinand Johann Frederick and Margretta Kleingown Steen, was born February 1, 1871

CHAPTER IV

Claus Matthias Steen was born in Schleswig, now in the northern province of Germany, but adjoining Denmark, and formerly in possession of the Danish King He was born about 1778 (?), and was married, about 1803, to Katherine Elizabeth —————, to whom two children were born, as follows

I.—Doris Steen, a daughter of Claus Matthias and Katherine Elizabeth Steen, was born in Schleswig, in Northern Germany, about 1805, where she continued to reside

II —Johann Heinrich Christian Steen, a son of Claus Matthias and Katherine Elizabeth Steen was born in Schleswig, in Northern Germany, November 28, 1807, where he was brought up He was married at the same place, about 1835, to Anna Elizabeth Frederica Kiaer, she having been born in Schleswig June 30, 1806 To them were born three children, as follows:

1 Emilie Steen, the first child of Johann II. C and Anna Elizabeth Frederica Kiaer Steen, was born in Malden, in Schleswig then belonging to Denmark, June 14, 1837, where she was brought up She afterwards removed to America Residence, with her brother, 386 Twelfth Street, Brooklyn, New York

2 Peter Carl August Steen, the second child and only son of Johann H C and Anna Elizabeth Frederica Kiaer Steen, was born in Schleswig September 1 1840, which was then

under the Danish Government   He had to go through the campaign of 1863-1864 as a soldier in the Danish Army, after which he removed to America and located in Brooklyn, New York   He is an artist by occupation   He was married by the Rev H Sumner, in Brooklyn, New York, to Henrietta Katherine Frederica Voderberg, a daughter of Claus Heinrich and Franke Loase Voderberg, of Oldenburg, Holstein, she having been born at Rendsburg, Holstein, April 7, 1850   Residence, 386 Twelfth Street, Brooklyn, New York.

3 Frederica Wilhelmina Henrietta Steen, the third child and second daughter of Johann Heinrich Christian and Anna Elizabeth Frederica Kiaer Steen, was born in Schleswig, April 26, 1842, and brought up under the Danish Government   She afterwards removed to America, and now resides with her brother at 386 Twelfth Street, Brooklyn, New York

---

CHAPTER V

John Otto Steen was born in Denmark, probably about 1800 He was married possibly about 1828, and brought up a family of five children in Denmark

I.—Otto Steen, a son of John Otto Steen, was born in Denmark, probably about 1830, where he grew to manhood   He afterwards removed to America, and located in Enterprise, Clarke County, Mississippi

II —Christian Steen, a son of John Otto Steen, was born in Denmark, probably about 1833   He afterwards removed to the United States of America, and settled in St. Louis, Missouri.

III —William Steen, a son of John Otto Steen of Denmark, was born in Copenhagen, Denmark, December 28, 1835, and emigrated to America when he was a young man   He was married at West Point, Mississippi, January 31 1860, to Emma

Caroline Collins, and located in Columbus, Mississippi, where he died in 1884, in the 49th year of his age He was the father of two children, as follows

1 Fannie J Steen, the first child of William and Emma Caroline Collins Steen was born at Columbus Mississippi, August 9, 1867 Residence, Columbus, Mississippi

2 John William Steen, the second child of William and Emma Caroline Collins Steen, was born in Columbus, Mississippi, July 15, 1869 Residence, Columbus, Mississippi

IV —A daughter of John Otto Steen was born in Copenhagen, Denmark, about 1838 and still resides there

V —A daughter of John Otto Steen was born in Copenhagen, Denmark, about 1840, and still resides there

---

Hans Christian Frederick Steen was born in Denmark, and when a young man removed to the United States of America He is a carpenter and house builder by occupation Residence, 41½ Dorland Street, San Francisco, California

---

CHAPTER VI

Samuel Martin Steen was born in Bergen, Norway, in 1804, and died in 1849, aged 45 years He was a magistrate in Norway The family name was originally Dombe-Steen, but his father was given permission by the Storthing, or Parliament, of Norway to drop the Dombe from the name Samuel Martin Steen was married in Norway, about 1836, to Elsie Margrethe Kron Heiberg, she having been born in 1810 To them six children were born.

I —Gerhard Siverin Heiberg Steen, the eldest son of Samuel Martin and Elsie Margrethe Kron Heiberg Steen was born in Bergen, Norway, in 1838 where he spent his early life He was married at the same place, August 17, 1866, to Madsella

Lounze Madsen, she having been born in Bergen, Norway, November 25, 1848 Mr Steen is by occupation a bookkeeper and business correspondent   Residence, 229 South Washington Street, Baltimore, Maryland   To them nine children were born

1 Reinert Heiberg Steen, the eldest son of Gerhard S H and Madsella Lounze Madsen Steen, was born June 10 1867— a clerk by occupation   He was married and lives on Baltimore Street, near Central Avenue, Baltimore, Maryland

2 Sigurd M Steen, the second son of Gerhard S H and Madsella Lounze Madsen Steen, was born December 28, 1868 He is a traveling salesman   He was married, and resides in Baltimore, Maryland, 2010 East Gough Street

3 Gerhard Siverin Heiberg Steen, Jr, the third son of Gerhard Siverin Heiberg and Madsella Lounze Madsen Steen, was born August 23, 1870 — a salesman   Residence, 229 South Washington Street, Baltimore Maryland

4 Madsella Lounze Steen, the fourth child, a daughter of Gerhard S H and Madsella Lounze Madsen Steen, was born August 13, 1872 — a teacher   Residence, 229 South Washington Street, Baltimore, Maryland

5 S Steen, the fifth child and fourth son of Gerhard S H and Madsella Lounze Madsen Steen, was born June 11, 1874 — a telegraph operator   Residence, 229 South Washington Street, Baltimore, Maryland

6 Egil Steen, the sixth child and fifth son of Gerhard S H and Madsella Lounze Madsen Steen, was born April 8, 1877 Residence, 229 South Washington Street, Baltimore, Maryland

7 Edwin S Steen, the seventh child and sixth son of Gerhard S H and Madsella Lounze Madsen Steen, was born July 2, 1881   Residence, 229 South Washington Street, Baltimore, Maryland

8 Valborg Steen, the eighth child and seventh son of Gerhard S H and Madsella L M Steen, was born January 19, 1883 Residence, 229 South Washington Street, Baltimore, Maryland

9 Lily Cleveland Steen, the ninth child and second daughter of Gerhard S H and Madsella L M Steen, was born March

4, 1885   Residence, 229 South Washington Street, Baltimore, Maryland

II —Reinert Steen, the second son of Samuel Martin and Elsie
Margrethe Kron Heiberg Steen, was born in Bergen, Norway, in 1840   He is now dead

III —Henrikke Steen, the third son of Samuel Martin and Elsie
Margrethe Kron Heiberg Steen, was born in Bergen, Norway
in 1842, and died

IV —Valborg Steen, the fourth son of Samuel Martin and Elsie
Margrethe Kron Heiberg Steen, was born in Bergen Norway,
in 1844   Residence, Baltimore Maryland

V —Truth of Steen, the fifth child and the elder daughter of
Samuel Martin and Elsie Margrethe Kron Heiberg Steen, was
born in Bergen, Norway, in 1846, and is now dead

VI —Samuelle Steen, the youngest child of Samuel Martin and
Elsie Margrethe Kron Heiberg Steen was born in Bergen,
Norway, in 1849   She was married to a Mr Engberg   Resi-
dence, Salt Lake City, Utah

Henry H C Steen, belonging to a different family, lives in
Baltimore, Maryland   Residence, 1212 York Road

CHAPTER VII

Johannes Kundsen Steen was born in Christiansund, Norway, probably about 1786, and was married at the same place,
possibly about 1813, to Olave Bergithe Stoame, and brought up
a family of three children

I —Helen Margiette Steen, the eldest child of Johannes
Kundsen and Olave Bergithe Stoame Steen, was born in
Christiansund, Norway, September 5, 1814

II—Carl Andreas Steen, the second child and only son of Johannes Kundsen and Olave Bergithe Stoame Steen, was born in Christiansund, Norway November 14, 1816 He is by occupation a sailor, and has traveled extensively He was married by Wessel Berg, at Flodanger, Norway, April 1, 1853, to Magdalena Jacobia Schoenning, a daughter of Mons Gjentaft Schoenning and Kirsten Aas Leek, of Bar Island, she having been born at Bar Island, April 1, 1829 Residence, 28 Fifth Street South Boston, Massachusetts.

III—Johanna Barbara Steen, the third child and second daughter of Johannes Kundsen and Olave Bergithe Stoame Steen, was born in Christiansund, Norway, November 21, 1818

CHAPTER VIII

Peder O Steen was born in Ode Gaarden, Nordeshang, Norway, and brought up on a farm near Packveraein Norway He had an elder brother who was brought up with him whose name was Hans O Steen

Peder O Steen was born in the year 1810 He was married in the Kirke, in Nordeshang, Norway, in 1830, to Inger Frans Dotta Schoen They removed to the United States of America in 1854, and settled in Wisconsin He was a blacksmith by trade To them were born five children, as follows

I—Ole P Steen, the eldest child of Peder O and Inger Frans Dotta Schoen Steen was born in Norway, about 1827, and came to America with his parents in 1854, when about 27 years of age Residence, Steen, Rock County, Minnesota

II—Charles P Steen, the second son of Peder O and Inger Frans Dotta Schoen Steen, was born in Norway, about 1829, and brought up there He removed to the United States of America with his parents in 1854, when he was about 25 years of age Residence Manston, Juneau County, Wisconsin

III.—John Pederson Steen, the third son of Peder O and Inger Frans Dotta Schoen Steen, was born at Havefessen, Norway, four miles from Christiania, January 14, 1832 He came to America with his father's family in 1854, when he was about 22 years of age He is a blacksmith by trade. John Pederson Steen was married in Adams County, Wisconsin, March 10, 1864, to Lina Klemson Residence, Steen, Rock County, Minnesota To them was born one child, as follows

  1 Peder Nicolaus Steen, a son of John Pederson and Lina Klemson Steen, was born at Steen Rock County, Minnesota, about 1866 Residence, Steen, Rock County, Minnesota

IV.—Annette Steen, the fourth child and only daughter of Peder O and Inger Frans Dotta Schoen Steen, was born in Norway, about 1835, and came to America with her parents in 1854, when she was about 19 years of age She was married to August Kraus Residence, Milwaukee, Wisconsin

V—Gunnold Steen, the fifth child and youngest son of Peder O and Inger Frans Dotta Schoen Steen, was born in Norway about 1838, and died ————

CHAPTER IX

Anders Th Steen was born near Christiania, Norway, probably about 1763. He was married and brought up a large family there One of his sons in middle life removed to America with his family

I—Thrond A Steen, a son of Anders Th Steen, was born near Christiania, Norway, probably about 1795 He was married in Norway, some time about 1818, to Ingeborg Halvarsen Thorstad, and brought up a family of nine children In 1853 he removed with his whole family and settled permanently in the United States of America The following are their children

1 Andreas T Steen, the eldest son of Thrond A and Ingeborg H T. Steen, was born near Christiania Norway, about
1820, and came to America with his parents in 1853   Residence, Spring Grove, Minnesota

2 Ole Christian Steen, the second son of Thrond A and Ingeborg H T Steen, was born near Christiania, Norway, about
1822, and came with his parents to America, in 1853, but is
now dead

3 Martin T Steen, the third son of Thrond A and Ingeborg
H T. Steen, was born near Christiania, Norway, about 1824,
where he was brought up   He emigiated to America with
his father's family in 1853   Residence, Lake Mills, Iowa

4 Karen Kristie Steen, the fourth child and only daughter of
Thrond A and Ingeborg H T Steen, was born near Christiania, Norway, about 1826, and died in infancy

5 Theodore Steen, the fifth child and fourth son of Thrond A.
and Ingeborg H. T Steen, was born near Christiania, Norway, about 1828 and died ————.

6 John Steen, the sixth child and fifth son of Thrond A and
Ingeborg H T Steen, was born near Christiania, Norway,
about 1830, and came to America with his parents in 1853
Residence, Wahoo, Nebraska

7 Hildus Steen, the seventh child and sixth son of Thrond A
and Ingeborg H T Steen, was born near Christiania, Norway, about 1832, and came to America with the family in
1853   He now lives in Nebraska

8 Otto Frederick Steen, the eighth child and seventh son of
Thrond A and Ingeborg H T Steen, was born near Christiania, Norway, about 1834, and is now dead

9 Charles August Steen, the ninth child, the eighth and youngest son of Thrond A and Ingeborg Halvarsen Thorstad
Steen, was born near Christiania, Norway, August 20. 1836,
and died in Decorah, Iowa, July 31, 1877, in the 41st year
of his age   He came to America with his father's family in
1853, when he was about 17 years old   He was married in
Woodville, Winneshiek County, Iowa, March 27. 1867, to
Carrie M Paulsen, she having been born near Throndlyen,

Norway, August 17, 1843, and now (1900) resides with her children at 210 East Broadway, Decorah, Iowa

I—Josephine Matilda Steen, the elder daughter of Charles A and Carrie M Paulsen Steen, was born in Decorah, Iowa, in 1868

II—Emma Theressa Steen, the second daughter of Charles A and Carrie M Paulsen Steen, was born in Decorah, Iowa, in 1871.

BOOK TWENTY.

THE STEENS IN HOLLAND.

In the introduction to this work brief mention was made of Steens in Holland and their characteristics in the dark days of religious persecution. The following letter, from a prominent attorney in New York, will fully explain the Dutch coat of arms, including the Steen family in Holland.

NEW YORK, June 27, 1899

"My Dear Mr Steen

'According to Rietstap, the authority on Dutch coats of arms, there are three families of Steen—

"First —Holland Shield of gold, with eight-pointed red (vermilion) star, surmounted by a rose of same color

"Second —Arnheim Vermilion shield, with three triangular diamonds with gold edges This has a crest — a gold jewel crown, ornamented with a triangular diamond; the scroll work (or lambrequins) of the crest, vermilion. silver and gold

"Third —Holstein Blue with a silver shell (pilgrim's cockle shell) This has a crest, two projections, or rays, of blue, each one containing three silver cockle shells, one on the other

' There are additional families of 'Van den Steen ' I thought this would interest you and your friend

"Yours sincerely,
"GEORGE W VAN SICLEN "

The explanations here given, together with names taken from city directories in Holland, were furnished by Aire H Voorwinden, Esq, Vice Consul of the United States in Rotterdam

The old Dutch word for "Castle" is Steen, and the ancient

castle in Antwerp is still called "The Steen." The word "Van" means "of," and probably implies that the original bearers of the name "Van Steen" were men of stone, or strong men. The word "der" or "den" means "the," and indicates that the original bearers of the name "Van der Steen" or 'Van den Steen' were in some way connected with a castle. The name "Steen" following any other surname, as, for instance, "Brand Van der Steen," would show that the 'Brands' were ancient noblemen, and formerly owned a castle

---

STEENS IN AMSTERDAM

G. Steen, bloemist—florist. Kulverstraat, 91

T: Steen, deurwaarder—constable, Ceintuurbaan, 343

T T Steen, Bloemgracht. 169

T D Steen, comestibles—canned goods, Prinsenstraat. 6 en Singel, 176

A· B· Van Steen, broodbakker—baker, Gandbloemstraat, 74

L. Van Steen, Weteringstraat, 37

H· R Van den Steen, commissionaire. Singel Old Berg-straat, 140.

Wed M Van den Steen, tapster, Beth Amenstraat, 15

Wed W. Van der Steen, Bloemstraat, 76

STEENS IN ROTTERDAM

J· G Steen, Rembrandstraat, 60

E Steen, Vuendenlaan, F 88

L Steen, widow, Bloumerdykesleweg 263

J Steen, Annemarrastr, 26 3-2

D A Steen, Hafaade 18

A Steen, Erasmustraat, 33

L. L: Steen, teacher Erasmusstraat, 33

E Steen, Eleanorastraat 11

STEENS IN THE HAGUE

A Steen, carpenter. Wagenstraat, 153

A Steen, painter, Sumatiastraat. 125.

A Steen, printer, Habblemastraat, 63

G C Steen, Luideval, 3rd

Miss C Steen, lady tailor. Luideval, 3rd

J. J Steen, cork manufacturer, Doufletstraat, 34

J: W: C Steen, dealer in sewing machines, Trinsenstraat, 104

Mis G· Steen, groceries, Lage Niewstraat.

H Van Steen, storekeeper, Veenkade, 77

H Van Steen, milk dealer, Geest, 48

A P L: Van der Steen, bookkeeper, West Linde, 194 d

T· A Van der Steen, baker, Van Viemenstraat, 81

J H Van der Steen, mason, Buitemingel Z. W 8

W C Van den Steen, milk dealer, Kartenbosch, 21

Miss T H Van den Steen, teacher, Piel Hemstraat, 8

Miss G. W C. Van den Steen, teacher, Trinsenstraat 104

Isaac Van den Steen, Trinsenstraat, 104, dealer in sewing machines

W Van der Steen, carpenter, Konigstraat. 111

W Van der Steen, beer dealer, Skylinde 16

GENERAL INDEX.

BOOK ONE

BOOK TWO

BOOK THREE

BOOK FOUR

BOOK FIVE

BOOK SIX

BOOK SEVEN

BOOK EIGHT

BOOK NINE

BOOK TEN.

BOOK ELEVEN

BOOK TWELVE

BOOK THIRTEEN

BOOK FOURTEEN

BOOK FIFTEEN

BOOK SIXTEEN

Deeley, Eliza J Steen   Sixteen, Sec 2, I 1
Deeley, Benjamin E   Sixteen, Sec 2
Deeley, Mary J   Sixteen, Sec 2, I 1 1
Deeley, Sarah E .   Sixteen, Sec 2, I 1 2
Deeley, Stanton F   Sixteen, Sec 2, 1 1 3
Deeley, Annie Laurie   Sixteen, Sec 2, I 1 4

Graham, Ellen E Steen   Sixteen, VIII 3
Graham, Hiram   Sixteen
Graham, Jennie T   Sixteen, VIII 3 1
Graham, Lizzie I   Sixteen, VIII 3 2
Graham, William A   Sixteen, VIII 3 3
Graham, Laura F   Sixteen, VIII 3 4
Graham, Hiram M   Sixteen, VIII 3 5
Graham, Harriet V   Sixteen, VIII 3 6
Graham, Margaret E .   Sixteen, VIII 3 7
Graham, Raney   Sixteen, VIII 3 8
Graham, S Bertha   Sixteen VIII 3 9
Graham, John Steen   Sixteen, VIII 3 10

Hill, Mary O Steen   Sixteen, Sec 2, I 3
Hill, George F   Sixteen, Sec 2
Hill, M Belle   Sixteen Sec 2, 1 3 1
Hill, Inez A   Sixteen, Sec 2 1 3 2
Hill, Lysle Steen   Sixteen, Sec 2, 1 3 3
Hill, Harvey C   Sixteen, Sec 2, 1 3 4

Rose, Martha Steen   Sixteen, VIII 5
Rose, John M   Sixteen
Rose, Levi M   Sixteen VIII 5 1
Rose, William W   Sixteen, VIII 5 2
Rose, David I   Sixteen VIII 5 3
Rose, Nora V   Sixteen, VIII 5 4
Rose, Samuel H   Sixteen, VIII 5 5

Steen, David   Sixteen
Steen, ——— McGeorge   Sixteen
Steen, James   Sixteen, I
Steen, Martha   Sixteen, II
Steen, David .   Sixteen, Sec 2
Steen, Mary F Armstrong   Sixteen, Sec 2
Steen, John   Sixteen, Sec 2
Steen, Charles A   Sixteen, Sec 2, I
Steen, Lorenda S Sexton   Sixteen, Sec 2

Steen, David O   Sixteen Sec 2, I 2.
Steen, Julia A Weimar   Sixteen, Sec 2.
Steen, Herbert O   Sixteen Sec 2, I 2 1
Steen, William H .   Sixteen Sec 2, I 2 2.
Steen, Charles F   . Sixteen, Sec 2, I 2 3
Steen, Sarah L .   Sixteen, Sec 2 I 2 4
Steen, Robert A   Sixteen, Sec 2, I 2 5
Steen, Hattie E   Sixteen, Sec 2 I 2 6
Steen, Charles F   Sixteen, Sec 2, I 4
Steen, Sarah L Modine   Sixteen, Sec 2.
Steen, Harry M   .   Sixteen, Sec 2, I 4 1
Steen, Ada L   . Sixteen, Sec 2, I 4 2
Steen, Alpha H   Sixteen, Sec 2, I 4 3
Steen, Rollin E   Sixteen, Sec 2, I 4 4
Steen, Barbara   Sixteen, Sec 2, II.
Steen, Ellen   Sixteen, III
Steen, Margaret   Sixteen, IV
Steen, Mary Ann   Sixteen V
Steen, Jane   Sixteen, VI
Steen, Eliza   Sixteen VII
Steen, William W   Sixteen, VIII
Steen, Jane Conley   Sixteen.
Steen, David C   .   Sixteen, VIII 1
Steen, Daniel   Sixteen, VIII 2
Steen, Elizabeth M King   Sixteen.
Steen, William K   Sixteen, VIII 2 1
Steen, Inez I   Sixteen VIII 2 2
Steen, James M   Sixteen, VIII 2 3
Steen, Iona I   Sixteen, VIII 2 4
Steen, Reid W   Sixteen VIII 2 5
Steen, Mary   Sixteen, VIII 6
Steen, Harriet   Sixteen VIII 7
Steen, Mary Jane   .   Sixteen, VIII 8
Steen, Sarah A   Sixteen VIII 9
Steen, William J   Sixteen, VIII 10
Steen, James H   Sixteen, VIII 11
Steen, Emma L Roder   Sixteen
Steen, Willa May   Sixteen, VIII 11 1
Steen, Samuel R   Sixteen, VIII 12
Steen, Milla N Graham   . Sixteen
Steen, Ollie Henderson   Sixteen, VIII 12 1
Steen, Norman Edmund .Sixteen, VIII 12 2
Steen, John   Sixteen, IX

BOOK SEVENTEEN

Ferguson, Mary A Steen   Seventeen, V 7
Ferguson, Jonathan   Seventeen
Ferguson, Joseph Steen   Seventeen, V 7 3
Ferguson, Dewitt C   Seventeen, V 7 4
Ferguson, Alice Mellen   Seventeen
Ferguson, Jerome C   Seventeen, V 7 5
Ferguson, Mary Storm   Seventeen
Ferguson, Steen   Seventeen, V 7 5 1
Ferguson, Eva Streeter   Seventeen
Ferguson ———   Seventeen, V 7 5 1 1
Ferguson, Ettie   Seventeen, V 7 5 2
Ferguson, Franklin F   Seventeen, V 7 6
Ferguson, Addie Storm   Seventeen
Ferguson, Arthur   Seventeen, V 7 6 1
Ferguson Carrie F   . Seventeen, V 7 6 2
Flint, Ann E Steen   Seventeen, V 5
Flint, Frank F   Seventeen
Flint, Ethel Steen   Seventeen, V 5 1
Flint Bertha Steen   Seventeen V 5 2

Harvey, Louisa A Steen   Seventeen V 1 1
Harvey William W   Seventeen
Harvey, George C   Seventeen, V 1 1 1

Harvey, Helen W   Seventeen, V 1 1 2
Harvey, William Steen   Seventeen, V 1 1 3
Harvey, Laura A,   Seventeen, V 1 1 4
Harvey, Louisa   Seventeen, V 1 1 5.
Harvey, Wallace N   Seventeen, V 1 1 6

Mellen, Charlotte M Ferguson
    . . Seventeen, V 7 2
Mellen, Hezekiah H   Seventeen
Mellen, Frank H   Seventeen, V 7 2 1
Mellen, Mary M Hydorn   Seventeen
Mellen, Marguerite . Seventeen, V 7 2 1 1
Mellen Paul H   .   Seventeen V 7 2 1 2
Mellen, George H   Seventeen, V 7 2 1 3.
Mellen, Edith A   Seventeen, V 7 2 1 4.

Potter Mary F Ferguson Seventeen V 7 2
Potter, John   Seventeen

Ripsom Elizabeth Mellen   .
    Seventeen V 7 2 2
Ripsom, William F   Seventeen
Ripsom, Lulu B   Seventeen, V 7 2 2 1

BOOK EIGHTEEN

BOOK NINETEEN

n, Otto Frederick	Nineteen, IX 1 8	Steen, Josephine Matilda	Nineteen, IX 1 9 1,
n, Charles August	Nineteen, IX 1 9	Steen, Emma Theressa	Nineteen, IX 1 9 2
n, Carrie M Paulsen	Nineteen, IX		

BOOK TWENTY

STEENS IN HOLLAND

There are twenty Steens, four Van Steens, six Van den Steens and six Van Steens

CPSIA information can be obtained
at www.ICGtesting.com
Printed in the USA
BVHW031759160622
639860BV00001B/46

9 781298 506894